CRYSTAL POWER, CRYSTAL HEALING

Michael Gienger

CRYSTAL POWER, CRYSTAL HEALING

Translated by Astrid Mick

An Hachette UK Company
www.hachette.co.uk

First published in Germany by Neue
Erde titled *Die Steinheilkunde*

This revised edition published in 2015
by Cassell Illustrated, a division of
Octopus Publishing Group Ltd
Carmelite House,
50 Victoria Embankment
London EC4Y 0DZ
www.octopusbooks.co.uk
www.octopusbooksusa.com

First published in 1998 by Blandford
Reprinted in 2009 by Cassell Illustrated

Distributed in the US by
Hachette Book Group
1290 Avenue of the Americas
4th and 5th Floors
New York, NY 10020

Distributed in Canada by
Canadian Manda Group
664 Annette St.
Toronto, Ontario, Canada M6S 2C8

ISBN 978-1-84403-841-1

A CIP catalogue record for this book is
available from the British Library.

Printed and bound in China

10 9 8 7 6 5 4 3 2 1

Translation: Astrid Mick
Editing of the translated text:
  Anne Trevillion
Original graphics and artwork:
  Fred Hageneder/Dragon Designs
Original colour photograpy:
  Ines Blersch

Revised edition
Deputy Art Director:
  Yasia Williams-Leedham
Designer: Isabel de Cordova
Translation of new and updated text:
  JMS Books LLP (www.jmswords.com)

Publisher's note
The information in this volume has
been compiled according to the best
of our knowledge and belief, and the
healing properties of the crystal have
been tested many times over. Bearing
in mind that different people react in
different ways, neither the publishers
nor the author can give a guarantee
for the effectiveness or safety of use in
individual cases. In the case of serious
health problems, please consult your
doctor or naturopath.

This book is dedicated to my 'crystal healing friends'
of the early days and the members of the first
crystal healing research group in Stuttgart:

Marcella Balzer
Wolfgang Bregger
Sibylle Daeschler-Geyer
Anja Gienger
Walter von Holst
Eveline Kopp
Marion Molitor
Lisa Muntwiler
Barbara Newerla
Joachim Rieger
Heide Ruf
Dr Gerald Rollett
Ulrike Scheffler
Beate Simon
Silvia Weller

This book would not exist without their contributions.

Contents

Part 2: The art of healing with crystals

Part 3: Healing crystals

3.1 The healing properties of precious stones   219

Appendices

Advancing toe of lava at the front of a stream of pahoehoe lava, Hawaii, December 1992.

Foreword

Among my earliest memories are those of stones, inseparably linked in my mind with running water, and mountain streams in particular. I loved to divert the flow of water with the aid of dams built with large and small pebbles, and delighted in dividing one stream into many small ones, connecting these up again, erecting dams and waterfalls, or creating a quiet basin of water in the middle of a fast-flowing stream. My favourite materials in all these endeavours were stones and rocks. Where others used twigs, sticks, wood or soil to reinforce their elaborate structures, these were only substitutes for me – the challenge was to solve the problem using only rocks and stones!

With all these activities, which resulted in many a soaking wet pair of trousers for me and trials of patience and tolerance for my parents, grew a great love of the world of rocks and stones. First I was attracted by the spotted, striped, banded or peculiarly veined pebbles and stones in streams, but later my interest extended to all other stones and rocks that were in any way characterized by their shape or colour, or by any other special feature. Fortunately, my parents actively supported my growing collecting mania (by carrying my numerous finds home for me!).

Then, in the summer of 1972, I tripped over a very special stone on a field of scree in southern Tyrol, Austria. This particular stone was peculiarly angular and had an even, reddish-brown surface with a slight film of mica, and looked – well, different. It was too regular in shape to be an ordinary stone, at least as far as I was aware at the time. Just a broken piece of something, I thought, and threw it away again. A few minutes later, however, I came across it again and decided to take it with me.

I never looked at it again during the rest of the holiday, but it was among the other stuff I had collected when I showed it all to my friend Thomas back home. 'Where on earth did you find this garnet?' he asked, and among all the colourful bits of stone, he fished out this unusual piece. 'Garnet?' I asked. 'How do you know that's what it is?' He pulled out a slim, hardback entitled *My Little Book of Minerals*, and one of the pictures looked just like my find. So, this peculiar stone was a mineral, a garnet, definitely something very special!

Of course, I just had to own a copy of *My Little Book of Minerals*, and with it I began to discover a completely new world – the world of minerals. I learned that all rocks and stones consist of at least one but usually several minerals, which generally remain small and unobtrusive, rarely becoming beautiful or large with a conspicuous shape and colour like the piece of garnet I had found. I also found out that minerals actually grow, beginning with a small 'seed' and, over the course of many years, become larger and larger, while adhering to a wonderful 'construction plan' that ensures exact and regular shapes. These shapes, my little book informed me, are called crystals, of which there are only seven groups in the whole world.

The author at the age of six, collecting stones.

So as a child of eight I was already familiar with crystal systems, minerals, Mohs' hardness and systems of minerals. All this awoke the collector's passion in me and I began to collect minerals. No longer did I want 'ordinary stones' – they had to be minerals! Collecting became more targeted, my collection grew larger with every year, and I joined evening classes and went on outings to quarries.

Anything I was unable to collect for myself was supplied at Christmases and birthdays by my parents and relatives. What a shame it was that there were not far more occasions throughout the year for present-giving! My mineral collection became huge and soon I had taken over the boiler room in the cellar of our house with 'Cosmos' kits and my first 'mineralogical' laboratory, where I loved to identify, test and conserve my collection.

It was, therefore, not surprising that chemistry, the school subject most closely related to mineralogy, became my favourite subject and a firm foundation for a good grade average. When I left school, I began studying chemistry at university.

There, however, I came down to earth with a sinking feeling of disappointment. Chemistry, as practised there, led me into a dry, cold, sterile world that did not seem to have anything in common with the beauty of pebbles from streams or the fascination of minerals. Viewing the entire world as accidentally interacting matter seemed to rob our existence of all its magic and I was left with the strong conviction that this could not be all there was to our existence. I packed up my university studies.

During the next few years, I tried hard to find answers to the deeper questions: are we humans merely the end product of a chain of random mutations, or are we really beings with a spiritual source? Is this Earth, with all its beauty and cruelty, merely a planet lost in space, or perhaps after all a world that makes sense and has a purpose? My inner world became a battleground between materialism and a more spiritual view. These inner conflicts resulted in an extremely chaotic phase of my life, replete with a series of accidents and illnesses.

All this resulted in my meeting with rocks and stones again – but in a very different way. In 1985 – my year of accidents and illnesses – someone first suggested to me that I use a mineral for healing purposes. At the time I was suffering from regularly recurring, severe sinusitis infections against which both antibiotics and homeopathic remedies remained ineffective. I was very sceptical when an acquaintance mentioned that emerald was very helpful for infections. The view that stones and minerals were attractive and fascinating but otherwise consisted of dead matter still was still dominant in my mind.

Nevertheless, I decided to try it out. 'It can't do any harm' was my main thought at this point. I managed to borrow an emerald, stuck it to my forehead with a piece of sticking plaster and – it worked! Literally 'overnight' the persistent phase of illness just cleared up!

Initially, I tried to explain it away as a mere coincidence. I turned again to the study of stones and rocks, this time fully intending to dedicate myself to the study of the healing properties of minerals and precious stones. I collected all the literature I could on the subject, although there was not very much around at the time. Only a very few pioneers had so far involved themselves with the healing powers of stones – a situation that has changed only little to the present day.

Although the number of books available on the subject makes it appear otherwise, this turns out to be an illusion. Closer investigation reveals that, especially recently, these publications have mainly appeared through a process of 'editing', that is, by collecting together secondary source information. With very few exceptions, the pioneers of the last few decades are still merely being quoted and copied.

While studying the literature on healing stones, I noticed two things in particular: first, that there were great contradictions with respect to the healing properties described and the use of the relevant stones, and second, a noticeable consensus when it came to explaining the effects of minerals and precious stones in terms of their colours. Both these points created a conflict in my 'scientific soul'. These contradictions in the descriptions of healing properties, I reasoned, either meant the whole thing was humbug, or else subjective experiences were being generalized into objective truths.

Next, there seemed to be a dire lack of knowledge about minerals, as a mineral certainly consists of a great deal more than merely its colour! The circumstances of its origin, the structure and the mineral constituents of a given stone are of such great importance for the growth and later appearance of a mineral that all almost certainly must play a part in the acquisition of its specific healing properties!

For the moment, I could see no way of solving these contradictions, so I decided to study other natural healing remedies and methods and experiment with minerals 'on the side'. Again, it was a number of 'coincidences' that brought me into contact with *shiatsu*, the Japanese form of acupressure, as well as Chinese medicine and various traditional healing methods. I learned about the complete opposite to orthodox medicine at the School of Natural Healing, an experience which, with hindsight, I would certainly not have wished to miss. It was while I was studying there, in 1988, that I was encouraged by lecturer and outstanding homeopath, Wolfgang Bregger, to pass on the experiences I had with stones.

I was amazed by the response I received. The demand for information on this subject area was so overwhelming that a seminar developed out of it and, even more important, a research group was set up which, from 1989 to 1993, continuously investigated and recorded the healing properties of minerals and precious stones.

From then on, I dedicated myself entirely to the world of stones. The research group tested stones according to the established principle behind testing new medicines and drugs: over a period of four to six weeks all the members of the group would wear the same stone. All psychological, spiritual or physical phenomena that were observed were recorded and were reported on at regular meetings. The results were amazing!

With every stone tested, it became increasingly clear that a common thread seemed to run through the experiences of all those taking part. Mutual features and characteristics were so clearly demonstrated that coincidence could effectively be ruled out. By involving a large number of people of different types, from students to pensioners, and of all age groups as well as representatives of different fields of employment, the 'real' effects of the mineral or precious stone were easy to distinguish from other influences. In this way, the research group developed comprehensive, detailed descriptions that had never been encountered before.

The results of these experiences were initially offered to doctors and non-medical practitioners for trials in their own practices. After we had received more and more positive responses, they were also offered in the form of seminars, training units and lectures to the wider public. My own task during the course of research and teaching activity consisted of analysing the parallels between the real mineralogical facts associated with the stones and their healing properties. Based on the profusion of experimental material gathered by the research group, I was finally able to carry out this analysis.

The initially fairly vague supposition I had had when I first studied the existing healing crystals literature was now proved to be correct. The healing properties of minerals and all other types of stone can be traced back to the manner of their origin, their inner structure, their mineral elements and their colours. These four principles can be described separately and, in the case of each individual stone, can be combined to form an individual portrait of its healing characteristics.

In this way, we were able to create a foundation for the art of healing with crystals, a method in which the principles refer to the nature and characteristics of the stones themselves. Until then, the use of crystals had usually been only as a supplementary method to other medical systems. As therefore crystals were only employed in healing in the context of some other system, their use was also usually restricted to a particular aspect of their healing power. Now it has become possible to understand the effects of crystals in a truly comprehensive way and to apply them to the whole person, to their psychological state, their spirit, mind and body.

By the mid-1990s, these first findings had matured and began to bear fruit in rapid succession, so it was the right time for us to publish the results of our activities in a book. What followed surprised us all: after the appearance of the first edition in 1995, *Crystal Power, Crystal Healing* became a bestseller within weeks and proved a springboard to further research. The Steinheilkunde e.V. association, which was founded in the same year, took over and expanded our research project. Research groups sprang up all over German-speaking Europe with the result that at times up to 300 test subjects were involved in the experiments. The amount of practical experience gathered also grew exponentially and the 1990s saw the founding of the first teaching institutions and associations by healing crystal therapists.

Our understanding of the effects of stones and our knowledge of their practical applications have advanced step by step with the result that healing crystal therapy has now found a firm place beside homeopathy, herbalism and other practices as one of the natural healing techniques. *Crystal Power, Crystal Healing* has continued to provide a stable foundation for subsequent developments and, though new mineralogical findings now mean that after almost twenty years, a new, revised edition has become necessary, the essential findings depicted in this book are just as up-to-the-minute as ever – and if anything have gained in relevance. *Crystal Power, Crystal Healing* explains in clear and easy-to-understand terms how stones have healing properties and how you can identify the best healing crystal for you.

In order to understand completely these properties, we will need to become familiar with the world and nature of rocks, stones and crystals as well as that of humans. Only then will we be able to understand how and in what form communication between the two can be possible. As rocks and stones are by far the older partner in this, our earthly existence, I would like to introduce them first.

Michael Gienger, Spring 2014

1.1 The origins of minerals

The Earth's boiling interior

In the beginning there was magma. Not at the beginning of all things but at the beginning of many rocks and stones. As our solar system came into existence, the Earth evolved out of a cloud of gases into a dense fog of dust and then, through contraction, became denser and shrank into an intensely hot ball. This fiery spherical body consisted entirely of hot molten matter, a viscous glowing mass.

Very little has changed to this day. The Earth has now acquired a firm crust through cooling down but this crust is still comparatively thin. If you imagine the Earth to be an apple, then the Earth's firm outer crust is about as thick as the skin around it. That is not exactly thick! The rest is still molten and in constant movement. And it is from this 'rest' that magma is formed.

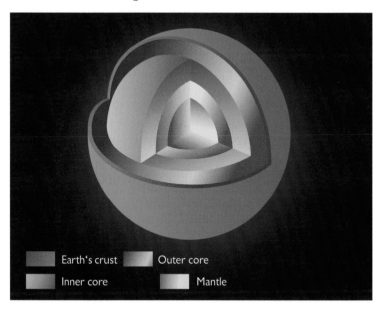

Earth's crust   Outer core
Inner core   Mantle

The internal structure of the Earth: the Earth is presumed to consist of metals, while the mantle is made up of movable, molten rocks; the crust (c. 0.1% of the diameter) is made up of solid rock.

(opposite) A nocturnal eruption of the volcano Krakatoa, Indonesia, 1993.

Although the thought of there being molten rock below the crust may be alarming, in fact there are several kilometres of rock between your feet and the Earth's hot mantle and the rock has outstanding insulating properties. As long as your house does not happen to be situated in the centre of an earthquake zone, on a tectonic fault (i.e. a deep crack reaching right down to the Earth's mantle), or in the middle of the crater of a periodically erupting volcano, you will notice very little of any activity within the Earth. Very occasionally an earth tremor may remind us that the ground beneath our feet is not quite as stable as it seems.

Indeed, the interior of the Earth is in constant flux. As rocks of the Earth's mantle near the centre of the Earth are considerably hotter and therefore lighter than rock nearer the surface, movable, molten rock slowly rises towards the Earth's crust. Here, they cool a little, become denser and heavier again, and gradually sink back down towards the centre of the Earth. These constant movements, known as convection, cause the crust of the Earth, which 'swims' on the top, to move as well. This is how cracks are formed where plates drift apart (as, for example, in the Atlantic Ocean, where Europe and the Americas are being pushed apart), or how mountains form where plates are pushed into each other (still happening now, for example in the Himalayas).

When water collects anywhere in the hot rocks of the upper mantle or lower crust of the Earth, the rocks melt and the molten rock created in this fashion is known as magma. As it takes up more volume than relatively solid rock, the increase in pressure pushes the magma upwards; this sometimes reaches the Earth's surface in a volcanic explosion, but more often it cools and solidifies again as it rises. In either case, this causes the formation of the first, so-called 'primary' minerals and rocks.

The formation of igneous rocks and materials

The formation of minerals from magma can be likened to the emergence of sugar crystals in jam that is oversaturated with sugar. Many of us may have observed this fascinating phenomenon when a home-made jam – particularly a jelly-like one like blackberry or quince – suddenly produced distinct crystals on its surface or on the sides of the jar. When this happened the crystals did not materialize immediately the jam was made, but, after it had been kept in a jam store for a while, they suddenly seemed to appear. And they carried on growing. What had happened to produce them out of a gooey, seimi-liquid substance?

While the jam was boiling, the added sugar was easily dissolved in it. It is a rule that hot liquids are able to dissolve larger quantities of solids than cold liquids. When the jam cooled down it turned into a 'supersaturated solution', which means that there was more sugar present in the jam than the now cooled liquid could hold. The sugar slowly began to precipitate out of the jam. Single, tiny grains of sugar formed, acting as nuclei for the growth of further new particles of sugar. This is how sugar crystals gradually grew in the home-made jam.

Minerals and rocks

The crystallization of minerals from magma occurs in exactly the same way. Magma is a mass of molten rock. Because of its high temperatures (more than a thousand degrees Celsius), all matter contained in it is in a liquid state.

Once the magma begins to cool down, it is unable to retain all the different substances in solution and some of the matter begins to precipitate out: here, too, the process begins with small 'seeds' that gradually grow into larger crystals. The process continues until, at the end of the cooling phase, all the liquid matter released has become solid. If the 'end product' consists of homogeneous matter, we speak of a mineral, but if it consists of a mixture of substances, that is of several minerals, it is called rock. The size of the crystals will depend on how quickly the magma cools down, or the length of time that the magma has had available for the mineral's growth.

As the analogy with the home-made jam has shown, the crystallization process requires time. This is why the crystals of minerals that are created during a volcanic eruption are considerably smaller than those formed deep in the Earth. This makes sense: magma that has been released as 'lava' from the interior of the Earth onto the surface will have cooled down in a matter of days or weeks, while millions of years may have passed during a cooling process taking place in the depths of the Earth.

Igneous rocks

In mineralogy the rocks and minerals that have formed directly from magma are called igneous or magmatic rocks and minerals. These magmatic minerals are characterized by the fact that they were formed through the cooling and solidification processes described above. Depending on where they were formed, whether at the surface or deep in the Earth, igneous rocks are divided into rocks or minerals of volcanic origin (vulcanites and volcanic minerals) and rocks of plutonic origin (plutonites, otherwise known as 'intrusive' rocks).

The term 'plutonic' is derived from Pluto, the name of the Lord of the Underworld in Roman mythology, and is used for those rocks that have formed deep within the Earth. Minerals that formed in plutonites are subdivided into a further three categories, called liquid-magmatic, pneumatolytic and hydrothermal. They will be described in more detail in what follows.

Vulcanites

Vulcanites generally form fine-grained rocks containing minerals that produce only minute crystals. Well known among these are the lightweight 'lava rocks', such as pumice, which owe their structure to gases contained in the lava, or the more solid basalt, a very hard rock without gas bubbles. Vulcanites applied in healing with crystals are porphyrites and rhyolite, with the latter being traded as leopard stone or rainforest stone. Fire opal is also formed during the course of volcanic activity.

In some cases, when lava cools extremely quickly, for example by streaming into cold water, it may even be that no crystals are formed at all. Instead, the entire lava mass is practically 'frozen' through the temperature shock experienced, and the molten mass solidifies into a glass-like mass.

This is how obsidian originates. Obsidian, being a mixture of many substances, is not strictly speaking counted among minerals, but is classified among the rocks; it is also called rock glass or volcanic glass. Owing to

The formation of vulcanites

its varied composition, the appearance of obsidian can vary greatly, from the simple black obsidian to mahogany, rainbow, silver and snowflake obsidian, to name just the most important.

Plutonites

Among the plutonites, not all of the minerals form at the same time. The first minerals start forming freely in viscous magma where, depending on their density, they are able to sink down or rise up. This is how magma differentiates, or divides up, and how certain minerals accumulate at certain depths and become concentrated there.

This initial step in mineral formation is called 'liquid-magmatic formation', which simply means 'the formation of minerals from liquid magma'. This process occurs at temperatures between 1100 degrees and 700 degrees Celsius and under enormous pressures (several hundred atmospheres). Examples of healing crystals

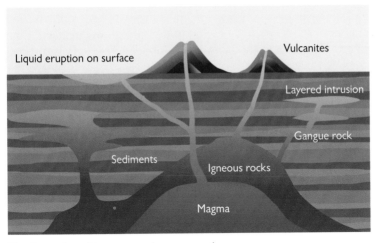

The formation of igneous and gangue rocks

formed in this way are amazonite, gabbro, olivine (peridot), rose quartz and hyacinth zircon.

Sometimes, gases or vapours from the magma penetrate neighbouring rock. This may also lead to mineral formation through substances dissolving out of the rock and forming compounds with the gases from the magma. Mineralogists call this process of formation 'pneumatolytic formation' (derived from the Greek words *pneuma*, 'vapour', and *lyein*, 'to dissolve'). Of these

21

pneumatolytic minerals, the following are applied in healing with crystals: lepidolite, muscovite, petalite, topaz and tourmaline.

During the ensuing cooling phase, once the 'critical temperature' of water at 375 degrees Celsius and below is reached, aqueous solutions result. At temperatures above the critical temperature, water is only present as a vapour, whatever the prevailing pressure. Below 375 degrees Celsius water can become liquid if the pressure is great enough. Further minerals are then formed out of the substances dissolved in the water. Their formation is called 'hydrothermal', derived from the Greek *hydro*, 'water', and *therme*, 'hot spring'. Well-known healing crystals that have been formed hydrothermally are, among others, rock crystal/crystal quartz, chalcedony, fluorite, carnelian, kunzite and larimar.

Because water is far more free-flowing than the viscous magma, it is able to penetrate more easily and quickly into cracks and fissures in the surrounding rocks. Here, the minerals are precipitated as druse on the walls of veins or pockets, forming so-called gangue rocks. The mineral solutions in these types of environment will only cool off very slowly owing to the insulating qualities of the surrounding rock (sometimes only by about 1 degree Celsius (33.8 degrees Fahrenheit) in more than 10 000 years). This means the minerals created here are able to form large, beautiful crystals.

Another important factor is that they have plenty of space to grow undisturbed. Some of the most beautiful and popular healing crystals, for example agate, apophyllite, rock crystal/crystal quartz, chalcedony, smoky quartz, tourmaline and many more, are formed in these fissures and clefts.

The principle of igneous rock formation

A liquid substance becomes solid. This is the simplest way of

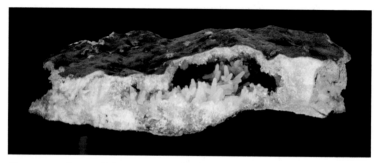

Gangue rock containing quartz and calcite crystals

describing the first and oldest formation principle of minerals. It is important – in order to understand the resulting effects of minerals on humans – to have a closer look at what the process really involves.

The first stage is represented by a free or non-ordered state. Free means mobile and non-ordered as all the substances contained are mingled and mixed together unbound in compounds. Magma, therefore, is like a thick soup containing many mineral-forming elements (chemical elements), but no mineral has yet been formed at this stage. Magma is the 'potential' out of which many minerals and rocks can be formed. According to the elements it contains, magma helps determine what particular minerals will eventually form, and which ones will not. Magma is not identical everywhere, which is why certain minerals are found only in certain parts of the world.

Apart from the magma itself, further factors will determine the formation of minerals: pressure and heat, as well as the speed of cooling. The same source substances may lead to very different final forms, depending on whether the magma reaches the surface in the form of lava and cools down very quickly, whether many 'closely packed' crystals are formed in liquid-magmatic formation, or whether the mineral has enough time in a cavity or cleft to develop, grow and form beautiful, large crystals.

In brief: The igneous formation principle demonstrates a crystallization process based on the cooling and solidification of liquid magma. The mineral-forming elements contained in magma represent the potential and predisposition for formation, as they already determine what can be formed.

The crystallization process itself, however, is determined by the factors of pressure, heat, space and time, all of which decide in which manner the existing potential will be realized. As this is the oldest method of formation of rock (although, of course, it has continued through geological time and is still going on today) we will call the minerals so formed 'primary' minerals.

We should take note of this principle as it will continue to be of great importance for healing with crystals. Let us first turn to the second formation process which occurs in quite a different manner from the first.

The formation of sedimentary rocks and minerals

From the depths of magmatic formations, our path will now take us up to the surface of the Earth: here it will become clear that even stones and rocks do not remain the same forever. The teeth of Time are gnawing away at even the hardest rock; in fact it is the sun and rain, heat and cold, frost and wind that are doing the 'gnawing' and gradually wearing the rock away. This action of wind and weather that leaves nothing untouched is called weathering or erosion. It leads to the second way that rock is formed.

Erosion
Mountains are worn away by weathering. Rocks are split off by the action of frost and turn into the rubble that is found on mountain slopes in the form of extensive gravel (scree) slopes. This gravel will

Sedimentary rock

not remain lying there forever, but will gradually gravitate towards the valley bottom – gravel avalanches are greatly feared in such regions – where it is transported away by streams and rivers.

The flowing water serves to transform the angular pieces of rock of all sizes into round pebbles, by rolling them about against each other, knocking off their corners, grinding them down, and polishing them. During the process, myriad small fragments are created; this is sand, right down to the finest, dust-like, floating particles that we find in mud. A small amount of some mineral-forming elements is completely dissolved in the water, particularly chalk, for example, or rock salt.

Sedimentation

Water can only transport matter as long as it is flowing. Wherever a river slows down, in lakes, river deltas or where it reaches the sea, it

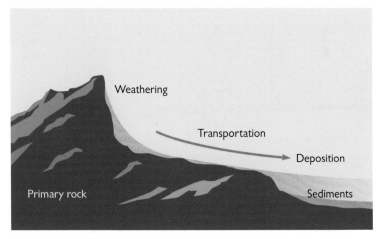

Formation of sediments

will deposit anything it has carried along. Vast quantities of deposits can be built up in this way, out of which new rocks are formed.

This kind of deposition is called sedimentation and the rocks formed in the process are called sedimentary rocks. Among these kinds of rocks we find such healing stones as anglesite, anhydrite, calcite, dolomite, oolite, selenite (gypsum) and pyrite, in particular the spherical pyrites known as 'pop rocks'.

Limestone sinter deposits

Small-scale weathering

Wherever rocks are close to the surface of the Earth, surface water, whether rainwater or other water, will penetrate them. This surface water carries oxygen, carbon dioxide or acids with it. It penetrates cracks and crevices and begins to dissolve the rock and release mineral-forming elements.

This, too, is a weathering process, although on a much smaller

scale. It is going on beneath our feet worldwide and completely independently of whether the rock is exposed to the air ('unlocked') or whether there is a layer of humus on top.

Cracks filled with chrysocolla

The zones between the surface and the water table

The mineral-forming elements that are released form compounds with other substances contained in the water and are then either deposited on the spot as new minerals or are transported away to be precipitated and deposited in deeper locations. This 'miniature sedimentation' causes the formation of many new minerals, particularly in rocks rich in ore. These processes occur in the zone between the surface of the Earth and the water table.

The region above the water table is called the 'weathering or oxidation zone', as oxygen from the air is still active at this depth. Chemically, oxidation means a release of electrons. By releasing electrons, metal atoms transform into charged particles (ions) and only in the form of ions are they able to form new compounds or can they can be dissolved in liquids. Typical minerals in the oxidation zone are, for example, azurite, malachite, chrysocolla, dioptase, turquoise and variscite.

The region next to the water table is called the 'cementation zone', as dissolved substances are precipitated out here (this process is also called cementation). In this zone, reduction processes occur during which, for example, metal ions turn back into neutral metal atoms. Chemically, 'reduction' means 'collecting electrons', so it is the opposite process to oxidation. Neutral metal atoms do not remain in solution, so this is where we find typical minerals of the cementation zone like copper or silver. Other minerals from this region are copper chalcedony and covellite.

The principle of sedimentary formation

'Weathering and deposition' are the main elements of this principle. The environment plays a decisive part not only in shaping rock but also in reforming it, both through the power of the wind and weather and through the work of weak acid solutions. Sedimentary formation starts with an already existing rock that is gradually dissolved, whether completely or partially, through the effect of outside forces. The rock itself represents only one element in what goes into possible later new formation.

Logically, only the mineral-forming elements already present in the rock can be involved in the process of dissolving and new formation, but watery solutions in the form of acids make up another equally important component. It is the combination of these two influences that determines the formation of new minerals. We shall call such minerals 'secondary' minerals.

In brief: The sedimentary formation principle represents a process in which the solid structures of certain rocks are dissolved through environmental influences. The mineral-forming elements released out of the rock, together with other substances brought there through environmental activity, create new minerals.

So much for this part; all good things usually come in threes – thus after the first two processes we have a third: the metamorphic formation process.

The formation of metamorphic rocks and minerals

Leaving the surface of the Earth behind, we will now go right back down again into the depths, kilometres deep into the Earth's mantle. And even here the rock has no peace, but the heat and the immense pressure of the Earth's core are ever present. Here again, there are various different factors at work, contributing to a state of affairs in which nothing remains exactly as it was before.

The nature of the Earth's crust

In order to understand what follows, we must first get rid of the superficial notion that the Earth's crust is evenly thick and firm all the way round. This is by no means the case. In reality, the crust consists of discrete 'shields' or 'plates' that float on top of the molten rocks of the Earth's mantle, in a similar manner to ice on the surface of water.

The individual plates vary in thickness: the oceanic plates are only about 5–10 kilometres (3–6 miles) thick, the continental plates, on the other hand, are more like 20–60 kilometres (13–38 miles) thick. As with icebergs, it is only the smaller portion that is visible at the top; the greatest part is below the surface.

For this reason, the continental plates also rise up farther than the oceanic ones; this is why we have the distinct separation of oceans and dry land on our planet.

The formation of mountains

Owing to the convection currents within the Earth's mantle (explained above), the various plates of the Earth's crust remain in constant motion. During this process they are pushed together and on top of each other in certain parts of the world. This creates zones where they cross each other and become buckled or folded up, forming mountains.

A glance at the world map will show these 'squashed' zones on the Earth as long chains and ranges of mountains. The largest, at present, are the Himalayas, then the Rocky Mountains and the Andes. These regions are also the places where the Earth's crust is at its thickest. According to the 'iceberg principle', only about 10 per cent of the total mass is pushed upwards; the rest is pressed down into the depths.

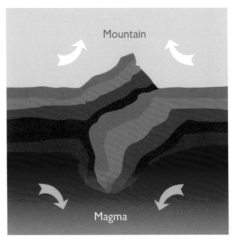

Regional metamorphosis during the formation of mountains.

Metamorphosis

These processes do not, of course, occur without leaving a trace on the rocks involved. A glance at our mountains will give you an inkling of the enormous power of the forces in the interior of the Earth that have accomplished these folding processes. Rocks that are involved in such a process under extreme pressures begin to restructure themselves. Crystals that were originally randomly interlocked with each other in all directions begin to order themselves, under the action of the great pressure.

As far as possible, they will organize themselves so they end up facing crossways to the direction of pressure. In some minerals, certain substances are quite literally 'squeezed out' of them; these accumulate and then form new, more resistant minerals. In some cases, neighbouring layers of rock are pressed together in such a way that they exchange elements with the moving rock and form new minerals in a kind of boundary layer. Any change in structure that will save space and provide more resistance to the pressure being exerted will inevitably take place: this is how a completely new rock is created.

The process is further promoted by heat acting upon the rock involved. The temperature of the rock in the interior of the Earth will begin to rise, particularly in layers of rock that are being pressed downwards by the formation of mountains. Temperatures even higher than those during the liquid magmatic phase of igneous rock formation may occur if the water required to turn the rock molten is not present.

The transformation of existing rock under extreme pressure and heat, without it becoming molten, is called metamorphosis, meaning it changes its shape and appearance. The newly formed

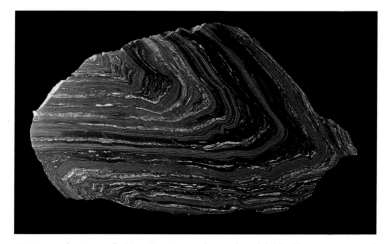

Metamorphosis: rock (tiger iron) transformed and folded by pressure and heat.

rocks are called metamorphic rocks and the minerals formed inside them are called metamorphic minerals.

Transformation of large areas

In addition to the example given above of the formation of mountains, metamorphosis also occurs if rocks become ever more compressed and hence heavier through overlaying with new layers, and thus end up sinking into the depths of the Earth. In both cases we speak of regional metamorphosis, as large areas are subjected to these transformations. Crystalline slate is typical of rocks formed in this way. Minerals formed in metamorphic rocks include disthene (kyanite), garnet, jade, nephrite, serpentine, thulite, tiger iron and zoisite. Another well-known example of a metamorphic rock is marble (transformed limestone), in which deposits of lapis lazuli or emeralds can sometimes be found.

Small-scale metamorphosis

Small-scale metamorphosis also occurs in the vicinity of rising magma. Owing to the enormously high temperatures, the rock around a volcanic chimney, for example, is subject to contact metamorphosis. This process can form ruby and sapphire, for example.

The addition of new elements

Wherever an additional exchange of elements in surrounding rocks takes place, for example through pneumatolytic vapours dissolving certain elements out of the rock and replacing them with others, this process is called 'metasomatism' (addition of new elements by migration in the rock). Examples of minerals formed in this way are charoite and rhodonite, as well as falcon's eye and tiger's eye.

The principle of metamorphic formation

Metamorphosis is the key word for the transformation of existing rock under the influence of heat and pressure in the interior of the Earth. The important point here is that the rock is not melted down again, but still undergoes alterations in its structure and mineral content. It takes on a completely different shape and appearance, but the transformation occurs essentially from the inside out. Metamorphosis subjects the rock to severe testing. Only what is impermeable to pressure and heat will be retained, everything else is transformed until a new, stable state is obtained.

In brief: The third formation principle represents a transformation process in which everything that cannot withstand the heat and pressure is changed into a new form from the inside out. In this way, new minerals are formed through metamorphosis and exchange of elements. We shall call these 'tertiary' minerals.

The cycle of rock formation

It now becomes clear that even rocks, together with their minerals, are by no means as eternal and unchangeable as they often appear to human observation. It is really only the enormous time scale in which these geological and mineralogical transformations take place, compared with the relatively short span of our earthly existence, that gives rise to this false notion. How could we, who in our short lives barely experience the span of three generations, be able to grasp time spans of millions of years?

Maybe an analogy will make the dimensions of these processes more obvious. If our allotted span of, say, 70 years were to represent symbolically one minute, an Alpine rock crystal, for example, would be almost a year old and the dinosaurs would have become extinct about two years ago, diamonds could boast 30 years or more, the oldest rocks would be regular Methuselahs of over 90 years and the Earth itself could boast as much as 150 years. Again, compare these figures with the minute of our lifespan!

When the processes are viewed as a model with these dimensions, it is clear that even rocks and minerals are in a constant process of

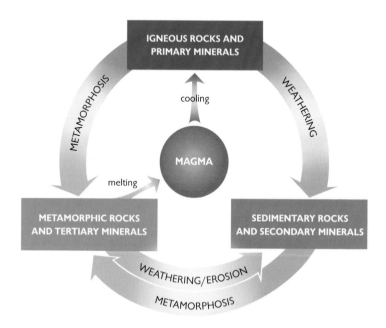

Cycle of rock formation

transformation. Here, too, there is creation, change and dissolution. From the magma arise igneous rocks with their primary minerals; through weathering these are transformed into sedimentary rocks and secondary minerals. Both formations may pass through a process of metamorphosis to become metamorphic rocks or tertiary minerals, which may then be transformed back into sedimentary rock or secondary minerals through weathering.

Finally, the heat of metamorphosis may become so great that the rock is melted down again. Thus the circle is closed if rock returns again to the state of magma.

The relationship between mineral origin and crystal healing

Very soon after the first results and experiences with the healing powers of minerals and precious stones had been established, I found myself asking the question as to how the ground beneath our feet might influence our human condition. Naturally, the rocks we walk about on daily contain a number of minerals and are present in such quantities that a possible influence could not be ruled out if a certain power were inherent in these minerals.

I dug out my old notebooks and diaries and gathered together geological maps of all my previous places of residence, remembering that I had moved house a total of six times between 1984 and 1987. I could be a useful research specimen myself for observing possible changes due to being subjected to different underground rocks. I was very surprised when I realized that of the total of seven different locations of residence, the first five had always been on the same type of rock strata.

Could this be a coincidence? Or had I, intuitively perhaps, without consciously realizing it, chosen the same types of homes on the same types of soil and rock? Even when I moved to Nürtingen, a slightly larger town than the others where I had lived, I had chosen one of only two streets in which the same rock was present underground.

I should like to give the sceptics among my readers the benefit of the same doubts and considerations I had at the time and which occupied me a great deal. When I use the term 'rock', I do not mean a basic, overall type that is present in great quantities (large mass), but a very specific strata: lias alpha, a very narrow band of black Jurassic that was only a few metres thick in several places where I lived. Furthermore, another glance at the geological map also yielded the information that the clinic in which I was born also lies on the same layer.

That moment, after a total of 23 years, when I 'left' the familiar rock strata in order to take up residence on a different strata, also brought a visible turning point in my life. It was the moment in which the conflict between materialism and a more spiritual view of our existence was decided in favour of the spirit, the moment in which encounters with important teachers began and the moment when I decided to dedicate myself to natural healing methods and to start studying at the School of Natural Healing. After that, my life changed so radically that it could hardly be mere coincidence.

Following on this realization came a very intense period during which I spent a great deal of time outdoors, sitting, eating and sleeping on the most varied kinds of rock strata, trying to work out their influences and properties. Here again, I had the problem of trying to separate the actual influence of the respective rock from other environmental factors, and to try and find out whether it was the ground or the weather, or even accompanying people, who were responsible for creating a particular mood or atmosphere. In the end, I went on long walks in order to experience the influence of different rocks under similar conditions.

During this period I was involved with seminars, in which I used not only to pass on my own experiences but also to check over them with other participants. These seminars all took place in the form of excursions during which we trained ourselves to the point where we were able to sense or perceive an exact transition from one rock strata to another in unknown terrain without first looking at a geological map (dowsing principle).

In spite of the fact that we had many enthusiastic participating seminar members and friends, it was still to take seven years until the connections between the manner of origin of rocks and minerals and their influences on human beings became clear and capable of being formulated. Several paths of research led us into cul-de-sacs; however, the repeatable experiences that were finally described in 1994 will be introduced here.

The healing properties of igneous rocks and primary minerals

 If we think back again to the principles of origin of these rocks and minerals, we will realize that our human lives are bound up with very similar processes.

The first formation principle demonstrates a crystallization process based on the cooling and solidification of liquid magma. The mineral-forming elements contained in magma represent the potential and predisposition for formation, as they already determine what can be formed. The crystallization process itself, however, is determined by the factors of pressure, heat, space and time, all of which decide in which manner the existing potential will be realized.

From the first moments of our existence, beside eating and sleeping, we are mainly occupied with learning. If you look at the huge learning accomplishments of a small child in its first years of life, they are without a doubt amazing: grasping, sitting, standing upright, walking, talking, recognizing other people, objects, situations and understanding them. These are all such complex matters and are learned in such a short space of time that certain tendencies have to have been there right from the start.

These natural abilities are what distinguishes us from other creatures. We can, for example, talk but not fly like a bird and will not live to be as old as a tree. These factors are simply part of our natural, inborn tendencies. These tendencies, whether they are part of a spiritual inheritance or genetic, are as determining for us as is magma for igneous rocks. They represent the potential for what or who we can become.

There is, however, a second factor: what good are natural tendencies if we do not have the space, time, the energy and the possibilities to unfold them and develop them further? Only if the inherent potential meets optimal conditions will it have the opportunity to unfold fully. As an analogy, what good is an inborn tendency to be a concert pianist for someone who is never able to take piano lessons, or why does not every student of the piano become a concert pianist?

Minerals and rocks may not change our inherent tendencies, but they may help us to develop our inner potential and to unfold it. Igneous rocks and primary minerals in particular, because of the similar manner of origin involved, will encourage learning processes. Every magmatic mineral represents certain spiritual values and will support and encourage their development in us as individuals.

In connection with this, the mineral will also encourage a certain kind of spiritual experience and corresponding thought and behaviour patterns, and may help with healing if these values, experiences, thought and behaviour patterns in any given case are conducive to overall good health.

In all of life's challenges, perhaps where we have just embarked on a new beginning in our life that is confronting us with many new ideas, or where we are faced with a host of learning experiences, the primary minerals are the first choice of healing stones. They will encourage the necessary growth processes and help with diseases that will typically arise in these situations.

The healing properties of sedimentary rocks and secondary minerals

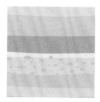

Sedimentary rocks and secondary minerals draw our attention to another aspect of our existence – the influences of the environment. Thanks to psychology, the fact that our environment – beginning with the home, kindergarten, school, training, profession, partner, children, friends and relatives and society, or even the total environment – has a massive effect on us is no longer a new idea.

It is, therefore, no surprise that sedimentary rocks and secondary minerals that originated through the influences of the environment will exactly reflect this aspect.

The second formation principle represents a process in which the solid structures of certain rocks are dissolved through environmental influences. The mineral-forming elements released out of the rock, together with other substances brought there through environmental activity, create new minerals.

The same processes occur in our lives: we are moulded and

shaped by the experiences of our past. Childhood experiences in particular play a determining role in all this. Here we make decisions based on pleasurable or painful experiences – what is 'good' and what is 'bad' for us.

We also develop survival strategies ('How do I get Mum and Dad to do what I want?') and during these years we are provided with 'explanations' for the way we find the world. As children, we are unable to check whether it is true that 'alcohol is evil' or whether 'beer is liquid bread'. We will tend to take on the opinions of those people whom we trust most.

In this way, first in childhood but also in later years, certain correspondences are created ('halt at red lights') and tenets of belief ('men only want one thing') that decisively shape our lives, behaviour and our feelings, as well as our imagination, ideals, goals and world views.

As long as this kind of shaping encourages our development in a positive way, there is nothing to be said against it. Very often, however, it so happens that the rigid patterns of behaviour that we have absorbed suddenly become useless at a later time or under different circumstances. For example, when we were children, if we learned the survival strategy 'Keep your mouth shut and you won't get hit in the teeth!' which might have been quite appropriate at a given time, we should not be surprised if, later on in our working lives, we get lumbered with the worst jobs because we are known for never protesting. Or if the strategy 'Cry loudly and I will get whatever I want!' worked with our parents when we were growing up, we should also not be surprised if nobody likes us much later on as adults because we never stop moaning.

Sedimentary rocks and secondary minerals make it easier for us to recognize this shaping based on learned correspondences, beliefs and painful experiences, to become fully aware of them, and then to dissolve them.

Sedimentary rocks and secondary minerals will help with new orientations, looking at new experiences from a different angle and with developing more suitable strategies tailored to present situations. In this way, our inner needs can more easily be brought in harmony with demands from our environment. Stress and tensions are dissolved, which will bring about healing of all diseases that result from conflicts with our environment.

There are many situations in which we are involved in conflict with our environment or with other people. Whether or not these conflicts are imminent or belong to the past, sedimentary rocks and secondary minerals will be our first choice for healing purposes. The healing of all diseases that have arisen through conflict or the avoidance of conflict is helped by them.

The healing properties of metamorphic rocks and tertiary minerals

 Just as their strength and durability were constantly being tested during their formation, metamorphic rocks and tertiary minerals appear to test aspects of our lives in terms of their durability.

Everything that is not of permanent value for us will begin to change and take on new shapes and forms. Many episodes in our lives will come to an end naturally, without there seeming to be any noticeable necessity for it. In theory we could have held onto many things for longer – a job, a home, a group or a partnership – but somehow a point came when it was all over, finished with and ended.

If we withdraw at that moment, make the break and begin something new, then as a rule the change will take place painlessly and without difficulties. Too often, however, we do not let go of the old but hold on to it because we are used to it, or because we do not (yet) know what the new thing is that is approaching us. We carry on as usual, only suddenly there is an unpleasant sense of 'something not being right'.

The sensation grows stronger and gradually materializes into a feeling that we have to change ourselves and our lives. We may have forgotten the point at which it should have been obvious, or we do not notice when it should have happened. It may be that the feeling of wanting this new thing has no particular direction, and pressures and heat arise in us that begin to question everything fundamentally.

The metamorphic formation principle represents a transformation process in which everything that cannot withstand the heat and pressure is changed into a new form from the inside out. In this way, through metamorphosis and exchange of elements, new minerals are formed.

The heat and pressure inside us may lead through a phase of dissatisfaction in which we are very self-critical. Everything is questioned as to whether it makes sense and is of value for our lives. We begin a radical clean-up. Lazy compromises, outworn habits, nostalgic relics from the past as well as meaningless rules and regulations are thrown out and replaced by genuine settlements, necessary activities, contemporarily useful attitudes and sensible agreements. In this way we transform our lives into completely new forms.

Metamorphic rocks and tertiary minerals stimulate this inner transformation process. They encourage critical self-reflection and help us to realize and understand those things in our lives that are not durable and what needs ending because it makes us feel dissatisfied. These minerals and rocks bring radical changes that lead to a more fulfilled, purposeful life. They will, therefore, help with all manner of diseases that are rooted in the fear of letting go, in necessary changes that have not been carried out, or in a lifestyle that no longer makes any sense. By stimulating an inner transformation they help us to overcome attachments, habits and compromises.

In all life situations in which we feel strong inner dissatisfaction, where we have a feeling that we should change something but do not know what, or if we are confronted with a change but are afraid because we do not know what will happen afterwards – in all these cases, metamorphic rocks or tertiary minerals are the first choice of healing crystals. The healing of all diseases that have come about through such inner conflicts is stimulated and accelerated by these materials.

The application of the formation principle to healing

The three types of origin of minerals and rocks is very clearly mirrored in typical life situations. The principle provides us with simple opportunities to find solutions for our problems or difficulties with the help of the right minerals or rocks. The curing of all the diseases that have arisen out of these situations is also enhanced. To identify correctly the minerals needed it is important to make an exact and careful analysis of the situation.

For this purpose, first make a sketch of the circumstances, that is, pick out the key issues and important features. Then, in your mind, run through all three possibilities: 'What should be present so that the primary/secondary/tertiary type of mineral may apply?' Once you have run through all three possibilities in your thoughts, it will become clearer which applies than if you just observe the given situation.

Once you have made a choice, matters become quite simple. Choose a location where the relevant rock is present in the ground and remain there for at least one day, and preferably at least three days at this location or in this area.

Typical rocks of igneous origin would be plutonites: granite, syenite, diorite and gabbro, for vulcanites: rhyolite, trachyte, basalt, phonolite and volcanic tuff (tufa) or 'lava stone'.

Typical sedimentary rocks (which give us secondary minerals) include: sandstone, breccia, conglomerates, clay-based rocks, as well as limestones, dolomites and gypsum rocks.

Typical metamorphic rocks (which give us tertiary minerals) include: gneiss, mica, phyllite, amphibolite, serpentine, hornfels and marble.

Geological or petrographic maps that will help you find the right strata can be obtained from Ordnance Survey offices, surveyors or the geological survey of the area.

Spend lots of time outside and moving about at these locations. You need not do anything else. The effects of the rocks are so strong that you will definitely experience changes very quickly. The third day is always the most interesting, on which the influence of the new type of ground becomes most clearly noticeable. It is also the so-called 'critical day', which is something all mountain guides and skiing instructors will be able to tell you about, as this is when the new 'feeling for life' begins, the urge to rebel against the old. People often lack concentration and become very careless and negligent at this time. The attention (unconsciously) turns inward and people tend to pay little attention to external demands and dangers. On the third day, you should definitely make time for yourself – even if you are already back at home!

The second possibility consists of choosing minerals of the correct formation from the table in the Chapter 2.2, The analytical art of healing with crystals (see page 151). You may even discover minerals that you already know and with which you already have a connection. If not, choose the suitable mineral according to the profile given in Part 3 of this book. Carry this mineral on you constantly. As the effect, in this case, will not be as strong as it would be if you were staying somewhere with the mineral in the ground beneath you, the influence will take longer to make itself felt. Here, pay attention on the third and seventh days.

During our research, these two days turned out to be ones with a special quality. It appears that renewal processes have an underlying rhythm of threes and sevens. Think, for example, of the fact that all the cells in our body are completely renewed over a span of seven years. And it may also be no coincidence that a cycle of exactly seven days was chosen for a weekly rhythm.

Let us now turn to a completely different aspect of our lives. Just as the manner of origin of minerals throws light on (and in) our present life situation, there is also a secondary principle in the kingdom of minerals that will illuminate our lifestyle. This principle is revealed to us in crystals

1.2 Crystals

The discovery of crystals

Throughout the ages people have noticed that minerals and precious stones display extremely conspicuous and fascinatingly regular shapes and forms in their naturally grown state. For a long time, these strange, precise shapes and forms were seen as evidence for the intervention of the gods during the formation of these stones. Who else would be in a position to create something as wonderful as this?

Only a little more than 300 years ago, in 1669, the Danish naturalist, Nils Stensen, known as Nicolas Steno, published some

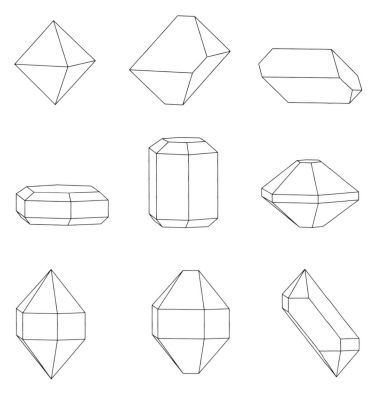

The crystal shapes of a mineral can look very different but the angles between the individual facets remain the same.

initial research concerning the mathematical regularity of crystals. Stenson had discovered that the angles between the surfaces of a particular mineral, independently of their size, appearance or location, are always the same. From these observations he formed the 'law of constant interfacial angles'.

From this time on, it became clear that it was not random influences from the place of origin that gave a mineral its shape, but that there was some inherent property that would always cause the mineral to take on certain shapes. It was then discovered that a particular, typical shape could often be a more reliable feature of a certain mineral than, for example, its rather variable colour. This presented the science of crystals with the presently accepted definition:

A crystal is a solid body with a geometrically regular shape.

The name 'crystal' had originally been given to rock crystal which the Greeks had christened *krystallos*, 'ice', as they believed rock crystal was deep-frozen water that could never melt again! This belief was still prevalent at the time of Nils Stensen. Four years later, in 1673, the British scientist Robert Boyle first cast doubts on the belief.

Nevertheless, scientists began to search enthusiastically for the laws governing the phenomenon of the 'crystal'. It was to take another 100 years until a French schoolmaster, Rene-Just Haüy, published his theory on the structure of crystals in 1784. A 'coincidence' had come to his aid: while handling a calcite crystal belonging to a friend, he dropped it and it split into several parts. Although this was very annoying, it allowed him to make an important discovery: the fragments of the shattered crystal all displayed a very similar appearance. Haüy concluded that crystals already have certain geometric shapes right down to their smallest 'elementary cells', that is, in the domain of atoms and molecules (the smallest building blocks of matter).

The crystal lattice

This realization had brought him very close to the truth. The atoms and molecules are not themselves geometrically shaped as Haüy assumed. However, they are organized spatially in exact, geometrical patterns, the so-called 'crystal lattices'.

This perfect order is explained by the fact that individual atoms and molecules (usually of varying sizes) of the mineral are packed

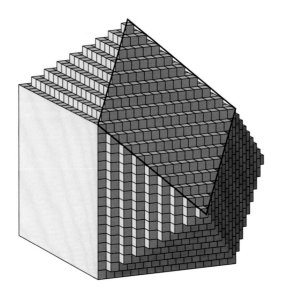

According to Haüy's theories, both the cube and the rhombo-dodecahedron (a twelve-sided object with diamond-shaped sides) can be formed out of smaller cubic elements.

together as closely as possible during their growth. This is partly because they are drawn together by strong electromagnetic forces, partly because pressure around them allows no space to be wasted. (Think back to the often extremely harsh conditions under which a mineral is formed!) A strictly ordered system will always offer a better use of space than a random muddle.

One small example may illuminate the nature of a crystal lattice: imagine you had to divide up an empty, white surface like that outlined below into lots of equal-sized fields without leaving any gaps. (The edges need not be taken into account.) What geometric shapes would be appropriate?

If you try this out for a while, you will discover that only the

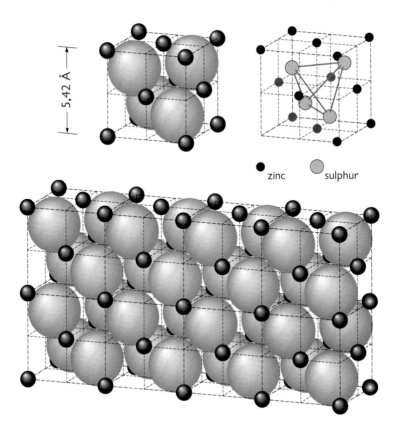

Above left: *The crystal structure of sphalerite (zinc blende); it is not the atoms themselves that are angled but their distribution in the crystal results in a severely geometrical lattice.*
Above right: *The atoms have not been shown here in their correct relative size to each other but merely as 'points of mass' in order to depict the lattice.*
Bottom: *A larger section of the crystal lattice; the lattice should be imagined to extend further into all three spatial dimensions.*

following seven geometric shapes can be used for the purpose: the square, hexagon, triangle, rectangle, rhombus, parallelogram and trapezium (see page 46).

Only with these shapes will you be able to fill out the surface without leaving any gaps. In the case of pentagons, heptagons, octagons, dodecahedrons, or even circles, there will always be gaps between the fields, meaning wasted space that cannot exist in a completely filled out crystal! For this simple reason, only crystal lattices exist that have squares, hexagons, triangles, rectangles, rhombuses, parallelograms and trapeziums as their basic structure. There are no other types!

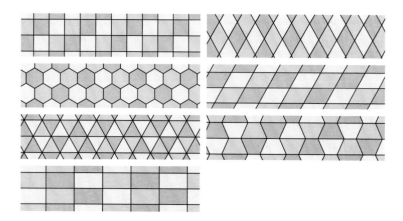

These basic structures ensure that crystals only ever display particularly defined shapes. This means that the basic structure of the square, for example, will typically lead to shapes like the cube, octahedron and rhombic dodecahedron, while a basic hexagonal structure leads to hexagonal pillars, and so on.

All crystals, not only those of minerals, but also crystals in the organic realm, as for example the sugar crystals mentioned earlier, are governed by these laws. Crystals can, therefore, be grouped according to their inner structure into seven distinct systems, the seven crystal systems.

The crystal systems

The **cubic crystal system** includes all crystals with a square inner structure. The word 'cubic' is derived from Latin *cubus*, hence our word cube. Cubic minerals often actually form cubes as crystals (for example diamond, fluorite, pyrite), octahedrons (diamond, fluorite, magnetite), rhombic dodecahedrons (garnet, lapis lazuli), tetrahedrons (pyrite, zinc blende (sphalerite)), pentagon-dodecahedron (pyrite) and others …

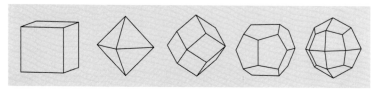

Crystal shapes based on the cube

The **hexagonal crystal system** includes all crystals with a hexagonal inner structure. The word 'hexagonal' is derived from the Greek for 'six-sided body'. Hexagonal minerals in the form of crystals will, as a rule, also form hexagonal pillars, such as apatite, aquamarine, beryl, morganite and emerald.

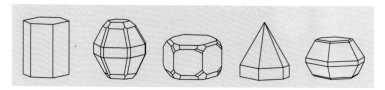

Hexagonal crystal shapes

The **trigonal crystal system** includes all crystals with a triangular inner structure. The word 'trigonal' is derived from the Greek *trigon*, 'triangle'. Trigonal minerals have crystals in the form of trigonal pillars (tourmaline) or hexagonal pillars, although the latter are not quite as regular as those formed in the hexagonal crystal system (for example amethyst, rock crystal, citrine, smoky quartz, ruby, sapphire, tourmaline), and also in rhombohedral forms (calcite, dolomite, magnesite, rhodochrosite). The inner trigonal structure is particularly beautiful and clearly visible in tourmaline slices that display triangular or trident-like colour zones.

Trigonal crystal shapes

The **tetragonal crystal system** includes all crystals with a rectangular inner structure. The word 'tetragonal' is derived from the Greek *tetragon*, 'rectangle'. Tetragonal minerals generally form crystals with rectangular pillars, sometimes with flat boundaries and sometimes with pyramidal points. Examples include apophyllite, rutile and zircon (hyacinth).

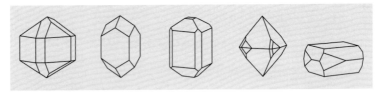

Tetragonal crystal shapes

The **orthorhombic crystal system** includes all crystals with a rhombic inner structure. The word 'rhombic' is derived from the Greek *rhombus*. Rhombic minerals form either rhombic crystals, for example aragonite, olivine (peridot) or topaz, but sometimes also hexagonal ones, as three rhombuses fitted together form a hexagon. This type of growth is quite aptly termed 'pseudohexagonal'; an example is aragonite.

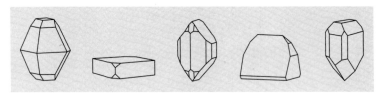

Rhombic crystal shapes

The **monoclinic crystal system** includes all crystals that have an inner structure in the shape of a parallelogram. The word 'monoclinic' means approximately 'with an inclined angle' (Greek *mono*, 'one', and *klinein*, 'to incline, bend'). Monoclinic crystals also display this 'crooked' angle. It is most obvious in gypsum that often has 'crooked' crystals with clearly visible parallelogram shapes (in this crystal form called selenite). Other monoclinic minerals include azurite, epidote, jade, kunzite, lepidolite, malachite, moonstone and nephrite.

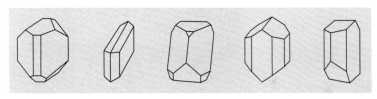

Monoclinic crystal shapes

The **triclinic crystal system** includes all crystals with an inner structure in the form of a trapezium. The term 'triclinic' means the equivalent of 'with three inclined angles' (Greek *tri*, 'three', and *klinein*, 'to incline, bend'). There is nothing quite like 'crooked' or 'bent' triclinic crystals that have no right angles at all. The inner structure of this crystalline system is most clearly displayed in amazonite crystals, which form the shape of two trapeziums joined together. Further triclinic minerals are disthene (kyanite), labradorite, rhodonite, sunstone and turquoise.

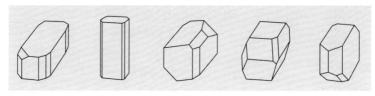

Triclinic crystal shapes

There seem to be no rules without exceptions! Sometimes, conditions are so extraordinary that a mineral has no possibility of forming a crystalline structure. These minerals are called **amorphous** (Greek *amorph*, 'without shape') and they do not possess any kind of inner structure. The reasons for this lack of structure are to be found in their too rapid creation, for example as in moldavite and obsidian, where there is no time for crystals to be formed, or because too many different substances are mingled together, as for example in amber and opal.

The appearance of amorphous minerals

Discovering the connections between crystalline structures and lifestyles

For me, crystals and their regular shapes were always the most interesting phenomena in the entire realm of minerals as it had been the strange, regular crystal facets of my piece of garnet that had started me off on my discovery of minerals.

This structure and order fascinated me and, even as a ten-year old, I was tossing around terms like 'lattice structure', 'crystal system', 'axis of symmetry' and so on. I would not maintain that I properly understood everything then, in as much as many modern books on mineralogy still suffer from the same defects that Franz of Kobell complained about in his *History of Mineralogy* in 1864:

Furthermore, at all times, it has been demonstrated that, although individual researchers have an unselfconsciously sharp eye for detail and a gift for explaining matters in simple terms, others place obstacles in the way of progress by demonstrating an even greater talent for passing on simple things in the most complicated manner and for seeing difficulties of all kinds where there are none!

So, whether I did or did not understand things then, at least the crystal systems were so familiar to me that I was rather surprised to find, during the early days of my studies on healing with crystals, that hardly any researchers or authors had taken much notice of them, let alone the possibility that they might incorporate these ideas into considerations of the healing properties of minerals and precious stones. There are only seven crystal systems in the whole world (not counting the amorphous exception). Surely there must be some kind of cosmic significance in this?

Fortunately, a remaining residue of scientific suspicion prevented me from immediately setting up a table to incorporate the crystal systems in a row with the seven planets of the classical world, the seven chakras, seven notes, and so on. Instead, I began observing which humans felt drawn towards certain minerals and what effects these minerals had on them.

One of the most impressive experiences I had was during a visit I paid to the home of an acquaintance who was known throughout his circle of friends for his exactness, correctness and thoroughness, and also for his extraordinary stamina, discipline, ability to learn, his immense knowledge and untiring 'know-it-all' attitude. In his living room, I unexpectedly came upon a shelf-ful of minerals – at the time, I did not even know that he collected minerals. This shelf accommodated fluorite exclusively.

At this point I must correct my earlier statement: he did not collect minerals – he collected fluorites. Only fluorites! Now, fluorites belong among the cubic crystals … Later, during the meal, when I noticed that I had never observed anyone sprinkling more salt (also cubic!) on his food than he did, a suspicion began to form in my mind … Could it be that there was a connection between the crystal structures of minerals and the lifestyle of humans? – that this inner structure of a mineral is mirrored in the way they conduct their lives?

Just as I began to come to grips with this idea, a bookseller in

Stuttgart offered me regular advisory sessions on the use of precious stones. I saw this proposition as a challenge, first to check out the conclusions I had come to and to see whether they were applicable practically, and second, to collect further experiences through contact with other people. This was the beginning of a very fruitful phase in my work with minerals and precious stones. Looking back, I am now very grateful that there was comparatively little information available during this period (1988–1989).

Because of this, there were very few opinions around and we were forced to research into the properties of relevant stones in these sessions by means of intense discussion. During the course of these sessions, I was able to observe very clearly the real connection between crystal structures and lifestyles. Minerals with particular crystal systems were always chosen by certain people with particular traits. With time, I became increasingly conscious of the connections, until eventually I was often able to guess in advance the crystal system that someone would intuitively gravitate towards by watching them from their first entrance into a room, their manner of walking, talking and moving.

Gradually, these observations led me to the conclusion that, even among the great variety of human lifestyles, there really were eight basic structures that corresponded to the seven crystal systems and the eighth amorphic state. The causes for this lie in the observed reality of each individual.

Human reality

Each one of us lives in his or her own reality. It is determined by our experiences and knowledge, by our opinions and observations and by the value systems we apply. This reality, which is defined by ourselves, will create mutual bonds with other humans or form boundaries between us and others. If you have shared experiences with someone, you will have the same reality. What do old friends do, for example? – They talk about 'the old days', that is, mutual experiences.

If you find someone who shares the same knowledge as you, you also share the same reality. Two experts in the same field will soon begin to exchange technical knowledge even if they have only just met five minutes earlier. An outsider (an interesting word!) who does not have this same knowledge will probably not understand very much about these conversations as he or she cannot share the same reality.

The same opinions or ways of looking at something create a reality, and this is how people who have the same political, world or religious views will quickly gravitate towards each other. The converse is also true, as there is hardly anything that will create deeper divisions between people. Thus, the example of religious wars shows that different realities can even lead to people into situations where they will kill each other, without gaining any significant advantage by doing so.

We are aware of this problem in everyday life: interview the witnesses of a traffic accident and you will be surprised how many different realities you come up with! Even shared experiences may lead to very different realities. A shared lesson at school will represent a very different reality to the star pupil than to the persistent problem pupil! Or how about the very different realities of optimists and pessimists? For the former a glass is half full, while for the other it is half empty.

This means reality is something completely subjective, yet the individual experiences it as absolute and valid. It is very important to understand this and to give it due attention. Particularly in the field of natural healing, it is extremely important to get to know the other person's reality. We will not be able to help anyone if we attack their reality, deny it or devalue it. Only if we accept another reality as given will we be able to help someone to change, if that person is having problems or difficulties and wishes to overcome them.

Crystals can be employed in this field in order to bring about changes or encourage them. A very interesting phenomenon is displayed when one is observing human realities. If we ignore all common factors that have arisen through shared experiences, knowledge, opinions, observations and values, there are still certain basic structures. Even then, humans can be distinguished by their nature and divided into different 'types'.

These 'basic structures of human reality' have been observed at all times and many systems have been created to explain the structures: the temperaments, Jung's archetypes, the principles of astrology, the picture cards of the tarot, and many others. All of these descriptions are valid within their own framework and when applied in the relevant system can work very well.

The difficulty always arises when one attempts to transfer a particular definition to another system. Here conflicts will arise between the different realities of the systems themselves. An example for this is the typical problem encountered by ethnologists arriving in a different cultural circle, where they investigate and then describe what they have found but are only very rarely able to discard the 'spectacles' of their own culture and lay aside the ways of observing they have brought along with them. This is where the necessary appreciation of a different reality is lacking.

For this reason, in spite of intensive studies of many different systems, I was always very careful not to be in a hurry to transfer knowledge gained from other systems to the realm of healing with crystals. The discovery of 'lifestyles' as a 'basic structure of human reality' and their correspondence with crystal systems was one of the happiest moments in the first ten years of healing crystal research; we now had a system that could be applied with a great deal of precision.

Crystal structures and lifestyles

Descriptions of different 'lifestyles' show eight distinct basic characteristics of human behaviour, of personal behaviour and of individual lifestyle. These characteristics are independent of age, background, gender, world view or life experience. They are basic structures out of which we have chosen one as a survival strategy for our entire life or for our present situation. As these basic patterns can be seen in connection with the crystal systems of minerals, those minerals that possess the crystal structure that corresponds to us are particularly suitable for us as healing stones.

The cubic lifestyle

Let us start with the cubic lifestyle, which was already briefly outlined in the earlier example of the 'fluorite collector'. Just as the cubic crystal system is characterized by a square structure and is therefore very regular, the corresponding lifestyle is also characterized by regular structures.

People who lead their lives in the cubic style never leave anything to chance. Order and an overview are very important to you. You will endeavour to create structure in all areas of your life in order to keep everything 'under control': your living space will be structured, for example, by making sure everything has its place. You know, both at home and at your work place, where everything can be found, at least in those task areas that you define or recognize as 'your' areas.

Time, too, has its own structure. Certain habits take up a fixed position in your daily schedule. You keep to daily rituals, whether they be the same sequence of morning hygiene, punctually timed meals, the evening news programme or anything else. You take your commitments seriously and are generally punctual – to the minute or always late by the same number of minutes, which is also a kind of punctuality. You like to plan things far in advance so that you can make detailed provisions for later events at an early stage.

Your actions are generally of a very regular nature. You love acting soberly with well-considered plans and are also in a position to anticipate the consequences of what you do, at least, as far as the consequences concern you.

You are quickly able to grasp the essentials of a situation and try to create order everywhere – your idea of order – and wherever necessary. Certain events and sequences that you have found to be sensible and effective will be adhered to, just as you prefer to stick to tried and tested ways of doing things instead of engaging in spontaneous experimentation.

Security is very important to you.

Logical thinking comes easily to you. You seldom have any difficulty in retaining an overview, even in complex systems, and you are able to look systematically for the causes of phenomena.

You are also very precise and exact in all your considerations of whatever will provide security and will strengthen your position in a conflict. You are extremely careful in any overly free associations or risky speculations. For you the inevitable outcome of cause and effect should be recognizable in all circumstances; even a risk should be calculable.

Feelings, too, have their place. You have deep feelings towards people you love, and even, depending on your inclinations, towards animals, plants, stones or even ideas that you feel enthusiastic about.

Still, you do not like to allow your actions to be led by your feelings. The terrain is too unfamiliar, lacking any landmarks, and the risk too great that you may allow yourself to be pushed into precipitous actions based on your feelings. Also, objectivity is too important for you to abandon it on a whim. You are, therefore, in a position to control your feelings and remain in charge of the situation.

You also prefer to maintain a constant appearance on the outside. You have certain favourite colours, preferred articles of clothing that you wear even when they are falling apart, and you like to stay in a certain kind of environment. You prefer to appear conservative rather than unorthodox.

The same goes for looking after your physical well-being: naturally, you are keen to remain healthy, have regular health check-ups, never miss the half-yearly dental checkup and stick to a regular regime of personal hygiene. Unfortunately, your bad habits are just as persistent! The main cause of illness in the cubic lifestyle is bad habits: poor diet, smoking, alcohol, an unhealthy lifestyle and many things you just cannot give up, no matter how hard you are pushed by your doctor.

Your greatest weakness is your lack of flexibility. On a mental level too, the biggest problems you have are connected with the fact that you cling too much to the familiar and show too little spontaneity if something unexpected happens. The collapse of a well-thought-out plan can create a deep crisis and a temporary sense of disorientation.

Defeats like this increase the urge to seek security and control to such a degree that there is a risk of becoming totally 'head-bound', resulting in overemphasis of the rational mind and logic and a suppression of intuition, feelings and emotions, to a degree that their existence can no longer be felt. This is just the beginning of a vicious circle that spirals downwards.

It then becomes utterly impossible to let go of habitual behaviour patterns, as you can now no longer see any other way of acting. Your thoughts and opinions become so rigid that they seem more important than reality itself. Under certain circumstances, you may even be ready to twist the reality of an event to make it conform to your view of it, rather than the opposite. In extreme cases, you will not balk at any means.

Depending on your individual character, you may find yourself subject to a strong missionary urge, or even experience a readiness to use violence to promote your own ideas. The desire to uphold your own system of order may lead to unnecessary complications: instead of handling a situation according to the obvious facts, you have to plan, think about it, grasp it, register it, analyse it, structure it, determine priorities, delegate, rule and secure. A simple garden party turns into a state reception …

All your rules and laws become even more problematic if you overemphasize them so much that you are really only able to live according to these preconceived patterns. Then any change coming from the outside becomes a threat, any criticism is seen as a personal attack, and all other lifestyles or world views become a danger that has to be fought against.

Your thinking is, therefore, polarized in an extremely negative way. You see nothing but mistakes, difficulties, failures and dangers, and your faculties for rational thought and logic are used exclusively to support these observations by collecting 'suitable' information that will back up your preconceived notions. Even help offered by others is viewed with suspicion. The opinion that 'the world is not treating me well' can be extended, forcing your own thought and behaviour patterns to be transformed into (small-scale) fortifications.

A climax is finally reached when the 'cubic' person might even be ready to commit suicide, merely in order to uphold an idea, world view or ideology. By this, I do not mean a kamikaze operation or the willingness to die for a good cause, but the daily mistake, repeated a million times over, of throwing away life on account of rigidly adhering to certain patterns of thought and behaviour: for example, being seriously ill and rejecting effective 'alternative' therapies, not going to the doctor in spite of pain, not changing your diet because you do not believe that it will help, driving a car under the influence of alcohol because you are absolutely sure of being in control, working yourself to death because money, position or a career are more important than good health or your life, and so on.

Things like this often happen for the simple reason that people of this disposition stubbornly hold on to certain set ways of looking at things, or do not allow themelves a new perspective. This is typically 'cubic'. But do not despair! You do not need to end up this way if you are a 'cubic' personality. A cubic lifestyle can allow both a negative development, as described above, and development in a positive direction.

In the latter case, there is development of precisely those characteristics that will allow you to 'think big' and generously. One of these abilities, for example, is being able to keep an overview of many different sequences: the working connections within a large firm, the complexities of a computer program, or even the many so-called 'coincidences' in one's own life that, seen as a whole, often seem clearly to demonstrate the finger of destiny – if you are able to see the connections. Then you have an opportunity to see yourself as part of a larger plan. Not merely to sense or feel how other lifestyles can make this possible, but to see clearly.

This starts with the possibility of seeing your own life 'pattern' as part of a higher structure. Along with the readiness not to stick stubbornly to your own ideas, you gain the opportunity to fit into the structures of family, community, human life and planetary life, as well as into the laws of a physical and spiritual universe. In this way, forming rigid boundaries, over-protecting yourself, suspicion and violent change become completely unnecessary.

Naturally, you do not blindly trust in God and the World, but are ready to allow yourself to be persuaded by new possibilities. You remain open to new experiences. In a typically 'cubic' fashion, you become extremely open to learning. Every new experience, any new piece of information is immediately linked with what is already known, fitted in, connected and is then ready to be applied.

Your ability to create order and oversee larger connections can also be employed in a way that is helpful to others. As you are able to see far ahead, you are in a position to 'switch the points' before others are able to see what is coming towards them. Your prognoses are, as a rule, well based and reliable.

No matter in what area of work you are involved, you will be concerned with making your work more effective, optimizing actions and improving results.

Large goals appear attractive to you, so you rapidly gravitate towards responsible positions and are able to fill them. Difficulties appear as challenges that can be mastered and problems merely help you to learn and grow. You gain fulfilment with the successful realization of each idea and – for a cubic personality who is able to foresee the consequences and results of their actions at the time of acting – success is bound to follow!

The hexagonal lifestyle

Among the seven shapes mentioned above, the hexagon is the one with the smallest perimeter in relation to the area enclosed. This efficient use of space has led bees to construct their honeycombs in hexagonal grid patterns, and this kind of efficiency is also a central theme of the hexagonal lifestyle. 'Hexagonal' humans have a great urge towards success and have plenty of direction. This goes for long-term goals as well as for individual daily stages.

If you are a 'hexagonal' person, anything you aim for you will ultimately reach. Your lifestyle is very consistent. You choose an idea consciously, know exactly who your role models are, and anything you have recognized as being right is made real through a step-by-step process. You love straightforwardness and honesty. The shortest path is your favourite path; diversions and distractions are anathema to you.

Time is one of your most precious commodities. You are anxious to use it as sensibly and usefully as possible; you abhor wasting time. As attaining the goal is more important to you than the path to it, you are able to distinguish very well between the necessary and the superfluous. You devote yourself to the former and ignore the latter. Your days are filled up, idle time or boredom are unknown to you. As a rule, you have a considerable amount ahead of you and once a goal is reached, you quickly look for and find another.

Your actions are well planned and well prepared. You will work tirelessly, with zeal and dedication, both physically and mentally, to achieve your goal, which may be of a personal, social, political or religious nature.

You never lose sight of the goal and this is what gives you the strength to carry on, no matter how steep the path or how difficult. Even if there are difficulties and obstacles along the way, the strength to overcome again and again is always available. You like having a career. You are spurred on by wanting to attain something that fills you with pride.

Your thinking processes are clear and analytical. You are quick on the uptake and are very motivated. As a rule, you determine for yourself what you are interested in and will rarely be distracted from it. You quickly understand the sense and usefulness of all matters so they can be incorporated into your plans, if they are appropriate.

Even though you are able to change strategies and tactics rapidly if necessary, you remain true to your fundamental persuasions. You are very thorough, sometimes even fussy, and only content if everything is working down to the last detail. As a rule, only the best is good enough for you.

Your life clearly emphasizes the rational side of things. You are able to experience feelings very intensely, but can detach yourself from them instantly if they hinder you or prevent you from acting. Here, too, the inborn faculty to overcome is a great advantage.

You are also very individualistic. The fact that you dislike being hemmed in by others and refuse to be slowed down, checked or oppressed is another reason for the urge to reach the top, the desire for a position in life in which you determine your own fate.

It is, however, an interesting fact that you usually stop just one step away from the top. Obviously, it appears more important to continue to have a goal in front of you than to sit at the top without a future prospect. The teacher's best pupil or the boss's right-hand man is a much more desirable position for some than being the teacher or the boss. Many Secretaries of State remain in office when the minister has to leave … the secret ruler rules longer!

Even your body displays this ideal. You love to have a well-trained, well-functioning body, and engage in just enough sporting activity to keep fit. As a rule, you look after your health and have a good diet, as long as other things do not become more important. If the time left to attain a projected goal is running out, you have no qualms about leaving out a meal here or there (or even several). Drinking coffee standing up and grabbing a quick snack on the hop can rapidly become a habit. Asceticism comes easily if it serves a purpose; you would, however, probably never sacrifice four weeks of holiday to go on a therapeutic diet.

If you do become ill, the main reason is generally overwork, too little self-consideration and too many demands on yourself. You often get very impatient during the get-well phase and the danger of having a lingering illness, suffering a relapse, or using acute suppression that results in an acute illness becoming chronic is far more prevalent with the hexagonal lifestyle than in any other. You also easily become accustomed to taking tablets to combat fatigue or bring sleep, as long as they appear to guarantee that you keep functioning.

Your greatest strengths can at the same time be your greatest weaknesses! You find it too easy to become fixated on a single goal, neglecting to look either to the right or the left. This results in a blinkered attitude that impoverishes your life and you are driven by the feeling that you are constantly lacking the time to do all you want. Hectic behaviour, impatience and stress increase constantly. Then you find you are lacking spiritual nourishment because you have not got enough leisure time, relaxation and variety, as well as the strength that can be derived from these. Even holidays are cut down to a minimum or they are used for another target-oriented and gruelling programme.

For a long time this stress will remain hidden, as you can make up for the deficiency in your life for a certain amount of time through sheer willpower, until finally the last reserves are used up. Then, you experience collapse.

The crisis will arrive just as certainly if you succeed in attaining one of the 'great goals' of your life. Suddenly, something seems to be missing: a sense, a task, the feeling of being needed or being important in some way. You need goals in front of you. This means that success is often not celebrated, the fruits of labour are not enjoyed. Instead of relaxing, taking a rest and enjoying peace, you immediately start looking for a new goal, a new direction, the next dimension. If you cannot find it quickly enough, the inner emptiness is bridged by outer activities, at least as long as it takes until your body pulls its emergency brake!

For this reason, 'hexagonal' goals or ideals are often set so high that it is almost certain they will never be attained. This means the risk of that 'great emptiness' arriving is eliminated, but woe betide anything that is in its path. During 'orientation crises', it is high ideals or 'salvation' teachings that will find fertile ground in the hexagonal personality: enlightenment, Nirvana, immortality or eternal bliss.

Wherever these ideals are promised, your own critical facilities will suddenly be switched off. You tend to accept the teachings offered without testing them; you lift them up to become a new goal, identify with them and find your way back to your strengths and habitual capacities. You often do not notice at all that it is only the fact that you have a new goal that has set the positive changes in motion, and the goal itself has taken second place.

If you then ascribe the positive changes to the content of this new ideal, fixation upon the new goal becomes very strong. Depending on what kind of content you are committing yourself to, your hexagonal tendency to fanaticism can lead to various different degrees of involvement.

In some ways, however, fanaticism is always destructive, as you begin to ignore your own needs and limits. Then it is only a matter of time before you start expecting or demanding it from others too. What was until now voluntary discipline and loyalty to your own principles is confused with ruthlessness and dogmatism. Here, too, in extreme cases, you find the willingness to sacrifice your life, and the lives of others, merely to follow an ideal or a flag.

The positive development of the hexagonal lifestyle begins with the simple principle – do as you say! The consistent way of acting that you have always had will automatically cause you to assimilate experiences while realizing the ideals that will either confirm what you are doing along the way, or send signals that changes are overdue.

Here, it is important that you always remain willing to reassess your goals in the light of your experiences. Goals can be changeable. The closer you get to the summit, the more clearly you will be able to see it. Perhaps the goal no longer corresponds to the image you had of it from a distance. This means it is important that you always leave an option open, daily, either to amend this image because new facts have come to light, or to embark on a different path. Both will make you freer.

The second aspect that will make a positive hexagonal development possible is an inner certainty that you will reach your goal. It simply lies in the nature of hexagonal personalities. You do not need to put such a great deal of effort into it. The frequently present feeling of 'being driven', the restlessness and overexerting yourself, often arise from a fear of not reaching the goal you have set for yourself. If you are certain, on an inner level, that you really possess the necessary abilities, you can approach the whole matter in a far more relaxed manner. This 'laid back' attitude is a better guarantee for success than any kind of effort. Naturally, you have to do some work, but you never could resist that anyway!

Freed of blinkers and armed with a consistent approach, inner certainty and a relaxed attitude, you are able to accomplish vast amounts each day. You storm up career ladders and the personal development that you desire moves along splendidly. Individualism and sociability are no longer seen as being opposed, but complement each other.

You also find that tolerance and acceptance of others' ways will never get in the way of your own personal self-realization; on the contrary, they will actually encourage it. The combination of foresight and a global view of life will offer such a host of experiences that you will gradually become aware of the truth: the path is the goal!

The trigonal lifestyle

The triangle is the simplest geometric form – likewise, the trigonal lifestyle is basically very simple. If this is your own lifestyle, you will lead a simple, uncomplicated life, very constant and tranquil. You are quite able to appreciate the comforts of luxury, if it is affordable, but you are never prepared to pay an overly high price for wealth or power.

Your principles in life are very pragmatic and realistic, the motto 'minimal effort – maximum success' dominate your actions. This is why negligence is much more familiar to you than ambition.

Where possible, you choose the path of least resistance but you are able to stick to a certain position or opinion and wait patiently until its hour arrives. Generally speaking, you are more inclined to let things come to you. Hasty action is foreign to you.

The trigonal personality has all the time in the world. You rarely rush and usually approach work and other projects at a comfortable pace, carrying out all necessary tasks with the simple motto: 'One thing after the other …'. As long as nobody demands impossible things of you, you are usually reliable.

You prefer to have a certain rhythm for doing things: there should be breaks – finishing off in time at the end of the day is very important. Nothing irritates you more than unnecessary hectic goings on and people who spread stress around them.

You are also very pragmatic in your actions. You like to learn by observing and are very skilled at simplifying things or procedures. Occasionally, you may be accused of being a bit lazy, but it may be worth remembering here that the greatest inventions were created out of a kind of laziness: the desire to make life easier!

For this reason, you are usually completely practical. Complicated theories are not your cup of tea. What counts in the end is whether something works or not. It is precisely with this attitude that you often become a master of your field or career as your results are accessible and applicable.

You do not create unnecessary complications on principle. Usually, you are able to arrive at acceptable solutions to your difficulties and problems without a great deal of thought. As a rule, you are, therefore, much valued by others who like to obtain practical advice or encouragement from you. If an immediate solution is not forthcoming, you are generally convinced 'it will work out', and are still able to sleep peacefully and remain relaxed until the saving idea arrives.

You love to indulge yourself and will occasionally let yourself go.

You still try to avoid conflicts and disagreements and you genuinely dislike quarrels and violent emotions. You are happy when domestic peace is maintained and if you have managed to arrange your life in such a way that you can be contented. The atmosphere in which you feel most at home is in one of tranquillity and comfort.

Often your physical self will also display this tendency. Active sports are not usually among your favourites, so you often have a 'rounder' figure than the average person, or at least have a tendency to have a 'spare tyre' or a flabby stomach. Usually, however, you can live with it, as maintaining a dream figure would be just too much effort!

On the other hand, laziness and laxness may often become factors in poor health or hinder healing. A complicated diet or a tiring programme of treatment will not exactly fill you with enthusiasm. A leisurely rest cure is quite a different matter.

Generally, there is a tendency to make things easy for yourself. In order to have your peace, you may often retreat into an 'island existence' with a horizon that is bounded by the garden fence. Bad or disturbing news is denied through lack of interest, conflicts are suppressed, complicated people or situations avoided.

This results in ever-increasing superficiality that is even encouraged nowadays through 'tele-communications': telephoning is simpler than visiting, faxing less effort than talking, adventures can be experienced on television in the comfort of the armchair, and the horror stories in the news remain at a sufficient distance to avoid spoiling the appetite for chips afterwards.

A quiet type of egotism becomes established: only your own well-being matters any more and only your own interests count, while mutual aid or becoming committed to a 'good cause' become less and less appealing. It is much simpler to donate some money on the doorstep now and then.

You tend to be less and less aware of the problems of others. For one thing, these people are nothing to do with you, while at the same time your attention is increasingly taken up by the functions of people you deal with on a one-to-one basis. Instead of feeling that you are surrounded by other human beings, you see them only in terms of the role they play: clients, customers, salespeople, civil servants, bosses, subordinates, or patients. This dehumanizing outlook can be found in some hospitals, where patients may be know only as 'appendixes' or 'fractures', etc.

If this superficiality finally reaches the level of indifference or apathy, things get worse: your feeling side atrophies completely and life becomes uniform, boring and empty.

Without feelings, you can only maintain the most necessary of life's functions: eating food becomes merely 'being full'; career becomes occupation; family life becomes a social safeguard; instead of ideas and interests, you have distractions; instead of communication, one-sided conversation; instead of a sense of living joyfully, there is only boredom. This spiritual death starts slowly and stealthily behind locked doors.

It need not be so! As long as you remain open and helpful towards your fellow human beings and retain for yourself an interest in a rich, fulfilled lifestyle, the gift of simplicity will create happiness for you and for others.

Your ability to find simple solutions makes you a valued advisor with an effective realism. Experiences and traditions are the foundation of your support. You find it easy to separate fantasy from fact, so where you do provide criticism, it will be well founded; if you recommend something, it can be relied on!

What really characterizes the trigonal personality is great commonsense – natural clarity of thought that is direct and honest and does not allow you to be deluded easily. Indeed, you are able to be neutral. You are able to listen without making value judgements and to understand what someone else is saying. This is precisely what enables you to help others best.

It is this neutrality that enables you to grow tolerant and acquire the ability to take others as they are, no matter whether you agree with what they say or do or not. Founded on this tolerance that people are able to sense, many feel they can trust you and your words will weigh more than the statements of enthusiastic proponents of particular opinions.

The result of this developmental process is harmony: actions and thoughts, understanding and feeling harmonize in a very simple fashion with each other. You feel good and are content with your life. Your family life, community life and working life are fulfilled. You enjoy having good friends without having to entertain on a lavish scale, and there is always something to do – you are unfamiliar with boredom.

A trust in God or Providence and a relaxed attitude encourage a healthy faith in the future, even in uncertain times, as there is one thing you are certain of: in simplicity lies truth!

The tetragonal lifestyle

The shape of a rectangle is similar to that of the square – but no more than similar. At a superficial glance the tetragonal lifestyle may seem to resemble the cubic lifestyle but at heart they are very different.

If you conduct your life in a 'tetragonal manner', it will appear to others that you are always certain about what you are doing and have everything under control. However, what appears as well planned to others is actually spontaneous, but at any time you are quite able to explain everything absolutely logically, even if it was undertaken simply because you felt like it.

The 'tetragonal lifestyle' can have two faces: an inner one and an outer one.

The tetragonal personality makes detailed plans and then throws them out again at the next moment, partly because of spontaneous changes and partly because of mistaken estimates regarding the actual time required for certain tasks.

While endeavouring to bring a certain amount of order into your life, you like to plan well ahead although you are certain from the start that everything will turn out differently from what you think. Personally, you do not find it difficult to make these constant changes, but those around you will often find it quite disconcerting because you appear to radiate such stability and reliability to the outside.

You love the new and the unknown. Every day is different; you dislike constant repetitions and routines. Once something is finished and done with, that is it! This means you are also willing to drop unworkable concepts immediately and replace them with new, better ones.

You are ready to learn from any new action or event and to improve on it next time. For yourself, this characteristic becomes an enormous capacity for personal development, but others often see it as unpredictability.

Your capacity for analytical thought and, on the other hand, the volatile nature of your emotional life are at the root of this type of behaviour. You are able to evaluate information very quickly and to interpret, with the interpretation being strongly coloured by your momentary feelings.

You do not, therefore, have much difficulty in explaining logically what you feel is right. You will change your mind very rapidly when the need arises, but you will then support the new opinion with the same kind of intensity as you did the old one the day before.

Whatever happens, you always have an answer for every question.

In principle, you feel secure, although you prefer always to remain in a position where you can decide whether and to whom you will reveal your feelings and thoughts. If necessary, you are able to cover up feelings and moods in order to appear to address a situation appropriately.

You are also capable of conscious deceit and living out several identities side by side without much trouble.

This dual nature is also mirrored in your outward appearance, which can be very variable. Just by changing your clothes and hairstyle, for example, you are able to alter your appearance and your image quite considerably. Even your body weight will rapidly alter, depending on the life situation and circumstances you find yourself in.

You look after your physical body in such a way that desirable features are emphasized and undesirable ones concealed. For this reason, your appearance is generally a statement about yourself, be it an expression of well-being, interest, wealth, power, protest, provocation or whatever.

This calculated way of presenting and expressing yourself does, however, contain a risk: if you are not careful, you will develop an unpenetrable facade that will provide you with a certain amount of protection, but occasionally it will need an enormous effort to maintain. This will make you dishonest, even towards the people who are closest to you.

You like to keep your little secrets that you do not wish to share with anyone but doing so run the risk of inner loneliness, even as at the same time you may appear sociable and friendly to people on the outside.

The tetragonal lifestyle is predestined to have a double life. Arising from a conflict between on the one hand wanting to give in to your feelings, and on the other hand wishing to keep your own life under control, situations will arise in which you are forced to lie and deceive.

In addition, there is a certain cowardice, so a lover is kept secret, a mistake glossed over or a bad habit concealed. As you tend to do things that you yourself do not really agree with, you create shame that has to be hidden.

The day of reckoning will finally arrive when you are forced to confess or one of your secrets is discovered. To begin with, you put a lot of effort into building a new facade, designing a new thought structure that can justify everything, or you use a great deal of artful persuasion to reinterpret all the visible evidence and draw a veil over it. Very often you are successful with this.

If you fail, however, you are so overwhelmed that a complete collapse is inevitable. You lose your self-confidence, are ashamed, feel inferior and tend to devalue everything, even the positive achievements in your life.

This 'loss of face' has a destructive effect: repressed aggressions are either directed outward so that you seek revenge on the person who exposed you, wishing them all manner of ills, or inward in the form of depression, self-punishment and, in extreme cases, as a flight into a 'better' world. Schizophrenia may even be the result of such a collapse; this is a 'typical tetragonal' disease – a life lived in several parallel realities.

If this low point, whatever it may be, is overcome in a negative fashion, you are likely to build even thicker walls around yourself in future, which are designed to protect you but instead become oppressive to everyone else around you. You may feel that as long as you do not allow anyone else to be strong beside you, the danger to yourself will be lessened.

The combination of feelings, spontaneity and analytical thinking common to the tetragonal lifestyle makes a positive development in your life possible, in which you no longer invest energy in erecting facades and maintaining them, but in which you penetrate them and discover the secrets lying behind them. As you know from your own experiences that the superficial appearance of things is not everything, you are always endeavouring to find a deeper sense and hidden connections.

Your interest is directed towards the 'Why?', the function and the intention behind all manifestations. When it is lived out in a positive manner, the tetragonal lifestyle could be that of a researcher or perhaps a scientist.

You are rarely ever content with what you have accomplished in life so far but are ready to keep re-examining everything, questioning results, daring to formulate new interpretations and try out new experiments. Your inner feelings are usually the driving force behind this: if you are lucky enough to be on the right path, you stick to it and will not allow yourself to be discouraged by any kind of failures.

The same commitment that a tetragonal person would use to hide things on your negative side is also made during a search for the truth. Imagination proves to be a particular gift here, fantasy – the art of making things visible (Greek *phainein*, 'making visible'). Without imagination, discoveries and inventions would be simply impossible.

Your own life will also be included in this search for truth: superficial contentment will not be sufficient as it is the deeper meaning of human existence that interests you. Intuition tells you that you have a task in this life, in whatever fashion this task may appear. Discovering it and fulfilling it provides a challenge to your capabilities and offers you a happy, joyful life.

Because of your natural versatility, you also find it easy to help others in this. You are able to analyse problems with your sharp intellect and develop creative solutions by using your imagination. Your way of helping may often be imaginative and unconventional but, in the end, new paths will always be more attractive to you than old, well-worn ones. This often means that the greater the challenge you are faced with, the more willing you are to accept it!

The rhombic lifestyle

A rhombus also has a certain similarity to a square, which is why the rhombic lifestyle also appears to outsiders as a condition in which everything appears to be in order. Life is like a long, tranquilly flowing river – this is how you could describe your feelings about it if you were someone who lives in this lifestyle. As a rule, life develops along a continuous line and without special events; only rarely do you experience massive intrusions or 'break-outs'.

A long cycle of daily occurrences that all seem much the same will suddenly bring you to a low point, seemingly for no particular reason. You may experience panic attacks, depression or simply bad moods of an unforeseen extent; just as suddenly as they turned up, these manifestations can disappear again without a trace.

'Break-outs' like this can arise in such a manner that things that seemed important to you until that moment suddenly seem to lose all their value and you are quite easily able to make far-reaching decisions that others find completely inexplicable. Without any regrets, you break off relationships, give notice to leave a job, move house, or throw security overboard. You suddenly start a new life – 'just like that'.

This perverse contrast between long, unchanging phases on the one hand, and unexpected changes on the other, determines your whole life's rhythm. Basically, you adjust yourself to the fact that everything will remain exactly as it is, so you never plan far ahead. There is no need to.

For you, Time is a constantly recurring phenomenon; every day the sun rises – it was always so and why should anything about it change? If something does suddenly change, as described above, then the very next day this constant attitude of taking things as a matter of course returns. Admittedly, recently everything was different, but from now on everything will be the way it is now.

Because of this attitude, you find it very easy to make decisions: a lot of money is invested in a new home, even if you do not know how long you will be staying there. A relationship spontaneously turns into marriage, or a task once taken on, often becomes a permanent commitment.

In all things, you possess enormous staying power, apart from the occasional intrusions or 'break-outs'. You are thorough and inconspicuous in all you do, and often perform most of the work in team situations without pushing into the limelight.

You are very self-sufficient and are not dependent on attention, praise or recognition.

You are ready to be enthusiastic about a good cause and, as a rule, show plenty of social awareness and commitment. You are basically helpful and often able to carry out the small details of a task. The 'big ideas' will often come from others but without your meticulous work on their realization, down to the last detail, very little would be accomplished.

Thoroughness and exactness are generally your strong points; you think all courses of action through quietly and objectively, but without falling into unnecessary introspection.

You are also very empathetic. You are quick to register the moods of others and find it easy to adjust to them.

You would be popular working in foreign countries and often find yourself engaged in caring work. You are happy if others, too, feel well and happy, and are always keen to create a pleasant atmosphere. You are known as a good listener among your friends, along the lines of: 'A sorrow shared is a sorrow halved. A shared joy is double the joy'. You are, therefore, able to subordinate your own interests to the greater goal of a community, provided that you identify with this community.

As you do not make a great deal of fuss about yourself, your appearance and the way you behave tend to be inconspicuous. You seldom like the limelight but prefer to stay in the background. You run the risk of going unnoticed so that, occasionally, after a party, you may be asked, 'Were you there, I don't remember seeing you?' or you may not climb the career ladder as fast as a loud-mouthed colleague. The other side of this is that, in the latter case, the risk of a 'fall' is also not so great.

The whole business becomes rather more dubious if you fit in too well and give up fulfilling your own interests for the sake of others. Sometimes this urge to fit in can result in an inner emptiness or insecurity that you try to secure through holding on to outer things – a partner, a community or a job.

It is precisely this disregard for your own wishes and dreams that reinforces this inner emptiness more and more until the 'intrusion' or 'break-out' occurs.

Intrusions happen when you suddenly become aware of the inner emptiness, but without being able to penetrate to the real cause. Then you find yourself no longer on solid ground; rather you are floundering in a 'mire'. As the cause is not recognized, this state will continue until you once more find your previous lifestyle acceptable and start adapting to your environment again. Suddenly, you begin to 'function' again and you seem to be able to continue with your life at exactly the point where you left off when the 'intrusion'/'break-out' took place.

Should you continue to put up resistance to the 'old game', depression will immediately follow. Any kind of help offered will just exacerbate the 'down' feeling. Sympathy, clever advice or psychopharmaceuticals will only succeed in perpetuating this state. Genuine help can only be provided by a recognition of the cause of your problem.

Such a recognition can, however, lead to a 'break-out': if you suddenly realize that you have not been living your own life for a very long time but (depending on circumstances), living through the life of your partner, your parents, children, friends, bosses, colleagues, gurus or whoever, then these bonds will, as a rule, be severed very quickly. The desire to be rid of this outside control can, however, sometimes lead to the 'baby being thrown out with the bathwater'.

By turning your life upside down, you also lose the positive things you have worked so hard for. Then you run the risk of fleeing into new (initially unrecognized) dependencies, looking for a new hold until the old game begins anew.

The real way out, or the beginning of a positive development in a rhombic lifestyle, consists of promoting your own life, strengthening your own interests and setting your own goals first. This may begin in the typical 'rhombic inconspicuousness' and is often even recommended: 'a young plant should be protected until its stem is strong enough to hold up to the wind'. Depending on the degree to which this inner hold is created and self-confidence is built up, you will be able to make visible change.

Interestingly enough, attacks from outside will be far fewer and further between than expected. On the contrary, your new way of making decisions will often be admired (I never thought that you would …') and supported ('It's great the way you have grown …') by others, and if attacks really do take place, it is now easier for you to distinguish between friend and foe. Making breaks with people who do not mean well or turn out to be false friends will surely not be harmful!

This new development makes it easy for you to employ your own abilities successfully for yourself and for others. Your capacity for understanding and empathy makes you into a good helper and perhaps even a healer, without having to deny your own identity. You will still be able to enjoy friendships and enjoy the well-being of others.

At the same time, all these qualities will also serve your own self-realization. In this way, you will gain permanent stability and fulfilment that is secure enough to stop you desiring more upheavals and changes. In this new state, you may again become inconspicuous, as often happens with people who are clear about themselves: you have no need to seek the limelight as you are happy and content.

The monoclinic lifestyle

A parallelogram often gives the impression of being just on the point of tipping to one side. This instability is fittingly also one of the essential characteristics of the monoclinic lifestyle, which features a continuous up and down movement.

Your life changes in almost regular rhythms, moods fluctuate, opinions are changed, even facts appear to keep on showing different facets. Something you really like today will not find favour tomorrow and what will happen next week is something you would rather not think about.

This permanent flux has something almost consistent about it. It appears so certain that you can plan for it. This is the reason why you make arrangements to meet people with reservations, never plan exact times but generally vaguer time slots for whatever you are intending to do, and are always ready to change everything at the drop of a hat.

You are extremely reluctant to make promises that you might be bound to without keeping a loophole – just in case. However, once you have given your word, you will stick to your promises even if great exertions are necessary at the last minute.

You find predictions for the future fascinating, on the one hand, as you would like nothing better than to know exactly what is awaiting you. On the other hand, you do not really believe them. According to your own life's experience, what actually happens is always different from what you thought would happen.

Your ideal would really be to be able to act in a prudent, thoughtful way. Still, you usually act very spontaneously and from a gut feeling. Depending on your moods, some days you are ready to run greater risks while at other times you are over-cautious.

In this way, you become completely unpredictable in the eyes of your family and friends, although you are used to it: 'this is me', you say, 'I am the way I am and that means different every day'. If you are told something you can understand, you are easily convinced by another's opinion.

Left to your own devices, you often torment yourself over making difficult decisions. If you have a choice between two equally valid possibilities, you can usually think yourself into both situations so you are able to recognize advantages and disadvantages in both. The longer you consider the matter, the more difficult the choice becomes. Even your very vivid imagination will not help you; on the contrary, when the decision has finally been made in favour of one thing, the advantages of the other suddenly seem to stand out even more clearly.

Then doubts begin – your constant companions. The changeover from one feeling to another is much more spontaneous: here, often a wrong word (not even meant seriously) is enough to propel you into a downward curve while another event can just as quickly ensure a 'high'. You would never think of yourself as moody as you are aware of very distinct triggers for your changes of mood.

Finally, this flexibility does have a positive side: anger and fury will dissolve very quickly, just as sorrow and sadness also disperse rapidly. As a rule you are never one to hold a grudge, certainly not as long as you are able to voice your feelings freely.

Inconstancy is also a feature of your physical state: your sleeping and eating patterns change all the time, sometimes you need more sometimes less. The same goes for your health; sometimes you are in top form, while at other times a gust of wind will knock you over and send you to bed with some ailment or the other. Sporty phases and lazy ones alternate. Your entire appearance can change so much that you are often told by people that that they 'nearly did not recognize you'.

This inconstancy is also the thing that creates the most problems for you. Disagreements with others, in particular with those who find it difficult to understand you, are the order of the day. Depending on how violent these disagreements are, you react in different ways to them: clear, direct confrontations are far more likely to explain your own way of doing things, help you gain trust again and to clarify different points of view (even in you). These discussions are often very necessary for your self-recognition and give you an opportunity, at the same time, to express your feelings. They will help you a great deal.

Constant needling and little intrigues, on the other hand, are pure poison. Because of your ability to be influenced, they gradually whittle away at your self-worth and encourage self-doubt. You begin to lose all feeling of security, start judging the changing sides of character with 'right' or 'wrong', while your fear of making mistakes grows all the time.

This causes you to lose all sense of objectivity, which you need to preserve some kind of overview over your life, and you sink into utter confusion. Things seem to become too much for you and growing doubts and difficulties with making decisions cause you to function less and less effectively.

This, in turn, causes ever more things to be left undone, until you are confronted with a mountain of unfinished tasks that appear unsurmountable. This engenders a risk of ignoring things for good while it does not help relieve any of the load. Resignation increases and that puts an end to the fluctuating moods, unfortunately fixing them at the down end of the emotional scale.

The only thing that will help here is to confront the situation as it is. Do not look away from it, but instead focus directly on it, however difficult that may be. Conversations with supportive friends are definitely a good idea. If you are then able to regain at least a small part of your self-worth, then it is time to strike and to deal with the unfinished business, step by step. Every small detail that is dealt with takes you another step forward.

Finally, your monoclinic nature will even help you: once you can look upon a few small successes, this will give you such a boost that the rest will seem more manageable. Your mood rises rapidly and you now only have to make sure that you keep at it until you have regained that feeling of freedom. The best sign for this is a return of that calm composure that is sure: 'Sunshine always follows after the rain'.

Then you are fully functional again, which is also the best natural protection against doubts: action always brings experience. Experience, in turn, prevents doubts. Your own experience is a secure island in the changeable world of the monoclinic reality – a firm standpoint.

If you make a habit of deciding quickly and without hesitation on important decisions, you will soon find that occasional wrong decisions are easier and quicker to correct than omissions caused through holding back. This will strengthen your feeling of self-value again and that, in turn, will make it possible to discover a new aspect of your feelings – trusting them.

Your feelings are often determined by triggers: events for which it is appropriate on the one hand to react with annoyance, rejection and fury or, on the other hand, with joy, trust or enthusiasm. As these triggers are often inaccessible to your conscious awareness, you can learn to use these your feelings as a finely calibrated barometer that will show you exactly whether a person or a situation is trustworthy or not, whether an endeavour will be successful or not or which decision you should make.

If you make a point of looking out for this, however, you will find that your feelings can be trusted, again and again. This creates security and what is really being developed here is nothing other than intuition! It is intuition that can reach perfection in the monoclinic lifestyle.

The triclinic lifestyle

The trapezium is a shape that has a broad base, symbolizing a stable, fixed nature which does, however, need to be turned upside down again and again to fit in the area to be filled. Turned upside down, the shape looks rather wobbly and insecure. Both realities are properties of the triclinic lifestyle, which manifests even more extremely than the monoclinic lifestyle as a fluctuation between two poles.

Volatile, spontaneous and unpredictable, even to yourself, the course of your life is erratic, with fate continuously and unexpectedly taking a hand and presenting new challenges.

This lifestyle contains an interesting phenomenon to do with time: subjective time. Without your being able to ascribe this to a particular cause, time flies on one day and on another appears to drag endlessly. Not only does this make planning of any kind very difficult – it makes it almost impossible! But then planning is not necessary.

Because of the lack of an objective means of measuring it, you are used to simply estimating periods of time and points in time and very often hit the mark surprisingly accurately. Those around you often watch this with great astonishment, considering that your estimates often turn out to be more precise – in spite of unforeseen obstacles and upsets – than would any complicated calculations.

A very similar situation exists with respect to your actions: there are days when everything just seems to fall into place, tasks are as easy as never before, everything works, and there are no problems to be seen anywhere.

The very next day, however, it may all be quite different. Even breakfast is beset with problems, and the rest of the day follows suit. You have obviously got out of the wrong side of the bed and if you risk leaving the house, in spite of the warnings, at the latest by midday, you will be fervently wishing that you had never even got up that day. It is almost as though fate or providence were doling out good or bad days to you.

Your manner of thinking is just as disjointed and inconstant. Although you are extremely creative and full of ideas, these ideas need to be held on to and realized as soon as they appear. If you hesitate for only a few moments, it may be too late!

Here again, days of unstoppable inspiration alternate with those featuring a complete lack of ideas, days on which any kind of effort seems to be for nothing and utterly frustrating. As long as the stream of pictures and ideas continues, you are effortlessly able to cope with many times the usual amount of work without being exhausted afterwards.

Your emotions flow up and down and cannot be influenced. Whereas this apparent fluctuation still manifests as a kind of wave motion in the monoclinic lifestyle, it becomes a strong zigzag motion in the triclinic lifestyle. Every change of mood seems to arrive unexpectedly and without any noticeable trigger or announcement.

On the contrary, it seems that moods consistently and suddenly tip over when they have reached a peak: at the climax of your own birthday party, you suddenly become desperately depressed; at the funeral of a dear friend, you suddenly find everything laughable. You oscillate between agony and ecstasy, apparently without rhyme or reason.

Even your body demonstrates the extreme contrasts of this

lifestyle: you are either tough and strong but appear rather delicate and weak, or you look like 'Mr Universe' but are by no means as sporty and strong as you appear. For the rest, your appearance generally mirrors your mood: from perfectly turned out to totally scruffy, you are a master of every nuance – something that can make someone who does not know you very well either wonderfully surprised or horrified.

Interestingly enough, all these changing appearances have very little to do with whether your life is happy or not. The basic mood is the really constant part of your existence, the stable aspect of the trapezium. Depending on whether you approach life in a generally positive, friendly manner, or in a negative and denigrating manner, it is possible you will experience these daily ups and downs as being either wonderfully varied or conversely as a dreadful trip through hell.

The negative aspect often begins with indifference. As everything changes constantly and you apparently have no influence over the happenings within you and around you, you develop a cloak of apathy as a protective mechanism. This does save you from getting too involved in events, but just drives you further into passivity, an attitude where you continue to suffer through everything and have to submit to it.

The result can be that you feel you are a victim: it is just fate that is giving you a bad time, you are unlucky and basically it is others who are nasty to you, wish you ill and are attacking you in some way. All negative things come from outside; you are threatened, struck down by fate or even attacked by evil forces. Finally, you actually need these imaginary enemies in order to justify your pitiable state.

At this point you give up showing any interest in things getting better, if you have not done so already. Any help you are offered is declined as you suspect further bad intentions.

Finally, help and healing also start to appear to you as forms of manipulation and you doubt the true motives of anyone trying to help or heal you. The moment of utter embitterment is reached: the down points of the original ups and downs stabilize, while the high points no longer arrive. This is a truly hellish state.

The only chance of once again attaining moments of high spirits is the decision to make a positive new start. The volatile nature of the triclinic lifestyle can make a leap of faith from the very depths possible. The crucial thing is making a decision to be a doer rather than a victim in your own life and believing the simple notion that 'there is no pure coincidence'. Then you will able to alter a 'triclinic life' quite radically.

Unlike the monoclinic lifestyle, the triclinic one does not have difficulties in making a decision. Any spiritual/mental decision is carried out consistently, even the decision to adopt either a negative or positive attitude towards life.

In a positive development, not much will change with respect to the tortuous paths of your life, but it is uncertainty itself that encourages the development of the so-called 'sixth sense' and other gifts.

As long as you are constantly confronted with new things, you remain wide awake and attentive. There are soothing securities in your life and, for this reason, the first thing that needs to be developed again is instinct, a very sure and targeted form of acting that you are often not even aware of but will always lead you to the right place at the right moment. You turn into a 'lucky beggar' and things seem to fall into your lap, once you are prepared to grasp them.

To the extent that you recognize that these moments are becoming much too frequent to be coincidences, you become more and more conscious of your talent. Instinct becomes clairvoyance, to begin with in the shape of vague inklings, but in the course of time these become more like foresight. Provided you nurture these talents, you can develop a fertile, mediumistic talent that will, at the same time, make you more stable.

At last you are able to see a meaning in your eventful life and realize that fate does not mean you any harm. The ups and downs become the winding course of a serpentine path that leads you consistently uphill. You realize you have been led on this path and this, in turn, expands your abilities further: you gain a faith in God that makes miracles possible …

The amorphous lifestyle

Describing amorphism, that is, giving it a 'shape', is not an easy task. Yet it is necessary to try, as there are mercifully few amorphous words in the English language that can describe everything or nothing at once.

For example, the word 'versatility'. Versatility is what characterizes a lifestyle that is amorphous. Everything constantly appears new and unrepeatable. You could not call it a change or a transformation, as both terms imply a past and a future, a causal development, a consistent course. All these things do not exist in an amorphous lifestyle. At least – not always.

For the 'amorphous' personality every moment is new. Every moment is unique. You are not interested in the 'Big Bang' or the end of the Universe – the former may never have happened and the latter may never happen, and neither is happening now! Time exists as a point, the very point you happen to be at now. Perhaps Time does not even exist, maybe it is just an invention of physics. In the end, it does not matter anyway.

Spontaneity is, therefore, not merely a feature of the amorphous lifestyle, but is its only way of expression. Between the impulse that motivates you and the action carried out, there appears to be no element of time or duration. Anything you think of is carried out immediately and ended at once if you lose sight of it or forget. This enables you to possess the freedom of the child to enjoy fully the present game you are playing, to live it out and when 'out' is reached, you let go without hesitation. You are one hundred per cent with something.

Every idea is an event. And yet you are still quite capable of thinking anything that can be thought. Your reservoir of creativity is boundless. Sometimes you give birth to ideas more quickly than you can hold on to them, speak them or write them down, and this is the only phenomenon during which you come into contact with Time; thinking seems to be quicker than speaking, speaking faster than acting, and that, paradoxically, all at the same moment.

You are in a position to experience all kinds of feelings but only one at a time. You are one hundred percent certain about this too. In a particular situation, no feeling can exist other than the one you are having right now. You like to show this feeling too; it is impossible for you to hide it because that would mean that two feelings could exist side by side (inside and outside). Amorphism also means being able to get right into any particular feeling. You are able to 'flow into' any situation, identify with it and leave it again. And you can enjoy a particular thing a hundred times over!

Of course, you do have a physical shape, a body, and it is

always in motion. At any given moment you are active and busy, 'buzzing' about, like your idol, the butterfly, but you can also be endlessly calm and tranquil, like its close associate, the flower. You love colourful things as they seem to be related to your versatility; you also love freedom and not being tied down.

The only time things get dangerous for you is if you suddenly want to hold on to a particular moment. Then the eternally new is lost and you try to keep the past and future away from you by closing your eyes to them. The effect of this is that you also lose sight of the colourful world of the present moment and become lost in darkness and fog.

You no longer know who you are, and begin to experience the shadow side of the amorphous lifestyle. Ideas no longer come to you, creativity disappears, emptiness arises, nothing motivates you any longer, nothing can make you happy, nothing beckons or seduces you. The rich life in the 'here and now' turns into 'no future', a kind of present you hate and which, for understandable reasons, you do not wish to continue with into the future. You would rather destroy it at once and, in keeping with your amorphous non-structural self, you start this process immediately. You become destructive and aggressive, and in the final stage, apathetic.

Thankfully this is only one of many possibilities that you 'amorphous' beings can fall into, but which you can also leave behind again very quickly, as soon as something turns up that makes you enthusiastic again. The deepest depth lasts only for a moment, quickly supplanted by another moment. Precisely because there is nothing final about the amorphous lifestyle (where there is no development, there is also no end), there is always hope of a new opportunity.

When living positively, the 'amorphous' personality possesses a kind of genius: to be able to think things that have never been thought before, create what has never been seen before, invent what has never been accomplished before. This is only possible if you can be playful and free, not bound to one-way tracks, conventions and rules.

You may be looked upon as an eccentric or a loner, but it is very easy to prove that in the history of mankind, far more innovative impulses have come from these people than from the majority of those who adapted themselves to circumstances. But all that is not important for you....

Note

Please do not expect to meet only people who are one hundred per cent like the types described here. For one thing, 'textbook examples' are always an exception. I have also exaggerated the characteristics of each type, almost as clichés, in order to emphasize the differences. So you will have to observe very carefully! Often, only single features in the lives or behaviour of a person will give you the right indicator.

Or, to formulate it freely after Samuel Hahnemann, the founder of homeopathic medicine:

▶ Three conspicuous, peculiar or odd features of a personal lifestyle will, as a rule, suffice to support any correspondences with the descriptions given here.

A little experiment

A simple way to make sure about the effect of the crystal systems is to look at one of the geometric shapes or a field of the same shapes for a minute and then read the above text on the description of the corresponding lifestyle. Afterwards, look at different shape or field and read the text again. You will find that after looking at a particular shape or field, you will suddenly be able to identify much more easily with the lifestyle of the relevant crystal system. What an amazing effect these simple structures have!

How crystal structures can affect us

As the descriptions above have clearly shown, each of the lifestyles described is, in principle, neutral. There is no 'better' or 'worse' one, merely a 'different' one. Each lifestyle basically contains two possibilities for development: either a personal development towards negativity, that is the growth of certain difficulties, problems or even illnesses, or a development towards the positive, that is, towards the development of specific capabilities and self-fulfilment.

The difference is very simple: negative development sets in if you are ruled by the relevant 'inner structure', if you are unable to live any other way, that is, when you are totally dependent on a certain lifestyle.

Positive development, on the other hand, begins once you are the master of your own life, if you know how to use certain talents and characteristics of yours and are able to handle your life sensibly! The first prerequisite for positive development is – wanting it! You have to be ready to take responsibility for your own fate and decide consciously to live out the positive side of your life, full stop.

It really is very simple: the effort and energy necessary for the development of all negative phenomena of a certain lifestyle are just as great as the effort and energy necessary for the development of positive phenomena.

The question is simply where to direct your attention and your energy. If you identify particularly strongly with one of the above descriptions, then please give a lot of thought and attention to the positive energies described there. Even on its own this will help encourage them.

Luckily you also have your 'helpers': healing stones. Minerals have an enormous effect as they are physical structures. Inconspicuously but nevertheless powerfully, they stimulate the corresponding lifestyle in two ways.

Healing with crystal structures

If you have created certain difficulties or problems based on your lifestyle, or have become ill because of this lifestyle, then minerals with the corresponding crystal structure can help to solve these difficulties and problems or heal the disease.

The effects of the mineral can be used to dissolve a blockage within the corresponding lifestyle and you will then become free to handle your life consciously. The mineral works according to the homeopathic principle, 'Like heals like'.

The healing process works very quickly. Provided you have found the right stone with a suitable structure, a strong effect may be noted after a few hours or days, or even moments. It will take a while until the newly attained state has become stabilized, but the first changes are very soon visible.

Learning through crystal structures

In addition to the healing described above, there is a second possibility: certain lifestyles will be completely alien to you, something you almost certainly will have noticed when reading the individual descriptions.

In spite of this, the relevant lifestyle can offer characteristics or abilities that would be quite interesting or useful for you. With the help of minerals of the corresponding crystal structure, you are in a position to get to know this lifestyle.

The effect of the mineral is to help you develop this unknown lifestyle. Like the crystallization process, during the course of time the characteristics and abilities of the relevant lifestyle become established, the whole process becoming more conscious, the more attention you give to it.

This learning process does take a certain amount of time. Crystals are rarely formed in a single day, and being able to play a musical instrument is rarely accomplished in a single week. For this reason, you will have to allow yourself some time for the process. As a rule, it will take one or a few months until the effect of the mineral becomes noticeable. Then it is like learning to walk – you need to use the newly acquired skill and practise it until it has become a part of you and can no longer be lost again.

The meaning and the goal of healing and learning processes

The prerequisite for a healing process, in which you choose the mineral with a crystal structure that corresponds to your lifestyle, is a situation in which you are no longer in control of your life.

Perhaps you are confronted with insurmountable difficulties or problems and can no longer see a way out, or you feel ill, either physically, mentally or spiritually. You are the only one who can measure this. If you are no longer content with your life, then healing becomes a necessity.

▶ The goal of the healing process is to bring back the control over your life that you had lost, so that you can become well again, are able to solve your difficulties and problems and be content with your life.

The prerequisite for a learning process is that you are happy with your life, but still wish to get to know new perspectives and abilities; you wish to expand your own opportunities and to develop further. As a rule it will first be necessary to get a grip on your own life (to stimulate healing processes, if warranted). Plunging into new experiences before the old ones have been digested can be equivalent to running away and may lead to even greater problems or confusion.

However, it is often necessary to add a learning process onto a completed healing process in order to lead the inner potential that has been released through the healing process in the right direction. If you have spent a long time mentally occupied with certain problems, it may often be the case that a kind of peculiar habit causes you to create new problems of a similar nature, after having got rid of the old, so that you can continue to be mentally occupied with them. Doctors or therapists often hear something like, 'For a while, everything went well, then the whole thing started up again!'

This can be avoided if you turn to something new right away, thus making the 'old games' superfluous. For this reason, it is also very important to be aware of exactly when a healing process has been completed, so you no longer address the old problem and change over to a learning process.

▶ The goal of a learning process is to expand your mental horizon and thereby to expand your abilities and opportunities. In the end, the goal is freedom! Freedom to think, communicate and act unhindered.

Imagine you could choose any of the lifestyles described above according to your preference. You could, for example, be 'cubic' at work if necessary, be 'amorphous' on holiday, 'rhombic' as a host, 'hexagonal' as a student, and so on. You could experience all the possibilities and use them. Nothing would restrict you: you would be free!

Wouldn't that be something?

How to heal with crystal structures

Learning and healing stones

Primarily, the crystal structures described in this chapter and the corresponding lifestyles are intended to help a particular person find the most helpful healing stone for a given moment in time. Determining the crystal structure first will narrow down the choice of minerals to an extent that the analysis of the life situation and the manner of formation, as described in this chapter, will usually offer enough reference points to enable you to choose the right stone. If, nevertheless, there are several available to choose from, then the minerals and colour effects described in the following chapters will give the final guidance in making a choice.

The crystal determined in this way should be worn for a while, shorter or longer depending on whether you are dealing with a healing or learning process, if possible without being influenced by wearing other jewellery. Once the desired result has been stabilized, the stone will no longer be necessary.

During healing processes, it is possible that a superficial structure can be replaced by a 'deeper-lying' one. As a rule, this is displayed very clearly through a marked change in the lifestyle of the person concerned. If the original problems or symptoms of illness do not disappear along with this change, the stone used will lose its effectiveness and a new one suitable for the changed circumstances needs to be determined.

Self-reflection

The characteristics described above can also help you interpret a stone you have chosen intuitively; this may help reflect your own lifestyle and help you become aware of your own weaknesses and strengths. Remember, 'Self-recognition is the first step towards betterment'.

Watching people in their own environments and discovering their structures and lifestyles will also visibly improve your understanding of your fellow human beings. It suddenly becomes clear that another person has his or her own idea of right or wrong, and his or her own idea of how to live their life and be happy. It also becomes clear that this 'other idea' does not threaten your own at all but that everyone is right about their own reality and that it is possible to allow both to stand side by side. Understanding, respect and tolerance towards others become more natural.

1.3 Mineral-forming elements

The chemistry of minerals

After dealing with their formation and crystal structure, now is the time to give some attention to the physical nature of minerals. Certain substances or elements in the right proportions and with the right surrounding conditions have to be present to form a certain mineral. Every one of these substances or elements has specific properties that together form the properties of the mineral and will have a noticeable bearing on its healing effects.

In order to understand these connections, first of all we need to take a little excursion into the world of chemistry. Please do not stop reading at this point – it really is all very simple! Unfortunately, chemistry has a very bad name. I can remember exactly how worried I was at the beginning of the year in which we took up chemistry. All I knew about the subject was that it had the reputation of being diabolically difficult, complicated and awful. I was then extremely surprised to discover that it is one of the easiest subjects if you are lucky enough to have a teacher who is able to explain the basics in a manner that is easy to understand. I was very lucky.

Chemistry is absolutely logical and describes the real world. This is great because it is not just a matter of believing what you are told – you can actually try it all out. As a student, I did this with enthusiasm; I set up a small experimental laboratory in my parents' boiler room in the cellar and occasionally made them nervous with explosions, smoke or clouds of chlorine gas. I always managed to placate them afterwards by getting good grades in chemistry.

The word 'chemistry' means 'knowledge of matter', or as described in the dictionary, 'a natural science that deals with researching the properties, connections and transformation of substances and their compounds'. Substances, in this context, are defined as 'matter present in a unified form and characterized by certain properties'. Chemistry is real enough, even in our own lives! Cooking is a chemical process in which different substances with characteristic properties are mingled, bound and transformed. The same goes for baking, gluing, heating and driving a car (combustion in the engine). So, chemistry is very much an everyday matter.

The structure of matter

Atoms

Several basic principles of matter need to be appreciated in order to understand why substances have different properties; why they can be combined, bound and transformed.

All matter known to us consists of three different types of 'building blocks', or elementary particles: these are, firstly, protons (Greek *proton*, 'the first, most important'); secondly, electrons (Greek *elektron*, 'amber', used here as a synonym for 'attraction' to other substances') and thirdly, neutrons (Latin *neuter*, 'neither of the other two'). These three types of particles form the most fascinating relationships with each other.

The protons and electrons are attracted towards each other, so physics defines them both as having 'electrical charges', meaning both are 'loaded with attraction' (Greek *elektron*, 'attractive force', see above). In order to differentiate between the two opposite types of attraction, a further definition is that protons are 'positively' charged (p+), and that electrons are 'negatively' charged (e–).

To attain a neutral or balanced state together, protons and electrons, as a rule, stand in a special relationship to each other. Should the proton and electron 'lose sight of each other' occasionally, for whatever reason, then their sole aim is to find a new 'partner' immediately.

The proton is a heavy, lazy particle. The electron, in contrast, is fast and mobile. For this reason, the proton always forms the quiet nucleus in this partnership of proton and electron, with the electron zipping around it like lightning, rather like a planet being orbited by satellites.

Then there is the neutron (n), which is basically neutral (as the name suggests) and is not particularly attracted either to the proton (p+) or the electron (e–). As the neutron is in many ways similar to the proton (almost equally heavy and lazy), it has the tendency to stay close to the proton and the dynamic electron orbits around both of them.

This is how simple it all really is. All known substances are built up around this basic foundation: a nucleus composed of protons and neutrons, which is orbited by electrons. A particle like this is called an atom (Greek *atmos*, 'indivisible') and forms the smallest building block of matter.

The elements

In nature, we find no more than 83 different, stable atoms; they are distinguishable from each other only by the number of their elementary particles. These 83 different atoms are also called 'chemical elements' (Latin *elementum*, 'basic matter, original matter'). They form the 'pure matter' out of which all compounds are formed.

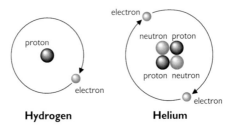

Internal structure of the atom: hydrogen and helium

The proton only received its name, 'the most important', because the number of protons in an atom determines what element you are dealing with. One hydrogen atom, for example, contains a single proton, oxygen contains eight, iron 26 and gold as many as 70 protons. As soon as there is one more or less proton in the nucleus, you are dealing with an entirely different new element, a new substance with quite different properties. Fluorine, for example, has only one proton more than oxygen, yet this seemingly small difference results in an aggressive, toxic gas instead of the one essential to life.

The neutron, however, may appear in atoms in varying numbers, without changing their chemical properties. It will not influence the nature of an element, so here, too, it displays neutrality.

An atom always has the same number of electrons as protons. This is logical, as each electron is attracted by a corresponding proton. The space in which the electrons orbit around the atomic nucleus is called the electron cloud. It is the particular structure of this 'cloud' that is responsible for allowing atoms to combine with each other. The 'cloud' consists of different 'shells' where only certain numbers of electrons can be accommodated. In most atoms, the outer shell contains a maximum of eight electrons, although the inner shells can contain other fixed numbers of electrons.

Number of protons	Chem. abbrev	Name of Element	Number of protons	Chem. abbrev	Name of Element
1	H	Hydrogen	42	Mo	Molybdenum
2	He	Helium	44	Ru	Ruthenium
3	Li	Lithium	45	Rh	Rhodium
4	Be	Beryllium	46	Pd	Palladium
5	B	Boron	47	Ag	Silver
6	C	Carbon	48	Cd	Cadmium
7	N	Nitrogen	49	In	Indium
8	O	Oxygen	50	Sn	Tin
9	F	Fluorine	51	Sb	Antimony
10	Ne	Neon	52	Te	Tellurium
11	Na	Sodium	53	J	Iodine
12	Mg	Magnesium	54	Xe	Xenon
13	Al	Aluminium	55	Cs	Caesium
14	Si	Silicon	56	Ba	Barium
15	P	Phosphorus	57	La	Lanthanum
16	S	Sulphur	58	Ce	Cerium
17	Cl	Chlorine	59	Pr	Praseodymium
18	Ar	Potassium	60	Nd	Neodymium
19	K	Kalium	62	Sm	Samarium
20	Ca	Calcium	63	Eu	Europium
21	Sc	Scandium	64	Gd	Gadolinium
22	Ti	Titanium	65	Tb	Terbium
23	V	Vanadium	66	Dy	Dysprosium
24	Cr	Chromium	67	Ho	Holmium
25	Mn	Manganese	68	Er	Erbium
26	Fe	Iron	69	Tm	Thulium
27	Co	Cobalt	70	Yb	Ytterbium
28	Ni	Nickel	71	Lu	Lutetium
29	Cu	Copper	72	Hf	Hafnium
30	Zn	Zinc	73	Ta	Tantalum
31	Ga	Gallium	74	W	Tungsten
32	Ge	Germanium	75	Re	Rhenium
33	As	Arsenic	76	Os	Osmium
34	Se	Selenium	77	Ir	Iridium
35	Br	Bromine	78	Pt	Platinum
36	Kr	Krypton	79	Au	Gold
37	Rb	Rubidium	80	Hg	Mercury
38	Sr	Strontium	81	Tl	Thallium
39	Y	Yttrium	82	Pb	Lead
40	Zr	Zirconium	83	Bi	Wismut
41	Nb	Niobium			

Chemical compounds

Once an electron shell possesses its full complement of electrons, the shell is stable. Consequently this shell cannot accept any more electrons, nor will it release any. If the outermost shell of an atom has exactly eight electrons, the atom itself is also stable and it will not display any chemical reactions.

This state occurs naturally only in the noble gases (helium, neon, argon, krypton and xenon). These elements are never found in any chemical compounds (they are too 'noble'). As long as an atom has

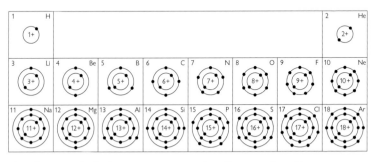

The electron 'shells' have a structure rather like an onion skin

less than eight electrons in its outer shell, it will form compounds with other elements that will allow it to achieve the stable state described above. It will try to fill up its outer shell with 'foreign' electrons, or shed electrons from its own outer shell so that the next shell in (which will already be completely filled) becomes the outer shell.

There are three main types of bonding that occur between atoms: ionic, covalent and metallic bonding.

Ionic bonds

Ionic bonds are formed when electrons are transferred from one atom to another. The ions created in this way are held together by electrical attraction. The bonding of chlorine and sodium is an example of ionic bonding. The chlorine atom has only seven electrons in its outer shell, exactly one electron short of the stable state. The sodium atom, on the other hand, has only one electron in its outer shell, so its aim is to get rid of it. If sodium and chlorine meet, a simple barter takes place: the sodium releases one electron to the chlorine so that both achieve the desired eight outer electrons and both are happy.

This trade does have certain consequences, however, as the attractive force of the exchanged electron remains. The sodium is now positively charged and the chlorine negatively charged. The electrical attraction between the two holds them together in a compound, sodium chloride, more commonly known as ordinary cooking salt!

As the atoms in these compounds now possess electrical charges ('attractive forces'), they are called ions ('charged particles'). Sodium chloride consists of one positively charged sodium ion (Na+) for each negatively charged chloride ion (Cl–). This information can be found, for example, on a mineral water bottle; the first item listed is usually the positively charged ions (the cations), followed by the negative ions (the anions). The bond that exists between cations and anions owing to their electrical attraction is, therefore, called an ionic bond.

Covalent bonds
Another kind of bonding occurs if two atoms meet, both of whose outer shells are lacking very few electrons, and when neither is 'ready' to release any electrons to form ions. In this case, the trade occurs in such a way that both atoms 'agree' to utilize certain electrons mutually, so that both can enjoy having eight electrons in the outer shell.

The mutually shared electrons then occur in pairs between the atoms and become attracted equally to both. This sharing of electrons creates a bond, called an electron pair bond or covalent bond. No ions (charged particles) are created, but rather both atoms remain neutral and merely bond together with their 'mutual possessions'.

An example may make this clearer: the chlorine atom with its seven outer electrons is lacking just one electron to be stable. If two of these chlorine atoms should happen to meet, both lacking just one electron, they agree that each will put one electron at the disposal of the other, so that there are two electrons shared between the atoms.

The result of this is to give both a complement of eight electrons, and a stable state is achieved. The mutually shared electron pair does, however, result in both atoms remaining wedded (until 'another chemical interaction shall part them').

Metallic bonds

A third possibility that certain elements, the metals (Greek *metallon*, 'mine, vein of ore'), like to use to achieve the desired stability is the metallic bond. Here, the excess outer electrons are simply generously put at the disposal of the general community. The atom distances itself from its outermost 'appendages', feels stable, and the freed electrons can move around between the atoms.

The bonding here occurs via a shared 'cloud' of electrons. The bonding is not as rigid as in ionic and covalent bonds, as no single atoms are joined together – instead, it is the entire structure that is held together. For this reason, metals can be bent and formed, and because of the 'free electrons' they are able to conduct electric current. (Electrical current is merely a 'current' or 'flow' of electrons.)

Metals and non-metals

Based on the bonding properties described above, all elements can be categorized into two main groups. The larger group, the metals, consists of elements that release electrons (can and will). In ionic bonds with non-metals they provide the 'cations' (positively charged ions), they create metallic bonds with each other, and they are only rarely found in covalent bonds.

The other group consists of the non-metals. These can accept electrons, provide 'anions' (negatively charged ions) in ionic bonds with metals and, as a rule, form compounds with each other via covalent bonds. Non-metals do not form metallic bonds.

In-between these groups there are a few elements that are neither distinctly metals nor non-metals, but have a mixture of properties. These are called metalloids. Depending on the circumstances they are capable of sometimes releasing electrons and sometimes accepting them, and they show the entire range of different bondings.

Mineral-forming elements

Not all of the elements in a chemistry book can be found in minerals. Some are missing because they do not form bonds (noble gases), and some because they were created by humans in laboratories and atomic reactors (plutonium, etc.). In order to limit ourselves to those elements that actually form minerals, they will be called mineral-forming elements from now on. After dividing them up again into the classification of metals and non-metals, the following list presents the most important mineral-forming elements.

Metals: aluminium, antimony, beryllium, lead, calcium, chromium, iron, gold, potassium, cobalt, copper, lithium, magnesium, manganese, sodium, nickel, silver, titanium, vanadium, bismuth, zinc, tin and zirconium.

Non-metals: boron, chlorine, fluorine, carbon, phosphorus, oxygen and sulphur.

Metalloids: the most important in this group, and in the entire mineral kingdom, is one of the most important and abundant of all elements, silicon. Other metalloids are boron, germanium, arsenic, selenium and tellurium.

From the compounds of these few elements, the overwhelming majority (over 95%) of the 4000 known minerals are formed. Quantitatively, these elements actually make up over 99.9% of the Earth's crust. Each of them has its own special properties and the compounds of these elements create the characteristic features of minerals. These properties are also extremely important in healing for the effect of the minerals on the human body, soul, mind and spirit.

The properties of mineral-forming elements

As a rule, minerals consist of two components, a metallic and non-metallic portion – only very rarely do we find a metal or non-metal 'alone' in nature. This polarization is a determining factor both in the mineralogical and healing properties of a mineral.

One fact that stands out from the start is that nature has far more metals than non-metals to offer. Looking more closely, we will also see that the non-metallic proportion of a mineral determines its basic qualities, while the metallic portion produces individual variations.

With all minerals that contain the same non-metallic proportion, we find common features as in a kind of relatedness. Using a rather free analogy from the human world, we can liken the non-metallic portion to the 'family name' of the mineral (in a chemical formula it always appears at the end).

Following this analogy through, the metals in a mineral correspond to the first name. The metals serve to distinguish the various members of the family from each other and visibly alter the basic properties of each mineral. The metals are also the part of the mineral that give it its characteristic colour, as we shall see later on.

The mineral classes and their properties

Just as biology distinguishes by groups such as genera or species, mineralogy proceeds as follows: all minerals are divided up into eight large classes, determined by the most frequent non-metallic proportions and the similarities that result from them.

These classes of minerals also demonstrate the first spectrum of effectiveness of minerals for healing purposes so, in the following text, mineralogical and healing aspects will be shown alongside each other.

Mineral classes	Non-metallic portion	Chemical symbol
I natural elements	consists of only one element	element's symbol
II sulphides	sulphur	S
III halides	fluorine, chlorine, bromine & iodine	F, Cl, Br, I
IV oxides	oxygen	O
V carbonates	carbonic acid	CO_3
VI sulphates	sulphuric acid	SO_4
VII phosphates	phosphoric acid	PO_4
VIII silicates	silicic acid	Si_nO_m

Class I. The minerals of the class of **natural elements** consist of only a single mineral-forming substance, a single element. This is very rare in nature, as only very few chemical elements are able to remain uncombined with other elements. Among the non-metals only carbon, which can be found in the form of graphite or diamond (formula: Cn), and sulphur (S8) appear as natural elements. Among the metals, only the precious metals gold (Au), silver (Ag), copper (Cu), etc. sometimes occur in a pure form.

The natural elements represent purity and the ability to remain uninfluenced. They help us to develop our personalities without interference from outside. They also stimulate us to distance ourselves from anything in life that is not really part of our essential nature. They help us recognize what will harm or help us. Depending on which element is involved, certain corresponding areas of life will be particularly addressed (more on this later on).

Class II. The minerals of the class of **sulphides** are derivatives of sulphur, or to be precise, of hydrogen sulphide. This highly toxic gas is often a product of decay and produces the well-known odour of 'rotten eggs'. Hydrogen sulphide is formed during volcanic activities and during the decay of organic matter, and is present almost all over the Earth in varying quantities.

The sulphides arising from its compounds with metals are generally opaque and are characterized by a metallic sheen, rather like the surface of a mirror. Their chemical formulas end in S (sulphur), for example pyrite is FeS_2 (iron sulphide).

Sulphides are the mirrors of hidden things. They help uncover repressed and forgotten matters and get rid of confusion and muddle, with precisely that area of our lives coming under scrutiny where something 'stinks' or is 'bad'. Sulphides are also known as the 'merciless awareness-makers', as they will, on the one hand, guide our attention to where changes are drastically necessary but, on the other hand, will not give any kind of help in setting these changes in motion. But then, knowing oneself is the first step towards bettering oneself.

The following sulphides are currently used as healing stones: antimonite, chalcopyrite, covellite, jamesonite, marcasite, pop rocks, schalenblende and sphalerite.

Class III. The minerals of the class of **halides** (Greek *halos genes*, 'salt-forming') are derivatives of a group of elements called halogens, which include fluorine and chlorine. In the pure state halogens are toxins, but they readily form compounds with other elements to become valuable salts (hence the name).

Combined with hydrogen they form, for example, hydrofluoric acid (HF) and hydrochloric acid (HCl). Both acids are extremely aggressive; hydrofluoric acid is even able to corrode quartz and dissolve glass. When these acids come into contact with metals they form transparent minerals, such as fluorite (CaF_2) or rock salt (NaCl).

Halides have a dissolving property, in accordance with the properties of acids from which they arise. Just as they are able to dissolve metals with which they would like to form compounds, so they can also help us to end restrictions and break down barriers. Patterns of thinking, behaving or living that are no longer any good for us but merely hinder us can be dissolved with their help. In the Middle Ages salt was thought to be capable of driving out demons! And what are demons, but circumstances in our lives that we cannot control but that control us?

Of the mineral class of halides only fluorite and halite (rock salt) are currently used as healing stones.

Class IV. The minerals of the class of **oxides** are derivatives of oxygen (Greek *oxys genes*, 'oxygen, the acid-former'). They can occur anywhere as oxygen is contained in magma, in water and in abundance in air. The formation of oxide minerals can take place in front of your very eyes – for example the formation of rust (iron oxide) on the bodywork of cars owing to oxygen in the air.

Oxygen is the most prevalent mineral-forming element on Earth: 50% of the solid crust consists of this element. The formula for oxides ends with oxygen, for example haematite is Fe_2O_3 (iron oxide).

Oxides have a transformative effect, and will convert unstable states into stable ones. Oxygen is the element that feeds combustion processes: anything from a campfire to energy consumption in our body cells. During this process, energy-rich unstable compounds are converted into energy-poor but more stable compounds (wood turns into ash). Wherever we need to invest energy constantly, in order to maintain an unstable state, oxides will become active to transform this state into a stable one. The energy bound up in this transformation (and therefore not available for use) is released and can be used. Hence oxides also advance all unfinished things in our lives that would otherwise be constantly draining away energy.

The most important healing stones from the class of oxides are hematite, magnetite and tiger iron, alexandrite and chrysoberyl, spinel and the corundum group containing ruby and sapphire. Older books on minerals also classify quartz and quartz-related minerals (obsidian and opal) with the oxides, as their formula (SiO_2) would suggest this (with silicon as the metallic and oxygen the non-metallic element).

In newer books, however, quartzes and their close relatives are classified as framework silicates, as silicium and oxygen form linked silicate lattices here via atomic bonds. This classification also corresponds with their crystal healing properties.

Class V. The minerals of the class of **carbonates** are derivatives of carbonic acid (Latin *carbo*, 'coal'). Carbonic acid (H_2CO_3) is a very unstable compound of liquid (water, formula H_2O) and gas (carbon dioxide, CO_2) that very easily breaks down in its liquid form. We can readily observe this: when a bottle of carbonated mineral water is opened carbon dioxide is released and immediately escapes.

When carbonic acid reacts with metals more stable compounds are formed – the bonds are firmer. Even then, a certain amount of reactivity is retained: carbonates are rarely a stable end product, rather a temporary transitional phase that is further developed when new influences begin to become effective. Their chemical formulas end in CO, (carbonate), for example calcite is $CaCO_3$ (calcium carbonate).

Carbonates influence developmental processes. During these processes carbonates that contain water, such as azurite and malachite, have an initiating effect, which means they stimulate new developments. Just as carbon dioxide gas escapes from the liquid in mineral water, unfamiliar thoughts may suddenly rise up into our conscious awareness.

In contrast 'dehydrated', dry carbonates stabilize developmental processes that have got out of balance, either because they were too fast (e.g. aragonite) or too slow (e.g. calcite). The shared theme in all cases is a permanent change.

Of the carbonates the following are currently used in healing: aragonite, azurite, azurite-malachite, calcite, dolomite, magnesite, malachite, rhodochrosite and smithsonite.

Class VI. The minerals of the class of **sulphates** are derivatives of sulphuric acid (not to be confused with sulphides). Sulphuric acid is a compound of hydrogen and a sulphide (H_2SO_4) and is a very dense liquid that flows much more slowly than water, for example, and hardly evaporates at all if it is kept in an open flask.

Sulphuric acid compounds are very stable and persistent. This property is used in pharmacology when, for example, unstable medications are crystallized out as sulphates. This makes the medications more persistent and they also keep longer. The formulas of sulphates end in SO_4 (sulphate), for example anglesite (anhydrite) is $CaSO_4$.

Sulphates make things constant or lasting. They fix a certain state and can maintain it over a long period of time. They also have an insulating effect, so they form a protection against outside influences. Depending on whether the fixed state is pleasant or unpleasant for us, this may represent heaven or hell. They have a dampening effect on developmental processes; this means they may afford us a period of rest, but using them for a long time requires caution!

Among the sulphates, anglesite (anhydrite), celestine and gypsum in the form of Mary glass and selenite are currently used as healing stones.

Class VII. Minerals from the class of **phosphates** are derived from phosphoric acid (H_3PO_4), the central element of which is phosphorus (Greek *phosphores*, 'light-carrying'). Phosphates are in fact carriers of energy in our own bodies (see below).

In addition, phosphates are an important 'buffer'; that is a substance that is able to neutralize both acids and bases (alkalis). The formulas of phosphates end in PO_4 (phosphate), for example variscite is $AlPO_4$ (aluminium phosphate).

Phosphates have a balancing effect and can mobilize energy reserves. The buffering effect of phosphates helps to preserve neutrality in our body fluids, thereby promoting stability in terms of health and a balance of mood.

In addition, when phosphates are deposited in our bodies in the form of certain organic compounds, their energy levels are raised; when these phosphate compounds are broken down, energy is released. Phosphate compounds are the energy carriers in our cells. Energy turnover is increased through the use of phosphates and this makes us awake, lively, active and ready for action.

From the mineral class of phosphates, apatite, turquoise, variscite and vivianite are currently used in healing.

Class VIII. Minerals from the class of **silicates** are derivatives of silicic acid (HxSiyOz). Silicic acid is one of the most versatile of acids, which is why its structure cannot be expressed in a single formula. The smallest unit of silicic acid consists of a single silicon atom surrounded by four oxygen atoms and to which, in turn, four hydrogen atoms are bound (H_4SiO_4).

Several of these units can be bound in groups, chains, rings, layers and lattice-like structures by splitting off water, which means that, in principle, there is not just 'one' but 'several different' kinds of silicic acid. For example:

$$2\ H_4SiO_4\ \rightarrow\ H_6Si_2O_7\ + H_2O$$

$$3\ H_4SiO_4\ \rightarrow\ H_8Si_3O_{10}\ +\ 2\ H_2O \text{ etc}$$

Silicates, therefore, possess the most versatile crystal lattices, which makes it impossible to give a general description of their properties and also makes further distinguishing features very necessary.

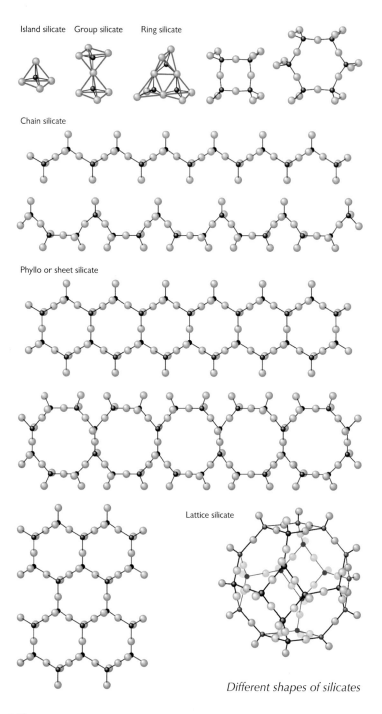

Island silicate Group silicate Ring silicate

Chain silicate

Phyllo or sheet silicate

Lattice silicate

Different shapes of silicates

Class VIII – 1. The crystal lattice of **nesosilicates or island silicates** contains individual silicate molecules, single tetrahedrons like 'islands' between the metal ions. Their formulas end in SiO_4, for example zirconium is $ZrSiO_4$ (zirconium silicate). The way the island silicates are structured results in very compact minerals with a high density.

Island silicates strengthen resistance and the desire to structure one's life according to one's own wishes. The individual island silicates represent individuality, the path one can travel alone. Island silicates also fortify one's health and are helpers in crises and emergencies so we are able to remain true to our convictions, even when under great stress.

At present the following island silicates are used for healing purposes: andalusite and chiastolite, disthene (kyanite), dumortierite, the garnet family with andradite, almandine, hessonite, grossular, melanite, pyrope, rhodolite, spessartite, tsavorite and uvarovite, as well as olivine (peridot or chrysolite), sillimanite, titanite (sphene), topaz and finally, the zirconium family with the variety called hyacinth.

Class VIII – 2. The crystal lattice of **sorosilicates or group silicates** contains silicate molecules that are bound together in pairs or small groups, as a rule, two to four connected tetrahedrons. The end of the formula can be derived as follows: Si_nO_{3n+1} where n is the number of silicon atoms, or the number of silicon tetrahedra. For example prehnite has the formula Ca_2Al_2 $[(OH)_2/Si_3O_{10}]$; this is calcium aluminium hydroxide silicate, an alkaline (OH) group silicate comprised of three connected silicate tetrahedrons.

Group silicates strengthen the power of regeneration. They encourage the healing process after an illness and help one find one's way back to the original wishes, goals and intentions that inspire us. They are helpful whenever we have to orientate ourselves again or are faced with a new beginning. They stimulate the energy flow inside and increase the speed of the healing process.

Of these group silicates only epidote, prehnite, vesuvianite (idocrase) and the zoisite family, including tanzanite, thulite and zoisite, are used for healing. With the exception of prehnite, these contain both island silicates and group silicate molecules, and so beautifully combine the properties of both classes.

Class VIII – 3. The crystal lattice of the **cyclosilicates or ring silicates** contains rings of three to twelve closed circles of silicate tetrahedrons. The end of the formula is Si_nO_{3n}, for example beryl: $Al_2Be_3[Si_6O_{18}]$ = aluminium beryllium silicate. Whenever these rings are arranged in 'pillar-like' structures in the mineral, the ring silicates become extremely good electrical conductors. If the rings are not in regular arrangements, the structure is 'sponge-like' and results in opaque minerals.

When these rings in the mineral are arranged as long, pillar-like structures, the ring silicates become good electrical conductors; if the rings instead form amorphous shapes, this creates a matrix in which opaque minerals are formed. The former can be used when energy flows in our bodies are blocked or if there is a general lack of vitality. Ring silicates with pillar-like structures have a stimulating effect, making the user active and dynamic, while ring silicates with a random structure will absorb excess energy. They have a calming, sobering effect and will lower a fever or reduce heat and pain.

Ring silicates with pillar formations used as healing stones are: the beryl family with aquamarine, beryl, bixite, golden beryl, heliodor, morganite and emerald, as well as cordierite (iolite), dioptase and the tourmaline family with dravite (brown tourmaline), indicolite (blue tourmaline), rubellite (red tourmaline), schorl (black tourmaline), verdelite (green tourmaline) and all their colourful mixed crystals. Ring silicates with random structures that are used as healing crystals are chrysocolla and sugilite.

Class VIII – 4. The crystal lattice of the **inosilicates or chain and band silicates** contains silicate tetrahedrons that are linked together in long chains. Their formulas show the same relationships as those of the ring silicates, Si_nO_{3n}, but owing to the length of the chains (which often cannot even be determined) only the quantity ratio between silicon and oxygen is given (2:6). This helps distinguish the chain and ring silicates by their formulas. An example of a chain silicate is kunzite: $LiAl[Si_2O_6]$ = lithium aluminium silicate.

Chain silicates stimulate energy flows in us and increase the speed of healing and developmental processes. They provide for a balanced distribution of energy in the organism and, in this way, they also have an emotionally balancing and harmonizing effect. At the same time, they improve spiritual and physical flexibility and encourage a spiritual movement towards goals and ideals.

Among the chain silicates the following minerals are used as healing stones: actinolite and nephrite, bronzite, chloromelanite, diopside (also chromium diopside), jadeite, the spodumene family with hiddenite and kunzite, as well as rhodonite.

Class VIII – 5. The crystal lattice of **phyllosilicates or sheet silicates** consists of silicate tetrahedrons that are connected in sheets. Their formulas end in $SinO_{2n+2}$, for example apophyllite: $KCa_4[F/(Si_4O_{10})_2] \cdot 8 H_2O$ = potassium calcium fluoride silicate containing water. These layers are very cohesive. They can be separated easily but it is very difficult to cut through them. The structure of the layers means that sheet silicates are easy to split but difficult or impossible to slice!

Sheet silicates have a protective effect and strengthen boundaries. These minerals display poor energy and warmth conducting properties at right angles to the layers or sheets (they are used as insulators in technology). They are able to shield us from energy forms affecting us from outside, while the flow of energy in ourselves is unaffected.

Healing stones used from the group of sheet silicates are apophyllite, biotite, charoite, lepidolite and serpentine.

Class VIII – 6. The crystal lattice of **tectosilicates or framework silicates** forms three-dimensional grids of silicate tetrahedrons, usually incorporating of further elements such as aluminium (Al), beryllium (Be) or boron (B) in the crystal lattice. These lattice structures are too complex to be reduced to a simple, generally applicable summary formula. Where there is doubt, we recommend consulting mineralogical specialist literature on the particular stone involved.

Framework silicates have a filtering effect that will absorb certain things and reflect others. Their three-dimensional structures can have an absorbing effect, producing opaque minerals that have absorbing properties, as in the 'unstructured' ring silicates. They also have a calming and sobering effect and reduce fever, heat and pain. These healing stones include the feldspars with gold orthoclase, labradorite, moonstone and sunstone, quartz-related minerals (obsidian and opal) and the entire quartz group: the crystal quartzes amethyst, ametrine, rock crystal, citrine, prase, smoky quartz, rutile quartz and tourmaline quartz; the coarse quartzes, aventurine quartz, tree quartz, blue quartz, budstone (prase quartz), rose quartz, falcon's eye and tiger's eye; the fibrous quartzes, chalcedony, chrysoprase, carnelian, heliotrope, moss agate, onyx, ocean chalcedony, sardonyx and fossilized wood; and the grainy quartzes, jasper and mookaite; as well as agate, which combines different quartzes in layers.

If the mineral remains transparent, we often see partial absorption and light reflections that result in a change in our perception: our usual 'filters' are adjusted and suddenly we see the world with 'new eyes' and are able to adopt new perspectives we could not have imagined possible until now. Framework silicates promote a broadening of our horizons. Among these healing stones are the minerals gold-orthoclase, labradorite, moonstone and sunstone (all of the feldspar family).

The metabolism of minerals

The second important range of effects of mineral-forming elements results from the direct influence they have on our bodies. Many mineral-forming substances have important key functions in the body: they are vital to the formation of many enzymes, which are substances that make chemical processes in the body possible and guide them, thereby regulating our entire metabolism.

Also some play an important role in the stimulation and conduction of our nerves, that is, in conducting sensory impulses, regulating the activity of the brain, and directing the function of the muscles and organs. Regulation of the water metabolism is also directly connected with these substances, as is the quality of the blood and body fluids.

Minerals cannot be produced by the body; they have to be absorbed through food. They could be looked upon as 'inorganic vitamins' – vitally important substances whose continuous supply from outside has to be ensured at all times. Mineral deficiency can arise if too few minerals are present in the diet, for example through poor eating habits with too many processed foods, fast foods and preserved foods, or if the small intestines are unable to absorb the necessary minerals. The last example is the most frequent cause of mineral deficiency.

The small intestine is a sensitive organ. The stress of a permanently bad diet will give it a hard time, as will emotional stress, traumatic experiences or negative attitudes towards life – in short, an unhealthy quality of life. These influences will perceptibly and negatively affect its function of absorbing vitamins, nutrients and minerals. As long as it is able to function without interference, the small intestine possesses a complicated system of many biochemical mechanisms that are responsible for absorbing precisely those substances into the bloodstream that are needed by the body while all superfluous or even harmful substances are kept out.

Under the type of stress described above, these mechanisms get muddled up. Vitally needed substances are no longer absorbed and others are absorbed in excess. The kidneys are often able to work against the excess substances by excreting more of these, but where vital substances are not absorbed in sufficient quantities there will be a deficiency that gradually uses up the reserves in the body and in the long term there can be no balance!

The consequences are fairly inconspicuous to begin with, the first signs being certain repetitious thoughts, ideas, feelings, moods and emotions, tiredness or hyperactivity and nervousness. Gradually the deficiency leads to more serious physical manifestations through to physical illness. The effect of lack of particular minerals may appear anywhere in the body; the importance of minerals to the whole body is clear from the description given above of the areas of function of minerals.

It has been found that minerals that contain certain mineral-forming substances stimulate their absorption via the small intestine and encourage their metabolism within the organism. The problem of disruptions to absorption from the small intestine can be solved with their help. As long as the food intake offers the necessary substances, the body should be in a position to absorb them adequately. In this way minerals fundamentally support our health.

Minerals stimulate all metabolic processes that are connected with the relevant mineral-forming substance and this activates the elimination of excess or harmful substances from the organism. Typical symptoms of irritation or toxicity right through to allergic reactions can be healed in this way. This aspect is very important as healing with crystals and stones opens up the possibilities of employing minerals whose compounds are not present in the human organism.

Acids and alkalis

Minerals are rarely formed directly from pure elements. In general they first form acids and alkalis (also called bases) and then comes a reaction with the mineral. Acids and alkalis arise from the bonding of a mineral-forming substance with water (H_2O) that is first split into the ions H^+ and OH^- ($H_2O \rightarrow H^+ + OH^-$). If the compound thus formed now contains H+ ions, or if it is able to release these, it is called an acid, for example:

$$\text{Hydrochloric acid} \quad HCl \rightarrow H^+ + Cl^-$$

$$\text{Carbonic acid} \quad H_2CO_3 \rightarrow 2\,H^+ + CO_3{}^{2-}$$

$$\text{Phosphoric acid} \quad H_3PO_4 \rightarrow 3\,H^+ + PO_4{}^{3-}$$

If the compound formed contains OH– ions, or is able to absorb H+ ions and bond them, it is called an alkali, for example:

$$\text{Sodium hydroxide} \quad NaOH + H^+ \rightarrow Na^+ + H_2O$$

$$\text{Calcium hydroxide} \quad Ca(OH)_2 + 2\,H^+ \rightarrow Ca^{2+} + 2\,H_2O$$

The reaction of an acid with an alkali is called a neutralizing reaction as a neutral substance is formed if both are present in the right quantities:

$$\text{sodium hydroxide} + \text{hydrochloric acid} \rightarrow \text{salt} + \text{water}$$
$$NaOH \quad + \quad HCl \quad \rightarrow \quad NaCl \quad + \quad H_2O$$

Nature is no sterile laboratory. This is why it rarely happens that acids and alkalis meet in exactly the right quantities necessary for complete neutralization. Usually, a certain quantity of one remains, and it is then often built into the crystalline lattice of the mineral being formed. The mineral then acquires an acidic or alkaline character. Acidic minerals tend to look transparent, while alkaline ones are more often dark or opaque.

These properties of a mineral are very important for healing as there are areas in our bodies that are more acidic (stomach), alkaline (small intestine) or neutral (blood). Minerals work according to their character on the milieu of the body fluids and make them either more acidic or alkaline. This determines, among other things, what diseases develop in the body, as they usually need a certain environment to 'flourish'. Rheumatic diseases or viruses, for example, require an acidic environment, bacteria a neutral one, and fungi an alkaline one.

This has implications on our spiritual health also. Not for nothing has the word 'humour' been derived from the Latin for 'moisture' and the word 'temperament' from *temperamentum*, 'the right proportion of a mixture', concepts which, in the Middle Ages, dealt with the 'mixing or balancing of the four humours or liquids in the body'. These corresponded to the four temperaments: choleric, sanguine, melancholic and phlegmatic. A more acidic metabolism tends to promote a choleric temperament (a sour disposition!), while an alkaline metabolism promotes a phlegmatic temperament. Accordingly, acidic minerals are more stimulating, alkaline ones more calming.

Substances such as phosphates, for example, are particularly interesting as they are able both to absorb H+ ions and release them. They are called buffers as they are able to keep acids and alkalis in a balance for a long time through the following reactions:

$$NaH_2PO_4 + OH^- \rightarrow NaHPO_4^- + H_2O$$
the buffer reaction if an alkali is introduced

$$NaH_2PO_4 + H^+ \rightarrow H_3PO_4 + Na^+$$
the buffer reaction if an acid is introduced

With these properties, minerals that contain buffers are able to stabilize the acid-alkali equilibrium in the body and promote a balance of emotions and temperament.

The principles of the effects that mineral-forming elements have on us

The absorption and metabolism of mineral-forming elements that have an important function in our bodies are stimulated by minerals that contain the same mineral-forming elements. Any deficiencies can be removed and the functioning of the organs improved in this way.

Mineral-forming elements that are in excess or harmful in the body will be increasingly eliminated under the influence of minerals that contain these or similar substances. This process stimulates purification and detoxification in the body which, in turn, alleviate or heal symptoms of irritation or poisoning, as well as any allergic reactions.

▶ The alkaline or acidic character of a mineral will influence the milieu of body fluids in a corresponding manner. As physical illnesses as well as mental perceptions correspond directly with the milieu of body fluids, minerals will influence the general tendency towards illness, and will also influence emotions and temperament.

These three principles are not limited to the body. Just as the mental and spiritual state have an effect on physical well-being, so physical changes also stimulate certain emotions, inner visions, thoughts and intentions. 'As above, so below' is an ancient saying derived from Hermetic wisdom, which is just as valid today.

Mineral-forming elements also activate spiritual and mental experiences, encourage the necessary processes of accepting, both an inner 'digesting' as well as the 'elimination' of thoughts, ideas, constructs, moods and emotions that bother us or harm us. Whether a mineral will be effective primarily on the physical, the mental/soul or spiritual level, will be decided for the most part by one important factor: the amount of mineral-forming substance contained in the mineral.

The principle of dilution

We make a distinction here between 'large or frequent' quantities, 'smaller' quantities or trace amounts. The larger the quantity of a certain mineral-forming element within a mineral, the more extensive its effect, extending from the material to the spiritual levels. The smaller the amount and the finer its distribution, the more discretely levels of effectiveness can be attained.

This distinction helps, on the one hand, to choose more precisely the suitable mineral for a particular situation, while on the other hand, it shows on which level an initial reaction to the use of the mineral can be expected. The emphasis here is on the 'initial reaction' as, in the end, all levels correspond with each other and holistic healing is aimed for in the long run.

We speak of a **frequent** component if the relevant mineral-forming element (X) is present in such large quantities in the mineral that it acts as one of the mineral-forming elements and can also be represented in the chemical formula (X_nY_m). Calcite $(CaCO_3)$ contains calcium (Ca) and carbonate (CO_3) as frequent components, for example.

Rose quartz (SiO_2), for example, contains silicon and oxygen as its most abundant components. The mineralogical formula does not take account of all the minerals present as every mineral contains a number of inclusions and 'foreign substances'. Including these would only lead to confusion. This circumstance can be used in healing with crystals and stones through looking at the formula to see which mineral-forming elements are particularly 'frequent'. Their effect then takes place primarily in the body, corresponding to the incidence in one's own metabolism, for example, in the momentary stress created by toxic or waste products. But it also includes mind/soul and spiritual effects.

We speak of the **'smaller'** component when a certain substance (Z) is present in such minute quantities that it is no longer part of the formula but can still be proven to be present. Here, too, we have an appropriate distinction taken from mineralogy: 'well proven' means the substance can be identified through chemical analysis. It has to be present in sufficient quantities to have a visible effect (energy levels) and to take part in the chemical reaction. These components, present in minute quantities, are only rarely mentioned in the mineralogical literature; they are added as follows to the chemical formulas of stones in this book: XnYm+ Z. Calcite ($CaCO_3$+ Mn,Fe,Mg) may contain manganese (Mn), iron (Fe) and magnesium in small quantities, for example. Its effect then takes place primarily on the mental/soul level. For every mineral-forming element, certain typical emotional, mental and spiritual properties are displayed.

A component is only present as a **trace** when the amount of mineral-forming element (A) is only just detectable on the borderline. 'Borderline' means that many chemical methods can no longer identify this substance; it may only be detectable using procedures in modern physics (spectral analysis, X-ray analysis, electron probe microanalysis).

Nevertheless, these substances are often of great importance as it is often these very trace elements that are responsible for the colour of crystals and stones, for example. In older mineralogical literature we often have no indications of these mineral-forming elements, as certain discoveries have only been made during the past few years. The trace element components have therefore been added to the end of the formulas in this volume: XnYm+ (A). Here again, the example of calcite: $CaCO_3$+ Mn,Fe,Mg + (Sr,Ba,Co,Zn) – strontium (Sr), barium (Ba), cobalt (Co) and zinc (Zn) may be contained as trace elements here. The effect of these trace elements is felt principally on the spiritual plane through changing patterns of life, thought and behaviour, spiritual structures and character.

The healing properties of mineral-forming elements

The effects described below can be observed when a mineral that contains the relevant mineral-forming element is worn close to the body (ideally next to the skin). On no account should the properties listed here be attributed to the pure chemical substance without checking. Also, we strongly recommend you do not take many mineral-forming elements internally as high doses are toxic and would have exactly the opposite effect to the one desired.

A healthy, balanced diet can supply the body with enough of the necessary mineral-forming elements and in exactly the right form for the body to deal with them, organically constituted. In order to achieve the desired effects, it will be quite sufficient to wear the appropriate mineral!

The chemical abbreviation for the mineral-forming element in the chemical formula of a mineral is given again for identification purposes. For those interested in chemistry, we also give the number of positive or negative charges of the element in the ionic bonds of the minerals.

Aluminium (Al^{3+})

Physical: Aluminium promotes alkaline metabolic processes. In this way, it will help with all problems that arise through over-acid conditions, for example rheumatism and gout, and will decrease excessive acid formation in the stomach. Aluminium supports the absorption of iron in the intestine and normalizes conductivity in the nerves. In this way, it helps with symptoms of weakness, slowed down perception and even with paralysis.

Psychological/mental: Aluminium has a very calming effect on nervousness, fears and feelings of guilt. A typical indicator is a feeling of impending madness. Aluminium encourages the facility to express feelings, and to release behavioural patterns of holding onto things and holding back. It also stimulates a desire for change and alteration.

Spiritual: Aluminium can help with a loss of identity, finding out again who we really are and what our task is in life. It encourages a sense of reality, soberness and alertness at any given moment. Aluminium aids the recognition of the seductions of modern life as the illusions they are and helps us to deal with them.

Antimony (Sb^{3+})

Physical: Antimony supports the digestion and helps with stomach problems, particularly heartburn, nausea and vomiting. It helps with skin diseases, dry, cracked skin, all kinds of rashes and spots, eczema and persistent itching. Antimony regulates all elimination through the skin and the gut.

Psychological/mental: Antimony promotes objective, logical/rational thinking and helps overcome anger, dissatisfaction, sadness and oppressive feelings. It helps with a retreat from sentimental emotions, love-sickness or world-weariness. Antimony dampens excessive sexual desire and helps us to give up habits that are merely substituted gratification for unfulfilled desires (for example, overeating out of frustration).

Spiritual: Antimony encourages a creative lifestyle. It facilitates following one's own inner voice and in overcoming limiting ideas. Antimony helps balance and harmonize personal interests and higher ideals, and makes life appear more meaningful and happy.

Beryllium (Be^{2+})

Physical: Beryllium helps with allergies, eczema and ulcers; also with rheumatic complaints and hormonal problems.

Psychological/mental: Beryllium encourages a far-seeing perspective, clear perception and concentration.

Spiritual: Beryllium helps create goals and encourages discipline and consistency in attaining these goals.

Bismuth (Bi^{3+})

Physical: Bismuth has disinfectant and contracting properties, so it is used for injuries and the healing of wounds. In its mineral form, it enhances the ability to regenerate the mucous membranes and is helpful with gastritis and stomach ulcers.

Psychological/mental: Bismuth enhances a natural, child-like lack of inhibition and a playful attitude towards life. It helps us accept our mortal existence when strong aversion to it exists and there is a predominant feeling of being lonely and not really at home on this planet.

Spiritual: Bismuth helps us to take up again forms of spiritual development that had been abandoned owing to external circumstances and bring them to completion.

Boron (B^{3-})

Physical: Boron helps with many diseases of the stomach and intestinal tract: nausea, vomiting, cramps, colic and diarrhoea. It dissolves energy blockages and leads to relaxation of the affected organs. It helps with skin problems, for example those caused by contact with irritating or toxic substances, and with problems of the nervous system, for example epilepsy or perceptual problems.

Psychological/mental: Boron has a balancing effect on nervousness and jumpiness, promotes equilibrium and prevents us from stumbling or dropping things. It helps with panic attacks and great fear, promoting harmony and trust.

Spiritual: Boron helps us gain control over our own life, that is, to get a grip on our life.

Calcium (Ca^{2+})

Physical: Calcium encourages the metabolism of the cells, absorption of nutrients by the cell membranes, and energy use in the cells. It is necessary for the formation of DNA (the carrier of genetic information) and RNA (the messenger that passes on information on proteins, enzymes and hormones).

Calcium supports the growth, firmness and flexibility of bones, teeth and tissue. It is important for the regulation of the acid/alkali balance and encourages the elimination of fluid (the antagonist of sodium). It supports blood clotting (the antagonist of magnesium).

Finally, calcium is important for the formation of transmitter substances in the sensory system from nerves to organs or muscles. It regulates the heart rhythm and strengthens the heart.

Psychological/mental: Calcium encourages receptivity, discrimination and memory. It has an emotionally stabilizing effect, lends self-confidence and helps to eliminate fear, particularly of accidents and illness. Calcium gives inner drive in cases of lethargy and clears up confusion.

Spiritual: Calcium regulates the development of the personality. It speeds up a development that is slowing down and normalizes situations where developmental processes have become over-accelerated and chaotic. Calcium promotes mental growth.

Chlorine (Cl⁻)

Physical: Chlorine helps with all feelings of weakness, including fainting and blackouts. It raises the blood pressure and regulates elimination through the kidneys. In addition, it encourages retention of water in the tissues and helps make them more elastic (works against 'stiffness') and encourages detoxification and the elimination of waste products in the cells. Chlorine encourages production of hydrochloric acid in the stomach and stimulates the digestion. Together with sodium and potassium it regulates the transmission of impulses in the nervous system.

Psychological/mental: Chlorine dissolves tension and illnesses caused by stress, constriction, sorrow or fear. It makes us less sensitive to outer influences and reduces irritability. Chlorine gives us tranquillity and encourages deftness.

Spiritual: Chlorine causes or promotes a positive, optimistic attitude towards life. It helps make us freer and able to unfold on an inner level without being bound.

Chromium (Cr³⁺, Cr⁴⁺, Cr⁶⁺)

Physical: Chromium helps diabetes in its early stage as it assists the insulin in maintaining an equilibrium in blood sugar and storing sugar in the muscles. Chromium stimulates the fat metabolism, lowers the cholesterol level and prevents arteriosclerosis. It encourages growth as it influences the formation of growth hormone.

Chromium has anti-inflammatory properties, particularly in the central organs (the liver, heart, stomach, intestine and kidneys), as well as in infections of the nose and nasal passages (sinuses). It stimulates detoxification of the organism, lowers acidity and encourages fever as a healing reaction. It regulates the energy and heat levels in the body and soothes pain, particularly in the case of 'wandering' pain or headaches caused by weakness. Chromium helps clear cloudiness in the cornea.

Psychological/mental: Chromium encourages mental regeneration and healing. It takes away the feeling of being under pressure. The richness of the world of ideas and creative imagination can be discovered and versatile ideas and enthusiasm are the result. Chromium brings colour into our life (Greek *chromos*, 'colour')!

Spiritual: Chromium encourages the desire for self-determination and individuality. It stimulates us to discover and develop our own capabilities and to realize those important dreams in life. Chromium promotes all processes of mental healing.

Cobalt (Co^{3+})

Physical: Cobalt increases the formation of red blood corpuscles in the bone marrow through the creation of a hormone in the kidneys. It accelerates maturation and extends the lifespan of blood cells. Cobalt also increases the ability of the small intestine to absorb iron.

Psychological/mental: Cobalt, like chromium, enhances a desire for change and new experiences. It awakens curiosity and joy in living, removes melancholy and strong yearnings, and promotes wit and cunning. Not for nothing has it been named after the German *Kobold*, a clever and mischievous type of gnome.

Spiritual: Cobalt helps to develop the view that all spiritual things are imbued with invisible being. It also promotes recognition of the spiritual universe.

Copper (Cu, Cu^{2+}, Cu^{3+})

Physical: Copper promotes absorption of iron in the small intestine and triggers the transformation of stored iron into a form that can be transported by the blood. It is a catalyst in the formation of haemoglobin and is responsible for the formation of enzymes that keep the blood vessels elastic. Copper promotes the development of the female sexual organs and helps with menstruation problems.

Copper promotes cell growth, cell respiration and pigmentation of hair and skin. The greatest concentrations of copper are in the liver, brain and blood and it stimulates all their activities. Copper is effective in lowering a temperature and loosening cramps; it is anti-inflammatory and detoxifying.

Psychological/mental: Copper increases dream activity and promotes the inner world of pictures and imagination and the creative potential resulting from it. Copper helps develop creative imagination and dissolve confusion. It creates neutrality and a balancing of mood and also promotes free expression of feelings. Copper makes it possible to live out and enjoy the senses and sexuality.

Spiritual: Copper encourages a sense of aesthetics and beauty, as well as the development of a spiritual culture. It fortifies a sense of justice and promotes friendship and love towards all beings.

Fluorine (F–)

Physical: Fluorine promotes firmness of bones and teeth and improves stiffness and problems with joints, even with arthritis (inflammation of the joints). It promotes the regeneration of the skin and mucous membranes, particularly in the respiratory tract and the lungs. Fluorine promotes the activity of the nervous system, particularly that of the cerebral cortex, and helps tone down allergies of psychological origin.

Psychological/mental: Fluorine helps us get rid of fixed behavioural patterns, fixed ideas, small thinking, narrow-mindedness and a generally uptight manner. It promotes flexibility, quick thinking, concentration and the ability to learn.

Spiritual: Fluorine promotes spiritual freedom.

Gold (Au)

Physical: Gold promotes the distribution of energy and vitality in the body. It is 'warming' and promotes a well-functioning circulation. It helps with problems and diseases of the sexual organs, generally supports the functioning of the glands, and helps heal damage to bones and tissues. Gold regulates conduction of impulses in the nervous system.

Psychological/mental: Gold helps us out of depression, fear of death and, in severe cases, inclination to commit suicide. It confers self-confidence and self-consciousness and releases us from destructive influences.

Spiritual: Gold brings our innermost core, our essence, to light. It helps give meaning to life and enables the realization of great deeds and projects. Gold represents generosity and magnanimity.

Iron (Fe2+,Fe3+,Fe4+)

Physical: Iron promotes the absorption of iron through the intestine, as well as the formation of haemoglobin and red blood corpuscles. This ensures transportation of oxygen to the cells of the muscles and organs, good energy transfer and physical vitality. It helps in cases of weakness, tiredness and exhaustion.

The functions of the liver, spleen, intestine and bone marrow are stimulated by iron. In addition, it fortifies the immune system – in silicon compounds mainly unspecifically, in oxides specifically the immune response.

Psychological/mental: Iron has a stimulating, activating effect, encourages activity, initiative, dynamism, endurance, willpower, the ability to assert ourselves and the ability to be enthusiastic about something. Iron promotes the warrior side of us, the urge to research and discover and to conquer. It also promotes an upright attitude and honesty.

Spiritual: Iron promotes inner calm and makes us unchallengeable. It will purify consciousness of painful and unpleasant contents, gives alertness and deepens meditations. Iron also stimulates the mental processing of perceptions and experiences and thereby helps to complete unfinished cycles.

Lead (Pb2+)

Physical: Lead stimulates the elimination of heavy metals in the body, in this way helping with disease in organs affected by harmful substances, particularly the stomach, the intestine, blood and nerves. It helps with dehydration, sclerosis, stone formation in organs, loss of weight, muscular atrophy and severe localized pain.

Psychological/mental: Lead promotes joy in living, particularly when we are depressed by a personal or social situation that seems to be hopeless (the feeling that everything is 'heavy as lead'). It stops hallucinations and obsessions and helps us to release ourselves from restricting habits and oppressive dogmas.

Spiritual: Lead provides life with structure and encourages self-control, a sense of duty, constancy and loyalty.

Lithium (Li$^+$)

Physical: Lithium reduces blood pressure and dampens oversensitivity in nerves and the motor nervous system, thereby alleviating restlessness, trembling and neural pains, for example in sciatica or neuralgia. It reduces the cholesterol levels and helps to prevent deposition of plaques in the blood vessels and joints. In this way, lithium also helps with kidney disorders, rheumatism and gout.

Psychological/mental: Lithium has a generally calming effect, is an effective anti-depressant and improves the memory. It also encourages self-confidence.

Spiritual: Lithium promotes devotion and humility, acceptance of what is unalterable. It teaches us to be able to bend and give in and still remain true to ourselves.

Magnesium (Mg^{2+})

Physical: Magnesium dampens irritation of the nerves and muscles. It loosens cramp and relaxes muscles, for example in migraine, cramp-like headaches, cramp in the circulation, stomach and intestinal cramps and gallbladder colic. It is the antagonist of calcium.

As such, it hinders blood-clotting and all kinds of processes connected with stimulation and secretion. It increases blood circulation, makes the walls of the blood vessels tough and elastic, and expands the blood vessels surrounding the heart, thereby improving the functioning of the heart muscle. Magnesium promotes the toughness and hardness of the bones and is also involved with the metabolism of carbohydrates, fat and proteins and prevents sclerosis of tissue and vessels.

Psychological/mental: Magnesium is calming and relaxing. It promotes a peaceful disposition and is effective against nervousness, fearfulness, hypochondria, schizophrenia and dampens excitability, irritability and aggression. Magnesium makes us more resilient towards stress.

Spiritual: Magnesium promotes a positive attitude towards life. It helps us accept ourselves for who we are and to love ourselves. This gives us the gift of cheering up others and encouraging them, solely through the atmosphere we create.

Manganese (Mn^{2+}, Mn^{3+}, Mn^{4+})

Physical: Manganese has a pain-relieving effect and fortifies the body's own defences by activating immunological and detoxifying enzymes. Fertility is increased as manganese stimulates the formation of the sexual organs. It influences the heart and the heart function, stimulates growth and the development of the skeleton. Manganese promotes fat metabolism and lowers blood sugar levels. It hinders the absorption of iron (and vice versa).

Psychological/mental: Manganese encourages empathy, and sometimes sensitivity. It brings out warmth of heart and generosity. Manganese allows psychological wounds and injuries to heal, reduces strife, feelings of revenge and grudges, promotes trust and affection, as well as inner growth and maturity.

Spiritual: Manganese promotes understanding of our own reality and of the reality of our environment. It stimulates a clearing of consciousness and of our relationships.

Nickel (Ni^{2+}, Ni^{3+})

Physical: Nickel promotes the absorption and utilization of iron. It promotes the activity of the liver and detoxification of the organism. Nickel helps with pain that arises periodically, for example, headaches.

Psychological/mental: Nickel promotes a feeling of security within us and helps with fearfulness, sadness and irritability. It helps us let go of oppressive images, particularly in the case of recurring nightmares. Nickel also fortifies the power of regeneration.

Spiritual: Nickel promotes creativity and inventiveness. Nickel keeps us young mentally and encourages a playful nature.

Oxygen (O2–)

Physical: Oxygen is the element that feeds all combustion processes in the body. It is, therefore, the energy supplier in all cells, tissues and organs. Oxygen is obtained from the air via the lungs, transported in the blood bound to iron (in haemoglobin), and is finally released to the cells. In this way, oxygen is the prerequisite for all metabolic processes.

Psychological/mental: Oxygen supplies vitality and alertness, promotes creativity and the desire to turn ideas into reality. It mobilizes states of mood that have become rigid or frozen and provides the possibility for change.

Spiritual: Oxygen represents the life principle. It promotes joy in living and the ability to be creatively active. Oxygen ensures survival in the sense of continuous further development towards optimal conditions.

Phosphorus (P^{3-}, P^{5+})

Physical: Phosphorus is the building block of bones and teeth. Calcium always occurs with phosphorus in compounds and can only be absorbed through the small intestine with its help. It is involved in the formation of the genetic carriers DNA and RNA and of the cell membranes. In this way, it fundamentally increases the ability to regenerate all cells, tissues and organs. In lecithin, phosphorus promotes the functioning of the brain and the nerves.

Phosphorus compounds play an important role in the energy metabolism of all cells. Without this substance, there could be no growth, procreation, no muscular strength, heat formation or perception through the senses. The latter, in particular, is very important: phosphorus helps with many eye and ear complaints and the sense of smell. Phosphoric acid provides the buffer in blood to maintain the balance between acid and alkali.

Psychological/mental: Phosphorus has a mood-lightening effect and is enlivening in cases of tiredness, dejection or despondency and states of exhaustion. It has a balancing effect on anger and irritability and protects from heightened sensitivity towards outer influences. Wherever complacency and lack of sensitivity have been developed as safety mechanisms, phosphorus brings openness and sympathy.

Spiritual: Phosphorus is the bringer of light. It promotes consciousness, perception and extrasensory perception. Phosphorus helps us to realize our life through self-determination.

Potassium (K+)

Physical: Potassium improves the solubility of nearly all compounds in body fluids; it influences metabolic processes in the cell membranes and thereby determines the pressure in the cells and blood. In this way, it also stimulates the function of the kidneys.

It further encourages (together with sodium) electrical conduction in the nervous system, as well as stimulation and contraction of the muscles. Stimulation of the heart muscles is particularly influenced by potassium. It is also concerned with transportation of nutrients (glucose) to the cells and is important for the synthesis of proteins. The functioning of the pineal gland is supported by potassium in its activity of 'translating' outer light (qualities) into inner, hormonal impulses.

Psychological/mental: Potassium helps to free us from fears, melancholy, depression and a feeling of failure. It promotes contentment and tranquillity, particularly with sensitivity to pain, noise and restlessness (a secret tip for morning 'grumps'). Potassium promotes a feeling of self-worth and removes the impression of being a victim of fate or of outside enemies.

Spiritual: Potassium improves perception, particularly with perceiving light. This promotes intuition and helps us to recognize illusions and imagination as such. Potassium helps develop a freer attitude towards religious matters without dogma and suppression.

Silicon (Si^{4+})

Physical: Silicon fortifies the skin, hair and nails and toughens up the connective tissues and the bones, the latter through stimulating the calcium metabolism. It fortifies the immune reactions in the blood and body fluids and encourages the activity of the lymph nodes, the spleen and the lungs. It is particularly helpful with a tendency to persistent colds.

Silicon has a stimulating effect on cell metabolism and cell division, promotes the healing of wounds or injuries, prevents scar formation and generally prevents premature ageing. It improves the elasticity of the blood vessels and has an anti-inflammatory effect. Silicon enhances the sensory organs.

Psychological/mental: Silicon makes us warm-hearted and generous. It promotes a feeling of inner well-being that makes us less affected by external difficulties. It also works against fearfulness, oversensitivity and exhaustion. Silicon gives us inner stability, security and determination. It helps us to let go of fixed ideas and to open ourselves to inspiration and new impulses.

Spiritual: Silicon helps us to be alert and ready to react in all situations. It enhances the facility to fit in with the rules of the physical and spiritual world and to work creatively in harmony with them.

Silver (Ag, Ag^+)

Physical: Silver appears cooling and directs heat and pain away (a typical indication, for example, is the inability to cope with heat).

It stimulates the vegetative nervous system, helps harmonize the functioning of the inner organs and encourages fertility in women. By balancing the functioning of organs, many types of headache, particularly left-sided ones, are dissolved. Silver stimulates the activity of body fluids, improves the skin's ability to cope with light, fortifies the ability to see and the sense of balance, and gets rid of dizziness.

Psychological/mental: Silver releases the emotions and encourages proper expression of feelings. It promotes generosity and empathy. Silver helps us to become more flexible mentally or to remain so and to let go of influences and dependencies, particularly if these go hand in hand with feelings of helplessness. The imagination and the ability to visualize are all stimulated by silver. Somnambulism (sleepwalking) is helped. Silver also helps maintain control and balance on a psychic level.

Spiritual: Silver promotes the receptive, mediumistic side of our nature. It encourages a sense of community and an interest in traditional values. Silver also enhances the ability to see varying qualities of light and to harmonize inner life rhythms with the cycles of nature.

Sodium (Na+)

Physical: Sodium regulates the water metabolism; it helps store water in the body and thus controls the osmotic pressure in the cells and body fluids. In this way, it increases blood pressure, stimulates the metabolic processes and the circulation, and eliminates dizziness and vertigo. Sodium stimulates functioning of the kidneys, thereby balancing the acid/alkali metabolism. Together with potassium, it ensures the correct stimulation of muscles and nerves.

Psychological/mental: Sodium provides structure. It binds free energy in fixed goals, in regular processes and inner order. Sodium helps us not to squander our own potential and inner strength, but to channel it properly. It helps us to grasp situations, conclusions and inner pictures and to preserve them.

Spiritual: Sodium promotes a sense of tradition, constancy and steadfastness.

Strontium (Sr2+)

Physical: Strontium is related to calcium, but forms stronger, unbreakable bonds, and so tends to have a harmful effect on the body. In the mineral form, however, it tends to have a dissolving effect in bones, tissues and organs; also in the case of contraction of the blood vessels. Strontium helps with inflammations of the nerves and post-operative shock, relieves chronic muscular tension and accelerates the healing of sprained joints.

Psychological/mental: Strontium helps counteract a feeling of constriction, also feelings of asphyxiation. It brings relief when everything in life seems to be in disarray. It helps overcome feelings of helplessness and with gaining a more positive outlook on life.

Spiritual: Strontium helps build healthy, spiritual structures that stabilize life without restricting it.

Sulphur (S2–)

Physical: Sulphur is the formative building block of many proteins, enzymes and hormones. It is a component of keratin, a protein vital to the formation of hair, nails and the external layer of skin. It develops healing effects when used for skin diseases, psoriasis and fungal infections.

Sulphur compounds (sulphates) are vitally involved in the formation of connective tissue and in detoxification processes. This is why sulphur is so helpful with rheumatic disorders, gout and liver problems. Sulphur is a particular antidote for heavy metal poisoning, encourages elimination processes and strengthens the body's defences.

Psychological/mental: Sulphur uncovers confusing and muddled matters, illusions and hidden contents of the consciousness. It clarifies symptoms of illness by eliminating secondary symptoms and emphasizing the causal psychological/mental background symptoms. Sulphur helps with forgetfulness, laziness, lack of interest and a moody nature.

Spiritual: Sulphur wakens our shadow sides and helps us confront them and overcome them. Then we find the shaft of light that makes it possible for us to accept things we rejected before and to integrate them.

Tin (Sn4+)

Physical: Tin encourages the development and activity of the cerebrum and harmonizes the nervous system. It encourages the healing of spasms, states of weakness and paralysis that can be traced back to disturbances in the nervous system.

Tin helps greatly with chronic problems, particularly in the area of the respiratory tract, secondarily also with liver and gallbladder problems (colic). Tin controls the sense of taste.

Psychological/mental: Tin helps us transform emotions into a concrete form; it helps us to put feelings into words. Tin encourages enthusiasm, tolerance, trust and a friendly attitude and gives us the courage to master everyday difficulties. It dissolves sorrow into relief.

Spiritual: Tin encourages us to realize our own life's dream. It has an inspiring effect and helps develop our innermost talents and abilities. Tin brings sociability and generosity to guests. It encourages musical talent, particularly the playing of music.

Titanium (Ti^{4+})

Physical: Titanium is found in its highest concentrations in the muscles and bones. There it promotes growth and an upright posture. It also has anti-inflammatory properties, particularly in the case of colds, bronchitis, pneumonia and kidney infections. Titanium fortifies the heart and the ability to regenerate the organism.

Psychological/mental: Titanium has an enlivening and freeing effect in the case of claustrophobia, fear and oppression. It promotes sexual fulfilment and is helpful with problems of impotency and premature ejaculation.

Spiritual: Titanium confers honesty, independence and spiritual greatness.

Vanadium (V^{5+})

Physical: As vanadium itself is a severe irritant toxin in its mineral form, it has a strongly anti-inflammatory effect, particularly in skin diseases, eye problems (for example, inflammation of the cornea or conjunctiva) and with inflammatory illnesses of the respiratory organs.

Psychological/mental: Vanadium helps us express feelings freely and to get rid of undue restraint and caution.

Spiritual: Vanadium makes it possible to transform destructive attitudes into a constructive way of life.

Zinc (Zn^{2+})

Physical: Zinc activates all kinds of different hormones and enzymes. It enhances the effect of insulin and helps with diabetes, supports the immune system and promotes production of growth hormones and sex hormones. The function of the male sexual organs (formation of the seminal vesicles) is stimulated; prostate disorders and problems with the ovaries are improved.

Zinc also regulates the development of the brain and sensory perception. It is extremely important for the retina (especially for vision in bad light) as well as for the senses of taste and smell. It encourages regeneration and healing of wounds, bone formation and toughening of the outer layer of skin, hair and nails. Zinc protects the organism against harmful substances and radiation.

Psychological/mental: Zinc promotes the development of intelligence (abstract thinking). It helps with exhaustion, weakness, loss of courage and fearfulness, restlessness, lack of concentration and sleep disturbance, particularly with difficulties sleeping because there are too many ideas and thoughts running through the mind. Zinc encourages spontaneity and intuition.

Spiritual: Zinc initiates great changes in life. It breaks up outworn structures and helps us use these upheavals in a meaningful way for creating better circumstances in our life. It brings idealism and intensifies our lives. Zinc encourages the ability to communicate.

Zirconium (Zr^{4+})

Physical: Zirconium has an antispasmodic effect, particularly with menstrual problems that are connected with delayed menstruation. It also stimulates the liver's synthesizing function.

Psychological/mental: Zirconium helps with the release of material worries and blocks and with letting go of suppressed and retained fears. It encourages symbolic and pictorial thinking and brings deep insights in dreams.

Spiritual: Zirconium reminds us of the meaning of our existence. It helps with developing a spiritual view of things and with seeing through the illusory values of materialism as such.

How to use mineral-forming elements

Knowing the mineral-forming element content of a precious stone or mineral will immediately give a clear picture of its healing properties. Which aspects will be prominent in each individual case, however, will be determined by the relevant correspondence to those properties that derive from the way the mineral was formed and from its crystal structure.

A mineral can be formed from a whole range of mineral-forming elements. Usually, only those that we actually need for a physical, psychological/mental or spiritual situation in our lives will be effective in their use for healing. A prior investigation of the life situation (manner of formation) and the lifestyle (crystal structure) is definitely a good idea when choosing the right stone for healing purposes.

If this is not possible for some reason, or if you are going to use a mineral primarily for its material properties, the following procedure is recommended in making your choice:

1. Determine the suitable mineral class – this helps the initial choice by matching the mineral to the dominnat theme of the person's life.

2. Find a correspondence between the acid or alkaline character of the mineral and the person's temperament – this helps narrow down the first choice.

3. Determine the degree of dilution – this will define whether you should target mineral-forming elements with a stronger or weaker concentration, or even look for trace components.

4. Consider the mineral forming-elements themselves – this will finally will give you information on the essential properties of the minerals in question. Then you can choose the most suitable one.

This mineral – it is recommended to choose only one initially – should, as far as possible, be worn or carried for several weeks. As substantial changes on all levels are involved with the effect of mineral-forming elements, a certain amount of time will be needed for it to work. Use of the mineral can be terminated the moment the original problem is clearly solved or if there appears to be a sudden aversion to continuing to wear it.

If no change is noticed, it is recommended to switch to another mineral containing the same mineral-forming elements or to check whether another, similar mineral-forming element would not be better.

Finally, if there are several colour variations of a chosen mineral, the next chapter will help you to make the right choice.

1.4 The colour of minerals

It is a strange fact that such colourful things as minerals and precious stones can be produced from the depths of the Earth, in what we think of as eternal darkness. This is precisely what has fascinated people over the centuries, in so far as minerals are in no way less colourful and spectacular than flowers.

On the contrary, while the latter are ephemeral, and will wilt and decay, the colour of precious stones is (usually) permanent. In ancient times, not only the inexplicable shapes of crystals but also their remarkable colours were looked upon as direct, divine manifestations. Countless mythological descriptions, assignments to groups of elements and powers, as well as manifold effects, were ascribed by the ancients to these colours.

Modern life has destroyed even this veil of magic. Today, colours are seen as specific parts of the spectrum of light and are defined as radiation of a certain frequency and wavelength. They are analysed according to their shade and nuance, saturation point and brightness, divided up in standardized colour systems, and can be produced at any time, in any variation; colours are just not that special any more.

Or are they? When the trees start sprouting in the spring, then those shades of green are not merely a shade of a colour, but an experience! Whenever we gaze at a harmoniously composed picture with glowing colours, this is not just perceived through the eye but felt with the entire soul. If you observe someone who is holding up a sparkling precious stone to sunlight, you will suddenly be able to see the glowing eyes of a child, even in the face of the very old!

This is something to contemplate before we turn to the physical/ scientific side of colours. Colours provide us with wonderful experiences, the depth of which risks being played down if we talk about it too much. Colours belong to the reality of the soul, rather than to the intellect, so I will endeavour to keep my remarks brief in this chapter.

Colour and light

Simply expressed, colours are part of light. Or put another way: our sunlight contains all the colours of the spectrum. 'Light' in its original meaning is 'the enlightening, vision giving', and is a name for the phenomenon that allows us to see. This is so taken for granted nowadays that we never think about it any more. It seems logical: in order to see, we need light – if the light is switched off, it becomes dark....

According to modern thinking, light is an energy form that spreads in all directions in the form of radiation from a source of light. If a ray of light meets a solid body, it is reflected ('radiated back') or absorbed ('swallowed'). The reflected light is what makes it possible for us to see things that do not themselves radiate light.

There is always something that radiates of its own accord (sources of light like the sun, stars, a candle, a light bulb) and something else that is illuminated (everything else, the visible world). The statement that initially sounds fairly simplistic will become enormously important a few lines on, when we attempt to understand the various forms of colour play.

In German, the word 'colour', *Farbe*, and the Old High German word, *farawa*, originally meant the 'property of a being or thing'. This can still be found in the expression 'to show one's true colour' (to tell the truth). Light is a prerequisite for seeing something. Colour, on the other hand, conveys a content, determines what we see.

The connection is fairly simple: if we break down a ray of sunlight into its spectrum, we obtain beautiful colours, ranging from red, through orange, yellow, green, blue to violet. Nature presents these as a rainbow (rays of light are broken in the atmosphere by finely distributed droplets of water and displayed 'fan-like'). We can recreate this process by using a glass prism.

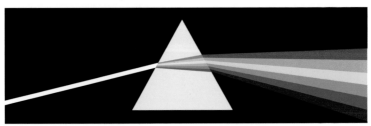

A prism

The reverse happens if the coloured rays are bundled together again, and we see white light. White light is the sum of all the colour rays and contains all colours.

Black is, therefore, the absence of all light (light off = darkness) and the absence of all rays of colour.

Colours are formed on a material object by the object absorbing a portion of the white light falling on it and reflecting the rest. We see the reflected light and this is what is perceived as the object's colour. This is how we perceive the colour of a mineral or precious stone, and this is how we see the colours from our paintbox, from painting pictures or painting the walls in the house.

However, there is a very different effect when we mix colours together. When you mix together pigments (Latin *pigmentum*, 'colour') of all the colours in a paintbox, the result will be black, not white.

This is because all the colours are combined in the pigment substances and, therefore, absorb all the light. Not much light is reflected, we cannot see much and the absence of light is recognized as black.

White colour is, therefore, a substance that does not absorb any light but reflects it all. White objects do not contain any colour substances; black objects contain all colour substances.

This seeming paradox to the above can be explained with the simple statement that we have to distinguish between bodies that actively illuminate and are sources of light and those that are illuminated. Here is a brief summary:

▶ When coloured rays that are transmitted from sources of light are 'gathered' together, we get white light (an additive mixture). White light contains all colours. Black arises through a complete absence of light.

▶ By mixing all the colours on an object we obtain the colour black, as it absorbs all the light falling on to it (a subtractive colour mixture). White is created through the absence of all colour pigments and reflection of all the light falling onto the body.

These simple laws of physics are illustrated in the figure below.

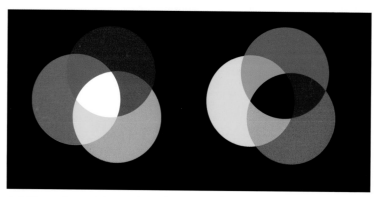

Additive colour mixing, right: subtractive colour mixing.

On the left, you can see an overlapping of coloured light rays and the resulting colour of the combined rays. On the right, you see the colours that are formed when coloured pigments are mixed.

Based on these simple laws of physics, we have to look upon the colour rays of a source of light and the reflected colours of a solid object as two very different phenomena. In the case of the visible colours of minerals and precious stones, we are dealing with the second phenomenon. In minerals, the colour is created through by absorbing certain portions of the light and reflecting the remainder.

This is also why we cannot find immediate correspondences between the colours of minerals and the colours of the human chakras and the aura, where we ourselves represent the source of light. These manifestations of colour are colour rays that are released through inner processes within ourselves and are not influenced by the reflected colours of a precious stone!

Even though appropriate tables of colours are widely published throughout the relevant literature, I would strongly recommend that you try out these tables: you will find out for yourselves that they do not work. There is a very different connection between stones, chakras and the aura which is our 'own light', light radiation from the stones (cf. Chapter 2.1 in Part 2). This connection will be discussed in more detail in a later book.

Colour variations

As shown in the graphic illustration of subtractive colour mixtures opposite, there are three basic colours, or primary colours, which yield all other colours through mixing. The three primary colours are red, yellow and blue, from which derive the mixed colours orange (red + yellow), green (yellow + blue) and violet (blue + red). These six colours produce a circle that can also be used as a basis for discussing mineral colours.

Now, in nature, we do not usually just come across pure colours, but most of the time a huge range of different variations of every colour, depending on how much white or black (or other colours) are mixed in. Red with a large proportion of white becomes pink, with a large proportion of black, it turns brown. This turns the colour circle into a sphere.

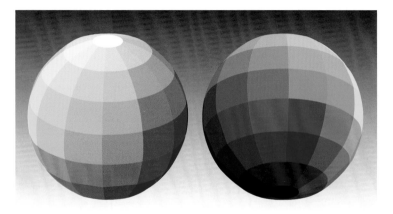

The colour sphere

Imagine there was a planet of colours with its axis running from north to south continuously from white through all shades of grey to black. Around the equator, we would find the 'pure' colours corresponding to a colour circle: red – orange – yellow – green – blue – violet. The colours of the equator are pure and undiluted as they are furthest away from the axis.

The closer the colours approach the axis in the north and the south, the more they are mixed with light grey or white (north), or dark grey or black (south). Thus we have pastel colours all around the white north pole and darker shades around the black south pole.

The illustration on page 133 shows this colour distribution, on the left dealing with the 'warm' colours (red – orange – yellow), and on the right with the 'cold' ones (green – blue – violet).

For our use in healing with crystals and stones, this pair of three-dimensional models can be radically simplified into a two-dimensional one with the 'north pole' moved to the centre and the 'south pole' represented as a dark ring around the 'equatorial' colour circle. This representation will be referred to in what follows as a colour wheel (below).

The colour wheel

The colour wheel provides a simplified overview of colour development as we find it among minerals: from black on the outside circle that absorbs all colours, then via dark grey on to the middle colour circle and further on all the way to silver, colourless,

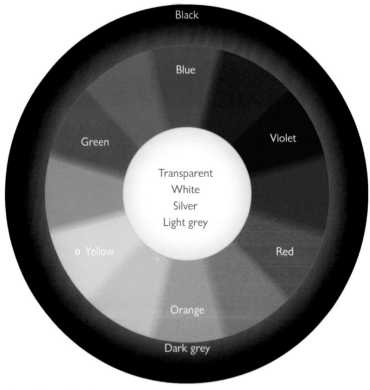

The colour wheel

white and clear, that reflect all the other colours.

The upper half of the middle circle displays the 'cold colours' green, blue and violet, while the lower half represents the 'warm' colours red, orange and yellow. These colour appearances are quite real: a red room that is the same temperature as a blue one will be felt to be warmer. This is already a small indicator that colour is not merely perceived with the eyes.

The complementary colours

Further, the wheel shows us that complementary colours are always situated opposite each other (Latin *complere*, 'to make complete, to add'), these being the colours that taken together as colour rays will produce white light, or when mixed as pigments, will produce black.

For example, a mineral that appears violet actually absorbs yellow light and reflects violet light. An orange-coloured stone will absorb the colour blue and reflect orange, and so on. The complementary colour plays an important part in healing with crystals and precious stones and when treating someone with minerals. The role that colour plays in healing will be discussed again in more detail at a later stage.

How mineral colours are formed

In order to produce a certain colour, a mineral has to be able to absorb certain portions of white light. This possibility exists when so-called colour centres are present in a mineral.

Colour centres are formed through mineral-forming elements that are electrically charged (usually metals), through free electrons trapped in the crystal lattice, or through a certain structural consistency, which ensures that incident light rays are broken up and partially absorbed. In all cases, the light energy of the incoming light is taken up by electrons that are stimulated and then transform the light energy into kinetic energy.

When the excitation of the electrons calms down again, the energy is released and given off in the form of warmth (infrared radiation), visible light and microwaves. This inherent radiation is, however, so weak that it is hardly perceptible. Only the infrared radiation is noticeable when a stone lying in the sun feels warm after a while.

Fluorescence (visible light energy) is a property of some minerals but will only become visible to the naked eye in darkened rooms under UV light. Microwaves are completely invisible to us. The only visible effect is that a portion of the white light falling upon an object 'disappears', the remaining reflected part gives a stone its colour.

Colour centres created by electrically charging mineral-forming elements

This is the most common source of colour. Many metals, particularly chromium, iron, copper, cobalt, manganese and nickel, are able to absorb certain wavelengths of light. For this reason they are also called 'colour carriers' or 'chromophores' (Greek *chroma*, 'colour' and *phoros*, 'carrying').

If any of these metals represent the largest component of a mineral, that is, if they also appear in its chemical formula, we speak of its 'self colour' in mineralogy or 'idiochromatic colouring' (Greek *idio*, 'own, self'). The colour is created by the mineral-forming elements characteristic of this mineral. If the colour is caused by fractional components or trace components, it is called a foreign colour (or xenochrome, from the Greek *xenos*, 'strange'), caused by foreign substances.

Idiochrome and xenochrome can be distinguished by the so-called streak test. This requires rubbing the mineral against a rough tablet of porcelain, or scratching the specimen with the tablet. Very hard minerals will be pulverized.

The resulting fine dust of scratching will only leave a coloured mark if the colour of the mineral is its own. Only then will the scratched off dust contain enough colour centres to make the colour visible. In the case of a xenochrome, insufficient colouring substance will be contained and the scratch will appear white.

The streak test is, therefore, a reliable method for identifying minerals. Idiochromes are rarer: hematite, for example, displays a red scratch, malachite a green one, azurite a blue one and pyrite a black one.

The multi-coloured fluorite, also the coloured quartzes, all display a white scratch as, in all these cases, we are dealing with xenochromes. Particularly colour variations in the same mineral usually arise through xenochromes.

Colour centres created by free electrons in the crystal lattice

The effect of ionizing (or radioactive) radiation, in particular during the formation of a mineral, can cause electrons to be precipitated out of an atom and then re-deposited in another part of the lattice. The completed, compact crystal lattice then prevents the electron from returning to its original position.

These free electrons find it particularly easy to absorb light energy and become colour centres in this manner. In some cases, the entire light spectrum is absorbed which allows the stone to appear dark brown to black. The best example of this occurring is found in smoky quartz.

Minerals coloured through free electrons logically also display a white streak line. The colour will be destroyed again, as a rule, if the mineral is heated, because heating makes the crystal lattice resonate, making it possible for the electron to return to its original position.

Colours based on structural characteristics

Microscopically fine structures inside minerals also cause light to be bent and colours to be created. The 'Tyndall effect', named after its discoverer, the Irish physicist John Tyndall, is well known: light is scattered or bent on very small particles (for example microscopically small droplets or fibres) and is broken up into rays of different colours, with the red portion usually being absorbed and the blue portion being reflected. This is how the blue colour of chalcedony is created along its fine, crystal fibres.

Internal cracks, splits, lamella or irregular surfaces may also lead to colourful light reflections. The best example for this is the opal, which consists of minute SiO_2 globules. The light reflected by these globules is broken up into all the colours of the rainbow and gives the opal its unique play of colours.

A similar phenomenon occurs along the fine lamellar structure of moonstone and labradorite. Here, too, when rays of light meet the surface of the stone they are scattered and reflected, which leads to the appearance of a play of lights in a blue hue as well as other colours.

Colours based on inclusions

Inclusions are deposits of a solid, liquid or gaseous nature in minerals. Inclusions, too, can have an effect on the light falling upon them.

In this way, the tiny, fine rutile needles contained in many minerals provide a light-scattering effect that is displayed as asterism (star formation), for example, in star rubies, star sapphires or star rose quartz. In certain blue quartzes, for example, fine inclusions of tourmaline result in the Tyndall effect and a blue colouring. Finely distributed gas and glass inclusions will make obsidian shine with a golden or silver sheen (gas), while inclusions of tiny crystals will display all the colours of the rainbow.

The interesting thing about this is that colour is not a phenomenon denoting purity or perfection, but actually occurs precisely through these deposits of foreign substances or faults in the lattice structure. Apparently incomplete absorption or reflection of light corresponds with the imperfection of the mineral.

This brings us back to the original, Old High German meaning of the word *farawa*. Colour actually does demonstrate the property of a being or thing, the only question being which property or quality is owned by the individual mineral colour?

The effects of mineral colours

We experience colours in a deep way: whether we 'see red', 'go green with envy' or are 'yellow' (cowardice), our use of language shows that colours have been endowed with more properties than physics books allow.

The healing properties of colours are no longer news these days. Colour therapy can be successfully employed for allergies, chronic problems and psychic illnesses, and shows results that orthodox medicine can only dream of. The reasons for these comprehensive, positive results are very simple.

Colour balancing

All of our inner processes are linked with each other and create energy phenomena. Our mental activities influence our spiritual experiences and vice versa. The latter definitely cause certain emotions that, in turn, create interactions with physical perceptions, the functioning of the nerves and the endocrine system (hormone metabolism). In this way, every thought and every feeling go hand in hand with certain metabolic processes and chemical reactions in our body.

Also during these processes, energy is either created or used up –

depending on the situation. To sum it up: our entire experience leads to a kind of 'colour formation' (colour = light = energy) in our bodies that naturally seeks a balance in order to attain the neutral 'white' state (or black). This balance simply occurs through externally adding on another colour, namely the complementary colour!

This is the reason our taste in colour changes: an article of clothing that we absolutely have to have today can perfectly well appear as 'impossible' on another day. A different colour would muddle us completely today, even though it appeared calming and harmonious a few days ago. Usually, we unconsciously follow these impulses by dressing in a certain way or, without noticing it, tend to linger in places with certain colours, or prefer to gaze at certain colours.

It is never the eyes alone that perceive colour. As already mentioned above, feelings about temperatures depend on the colour. Our skin is the largest sensory organ and can absorb colour and conduct it inside the body.

If we 'perceive' colour in this manner, and it helps balance our inner state, we will attain a comprehensive feeling of well-being. Tensions disappear, disharmony evaporates, and we are able to cope better with different kinds of psychological problems and physical disorders.

Seen another way, colours that appeal to us and create a feeling of well-being will help us identify and understand our inner state of mind: just as fresh spring green balances the red that accumulated through a heightened energy requirement in winter, gazing at a complementary colour will always indicate how a particular colour deficiency came about.

The colour wheel will be helpful with this: if we are drawn towards two colours, we can first of all determine the mixture of these colours that is located exactly between them on the colour wheel. Their complementary colour to this then corresponds to our inner state of the moment.

Wearing or having coloured minerals or precious stones next to the skin can be used in healing with stones to attain this colour balance, as well. If we apply a certain mineral for a lengthy period of time directly on our skin, the colour radiation will gradually percolate from that spot throughout the whole body. If we place the stone only briefly on a particular spot, the effect will remain more localized. In this way, the colour effect can helpfully be targeted exactly as desired.

In the following section, I should like to summarize the effect of the different mineral colours as I have experienced them through my own research over the years. Bear in mind that the list will not attempt to encompass every single healing effect known in colour therapy, and in some points it may even contradict some statements from colour therapy.

However, conversations with colour therapists have shown that different uses of colour will also produce different results. And if there is a difference between using coloured pieces of cloth, coloured foil and colour rays, then we may also assume that the colours of minerals, some of them very specific, will have their own special effects too.

■ Black minerals

Black minerals absorb all the light and are, therefore, suitable for 'stripping off' excess energies. This effect is particularly noticeable with pain: pain arises – looked at from the point of view of energy – wherever there is a blockage, and therefore, an energy back-up or bottleneck. Black minerals, for example smoky obsidian, smoky quartz or black tourmaline, will absorb this excess energy, causing pain to disappear and relaxation to set in. This does not always mean that the cause is also eliminated; however, freedom from pain is the best prerequisite for further treatment.

Black, therefore, does not apply to any organ in particular, but works for relaxation in the entire organism. The mental state is similarly affected: here too, tensions are eliminated and this makes us more resistant, resilient and more able to cope with stress. Black minerals give us security and stability.

Psychologically, black keeps away distractions and helps us concentrate on what is important and essential. Black helps bring hidden matters out into the open, pleasant as well as unpleasant ones, and through the absence of outer light, leads us to discover our own inner source of light.

■ Red minerals

Red minerals have a strongly stimulating effect, produce heat and speed up things. They stimulate the circulation, the blood vessels and the blood itself. Dark red stimulates the activity of the heart, while light red (pink) helps create harmony in the heart. Red and reddish brown minerals stimulate the small intestine and improve the absorption of nutrients, vitamins and mineral-forming elements. This, too, is good for the blood and improves its quality.

In a similar manner, our psychological experiences also become more intense. Our inner world of images is fortified and feelings are expressed more clearly; in particular the elementary emotions such as love or hate are enhanced. Red minerals make us more impulsive and extrovert. They strengthen the willpower and the ability to persevere. Pink is a little different in this respect: the large proportion of white makes its effect more peaceful, more sensitive to others and sometimes slightly oversensitive.

Red stimulates the inner fire. It encourages all processes of learning, and the processing of experiences in the mind, and, in this way, accelerates our spiritual growth. Red encourages willingness to help others as a basic prerequisite for living together with all other beings. Pink minerals encourage sympathy.

■ Orange minerals

Orange minerals have a vitalizing effect. They strongly stimulate the circulation, fortify the blood vessels and encourage an even distribution of energy throughout the body. The function and sensitivity of the sexual organs is improved. Dark orange and brown stimulate the body's sensitivity and regulate the metabolism and growth of tissues. The entire organism is strengthened and protected in this way.

On a mental level, orange enhances the quality of life and puts us in a cheerful, happy frame of mind. There is room for sensuality and spontaneity. Orange minerals help us to move out of apathetic states and they encourage creativity. Dark orange and brown help us to collect ourselves on an inner level, providing a feeling of security, peace, relief and down-to-earth realism.

Orange lends joy to life and a certainty of existing in harmony with a higher order and being on the right course in our life. Orange minerals help us find harmony and balance and encourage a sense of justice.

Yellow minerals

Yellow and gold-coloured minerals generally have a cheering effect and help produce a positive attitude towards life. They stimulate the digestion and the activity of the stomach, spleen and pancreas. Yellow improves the digestion of food in many ways and the supply of energy to the body. The vegetative nervous system (the nerves that control the inner organs) is supported in its work, likewise the immune system.

Yellow lends happiness, a carefree attitude and energy to do things. It makes us aware of our needs and desires and helps fight off harm. Yellow and gold-coloured minerals help us overcome depression and lend self-confidence, trust and belief in our own success.

On a mental level, yellow encourages an understanding of our daily experiences (mental digestion). From this arises a certainty of being able to shape our own life, that is, the ability to take on responsibility. Yellow minerals help us discover the meaning in our own existence and in this way lead us to spiritual maturity.

Green minerals

Green minerals have a harmonizing, neutralizing effect. They stimulate the liver and gallbladder and thus encourage detoxification and regeneration of the body. The liver here has a central function, as the organ of building up (synthesis of proteins, blood formation, formation of enzymes, etc.), storing (energy and nutrient storage) and cleansing, and it regulates the most important metabolic processes.

Green releases emotions and makes emotions more intense, in particular anger and fury, although by discharging the latter, in the long term it leads to an inner peace. Green minerals enhance speed and the ability to react and awaken interest and enthusiasm. They stimulate the inner world of pictures, clarify our dream experiences and encourage the imagination.

Green brings initiative and the will to live. It encourages the senses and perceptions and draws our attention to the material world. Green minerals help us to deal with 'spiritual toxins' and encourage a healthy optimism. This is the reason that green is the colour of hope.

■ Blue minerals

Blue minerals have a cooling, calming effect. They regulate the activities of the kidneys and the bladder and thereby the balance of liquids, hormones, acid/alkali and mineral-forming elements. Blue activates elimination and the movement of body fluids.

On the mental plane, blue encourages relaxation, openness and honesty, accelerates instinctive reactions and keeps things in motion. Blue minerals help us to overcome fear and take courage. They promote the ability to form partnerships.

Blue encourages a balanced flow by helping us to recognize and overcome barriers and external influences. Blue minerals help us develop strength and an inner equilibrium. They encourage striving for knowledge and a search for truth.

■ Violet minerals

Violet minerals have a cleansing, freeing effect. They encourage brain activity, the sensory and motor nervous systems, the skin and the lungs and respiratory tract. In this way, they regulate breathing (including the breathing of the cells) and absorption of oxygen, and they help overcome acidity by releasing carbon dioxide. In the large intestine, the colour violet stimulates the absorption and elimination of water.

Violet lends relief in sorrow and helps dissolving traumas. It encourages memory, a wealth of ideas and consciousness, as well as communication and interactions with others. Violet minerals encourage an understanding of the problems of others, even if they are foreign to our personality. Violet protects us from foreign influences of an energetic and psychological nature.

Violet lends spiritual freedom. It awakens our deep innate knowledge, encourages the absorption of information and helps us distinguish between what is useful and what is harmful. Violet minerals promote inner calm and composure and help us recognize who we are.

☐ Clear, white and silver minerals

All of these are characterized by the fact that they do not absorb light or colours but reflect everything. This means they are completely neutral and guide the light to us that contains all possibilities that there are. In this way they support and enhance whatever happens to be already present. Clear, white and silver minerals are suitable for conducting energy in cases of deficiency (feelings of coldness, lack of feelings, weakness, paralysis) and for promoting the effect of other minerals.

On a psychological level, these minerals promote the very properties we see in them: clear minerals encourage clarity and purity, white minerals promote neutrality, silver minerals work like a mirror: they promote self-recognition.

Spiritually speaking, clear, white and silver represent purity and the creative power that contains all possibilities and can realize all things. Consequently clear, white and silver minerals bring to the user abundance and wholeness (if they were not whole, they would be a colour).

Coloured and colourfully scintillating minerals

These minerals reveal the playful side of nature. Minerals like opals, labradorite or rainbow obsidian reveal plays of colour that are more than just the sum of the colours involved. They stimulate activity in the entire organism and accelerate the healing process.

Psychologically, coloured and scintillating minerals have an enlivening effect. They provide joy, desire and enjoyment, may awaken old memories or offer relief and relaxation through pleasant pastimes. Colourful and scintillating minerals are 'holiday' stones.

On a spiritual plane, coloured and scintillating minerals lend us the ability to play. This means that we voluntarily devote all our attention to a certain idea, undertaking or task and are completely absorbed in it. In such a 'playful' life, we are the source of our own fate; this will, in turn, bring unimaginable possibilities.

Colour healing with minerals

According to the descriptions given above, the suitable mineral colour can be found in two ways:

1. If one of the descriptions exactly fits the state you would like to experience, it will be sufficient to choose a stone of the right colour and to wear it, close to the skin if possible. You should be very careful when choosing among the many different nuances of colour – make the choice that gives you the best feeling. According to the laws of colour balance, you should be guaranteed to pick exactly the right shade. The correctness of your choice will soon

be proven to you through an improvement in your feeling of well-being.

2. If you recognize your own state in one or two of the descriptions given here and wish to change your life but do not know how, then choose a colour complementary to that of your present state. If two descriptions fit you, work out the colour that results from a mixture of the two, then choose the relevant complementary colour. The crystal, stone or gem chosen in this manner should, as far as possible, be worn next to the skin.

In the second case, it may be that you do not like the complementary colour at all. This means you have an inner aversion to this colour and, unfortunately, also towards the qualities and properties associated with it. This aversion, however it may have arisen, is hindering you from changing the circumstances that you do not like.

By confronting the complementary colour with the help of the respective crystal or stone, you will be able to overcome this aversion in time and change your life in the desired way. In the second case, it may well be that you will not feel at all well to begin with, but speaking bluntly – you need to go through with it! It is very important simply to observe what is happening: what do you want, feel, think and do, what do you remember and what do you encounter? On no account judge or evaluate, accept yourself during this period just as you experience yourself. Then a change will come about much more quickly.

With this last aspect of colour, the world of crystals and stones has now been described fairly comprehensively. From their formation to their structure, minerals and colours, you have now become acquainted with the most important basic concepts from both the field of mineralogy as well as from the field of healing.

Provided you immerse yourself and absorb the contents of this first part to the point where you have understood and can apply them, you will be in a position to work out the inherent healing effects of practically any mineral. I emphasize – these are the basic principles!

Every stone is an individual. What has been described so far has demonstrated the mutual features of a particular type of stone, the individual stones themselves can still be very different. Let me illustrate this with an analogy.

When studying embryonic development in humans, we study anatomy, physiology and biochemistry. Even when we have some knowledge of the individual environment, all we know is that a human is, in principle, an upright two-legged creature who uses tools, shapes his or her own environment and is able to speak. These are important basic principles, but they do not, however, give us much information on what the very next person we happen to come across will have to say to us!

This is how we will end Part 1. We have dealt with the most important things that can be described about minerals and healing crystals and stones. The remaining part of the story, which is even more important, will have to be told by the stones themselves, when you carry or wear them, surround yourself with them or use them for healing purposes. What you encounter then is the truly lived experience of the world of crystals. The second part of this book is intended to introduce you to this aspect.

2.1 The phenomenon of light

The source of the healing properties of minerals

As you may have already experienced, through being stimulated by the information in the first part of this volume, minerals and precious gems do indeed have healing effects, the mineralogical connections of which have been researched and are known.

The question remains unanswered, however, as to how and through what devices minerals are actually able to unfold their healing effects. What does this communication between stone and human being consist of? How can a piece of matter exert an influence on our organism? If one were able to ingest a mineral or stone, inhale it or absorb it into the body in some other way, one could perhaps imagine an effect taking place, but how can just placing it on our skin or wearing it as an ornament work – how does the effect take place?

The healing effect of a crystal becomes more easily understandable if we put aside the notion that the limits of our being are identical with the limits of our physical bodies. This notion is definitely a fallacy. Even in physics, it has been known for well over a hundred years that every body, every organism, every 'material object', be it a stone, a plant or a plastic bucket, possesses what is referred to variously as an 'emanation' or aura. Many physical and all chemical processes involve the absorption and emanation of radiation, which means that, whatever takes place, heat, light or another form of electromagnetic radiation is either absorbed or heat, light or another form of electromagnetic radiation is released.

This means we ourselves, and everything around us, are constantly surrounded by energy fields. This also means we are involved in a constant energy exchange with our environment. It all begins with the sunlight that we absorb and radiate out again in the form of heat, and ranges right through to the influences of energy from electrical currents, radio transmitters and microwaves.

Maybe you have seen something similar with an internal aerial on a portable television set. You may have had those annoying evenings when a perfectly adjusted picture appeared to suffer permanent interference merely through your presence. Not always, but on some days, it is difficult to find the right position in the room where you will not disturb the reception. The problem is not solely due to physical shielding of the signal, as sometimes another person can sit down in the very same armchair from which you have managed to ruin the entire reception without causing any effect at all! It appears from this that it is your very own 'radiation' that interacts with the box.

As this example makes clear, all of us are constant receivers and transmitters of radiation. In recent years evidence has emerged from various tests that 'electrosmog', caused by electrical currents and radio transmitters, can affect people's health, as can the influence of electromagnetic fields and radiation sources, or the effects of watercourses or faults in the ground.

Radiation from stones

Stones, minerals and crystals also possess this kind of radiating property, as has already been discussed in Chapter 1.4, The colour of minerals (see page 129). Their radiation results from the transformation of absorbed light, lying mainly in the infrared region and only to a very small degree in the visible and microwave regions of the spectrum. But despite their lesser quantity, the latter are of great importance. Infrared radiation is absorbed by the outermost layers of skin into the body, which is why we feel it as heat. Microwaves, however, penetrate the entire organism so, in principle, reach all tissues and organs.

The fact that we cannot normally perceive the visible portion of radiation of precious gems and minerals with the naked eye is simply due to the low intensity (Latin *intensus*, 'violent') of this radiation.

Radiation from our bodies, for example, is comparable to the glimmer of light from a candle about 20 kilometres (12.5 miles) away. During the daytime it cannot, of course, be seen. However, in total darkness, we would gradually become aware of this light. This radiation is a real effect; the difficulties experienced in science with measuring this subtle radiation has little to do with the radiation itself but rather more with the limitations of the measuring equipment available.

The role of light in the human body

Nowadays, even children know that the stars are still in the sky in the daytime, even though they are not visible because the intensity of the sunlight blots them out. The same goes for us: in principle we, too, are all sources of light. Our organisms glow: every cell, every tissue and every organ has its own specific radiation and also produces its own specific magnetic field. These are now made use of in medicine for the diagnosis of illnesses: the technique of magnetic resonance imaging is used to measure such radiation using pulsed magnetic fields and can produce three-dimensional images of all our inner organs that are considerably more accurate and precise than X-ray images.

There is more: further results of biochemical research first published in 1993 have proven that this radiation is actually used for communication. Every cell nucleus emits photons (the tiniest light particles or packages) with great consistency and in this way communicates with neighbouring cells.

This is how metabolic processes, growth, development and the differentiation of cells, tissues and organs are coordinated in the body. The nervous system and hormones only intervene in a guiding capacity in processes that are normally regulated automatically. This 'conversation' from cell to cell, this 'chatting over the garden fence', actually occurs via the medium of light.

Radiation as an information carrier

What can light really do? What we refer to as 'light' is only a small part of all existing electromagnetic radiation – merely the portion that is visible to our eyes.

This portion is also called the 'visible spectrum' (Latin *spectrum*, 'appearance'). In addition to the visible spectrum, there are other types of electromagnetic radiation: radio waves, infrared rays (heat radiation), ultraviolet light (UV light), microwaves and radiation given off by some radioactive materials (gamma rays). All of these have something in common: every type of radiation is an information carrier!

We make use of these properties in everyday life: whether it is for information sent via radio and television transmitters or mobile phones, or for remote control devices of every kind, the relevant information is always transmitted via a particular type of radiation, so that it passes from the transmitter to the receiver completely invisibly.

Healing with crystals as a form of information therapy

This is exactly what is taking place between stones and humans! Stones, too, emit radiation and, being extremely durable and permanent (at least, as a rule), they emit the same information in a very constant way.

They could be compared to radio transmitters that constantly broadcast the same programme. Every stone or crystal has its own specific light, or put another way, its specific radiation that naturally influences our organisms. If contact is made between a crystal and our bodies, the absorbed light will inevitably have an influence on the 'light communication' between the cells and cause certain reactions.

An effect therefore definitely exists. Whether this influence becomes a healing influence will depend upon two factors: (1) what we require at the moment, and (2) what the stone, or rather the information radiated by the stone, can offer us. If a need is fulfilled, healing will take place. This means that healing with crystals, just like homeopathy, Bach flower remedies or aromatherapy, belongs with the information therapies. It is not the chemical substance that is effective, but the information emitted by it.

What information exactly the crystals are able to supply us with in each individual case was discussed in detail in Part 1. Based on the mineralogical data on the crystal system, manner of formation, mineral class, content of mineral-forming elements and colour, we will know what basic programme is involved in each case.

In this way, we have exact instructions at our disposal as to how to identify exactly the right information transmitter (the right mineral) for us from our personal lifestyle, the given situation, the desired change, and so on. The systematic structure needed to do this will be found in the next chapter, The analytical art of healing with crystals.

2.2 The analytical art of healing with crystals

The basic principles of healing with crystals discussed in Part 1 of this volume – manner of formation/life situation, crystal system/ lifestyle, mineral-forming element effect and colour effects – make it possible for us to analyse and choose precisely the right mineral for any project, any problem or illness. This means that the analytical art of healing with crystals differs considerably from the usual symptomatic correspondences used in other therapeutic literature. A thorough examination of the nature and the given situation makes it possible to understand why a certain problem or a particular illness has arisen and can thus help to heal the root cause.

A mineral identified in this manner will activate your own inherent powers of self-healing and can, therefore, help with situations for which the literature – and even this volume – will not yield any suggestions. Providing the analysis is carried out thoroughly, the mineral will, in all probability, help as it will deliver the appropriate information. So, trust in your choice, even if you should pick out a seemingly unusual or atypical mineral. Also, remember that the modern art of healing with crystals is in its infancy and that we can almost certainly say that only a fraction of all possibilities have, so far, been investigated.

It is for this very reason that the following table includes not only the healing crystals described in this volume, but also a large proportion of all the crystals and minerals that are currently obtainable and are known to have been used for therapeutic purposes. Short descriptions of all these minerals can be found in my book *Healing Crystals: the A – Z Guide to 555 Gemstones*, Findhorn Press, 2014). In the present volume, I shall be describing only a selection of those minerals that have proved themselves to be the most important healing stones over what is now 25 years of analytical crystal healing. As with any branch of naturopathy, it is also the case with crystal healing that certain stones are used more frequently and achieve a wider spectrum of effects than others, and I would like to push these to the top of the list – with no claim to completeness.

In principle, there is no dividing line between healing crystals and 'ordinary minerals' in the art of healing. Every mineral, because of its inherent properties, may have an effect upon us. Whether this will turn into a healing effect will simply depend upon what we require at that moment. You could, therefore, extend all the principles described in Part 1 and apply them to all known minerals. The most important thing is to work out very thoroughly and exactly each principle in turn. The more precisely the chosen mineral suits the individual person in a given situation, the greater the success.

The following table is intended to serve initially as a concise, easy-to-scan analysis of crystal systems, formation principles and mineral classes, to help you to choose a suitable mineral for each case. Where the choice is between several minerals, the indication of the mineral-forming substance and the colours will provide further means of differentiating. Some minerals are formed in different ways, so certain ones may be referred to several times; however, only the most common and frequent types of formation are presented here, being those of the minerals that are obtainable in the trade. Descriptions in the mineralogical literature may, therefore, differ somewhat from those given in the table.

Chemical formulas have been presented according to current nomenclature. Mineral-forming substances that are present in a given mineral in small quantities have been indicated by '+ X', while traces are indicated as '+ (X)'. As the following table is principally arranged by crystal system (CS), only stones whose minerals are entirely (or at least almost entirely) part of the same crystal system (e.g. marble or obsidian) can be listed (in addition to pure minerals). Other stones used in crystal healing with minerals of differing crystal systems are to be found at the end of the table.

Analytical crystal healing: A systematic classification of the known healing crystals

(as of: June 2014)

Cubic structure/magnetic origin (primary)

Mineral/Rock Mineral class	Colours Chemical formulae
Iron nickel meteorite Natural elements	iron grey to rust brown $Fe + Ni$
Gold Natural elements	golden yellow $Au + Ag,Cu,Pa,Rh,Bi$
Copper Natural elements	red to brown $Cu + Ag,Au,Fe + (As,Bi,Ge,Sb)$
Pallasite Natural elements and others	yellow-brown inclusions in an iron grey matrix $Fe_mNi_n + (Mg,Fe)_2[SiO_4]$
Silver Natural elements	light grey, frequently suffused with brown to black $Ag + As,Au,Bi,Cu,Hg,Pb,Sb,Te$
Galenite Sulphides	lead grey $PbS + Ag,As,Bi,Cd,Cu,Fe,Sb,Tl,Zn,Se,Te$
Pyrite Sulphides	brass yellow, greenish-yellow, grey $FeS_2 + Mn,Ni,Co + (Pb,Zn,Cu,As)$
Pyrite agate Sulphides and others	dark grey with brass yellow inclusions $SiO_2 \cdot n\ H_2O + FeS_2 + Mn,Ni,Co + (Pb,Zn,Cu,As)$
Sphalerite Sulphides	white, yellow, red, brown, black $ZnS + Cd,Fe,Ga,Ge,Hg,In,Mn,Se + (As,Cu,Sn)$
Fluorite Halogenides	clear, blue, green, yellow, violet, also multi-coloured $CaF_2 + C,Ce,Cl,Fe,Mn,Y$
Magnetite Oxides	lead grey to black $Fe_3O_4 + Al,Mg,Co,Cr,Ni,Ti,V,Zn$
Spinel Oxides	black, red, violet, blue $MgAl_2O_4 + Co,Cr,Fe,Mn,Ti,V,Zn$
Garnet Nesosilicates	spessartite yellow, red-brown, brown $Mn_3Al_2(SiO_4)_3 + Cr,Fe,Mg,V,Y$
Hilutite Nesosilicates and others	clear with numerous red-brown inclusions $SiO_2 + (Fe,Mg)_3Al_2(SiO_4)_3 + ZrSiO_4 + Al,Fe,P,Hf,Th,U,Y$
Kimberlite Nesosilicates and others	grey to greenish-grey breccia $Mg_6[(OH)_8\|Si_4O_{10}] + (Mg,Fe)_2[SiO_4] + (Mg,Fe)_2[Si_2O_6] +$ $Ca(Mg,Cr)[Si_2O_6] + (Fe,Mg)TiO_3 + Mg_3Al_2(SiO_4)_3$ and others
Analcime Framework silicates	clear, white, grey, yellowish, reddish $Na[AlSi_2O_6] \cdot H_2O + K,Ca,Mg,Fe$
Hauyne Framework silicates	clear, greenish, green-blue, blue $(Na,Ca)_{4-8}[(SO4)_{1-2}/(AlSiO_4)_6] + Fe,K,Cl,CO_2,H_2O$
Sodalite Framework silicates	dark blue $Na_8[Cl_2(AlSiO_4)_6] + K,OH,Ca,Mg,Fe,Mn,CO_3,SO_4,H_2O$

Cubic structure/sedimentary origin (seconadary)

Mineral/Rock	Colours
Mineral class	Chemical formulae

Mineral/Rock / Mineral class	Colours / Chemical formulae
Gold	golden yellow
Natural elements	$Au + Ag,Cu,Pa,Rh,Bi$
Copper	copper red to brown
Natural elements	$Cu + Ag,Au,Fe + (As,Bi,Ge,Sb)$
Silver	light grey, frequently suffused with brown to black
Natural elements	$Ag + As,Au,Bi,Cu,Hg,Pb,Sb,Te$
Galenite	lead grey
Sulphides	$PbS + Ag,As,Bi,Cd,Cu,Fe,Sb,Tl,Zn,Se,Te$
Pop rocks (boji stones)	dark grey to rust brown
Sulphides	$FeS_2 + FeOOH \cdot n\,H_2O$
Pyrite	brass yellow, greenish-yellow, grey
Sulphides	$FeS_2 + Mn,Ni,Co + (Pb,Zn,Cu,As)$
Schalenblende	yellow and grey layering
Sulphides	$ZnS + PbS + FeS_2$
Sphalerite	white, yellow, red, brown, black
Sulphides	$ZnS + Cd,Fe,Ga,Ge,Hg,In,Mn,Se + (As,Cu,Sn)$
Fluorite	clear, blue, green, yellow, violet, also multi-coloured
Halogenides	$CaF_2 + C,Ce,Cl,Fe,Mn,Y$
Halite (rock salt)	clear, pink, orange, blue, violet, brown, black
Halogenides	$NaCl + K,F,Br,J$
Tiffany	stone beige-violet
Halogenides and others	$CaF_2 + SiO_2 \cdot n\,H_2O$
Cuprite	red to red-brown
Oxides	$Cu_2O + Fe$
Sonora	Sunrise red, black, green, blue
Oxides and others	$Cu_2O + CuO + Cu_4[(OH)_6 \,|\, SO_4] + (Cu,Al)_2[H_2Si_2O_5(OH)_4] \cdot n\,H_2O$

Cubic structure/metamorphic origin (tertiary)

Mineral/Rock	Colours
Mineral class	Chemical formulae

Mineral/Rock / Mineral class	Colours / Chemical formulae
Diamond	clear, grey, yellow, brown, black, blue, red, green
Natural elements	$C_n + (N,B)$
Gold	golden yellow
Natural elements	$Au + Ag,Cu,Pa,Rh,Bi$
Galenite	lead grey
Sulphides	$PbS + Ag,As,Bi,Cd,Cu,Fe,Sb,Tl,Zn,Se,Te$
Lapis lazuli	blue with small white or golden spots
Sulphides and others	$(Na,Ca)_8[(SO_4,S,Cl)_2 \,|\, (AlSiO_4)_6] + CaCO_2 + FeS_2 + CaMg[Si_2O_6]$
Pyrite	brass yellow, greenish-yellow, grey
Sulphides	$FeS_2 + Mn,Ni,Co + (Pb,Zn,Cu,As)$
Sphalerite	white, yellow, red, brown, black
Sulphides	$ZnS + Cd,Fe,Ga,Ge,Hg,In,Mn,Se + (As,Cu,Sn)$
Sphalerite magnetite in serpentine	greenish-yellow with brown inclusions
Sulphides and others	$Mg_6[(OH)_8 \,|\, Si_4O_{10}] + ZnS + Fe_3O_4$
Fluorite	pink
Halogenides	$CaF_2 + C,Ce,Cl,Fe,Mn,Y$
Magnetite	lead grey to black
Oxides	$Fe_3O_4 + Al,Mg,Co,Cr,Ni,Ti,V,Zn$

Sphalerite magnetite in serpentine greenish-yellow with brown inclusions
Oxides and others $Mg_6[(OH)_8 | Si_4O_{10}] + ZnS + Fe_3O_4$

Spinel black, red, violet, blue
Oxides $MgAl_2O_4 + Co,Cr,Fe,Mn,Ti,V,Zn$

Eclogite grey-green to green with red-brown inclusions
Nesosilicates and others $(Na,Ca)(Mg,Fe,Al)[(Si,Al)_2O_6] + Cr,Ti,K +$
$(Mg,Fe,Ca)_3Al_2[Si_3O_{12}] + Mn,Cr,Ti$

Glaucophane schist blue-grey with red-brown and other inclusions
Nesosilicates and others $Na_2(Mg,Fe)_3(Al,Fe)_2[(OH)_2 | Si_8O_{22}] + F,Cl,Ti,Mn,Cr,Ca +$
$(Mg,Fe)_3Al_2(SiO_4)_3$ u.a.

Almandine garnet red, brown to black
Nesosilicates $Fe_3Al_2(SiO_4)_3 + Cr,Mg,Mn,Ti,Y$

Andradite garnet khaki, brown, blackish
Nesosilicates $Ca_3Fe_2(SiO_4)_3 + Al,Cr,Mn,Ti,V$

Grossular garnet clear, green, pink, orange to brown
Nesosilicates $Ca_3Al_2(SiO_4)_3 + Cr,Fe,Mn,V$

Hessonite garnet red, yellow, orange, brown
Nesosilicates $Ca_3(Al,Fe)_2(SiO_4)_3$

Hydrogrossular garnet clear, light green, reddish, with dark mottling
Nesosilicates $Ca_3Al_2[(OH)_{4m} | (SiO_4)_{3-m}] + Cr,Fe,Mn,V$

Melanite garnet black
Nesosilicates $Ca_3(Fe,Ti)_2(Si,Fe,Al)_3O_{12}$

Pyrope garnet dark red to red-violet
Nesosilicates $Mg_3Al_2(SiO_4)_3 + Cr,Fe,Ti,V$

Rhodolite garnet dark red to red-violet
Nesosilicates $(Mg,Fe)_3Al_2(SiO_4)_3 + Cr,Mn,Ti,Y$

Spessartite garnet yellow, red-brown, brown
Nesosilicates $Mn_3Al_2(SiO_4)_3 + Cr,Fe,Mg,V,Y$

Tsavorite garnet grass green to emerald green
Nesosilicates $Ca_3(Al,Cr,V)_2(SiO_4)_3 + Fe$

Uvarovite garnet dark green to emerald green
Nesosilicates $Ca_3Cr_2(SiO_4)_3 + Fe,Mg,Mn,Ti$

Amphibolite garnet black-and-white speckles with brown inclusions
Nesosilicates and others $(Na,K)_{0-1}Ca_2(Mg,Fe,Al)_5[(OH)_2 | Si_{6-7.5}Al_{2-0.5}O_{22}] +$
$NaAlSi_3O_8/CaAl_2Si_2O_8 + (Fe,Mg)_3Al_2(SiO_4)_3$ and others

Mica schist garnet silver-grey to brown with red-brown inclusions
Nesosilicates and others $KAl_2[(OH,F)_2 | AlSi_3O_{10}]$ and/or
$K(Mg,Fe,Mn)_3[(OH,F)_2 | (Al,Fe)Si_3O_{10}] + (Fe,Mg)_3Al_2(SiO_4)_3$ u.a.

Peridotite garnet dark green, olive green, grey with red inclusions
Nesosilicates and others $(Mg,Fe)_2[SiO_4] + Mn,Ca,Ni,Cr + Mg_3Al_2(SiO_4)_3$ u.a.

Pyroxenite garnet black, grey to green with red inclusions
Nesosilicates and others $CaMg[Si_2O_6] + (Mg,Fe)_2[Si_2O_6] + (Mg,Fe)_2[SiO_4] +$
$(Mg,Fe)_3Al_2(SiO_4)_3$ and others

Garnet schist staurolite silver-grey with brown and red-brown inclusions
Nesosilicates and others $KAl_2[(OH,F)_2 | AlSi_3O_{10}] + (Fe,Mg)_3Al_2(SiO_4)_3 +$
$FeAl_4[O | OH | SiO_4]_2 + Li,Mg,Cr,Zn,Mn,Ti,Co$

Lapis lazuli blue with small white or golden spots
Framework silicates & others $(Na,Ca)_8[(SO_4,S,Cl)_2 | (AlSiO_4)_6] + CaCO_2 + FeS_2 + CaMg[Si_2O_6]$

Sodalite dark blue
Framework silicates $Na_8[Cl_2(AlSiO_4)_6] + K,OH,Ca,Mg,Fe,Mn,CO_3,SO_4,H_2O$

⬡ Hexagonal structure/magmatic origin (primary)

Mineral/Rock Mineral class	Colours Chemical formulae
Molybdenite Sulphides	silver-grey $MoS_2 + W$
Apatite Phosphates	black, blue, green, yellow, rarely pink or red $Ca_5[(F,Cl,OH)|(PO_4)_3] + Na,Mg, Mn,Sr,Y,SE,CO_3,SO_4$
Aquamarine Ring silicates	blue-green to sky blue $Be_3Al_2[Si_6O_{18}] + Na,K,Li,Cs,Mg,Fe,Ti,Sc,H_2O$
Beryl Ring silicates	clear, yellow, green, light blue, pink, red, black $Be_3Al_2[Si_6O_{18}] + Na,K,Li,Cs,Mg,Ca,Rb,Mn,Sc,H_2O + (Cr,Fe,N,U,Ti,V)$
Golden beryl Ring silicates	yellow to golden yellow $Be_3Al_2[Si_6O_{18}] + Na,K,Li,Cs,Mg,Ca,Rb,Mn,Sc,H_2O + (Cr,Fe,N,U,Ti,V)$
Heliodor Ring silicates	yellow, golden yellow to yellow-green $Be_3Al_2[Si_6O_{18}] + Na,K,Li,Cs,Mg,Ca,Rb,Mn,Sc,H_2O + (Cr,Fe,N,U,Ti,V)$
Morganite Ring silicates	pale pink, pink to apricot $Be_3Al_2[Si_6O_{18}] + Li,Mn + (Cs,Fe)$
Emerald Ring silicates	grey-green to intense emerald green $Be_3Al_2[Si_6O_{18}] + K,Li,Na,Cr,V$

⬡ Hexagonal structure/sedimentary origin (secondary)

Mineral/Rock Mineral class	Colours Chemical formulae
Covellite Sulphides	metallic blue-black, wet metallic violet $CuS + Fe + (Ag,Pb,Se)$
Schalenblende Sulphides	yellow and grey layering $ZnS + PbS + FeS_2$
Pyromorphite Phosphates	orange, brown, grey, green, white $Pb_5[Cl/(PO_4)_3] + As,OH,F,V,Cr,Ca$
Mimetesite Arsenates	yellow, orange-red, brown, grey, greenish, white $Pb_5[Cl|(AsO_4)_3] + Ba,Ca,P,V + (Mn,Sr,SE)$
Vanadinite Vanadates	red, orange, yellow or brown $Pb_5[Cl/(VO_4)_3] + As,Ca,P,OH$
Emerald Ring silicates	grey-green to intense emerald green $Be_3Al_2[Si_6O_{18}] + K,Li,Na,Cr,V$
Sugilite Ring silicates	pale violet to intense violet $KNa_2(Fe,Mn,Al)_2Li_3[Si_{12}O_{30}] + Ba,Ca$

⬡ Hexagonal structure/metamorphic origin (tertiary)

Mineral/Rock Mineral class	Colours Chemical formulae
Molybdenite Sulphides	silver-grey $MoS_2 + W$
Apatite Phosphates	black, blue, green, yellow, rarely pink or red $Ca_5[(F,Cl,OH)|(PO_4)_3] + Na,Mg, Mn,Sr,Y,SE,CO_3,SO_4$
Benitoite Ring silicates	sapphire-blue, pale blue, clear $BaTi[Si_3O_9] + Na,Fe,Zr$
Emerald Ring silicates	grey-green to intense emerald green $Be_3Al_2[Si_6O_{18}] + K,Li,Na,Cr,V$

Sugilite	pale violet to intense violet
Ring silicates	$KNa_2(Fe,Mn,Al)_2Li_3[Si_{12}O_{30}]$ + Ba,Ca
Shungite	black
Organic rock	C_n (containing graphite)

⚠ Trigonal structure/magmatic origin (primary)

Mineral/Rock Mineral class	Colours Chemical formulae
Bismuth	silvery white, yellowish, reddish, occasional tinges of colour
Natural elements	Bi + As,Sb
Cinnabarite	vermillion
Sulphides	HgS + Zn,Sb,Cu
Cinnabarite	opal clear-grey with red inclusions
Sulphides and others	$SiO_2 \cdot n\ H_2O$ + HgS + Zn,Sb,Cu
Nickeline	copper red, pink to brass yellow
Arsenides	NiAs + Fe,Co,Sb,S
Hematite	iron grey, red-brown
Oxides	Fe_2O_3 + Al,Mg,Ti
Ilmenite	black
Oxides	$FeTiO_3$ + Mg,Mn,Nb
Ilmenite quartz	grey-black threads in clear quartz
Oxides and others	SiO_2 + $FeTiO_3$ + Mg,Mn,Nb
Kimberlite	grey to greenish-grey breccia
Nesosilicates and others	$Mg_6[(OH)_8 \| Si_4O_{10}]$ + $(Mg,Fe)_2[SiO_4]$ + $(Mg,Fe)_2[Si_2O_6]$ + $Ca(Mg,Cr)[Si_2O_6]$ + $(Fe,Mg)TiO_3$ + $Mg_3Al_2(SiO_4)_3$ and others
Ruby	red to red-violet
Oxides	Al_2O_3 + Cr,Fe
Sapphire	blue, black, clear, green, yellow, pink
Oxides	Al_2O_3 + Cr,Fe,Ti,V
Rhodochrosite	pink to raspberry red
Carbonates	$MnCO_3$ + Ca,Mg,Fe
Siderite	white, yellowish, grey, brown, black-brown
Carbonates	$FeCO_3$ + Ca,Mg,Mn,Zn
Alunite	clear, white, grey, reddish, yellowish
Sulphates	$KAl_3[(OH)_6 \| (SO_4)_2]$ + Na,Fe
Phenakite	clear, wine yellow, pink, brown, greenish-blue
Nesosilicates	Be_2SiO_4 + Na,K,Mg,Ca,H_2O
Dalmatian stone (aplite)	black inclusions in a beige-grey matrix
Chain silicates and other	SiO_2 + $Kal[Si_3O_8]$ + $NaFe[Si_2O_6]$ and others
Wollastonite	white, grey, reddish
Chain silicates	$Ca_3Si_3O_9$ + Al,Mn,Sr,Fe,Mg,Na
Blue quartz	blue (indigolite quartz)
Ring silicates and others	SiO_2 + $(Na,Ca)(Li,Al,Fe)_3(Al,Fe)_6[(OH,O,F)_4 \| (BO_3)_3 \| Si_6O_{18}]$
Dioptase	emerald green to dark green
Ring silicates	$Cu_6(Si_6O_{18}) \cdot 6\ H_2O$ + (Zn)
Eudialyte	pink, red, yellow, brown to violet
Ring silicates	$Na_4(Ca_2FeZr[(OH)_2 \| (Si_8O_{22}]$ + Ce,La,Y,K,Mn,Sr,Ti,Nb,Al,Cl,F,P,S,Th,U
Dravite tourmaline	brown to black
Ring silicates	$NaMg_3(Al,Fe,Cr)_6[(OH)_4 \| (BO_3)_3 \| Si_6O_{18}]$
Elbaite tourmaline	all colours
Ring silicates	$Na(Li,Al)_3Al_6[(OH,F)(OH)_3 \| (BO_3)_3 \| Si_6O_{18}]$

Indigolite tourmaline blue
Ring silicates $(Na,Ca)(Li,Al,Fe)_3(Al,Fe)_6[(OH,O,F)_4 | (BO_3)_3 | Si_6O_{18}]$

Liddicoatite tourmaline all colours
Ring silicates $Ca(Li,Al)_3Al_6[FO(OH)_2 | (BO_3)_3 | Si_6O_{18}]$

Paraiba tourmaline garish green to turquoise
Ring silicates $(Na,Ca)(Li,Al,Cu)_3(Al,Mn)_6[(OH)_4 | (BO_3)_3 | Si_6O_{18}]$

Rubellite tourmaline red, pink
Ring silicates $(Na,Ca)(Li,Al,Mn)_3(Al,Mn)_6[(OH,O,F)_4 | (BO_3)_3 | Si_6O_{18}]$

Schorl tourmaline black
Ring silicates $NaFe_3(Al,Fe)_6[(OH,F)_4 | (BO_3)_3 | Si_6O_{18}]$

Uvite tourmaline brown to olive green
Ring silicates $CaMg_3(Al_5Mg)[(OH)_4 | (BO_3)_3 | Si_6O_{18}]$

Verdelite tourmaline green
Ring silicates $(Na,Ca)(Li,Al,Fe)_3(Al,Cr,V)_6[(OH,O,F)_4 | (BO_3)_3 | Si_6O_{18}]$

Tourmaline quartz black tourmaline crystals in clear quartz
Ring silicates and others $SiO_2 + NaFe_3(Al,Fe)_6[(OH,F)_4 | (BO_3)_3 | Si_6O_{18}]$

Dalmatian stone (aplite) black inclusions in a beige-grey matrix
Framework silicates and others $SiO_2 + Kal[Si_3O_8] + NaFe[Si_2O_6]$ and others

Agate white, grey, blue, yellow, red, brown, black
Oxides/framework silicates $SiO_2 + Al,Fe$

Actinolite quartz green crystals in clear quartz
Oxides/framework silicates $SiO_2 + Ca_2(Mg,Fe)_5[(OH)_2 | Si_8O_{22}] + Na,K,Al,Cr,Cl,F,Mn,H_2O$

Amethyst pale violet, violet to violet-black
Oxides/framework silicates $SiO_2 + (Fe,Al,Ti,Na,Li)$

Ametrine violet and yellow divided into zones
Oxides/framework silicates $SiO_2 + (Fe,Al,Ti,Na,Li)$

Tree agate white with green inclusions
Oxides/framework silicates $SiO_2 + (Mg,Fe,Al)_{12}[(Si,Al)_8O_{20}(OH)_{16}]$

Rock crystal clear (as transparent as glass)
Oxides/framework silicates $SiO_2 + (Al,Li,Na,H)$

Blue quartz blue (indigolite quartz)
Oxides/framework silicates $SiO_2 + (Na,Ca)(Li,Al,Fe)_3(Al,Fe)_6[(OH,O,F)_4 | (BO_3)_3 | Si_6O_{18}]$

Chalcedony pale blue to light blue, partially striated
Oxides/framework silicates $SiO_2 \cdot n\ H_2O$

Chrome chalcedony light green to dark green
Oxides/framework silicates $SiO_2 \cdot n\ H_2O + Cr$

Dendritic chalcedony white, light blue with black dendrites
Oxides/framework silicates $SiO_2 \cdot n\ H_2O + MnO_2$

Yellow chalcedony yellow to yellow-brown
Oxides/framework silicates $SiO_2 \cdot n\ H_2O + FeOOH$

Green chalcedony light green to dark green
Oxides/framework silicates $SiO_2 \cdot n\ H_2O + Al,Fe$ + green silicates

Pink chalcedony pink to pink-violet
Oxides/framework silicates $SiO_2 \cdot n\ H_2O + (Mn)$

Red chalcedony dark red
Oxides/framework silicates $SiO_2 \cdot n\ H_2O + Fe$

Chlorite quartz clear with green inclusions
Oxides/framework silicates $SiO_2 + Mg_5AlSi_3AlO_{10}(OH)_8 + Fe,Cr,Mn,Ni,Zn,Ti$

Citrine light yellow, golden yellow, brownish-yellow, greenish-yellow
Oxides/framework silicates $SiO_2 + (Al,Fe)$

Dalmatian stone (aplite) black inclusions in a beige-grey matrix
Oxides/framework silicates $SiO_2 + Kal[Si_3O_8] + NaFe[Si_2O_6]$ and others

158

Ferruginous quartz   red, brown, more rarely yellow
Oxides/framework silicates SiO_2 + Fe,O,OH

Eldarite   light green/dark green with round aggregates
Oxides/framework silicates $NaFe[Si_2O_6]$ + SiO_2 + $KAlSi_3O_8$ + $NaAlSi_3O_8$

Strawberry quartz   pale pink to red
Oxides/framework silicates SiO_2 + (Fe,Mn,Ti)

Girasol quartz   clear to cloudy
Oxides/framework silicates SiO_2 + (Al,Li,Na,H)

Goethite quartz   clear or violet with yellow-brown clumps and nodules
Oxides/framework silicates SiO_2 + FeOOH

Granite   grey, brown, red, pink, yellow, green, blue speckles
Oxides/framework silicates $KAlSi_3O_8$ + $NaAlSi_3O_8/CaAl_2Si_2O_8$+ SiO_2 + $K(Mg,Fe,Mn)_3[(OH,F)_2 | (Al,Fe)Si_3O_{10}]$

Hematite quartz   clear with red or dark grey inclusions
Oxides/framework silicates SiO_2 + Fe_2O_3 + Al,Mg,Ti

Heliotrope   moss green to dark green with red mottling
Oxides/framework silicates $SiO_2 \cdot n\ H_2O$ + Al,Fe

Hilutite   clear with numerous red-brown inclusions
Oxides/framework silicates SiO_2 + $(Fe,Mg)_3Al_2(SiO_4)_3$ + $ZrSiO_4$ + Al,Fe,P,Hf,Th,U,Y

Ilmenite quartz   grey-black threads in clear quartz
Oxides/framework silicates SiO_2 + $FeTiO_3$ + Mg,Mn,Nb

Jamesonite quartz   grey threads in clear quartz
Oxides/framework silicates SiO_2 + $Pb_4FeSb_6S_{14}$ + Ag,Bi,Cu,Zn

Jasper   beige, brown, grey, red, yellow, sand-coloured, green
Oxides/framework silicates SiO_2 + Fe,O,OH

Carnelian   red-brown, orange to a meaty red
Oxides/framework silicates $SiO_2 \cdot n\ H_2O$ + (Fe,O,OH)

Lavender quartz   lilac to lavender
Oxides/framework silicates $SiO_2 \cdot n\ H_2O$ + Fe,Mn

Lemon quartz   greenish-yellow
Oxides/framework silicates SiO_2 + (Al,Fe)

Mandarin quartz   clear with an orange coating
Oxides/framework silicates SiO_2 + Fe_2O_3

Metarhyolite grey   brown, beige, yellowish, reddish, green
Oxides/framework silicates SiO_2 + Fe,Al and others

Moss agate green   clear-brownish with pink to brown inclusions
Oxides/framework silicates $SiO_2 \cdot n\ H_2O$ + Al,Fe + green silicates

Moss agate pink   clear-brownish with pink to brown inclusions
Oxides/framework silicates $SiO_2 \cdot n\ H_2O$ + Al,Fe

Nickel quartz   pale green to grey-green
Oxides/framework silicates SiO_2 + Ni,Al,Fe

Onyx   black
Oxides/framework silicates $SiO_2 \cdot n\ H_2O$ + Mn,Fe

Ocean chalcedony   white, yellow, orange, reddish, brown, green, light blue
Oxides/framework silicates $SiO_2 \cdot n\ H_2O$ + Al,Fe

Plasma   green to dark green
Oxides/framework silicates $SiO_2 \cdot n\ H_2O$ + Al,Fe + grüne Silikate

Prasiolite   pale green to light green
Oxides/framework silicates SiO_2 + (Fe,Al,Ti,Na,Li)

Pyrite agate   dark grey with brass yellow inclusions
Oxides/framework silicates $SiO_2 \cdot n\ H_2O$ + FeS_2 + Mn,Ni,Co + (Pb,Zn,Cu,As)

Smoky quartz   brown, dark brown, blackish-grey, black
Oxides/framework silicates SiO_2 + (Al,Li,Na,Fe,Mn,Ti)

Pink quartz pink
Oxides/framework silicates SiO_2 + Al,P
Rose crystal clear quartz with a reddish coating
Oxides/framework silicates SiO_2 + Fe_2O_3
Rose quartz pink, rarely with a hint of lilac
Oxides/framework silicates SiO_2 + $(Al,Fe)_7[O_3 | BO_3 | (SiO_4)_3]$
Rutile quartz clear/smoky brown with yellow/red fibres
Oxides/framework silicates SiO_2 + TiO_2 + Fe,Sn,V,Cr,Nb,Ta
Sard red-brown to brown
Oxides/framework silicates $SiO_2 \cdot n\ H_2O$ + (Fe,O,OH)
Sardonyx black, white, red-brown
Oxides/framework silicate $SiO_2 \cdot n\ H_2O$ + Mn,Fe
Snow quartz snow white
Oxides/framework silicates SiO_2 + (Al,Li,Na,H)
Sulphur quartz sulphur yellow
Oxides/framework silicates SiO_2 + Al,Fe + S_8 (sulphur is not always included)
Tourmaline quartz black tourmaline crystals in clear quartz
Oxides/framework silicates SiO_2 + $NaFe_3(Al,Fe)_6[(OH,F)_4 | (BO_3)_3 | Si_6O_{18}]$

△ Trigonal structure/sedimentary origin (secondary)

Mineral/Rock	Colours
Mineral class	Chemical formulae

Cinnabarite	vermillion
Sulphides	HgS + Zn,Sb,Cu
Hematite	iron grey, red-brown
Oxides	Fe_2O_3 + Al,Mg,Ti
Kalahari picture stone	sand-coloured to brown
Oxides and others	SiO_2 + FeOOH + Fe_2O_3
Printstone	beige, red, brown stripes
Oxides and others	SiO_2 + $Al_4[(OH)_8/Si_4O_{10}]$ + Fe_2O_3 + FeOOH
Shiva lingam	beige/red/brown zones
Oxides and others	SiO_2 + $Al_4[(OH)_8/Si_4O_{10}]$ + FeOOH + Fe_2O_3
Calcite	white, grey, red, orange, yellow, green, blue, violet
Carbonates	$CaCO_3$ + Mn,Fe,Mg + (Sr,Ba,Co,Zn)
Chrysanthemum	stone white-grey crystals in a grey-black matrix
Carbonates and others	$SrSO_4$ + Ba,Ca + $CaCO_3$ + C
Dolomite	white, grey, beige, brown, orange, pink, red, violet
Carbonates	$CaMg(CO_3)_2$ + Fe,Mn + (Co,Pb,Zn)
Gaspeite	yellow-green, pale green, dark green
Carbonates	$(Ni,Mg)CO_3$ + Fe
Calcoolite	brown with small reddish or beige nodules
Carbonates	$CaCO_3$ + Fe oder $CaMg(CO_3)_2$ + Fe
Limestone	white, yellow, brown, grey
Carbonates	$CaCO_3$ + Fe,Mn
Magnesite	white to beige
Carbonates	$MgCO_3$ + Ca,Fe,Mn
Oncolite (leopardite)	light brown with grey to brown oncoids
Carbonates	$CaCO_3$ + Mn,Fe,Mg + (Sr,Ba,Co,Zn)
Onyx marble	white, yellow, brown and greenish stripes
Carbonates	$CaCO_3$ + Fe oder $CaMg(CO_3)_2$ + Fe
Rhodochrosite	pink to raspberry red
Carbonates	$MnCO_3$ + Ca,Mg,Fe

Sandstone	white, beige, yellow, greenish, brown, red, black
Carbonates and others	$SiO_2 + CaCO_3$ u.v.m.
Snake stone	dark brown with yellow-brown fossils
Carbonates and others	$CaCO_3 + Al_4[(OH)_8/Si_4O_{10}] + FeOOH$
Septarian	stone grey to brown with white to yellow filling
Carbonates and others	$CaCO_3 + Al_4[(OH)_8/Si_4O_{10}] \cdot n\ H_2O + K,Fe,Mg$
Siderite	white, yellowish, grey, brown, black-brown
Carbonates	$FeCO_3 + Ca,Mg,Mn,Zn$
Smithsonite	white, grey, yellow, green, blue, violet, pink, brown
Carbonates	$ZnCO_3 + Fe,Ca,Co,Mn,Cu,Mg,Cd,Pb$
Stichtite	dark pink to light pink
Carbonates	$Mg_6Cr_2[(OH)_{16}\,|\,(CO_3)] \cdot 4\ H_2O + Al,Fe,Ni$
Stichtite serpentinite	dark pink to light pink in a green-yellow matrix
Carbonates and others	$Mg_6[(OH)_8\,|\,Si_4O_{10}] + Mg_6Cr_2[(OH)_{16}\,|\,(CO_3)] \cdot 4\ H_2O + Al,Fe,Ni$
Stromatolite	brown-black stripes
Carbonates and others	$SiO_2 + CaCO_3 + Al_4[(OH)_8/Si_4O_{10}] \cdot n\ H_2O + FeOOH$
Fossilized coral	white, beige, reddish, brown
Carbonates	$CaCO_3 + Fe,Mn$
Lemon chrysoprase	pale green to yellow-green
Carbonates and others	$(Mg,Ni)CO_3 + SiO_2 + Ca,Fe,Mn$
Lemon magnesite	pale green to yellow-green
Carbonates	$(Mg,Ni)CO_3 + Ca,Fe,Mn$
Alunite	clear, white, grey, reddish, yellowish
Sulphates	$KAl_3[(OH)_6\,|\,(SO_4)_2] + Na,Fe$
Dioptase	emerald green to dark green
Ring silicates	$Cu_6(Si_6O_{18}) \cdot 6\ H_2O + (Zn)$
Agate	white, grey, blue, yellow, red, brown, black
Oxides/framework silicates	$SiO_2 + Al,Fe$
Amethyst	pale violet, violet to violet-black
Oxides/framework silicates	$SiO_2 + (Fe,Al,Ti,Na,Li)$
Ametrine	violet and yellow divided into zones
Oxides/framework silicates	$SiO_2 + (Fe,Al,Ti,Na,Li)$
Aurora quartz	clear with iridescent zones
Oxides/framework silicates	$SiO_2 + (Fe,Al,Ti,Na,Li)$
Rock crystal	clear (as transparent as glass)
Oxides/framework silicates	$SiO_2 + (Al,Li,Na,H)$
Chalcedony	pale blue to light blue, partially striated
Oxides/framework silicates	$SiO_2 \cdot n\ H_2O$
Chrome chalcedony	light green to dark green
Oxides/framework silicates	$SiO_2 \cdot n\ H_2O + Cr$
Dendritic chalcedony	white, light blue with black dendrites
Oxides/framework silicates	$SiO_2 \cdot n\ H_2O + MnO_2$
Copper chalcedony	blue-green with copper inclusions
Oxides/framework silicates	$SiO_2 \cdot n\ H_2O + Cu + (Cu)$
Pink chalcedony	pink to pink-violet
Oxides/framework silicates	$SiO_2 \cdot n\ H_2O + (Mn)$
Red chalcedony	dark red
Oxides/framework silicates	$SiO_2 \cdot n\ H_2O + Fe$
Chrysoprase	apple green
Oxides/framework silicates	$SiO_2 \cdot n\ H_2O + Ni,Fe,Cr$
Citrine	light yellow, golden yellow, brownish-yellow, greenish-yellow
Oxides/framework silicates	$SiO_2 + (Al,Fe)$

Ferruginous quartz   red, brown, more rarely yellow
Oxides/framework silicates $SiO_2 + Fe,O,OH$

Hawk's eye   blue-grey to blue-black, also green-black
Oxides/framework silicates $SiO_2 + Na_2Mg_3Fe_2(OH/Si_4O_{11})_2 + Al,Ti$

Flint   black, grey, brown, red-brown, bluish
Oxides/framework silicates $SiO_2 \cdot n\ H_2O + Al,Fe$

Gem silica   light blue to turquoise
Oxides/framework silicates $SiO_2 \cdot n\ H_2O + (Cu,Al)_2[H_2Si_2O_5(OH)_4] \cdot n\ H_2O$

Goethite quartz   clear or violet with yellow-brown clumps and nodules
Oxides/framework silicates $SiO_2 + FeOOH$

Gold quartz   (tiger eye) golden yellow to brown
Oxides/framework silicates $SiO_2 + FeOOH$

Hematite quartz   clear with red or dark grey inclusions
Oxides/framework silicates $SiO_2 + Fe_2O_3 + Al,Mg,Ti$

Hornstone   brown, grey, yellow, red, also colourful/multi-coloured
Oxides/framework silicates $SiO_2 \cdot n\ H_2O + Al,Fe$

Jasper   beige, brown, grey, red, yellow, sand-coloured, green
Oxides/framework silicate $SiO_2 + Fe,O,OH$

Kalahari picture stone sand-coloured to brown
Oxides/framework silicates $SiO_2 + FeOOH + Fe_2O_3$

Carnelian   red-brown, orange to a meaty red
Oxides/framework silicates $SiO_2 \cdot n\ H_2O + (Fe,O,OH)$

Lavender quartz   lilac to lavender
Oxides/framework silicates $SiO_2 \cdot n\ H_2O + Fe,Mn$

Mondolite   red to red-brown
Oxides/framework silicates $SiO_2 + Fe,O,OH$

Mookaite   white, beige, yellow, red, red-violet
Oxides/framework silicates $SiO_2 + Fe,O,OH$

Onyx   black
Oxides/framework silicates $SiO_2 \cdot n\ H_2O + Mn,Fe$

Oolite   light brown with small rust brown nodules
Oxides/framework silicates $SiO_2 + FeOOH \cdot n\ H_2O + Al,Ba,Ca,Mg,Mn,Ni,P,Si,V$

Pietersite   blue-black and/or yellow-brown brecciation
Oxides/framework silicates $SiO_2 + Na_2Mg_3Fe_2(OH/Si_4O_{11})_2 + Al,Ti + FeOOH$

Plasma   green to dark green
Oxides/framework silicates $SiO_2 \cdot n\ H_2O + Al,Fe +$ green silicates

Printstone   beige, red, brown stripes
Oxides/framework silicates $SiO_2 + Al_4[(OH)_8/Si_4O_{10}] + Fe_2O_3 + FeOOH$

Sand rose   sand-coloured to brown
Oxides/framework silicates $SiO_2 + CaSO_4$

Sandstone   white, beige, yellow, greenish, brown, red, black
Oxides/framework silicates $SiO_2 + CaCO_3$ u.v.m.

Sard   red-brown to brown
Oxides/framework silicates $SiO_2 \cdot n\ H_2O + (Fe,O,OH)$

Sardonyx   black, white, red-brown
Oxides/framework silicates $SiO_2 \cdot n\ H_2O + Mn,Fe$

Shiva lingam   beige/red/brown zones
Oxides/framework silicates $SiO_2 + Al_4[(OH)_8/Si_4O_{10}] + FeOOH + Fe_2O_3$

Stromatolite   brown-black stripes
Oxides/framework silicates $SiO_2 + CaCO_3 + Al_4[(OH)_8/Si_4O_{10}] \cdot n\ H_2O + FeOOH$

Tiffany stone   beige-violet
Oxides/framework silicates $CaF_2 + SiO_2 \cdot n\ H_2O$

Tiger's eye golden yellow to brown
Oxides/framework silicates $SiO_2 + FeOOH$
Fossilized coral white, beige, reddish, brown
Oxides/framework silicates $SiO_2 \cdot n\ H_2O + Fe,O,OH$
Fossilized wood yellow-brown, red-brown, brown-grey
Oxides/framework silicates $SiO_2 \cdot n\ H_2O + Fe,O,OH$
Lemon chrysoprase pale green to yellow-green
Oxides/framework silicates $(Mg,Ni)CO_3 + SiO_2 + Ca,Fe,Mn$

△ Trigonal structure/metamorphic origin (tertiary)

Mineral/Rock   Colours
Mineral class   Chemical formulae

Red aventurine quartz brown-red, red to orange-brown (hematite quartzite)
Oxides and others $SiO_2 + Fe_2O_3 + Mg,Ti\ /\ FeOOH$
Cordierite sunstone blue, blue-grey with brown inclusions
Oxides and others $(Mg,Fe)_2Al_3[AlSi_5O_{18}] + Na,K,Mn,H_2O + Fe_2O_3$
Hematite iron   grey, red-brown
Oxides $Fe_2O_3 + Al,Mg,Ti$
Ilmenite   black
Oxides $FeTiO_3 + Mg,Mn,Nb$
Ruby   red to red-violet
Oxides $Al_2O_3 + Cr,Fe$
Ruby disthene   red to red-violet in a blue coating
Oxides and others $Al_2O_3 + Al_2SiO_5 + Cr,Fe$
Ruby disthene fuchsite red/blue/green
Oxides and others $Al_2O_3 + Al_2SiO_5 + K(Al,Cr)_2[(OH,F)_2\,|\,AlSi_3O_{10}] +$
                       Ca,Fe,Mg,Mn,Na,Ti,V,Cr
Sapphire   blue, black, clear, green, yellow, pink
Oxides $Al_2O_3 + Cr,Fe,Ti,V$
Zoisite with ruby (anyolite) green with red inclusions
Oxides and others $Ca_2Al_3[O\,|\,OH\,|\,SiO_4\,|\,Si_2O_7] + Ba,Cr,Fe,Mg,Mn,Sr,V + Al_2O_3 + Cr,Fe$
Calcite   white, grey, red, orange, yellow, green
Carbonates $CaCO_3 + Mn,Fe,Mg + (Sr,Ba,Zn)$
Dolomite   white, grey, beige, yellow, brown, orange, pink, red
Carbonates $CaMg(CO_3)_2 + Fe,Mn + (Pb,Zn)$
Lapis lazuli   blue with small white or golden spots
Carbonates and other $(Na,Ca)_8[(SO_4,S,Cl)_2\,|\,(AlSiO_4)_6] + CaCO_2 + FeS_2 + CaMg[Si_2O_6]$
Magnesite   white to beige
Carbonates $MgCO_3 + Ca,Fe,Mn$
Marble   white, beige, yellow-green, reddish, brown, black
Carbonates $CaCO_3 + Mg,Fe,Sr$ oder $CaMg(CO_3)_2 + Fe$
Ophicalcite   light green to dark green with white veins
Carbonates and others $Mg_6[(OH)_8\,|\,Si_4O_{10}] + Fe,Ni,Al + CaCO_3 +$
                       Mg,Fe,Sr oder $CaMg(CO_3)_2 + Fe$
Porcellanite   light grey, grey-green, brown, black
Carbonates and others $Al_4[(OH)_8/Si_4O_{10}] + FeOOH + FeS \cdot n\ H_2O + CaCO_3$
Rhodochrosite   pink to raspberry red
Carbonates $MnCO_3 + Ca,Mg,Fe$
Siderite   white, yellowish, grey, brown, black-brown
Carbonates $FeCO_3 + Ca,Mg,Mn,Zn$
Stichtite   dark pink to light pink
Carbonates $Mg_6Cr_2[(OH)_{16}\,|\,(CO_3)] \cdot 4\ H_2O + Al,Fe,Ni$

163

Stichtite serpentinite   dark pink to light pink in a green-yellow matrix
Carbonates and others $Mg_6[(OH)_8 | Si_4O_{10}] + Mg_6Cr_2[(OH)_{16} | (CO_3)] \cdot 4\,H_2O + Al,Fe,Ni$
Wollastonite   white, grey, reddish
Chain silicates $Ca_3Si_3O_9 + Al,Mn,Sr,Fe,Mg,Na$
Dravite tourmaline   brown to black
Ring silicates $NaMg_3(Al,Fe,Cr)_6[(OH)_4 | (BO_3)_3 | Si_6O_{18}]$
Schorl tourmaline   black
Ring silicates $NaFe_3(Al,Fe)_6[(OH,F)_4 | (BO_3)_3 | Si_6O_{18}]$
Uvite tourmaline   brown to olive green
Ring silicates $CaMg_3(Al_5Mg)[(OH)_4 | (BO_3)_3 | Si_6O_{18}]$
Tourmaline quartz   black tourmaline crystals in clear quartz
Ring silicates and others $SiO_2 + NaFe_3(Al,Fe)_6[(OH,F)_4 | (BO_3)_3 | Si_6O_{18}]$
Serpentine lizardite   yellow-green, green, olive green to black
Sheet silicates $Mg_6[(OH)_8 | Si_4O_{10}] + Fe,Ni,Al$
Actinolite quartz   green crystals in clear quartz
Oxides/framework silicates $SiO_2 + Ca_2(Mg,Fe)_5[(OH)_2 | Si_8O_{22}] + Na,K,Al,Cr,Cl,F,Mn,H_2O$
Ametrine   violet and yellow divided into zones
Oxides/framework silicates $SiO_2 + (Fe,Al,Ti,Na,Li)$
Blue aventurine quartz light blue, dark blue, violet-blue, blue-black
Oxides/framework silicates $SiO_2 + (Al,Fe)_7[(O,OH)_3 | BO_3 | (SiO_4)_3]$
Green aventurine quartz light green to glittering dark green
Oxides/framework silicates $SiO_2 + K(Al,Cr)_2[(OH,F)_2 | AlSi_3O_{10}]$
Red aventurine quartz brown-red, red to orange-brown (hematite quartzite)
Oxides/framework silicates $SiO_2 + Fe_2O_3 + Mg,Ti$ / $FeOOH$
Red aventurine quartz raspberry red to vintage pink (manganese mica quartzite)
Oxides/framework silicates $SiO_2 + K(Al,Mn)_2[(OH,F)_2 | AlSi_3O_{10}]$
Red aventurine quartz raspberry red to violet-brown (piemontite quartzite)
Oxides/framework silicates $SiO_2 + (Ca,Mn)_2Al_3[O | OH | SiO_4 | Si_2O_7]$
White aventurine quartz white to light grey
Oxides/framework silicates $SiO_2 + KAl_2[(OH,F)_2 | AlSi_3O_{10}]$
Rock crystal clear   (as transparent as glass)
Oxides/framework silicates $SiO_2 + (Al,Li,Na,H)$
Blue quartz   light blue, dark blue (dumortierite quartzite)
Oxides/framework silicates $SiO_2 + (Al,Fe)_7[(O,OH)_3 | BO_3 | (SiO_4)_3]$
Chlorite quartz   clear with green inclusions
Oxides/framework silicates $SiO_2 + Mg_5AlSi_3AlO_{10}(OH)_8 + Fe,Cr,Mn,Ni,Zn,Ti$
Citrine light yellow,   golden yellow, brownish-yellow, greenish-yellow
Oxides/framework silicates $SiO_2 + (Al,Fe)$
Ferruginous quartz   red, brown, more rarely yellow
Oxides/framework silicates $SiO_2 + Fe,O,OH$
Epidote quartz   clear with green-black or silvery threads
Oxides/framework silicates $SiO_2 + Ca_2(Fe,Al)Al_2[O | OH | SiO_4 | Si_2O_7] + Cr,Mg,Mn,Sr,Ti,Pb,V,Th$
Gneiss   white, grey, greenish, yellow, pink, red stripes
Oxides/framework silicates $SiO_2 + KAlSi_3O_8 + NaAlSi_3O_8 + KAl_2[(OH,F)_2 | AlSi_3O_{10}]$
     and/or $K(Mg,Fe,Mn)_3[(OH,F)_2 | (Al,Fe)Si_3O_{10}]$ u.a.
Green quartz   light green to glittering dark green
Oxides/framework silicates $SiO_2 + K(Al,Cr)_2[(OH,F)_2 | AlSi_3O_{10}]$
Hematite quartz   clear with red or dark grey inclusions
Oxides/framework silicates $SiO_2 + Fe_2O_3 + Al,Mg,Ti$
Jamesonite quartz   grey threads in clear quartz
Oxides/framework silicates $SiO_2 + Pb_4FeSb_6S_{14} + Ag,Bi,Cu,Zn$
Jasper   beige, brown, grey, red, yellow, sand-coloured, green
Oxides/framework silicates $SiO_2 + Fe,O,OH$

Mandarin — quartz, clear with an orange coating
Oxides/framework silicates $SiO_2 + Fe_2O_3$

Prase — grass green to leek green
Oxides/framework silicates $SiO_2 + Ca_2(Mg,Fe)_5[(OH)_2|Si_8O_{22}]$

Smoky quartz — brown, dark brown, blackish-grey, black
Oxides/framework silicates $SiO_2 + Ca_2(Na,K)(Mg,Fe)_3(Fe,Al)_2[(O,OH,F)_2/Al_2Si_6O_{22}]$

Rose crystal — clear quartz with a reddish coating
Oxides/framework silicates $SiO_2 + (Al,Li,Na,Fe,Mn,Ti)$

Rose crystal — clear quartz with a reddish coating
Oxides/framework silicates $SiO_2 + Fe_2O_3$

Rutile quartz — clear/smoky brown with yellow/red fibres
Oxides/framework silicates $SiO_2 + TiO_2 + Fe,Sn,V,Cr,Nb,Ta$

Snow quartz — snow white
Oxides/framework silicates $SiO_2 + (Al,Li,Na,H)$

Tiger iron — grey, yellow-brown, red to yellow stripes
Oxides/framework silicates $SiO_2 + SiO_2/FeOOH + Fe_2O_3$

Tourmaline quartz — black tourmaline crystals in clear quartz
Oxides/framework silicates $SiO_2 + NaFe_3(Al,Fe)_6[(OH,F)_4|(BO_3)_3|Si_6O_{18}]$

▢ Tetragonal structure/magmatic origin (primary)

Mineral/Rock Mineral class	Colours Chemical formulae
Bornite Sulphides	reddish-brown, occasional colourful tinting $Cu_5FeS_4 + Zn,Ag,Ge,Bi,In,Pb,Se$
Chalcopyrite Sulphides	brass yellow to golden yellow, also with colourful tinting $CuFeS_2 + Ag,Au,In,Tl,Se,Te,Zn$
Cassiterite Oxides	black, yellowish to reddish-brown, grey, white $SnO_2 + Fe,Mn,Nb,Ta,Ti,W,Zn,Sc,In,Ge,Ga,OH$
Pyrolusite Oxides	grey to black $MnO_2 + Fe,Ti,Al,H_2O$
Rutile quartz Oxides and others	clear/smoky brown with yellow/red fibres $SiO_2 + TiO_2 + Fe,Sn,V,Cr,Nb,Ta$
Scheelite Wolframates	clear, yellow, brown, orange, greenish $CaWO_4 + Mo,Nb,Ta,SE$
Hilutite Nesosilicates and others	clear with numerous red-brown inclusions $SiO_2 + (Fe,Mg)_3Al_2(SiO_4)_3 + ZrSiO_4 + Al,Fe,P,Hf,Th,U,Y$
Zircon Nesosilicates	brown, red-brown, red-orange $ZrSiO_4 + Al,Fe,P,Hf,Th,U,Y$
Analcime Framework silicates	clear, white, grey, yellowish, reddish $Na[AlSi_2O_6] \cdot H_2O + K,Ca,Mg,Fe$
Scapolite Framework silicates	clear, yellow, pink, violet, blue $(Na,Ca,K)_4[(Cl,CO_3,SO_4)|Al_3(Al,Si)_3Si_6O_{24}] + F,P,Fe,Mg,Mn,Ti$
Tugtupit Framework silicate	white, pink, red $Na_8[(Cl,S)_2/Be_2Al_2Si_8O_{24}]$

▢ Tetragonal structure/sedimentary origin (secondary)

Mineral/Rock Mineral class	Colours Chemical formulae
Bornite Sulphides	reddish-brown, occasional colourful tinting $Cu_5FeS_4 + Zn,Ag,Ge,Bi,In,Pb,Se$

Chalcopyrite	golden to brass yellow, partial colourful tinting
Sulphides	$CuFeS_2$ + Ag,Au,In,Tl,Se,Te,Zn
Pyrolusite	grey to black
Oxides	MnO_2 + Fe,Ti,Al,H_2O
Wulfenite	yellow, orange, brown, greenish, red, clear
Molybdate	$PbMoO_4$ + Ca,Cr,Mg,W,V
Apophyllite	clear, light green to blue-green
Sheet silicates	$(K,Na)Ca_4[(F,OH)|(Si_4O_{10})_2] \cdot 8\,H_2O$ + Al,V

▢ Tetragonal structure/metamorphic origin (tertiary)

Mineral/Rock Mineral class	Colours Chemical formulae
Bornite	reddish-brown, occasional colourful tinting
Sulphides	Cu_5FeS_4 + Zn,Ag,Ge,Bi,In,Pb,Se
Chalcopyrite	golden to brass yellow, partial colourful tinting
Sulphides	$CuFeS_2$ + Ag,Au,In,Tl,Se,Te,Zn
Cassiterite	black, yellowish to reddish-brown, grey, white
Oxides	SnO_2 + Fe,Mn,Nb,Ta,Ti,W,Zn,Sc,In,Ge,Ga,OH
Rutile quartz	clear/smoky brown with yellow/red fibres
Oxides and others	SiO_2 + TiO_2 + Fe,Sn,V,Cr,Nb,Ta
Scheelite	clear, yellow, brown, orange, greenish
Wolframates	$CaWO_4$ + Mo,Nb,Ta,SE
Vesuvian	brown, red-brown, yellow, green, pink, violet
Group silicates	$Ca_{10}(Mg,Fe)_2Al_4[(OH)_4/(SiO_4)_5/(Si_2O_7)_2]$ + B,Be,Ce,Cr,F,Fe,Li,K,Na,Mn,Sr,Ti,Zn,SE + (Cu,Ni,V)
Scapolite	clear, yellow, pink, violet, blue
Framework silicates	$(Na,Ca,K)_4[(Cl,CO_3,SO_4)|Al_3(Al,Si)_3Si_6O_{24}]$ + F,P,Fe,Mg,Mn,Ti

◇ Rhombic structure/magmatic origin (primary)

Mineral/Rock Mineral class	Colours Chemical formulae
Sulphur	sulphur yellow, greenish, brownish
Natural elements	S_8 + C,Se,Te + hydrocarbons
Sulphur quartz	sulphur yellow
Natural elements and others	SiO_2 + Al,Fe + S_8
Markasite	brass yellow, possibility of colourful tinting
Sulphides	FeS_2 + As,Co,Ni,Cr
Chrysoberyl	yellow, brownish to greenish
Oxides	Al_2BeO_4 + Cr,Fe,Ti,V
Goethite quartz	clear or violet with yellow-brown clumps and nodules
Oxides and others	SiO_2 + FeOOH
Strontianite	white, grey, pale yellowish, greenish or pink
Carbonates	$SrCO_3$ + Ca,Ba
Adamine	clear, white, light blue, yellow, green, pink, violet
Arsenates	$Zn_2[OH/AsO_4]$ + Al,Cu,Co,Fe,Mn,Ni
Conichalcite	pistachio green to apple green
Arsenates	$CuCa[OH/AsO_4]$ + Fe,Pb,Zn
Barytes	clear, brown, yellow, greenish, red, grey, bluish
Sulphates	$BaSO_4$ + Ca,Pb,Sr
Dumortierite	blue, grey, green, brown
Nesosilicates	$(Al,Fe)_7[O_3|BO_3|(SiO_4)_3]$ + Mn,Ti

Gabbro	brown-black with white inclusions
Nesosilicates and others	$(Mg,Fe)_2([Si_2O_6] + NaAlSi_3O_8/CaAl_2Si_2O_8 + (Mg,Fe)_2[SiO_4]$
Kimberlite	grey to greenish-grey breccia
Nesosilicates and others	$Mg_6[(OH)_8 \| Si_4O_{10}] + (Mg,Fe)_2[SiO_4] + (Mg,Fe)_2[Si_2O_6] +$
	$Ca(Mg,Cr)[Si_2O_6] + (Fe,Mg)TiO_3 + Mg_3Al_2(SiO_4)_3$ u.a.
Olivine (peridot)	yellow-green, bottle green, olive green
Nesosilicates	$(Mg,Fe)_2[SiO_4] + Mn,Ni,Ca$
Pallasite	yellow-brown inclusions in an iron grey matrix
Nesosilicates and others	$Fe_mNi_n + (Mg,Fe)_2[SiO_4]$
Rose quartz	pink, rarely with a hint of lilac
Nesosilicates and others	$SiO_2 + (Al,Fe)_7[O_3 \| BO_3 \| (SiO_4)_3]$
Topaz	clear, light blue, light brown, light yellow
Nesosilicates	$Al_2[(F,OH)_2 \| SiO_4] + Fe,Ca,Mg + (Cr,Mn)$
Topaz gold	topaz golden yellow
Nesosilicates	$Al_2[(F,OH)_2 \| SiO_4] + Fe,Ca,Mg + (Cr)$
Imperial topaz	pink-yellow
Nesosilicates	$Al_2[(F,OH)_2 \| SiO_4] + Fe,Ca,Mg + (Cr,P)$
Topaz pink topaz	pink
Nesosilicates	$Al_2[(F,OH)_2 \| SiO_4] + Fe,Ca,Mg + (P)$
Prehnite	clear, pale green, yellow
Group silicates	$Ca_2Al[(OH)_2 \| AlSi_3O_{10}] + Fe,Na,H_2O$
Bronzite	bronze, brown with golden yellow sparkles
Chain silicates	$(Mg,Fe)_2[Si_2O_6] + Al,Ca,Mn,Ti,Cr,Na$
Bronzite gabbro	black with glittering, suspended copper particles
Chain silicates and others	$NaAlSi_3O_8/CaAl_2Si_2O_8 + (Mg,Fe)_2[Si_2O_6]$
Enstatite	white, yellowish, green to brownish-green
Chain silicates	$Mg_2[Si_2O_6] + Al,Ca,Fe,Mn,Ni,Cr,Ti$
Galaxite	black with labradorescent inclusions
Chain silicates and others	$(Mg,Fe)_2[Si_2O_6] + NaAlSi_3O_8/CaAl_2Si_2O_8$
Hypersthene	black with a brownish silvery gleam
Chain silicates	$(Mg,Fe)_2[Si_2O_6] + Al,Ca,Mn,Ti,Cr,Na$
Porphyrite	dark grey with white or greenish phenocrysts
Group silicates and others	$Ca_2(Na,K)(Mg,Fe)_3(Fe,Al)_2[(O,OH,F)_2/Al_2Si_6O_{22}] +$
	$(Mg,Fe)_2[Si_2O_6] + K(Mg,Fe,Mn)_3[(OH,F)_2 \| (Al,Fe)Si_3O_{10}]$
	$+ NaAlSi_3O_8/CaAl_2Si_2O_8 + Ca_2(Fe,Al)Al_2[O \| OH \| SiO_4 \| Si_2O_7]$
Analcime	clear, white, grey, yellowish, reddish
Framework silicates	$Na[AlSi_2O_6] \cdot H_2O + K,Ca,Mg,Fe$
Danburite	clear, white, yellow, pale pink, greenish, brown
Framework silicates	$Ca[B_2Si_2O_8] + Al,Fe,Mg,Mn,Na$
Natrolite	white, yellow, reddish, brown
Framework silicates	$Na_2[Al_2Si_3O_{10}] \cdot 2\ H_2O + K,Ca,Ba,Sr,Fe$

◇ Rhombic structure/sedimentary origin (secondary)

Mineral/Rock	Colours
Mineral class	Chemical formulae
Sulphur	sulphur yellow, greenish, brownish
Natural elements	$S_8 + C,Se,Te$ + hydrocarbons
Markasite	brass yellow, possibility of colourful tinting
Sulphides	$FeS_2 + As,Co,Ni,Cr$
Schalenblende	yellow and grey layering
Sulphides	$ZnS + PbS + FeS_2$

Goethite quartz   clear or violet with yellow-brown clumps and nodules
Oxides and others $SiO_2 + FeOOH$

Gold quartz (tiger eye) golden yellow to brown
Oxides and others $SiO_2 + FeOOH$

Kalahari picture stone sand-coloured to brown
Oxides and others $SiO_2 + FeOOH + Fe_2O_3$

Limonite   black, brown to yellow-brown
Oxides $FeOOH \cdot n\ H_2O + Al,Ba,Ca,Mg,Mn,Ni,P,Si,V$

Moqui marbles   rust brown
Oxides $FeOOH \cdot n\ H_2O + Al,Ba,Ca,Mg,Mn,Ni,P,Si,V$

Oolite   light brown with small rust brown nodules
Oxides and others $SiO_2 + FeOOH \cdot n\ H_2O + Al,Ba,Ca,Mg,Mn,Ni,P,Si,V$

Pietersite   blue-black and/or yellow-brown brecciation
Oxides and others $SiO_2 + Na_2Mg_3Fe_2(OH/Si_4O_{11})_2 + Al,Ti + FeOOH$

Pop rocks (boji stones) dark grey to rust brown
Oxides $FeS_2 + FeOOH \cdot n\ H_2O$

Printstone   beige, red, brown stripes
Oxides and others $SiO_2 + Al_4[(OH)_8/Si_4O_{10}] + Fe_2O_3 + FeOOH$

Snake stone   dark brown with yellow-brown fossils
Oxides and others $CaCO_3 + Al_4[(OH)_8/Si_4O_{10}] + FeOOH$

Shiva lingam   beige/red/brown zones
Oxides and others $SiO_2 + Al_4[(OH)_8/Si_4O_{10}] + FeOOH + Fe_2O_3$

Stromatolite   brown-black stripes
Oxides and others $SiO_2 + CaCO_3 + Al_4[(OH)_8/Si_4O_{10}] \cdot n\ H_2O + FeOOH$

Tiger eye   golden yellow to brown
Oxides and others $SiO_2 + FeOOH$

Tsesite   brown to blackbrown
Oxides $FeOOH \cdot n\ H_2O + Al,Ba,Ca,Mg,Mn,Ni,P,Si,V$

Abalone (mother-of-pearl) colourful mussel shell
Carbonates $CaCO_3 + H_2O$ + conchiolin (organic compound)

Ammolite   brown with colourful fluorescence
Carbonates $CaCO_3 + Al,Ba,Cu,Fe,Mg,Mn,Sr,Pb,S$

Aragonite   white, yellow, brown, greenish, blue
Carbonates $CaCO_3 + Sr,Pb,Ba$

Calcoolite   brown with small reddish or beige nodules
Carbonates $CaCO_3 + Fe$

Onyx marble   white, yellow, brown and greenish stripes
Carbonates $CaCO_3 + Fe$

Pearls   white, creamy, grey, black
Carbonates $CaCO_3 + H_2O$ conchiolin (organic compound)

Mother-of-pearl   white, beige with a delicate or colourful gleam
Carbonates $CaCO_3 + H_2O$ + conchiolin (organic compound)

Septarian   stone grey to brown with white to yellow filling
Carbonates and others $CaCO_3 + Al_4[(OH)_8/Si_4O_{10}] \cdot n\ H_2O + K,Fe,Mg$

Strontianite   white, grey, pale yellowish, greenish or pink
Carbonates $SrCO_3 + Ca,Ba$

Purpurite   deep purple to red-violet
Phosphates $(Mn,Fe)PO_4 + Li,Na,Ca,H_2O$

Variscite   pale green to grass green
Phosphates $AlPO_4 \cdot 2\ H_2O + Fe,As,Cr,V$

Wavellite   white, greenish, yellow
Phosphates $Al_3[(OH)_3/(PO_4)_2] \cdot 5\ H_2O + Ca,Cr,F,Fe,Mg,Si,Sn$

Anhydrite	clear, white, grey, brown, reddish, bluish, light pink
Sulphates	$CaSO_4 + Ba,Sr$
Barytes	clear, brown, yellow, greenish, red, grey, bluish
Sulphates	$BaSO_4 + Ca,Pb,Sr$
Chrysanthemum stone	white-grey crystals in a grey-black matrix
Sulphates and others	$SrSO_4 + Ba,Ca + CaCO_3 + C$
Celestine	clear, white, yellowish, light blue, reddish, green
Sulphates	$SrSO_4 + Ba,Ca$
Hemimorphite	clear to turquoise blue, pink or brown
Group silicates	$Zn_4[(OH)_2/Si_2O_7] \cdot H_2O + Cu,Fe,Pb,Cd$
Cavansite	sky blue to greenish-blue
Sheet silicates	$Ca[VO/Si_4O_{10}] \cdot 6\ H_2O$
Sepiolite	white, yellowish, grey, reddish
Sheet silicates	$Mg_4[(OH)_2/Si_6O_{15}] \cdot 2\ H_2O + 4\ H_2O + Fe,Ca,Al,Ni$
Danburite	clear, white, yellow, pale pink, greenish, brown
Framework silicates	$Ca[B_2Si_2O_8] + Al,Fe,Mg,Mn,Na$
Natrolite	white, yellow, reddish, brown
Framework silicates	$Na_2[Al_2Si_3O_{10}] \cdot 2\ H_2O + K,Ca,Ba,Sr,Fe$

◇ Rhombic structure/metamorphic origin (tertiary)

| Mineral/Rock | Colours |
Mineral class	Chemical formulae
Antimonite	grey
Sulphides	$Sb_2S_3 + As,Bi,Se + (Au)$
Porcellanite	light grey, grey-green, brown, black
Sulphides and others	$Al_4[(OH)_8/Si_4O_{10}] + FeOOH + FeS \cdot n\ H_2O + CaCO_3$
Alexandrite	green in sunlight, red to violet under artifical light
Oxides	$Al_2BeO_4 + Cr,Fe,V$
Chrysoberyl	yellow, brownish to greenish
Oxides	$Al_2BeO_4 + Cr,Fe,Ti,V$
Diaspore	white, beige, pink or greenish
Oxides/Hydroxides	$AlO(OH) + Fe,Mn,Cr$
Porcellanite	light grey, grey-green, brown, black
Oxides and others	$Al_4[(OH)_8/Si_4O_{10}] + FeOOH + FeS \cdot n\ H_2O + CaCO_3$
Tiger iron	grey, yellow-brown, red to yellow stripes
Oxides and others	$SiO_2 + SiO_2/FeOOH + Fe_2O_3$
Sinhalite	yellowish-brown, greenish-brown
Borates	$MgAl[BO_4] + Fe$
Barytes	clear, brown, yellow, greenish, red, grey, bluish
Sulphates	$BaSO_4 + Ca,Pb,Sr$
Andalusite	grey, brown, yellowish, pink, greenish
Nesosilicates	$Al_2SiO_5 + Fe,Mn$
Blue aventurine quartz	light blue, dark blue, violet-blue, blue-black
Nesosilicates and others	$SiO_2 + (Al,Fe)_7[(O,OH)_3/BO_3/(SiO_4)_3]$
Blue quartz	light blue, dark blue (dumortierite quartzite)
Nesosilicates and others	$SiO_2 + (Al,Fe)_7[(O,OH)_3/BO_3/(SiO_4)_3]$
Bronzite peridotite	dark green-blue-grey
Nesosilicates and others	$(Mg,Fe)_2[SiO_4] + (Mg,Fe)_2[Si_2O_6]$
Chiastolite	white, grey, yellow, brown with a black cross
Nesosilicates	$Al_2SiO_5 + Fe,Mn,Cr + C$
Peridotite garnet	dark green, olive green, grey with red inclusions
Nesosilicates and others	$(Mg,Fe)_2[SiO_4] + Mn,Ca,Ni,Cr + Mg_3Al_2(SiO_4)_3$ and others

Pyroxenite garnet black, grey to green with red inclusions
Nesosilicates and others $CaMg[Si_2O_6] + (Mg,Fe)_2[Si_2O_6] + (Mg,Fe)_2[SiO_4] + (Mg,Fe)_3Al_2(SiO_4)_3$ and others

Sillimanite clear, grey, brownish, pale green
Nesosilicates $Al[AlSiO_5] + Fe$

Prehnite clear, pale green, yellow
Group silicates $Ca_2Al[(OH)_2|AlSi_3O_{10}] + Fe,Na,H_2O$

Tanzanite blue, blue-grey
Group silicates $Ca_2Al_3[O|OH|SiO_4|Si_2O_7] + Fe,Ti,V$

Thulite vintage pink, red to blackberry red
Group silicates $(Ca,Mn)_2Al_3[O|OH|SiO_4|Si_2O_7] + Na,Ba,Cr,Fe,Mg,Sr$

Zoisite brown, grey, green
Group silicates $Ca_2Al_3[O|OH|SiO_4|Si_2O_7] + Ba,Cr,Fe,Mg,Mn,Sr,V$

Zoisite with ruby (anyolite) green with red inclusions
Group silicates and others $Ca_2Al_3[O|OH|SiO_4|Si_2O_7] + Ba,Cr,Fe,Mg,Mn,Sr,V + Al_2O_3 + Cr,Fe$

Anthophyllite black, occasionally blue or yellow iridescence
Chain silicates $(Mg,Fe)_7[OH_2|Si_8O_{22}] + Fe,Al,Ti,Ca,Mn,Ni,Na,K,F$

Bronzite bronze, brown with golden yellow sparkles
Chain silicates $(Mg,Fe)_2[Si_2O_6] + Al,Ca,Mn,Ti,Cr,Na$

Bronzite peridotite dark green-blue-grey
Chain silicates and others $(Mg,Fe)_2[SiO_4] + (Mg,Fe)_2[Si_2O_6]$

Enstatite white, yellowish, green to brownish-green
Chain silicates $Mg_2[Si_2O_6] + Al,Ca,Fe,Mn,Ni,Cr,Ti$

Hermanov's sphere silver-grey to dark brown
Chain silicates and others $KMg_3[(F,OH)_2|AlSi_3O_{10}] + (Mg,Fe)_7[OH|Si_4O_{11}]_2 + Al,Ca,F,K + (Na,Mn,Ti)$

Nuummite black with golden yellow or colourful iridescence
Chain silicates $Mg_7(Si_8O_{22})(OH)_2 + Mg_5Al_2(Si_6Al_2O_{22})(OH)_2 + Fe,Ni,Mn,Ti,Ca,Na,K$

Cordierite blue, blue-grey, yellow
Ring silicates $(Mg,Fe)_2Al_3[AlSi_5O_{18}] + Na,K,Mn,H_2O$

Cordierite sunstone blue, blue-grey with brown inclusions
Ring silicates and others $(Mg,Fe)_2Al_3[AlSi_5O_{18}] + Na,K,Mn,H_2O + Fe_2O_3$

Serpentine chrysotile silvery green fibres
Sheet silicates $Mg_6[(OH)_8|Si_4O_{10}] + Fe,Ni,Al$

Danburite clear, white, yellow, pale pink, greenish, brown
Framework silicates $Ca[B_2Si_2O_8] + Al,Fe,Mg,Mn,Na$

Natrolite white, yellow, reddish, brown
Framework silicates $Na_2[Al_2Si_3O_{10}] \cdot 2\ H_2O + K,Ca,Ba,Sr,Fe$

Stellerite white, yellow pink, salmon pink, red, brown
Framework silicates $Ca[Al_2Si_7O_{18}] \cdot 7\ H_2O + Fe,K,Na$

▱ Monclinic structure/magmatic origin (primary)

Mineral/Rock	Colours
Mineral class	Chemical formulae

Orpiment golden yellow, orange, red to red-brown
Sulphides $As_2S_3 + Hg,Ge,Sb$

Eclipse golden yellow, orange in a grey-black matrix
Sulphides and others $As_2S_3 + Hg,Ge,Sb + CaCO_3$

Jamesonite lead grey, brown to grey-black
Sulphides $Pb_4FeSb_6S_{14} + Ag,Bi,Cu,Zn$

170

Jamesonite quartz
Sulphides and others

grey threads in clear quartz

$SiO_2 + Pb_4FeSb_6S_{14} + Ag,Bi,Cu,Zn$

Realgar
Sulphides

glowing red to red-orange

$As_4S_4 + (Ge,Sb,Se,V)$

Creedite
Halogenides

clear, white, pink to lilac

$Ca_3Al_2[F_8(OH)_2(SO_4)] \cdot 2\,H_2O + Cl,Fe,Sr$

Cryolite
Halogenides

white, grey, brown

$Na_3AlF_6 + (Ca,Fe)$

Psilomelane
Oxides

grey to black

$(Ba,H_2O)_2Mn_5O_{10} + K,Na,Ca,Mg,Sr,Fe,Ti$

Azurite
Carbonates

light blue, azure blue to blue-black

$Cu_3[(OH)_2|(CO_3)_2] + (Ca,Fe,Mg,Co,Zn,Mn)$

Azurite malachite
Carbonates

blue and green

$Cu_3[(OH)_2|(CO_3)_2] + Cu_2[(OH)_2/CO_3] + H_2O + (Ca,Fe,Mg,Co,Zn,Mn)$

Eclipse
Carbonates and others

golden yellow, orange in a grey-black matrix

$As_2S_3 + Hg,Ge,Sb + CaCO_3$

Eilat stone
Carbonates and others

green/turquoise blue

$(Cu,Al)_2[H_2Si_2O_5(OH)_4] \cdot n\,H_2O + Cu_2[(OH)_2|CO_3] + Cu_3[(OH)_2|(CO_3)_2]$

Malachite
Carbonates

pale green to a powerful dark green

$Cu_2[(OH)_2|CO_3] + H_2O + (Zn,Co,Ni)$

Brazilianite
Phosphates

clear, pale yellow to yellowish-green

$NaAl_3[(OH)_2/PO_4]_2 + K,Fe,Cl,F$

Lazulite
Phosphates

light blue to dark blue

$(Mg,Fe)Al_2[OH/PO_4]_2 + Ca,Mn$

Wolframite
Wolframates

brownish-black

$(Fe,Mn)WO_4 + Ca,Nb,Sc,Sn,Ta,Ti + (In)$

Euclase
Nesosilicates

clear, sea green, light blue to deep blue

$AlBe[OH|SiO_4] + Fe,Zn,F$

Titanite (sphene)
Nesosilicates

yellow, green, brown, black, rarely pink, violet

$CaTi[O/SiO_4] + Al,Ce,Cl,Cr,F,Fe,K,Mn,Mg,Na,Nb,Sn,Sr,Th,V,Y,Zr,SE$

Porphyrite
Group silicates and others

dark grey with white or greenish phenocrysts

$Ca_2(Na,K)(Mg,Fe)_3(Fe,Al)_2[(O,OH,F)_2/Al_2Si_6O_{22}] + (Mg,Fe)_2[Si_2O_6] + K(Mg,Fe,Mn)_3[(OH,F)_2|(Al,Fe)Si_3O_{10}] + NaAlSi_3O_8/CaAl_2Si_2O_8 + Ca_2(Fe,Al)Al_2[O|OH|SiO_4|Si_2O_7]$

Aegirine
Chain silicates

dark green, greenish-black, black, brown

$NaFe[Si_2O_6] + Al,Ca,Mg,Mn,Ti,V,Zr$

Aegirine augite
Chain silicates

black

$(Na,Ca)(Fe,Mg,Al)[Si_2O_6]$

Actinolite quartz
Chain silicates and others

green crystals in clear quartz

$SiO_2 + Ca_2(Mg,Fe)_5[(OH)_2|Si_8O_{22}] + Na,K,Al,Cr,Cl,F,Mn,H_2O$

Augite
Chain silicates

black, more rarely dark green or brown

$(Ca,Na)(Mg,Fe,Ti,Al)[(Si,Al)_2O_6] + Na,Mn,Zn,Cr,V$

Basalt
Chain silicates and others

dark grey, greenish, brown to red

$Na[AlSi_3O_8] + Ca[Al_2Si_2O_8] + (Ca,Na)(Mg,Fe,Ti,Al)[(Si,Al)_2O_6]$

Diopside
Chain silicates

white, grey, green, light blue, blue-violet, black

$CaMg[Si_2O_6] + Cr,Fe,Na,Al,Mn,Zn,Ti$

Eldarite
Chain silicates and others

light green-dark green with round aggregates

$NaFe[Si_2O_6] + SiO_2 + KAlSi_3O_8 + NaAlSi_3O_8$

Gabbro
Chain silicates and others

brown-black with white inclusions

$(Mg,Fe)_2[Si_2O_6] + NaAlSi_3O_8/CaAl_2Si_2O_8 + (Mg,Fe)_2[SiO_4]$

Hiddenite green to yellow-green
Chain silicates $LiAl[Si_2O_6]$ + Na,K,Cr,Fe,Mn

Hornblende dark green, dark brown or black
Chain silicates $Ca_2(Na,K)(Mg,Fe)_3(Fe,Al)_2[(O,OH,F)_2/Al_2Si_6O_{22}]$ + Mn,Ti

Kimberlite grey to greenish-grey breccia
Nesosilicates and others $Mg_6[(OH)_8|Si_4O_{10}]$ + $(Mg,Fe)_2[SiO_4]$ + $(Mg,Fe)_2[Si_2O_6]$ +
　　　　　　　　　　　$Ca(Mg,Cr)[Si_2O_6]$ + $(Fe,Mg)TiO_3$ + $Mg_3Al_2(SiO_4)_3$ u.a.

Kunzite pale to intense pink or pink-violet
Chain silicates $LiAl[Si_2O_6]$ + Fe,Mn

Porphyrite dark grey with white or greenish phenocrysts
Group silicates and others $Ca_2(Na,K)(Mg,Fe)_3(Fe,Al)_2[(O,OH,F)_2/Al_2Si_6O_{22}]$ + $(Mg,Fe)_2$
　　　　　　　　　　　　$[Si_2O_6]$ + $K(Mg,Fe,Mn)_3[(OH,F)_2|(Al,Fe)Si_3O_{10}]$ + $NaAlSi_3O_8$/
　　　　　　　　　　　　$CaAl_2Si_2O_8$ + $Ca_2(Fe,Al)Al_2[O|OH|SiO_4|Si_2O_7]$

Richterite blue, green, yellow, brown
Chain silicates $NaCaNaMg_5(Si_8O_{22})(OH)_2$ + K,Fe,Mn,Al,Ti

Chrysocolla blue-green, turquoise
Ring silicates $(Cu,Al)_2[H_2Si_2O_5(OH)_4]\cdot$ n H_2O

Eilat stone green/turquoise blue
Ring silicates and others $(Cu,Al)_2[H_2Si_2O_5(OH)_4]\cdot$ n H_2O + $Cu_2[(OH)_2|CO_3]$ +
　　　　　　　　　　　$Cu_3[(OH)_2|(CO_3)_2]$

Tree agate white with green inclusions
Sheet silicates and others SiO_2 + $(Mg,Fe,Al)_{12}[(Si,Al)_8O_{20}(OH)_{16}]$

Biotite dark grey, brownish, black
Sheet silicates $K(Mg,Fe,Mn)_3[(OH,F)_2|(Al,Fe)Si_3O_{10}]$ + Ca,Ba,Li,Na,Rb,Ti

Chlorite quartz clear with green inclusions
Sheet silicates and others SiO_2 + $Mg_5AlSi_3AlO_{10}(OH)_8$ + Fe,Cr,Mn,Ni,Zn,Ti

Granite grey, brown, red, pink, yellow, green, bluish speckles
Sheet silicates and others $KAlSi_3O_8$ + $NaAlSi_3O_8/CaAl_2Si_2O_8$+ SiO_2 +
　　　　　　　　　　　　$K(Mg,Fe,Mn)_3[(OH,F)_2|(Al,Fe)Si_3O_{10}]$

Kimberlite grey to greenish-grey breccia
Nesosilicates and others $Mg_6[(OH)_8|Si_4O_{10}]$ + $(Mg,Fe)_2[SiO_4]$ + $(Mg,Fe)_2[Si_2O_6]$ +
　　　　　　　　　　　$Ca(Mg,Cr)[Si_2O_6]$ + $(Fe,Mg)TiO_3$ + $Mg_3Al_2(SiO_4)_3$ u.a.

Lepidolite red-violet to blue-violet
Sheet silicates $K(Li,Al)_3[(OH,F)_2|AlSi_3O_{10}]$ + Na,Rb,Cs,Fe,Mn,Mg,Ca,Ba,Sr,Nb,Ti

Muscovite clear, silver-grey, yellow
Sheet silicates $KAl_2[(OH,F)_2|AlSi_3O_{10}]$ + Na,Rb,Cs,Ca,Ba,Mg,Fe,Mn,Li,Cr,Ti,V

Green opal (chloropal) yellow-green, grass green to dark green
Sheet silicates and others $SiO_2\cdot$ n H_2O + $Na_{0.3}Fe_2(Si,Al)_4O_{10}(OH)_2\cdot$ 4 H_2O

Petalite clear, white, grey, greenish, yellowish, pink
Sheet silicates $LiAl[Si_4O_{10}]$ + Na,Fe,Mn

Phlogopite grey to brown
Sheet silicates $KMg_3[(F,OH)_2|AlSi_3O_{10})$ + Ca,Ba,Li,Na,Rb,Ti

Porphyrite dark grey with white or greenish phenocrysts
Group silicates and others $Ca_2(Na,K)(Mg,Fe)_3(Fe,Al)_2[(O,OH,F)_2/Al_2Si_6O_{22}]$ + $(Mg,Fe)_2[$
　　　　　　　　　　　　$Si_2O_6]$ + $K(Mg,Fe,Mn)_3[(OH,F)_2|(Al,Fe)Si_3O_{10}]$ + $NaAlSi_3O_8/CaAl$
　　　　　　　　　　　　$_2Si_2O_8$ + $Ca_2(Fe,Al)Al_2[O|OH|SiO_4|Si_2O_7]$

Amazonite green to turquoise
Framework silicates $(K,Na)[AlSi_3O_8]$ + Ca,Ba,Pb,Fe,H_2O

Analcime clear, white, grey, yellowish, reddish
Framework silicates $Na[AlSi_2O_6]\cdot H_2O$ + K,Ca,Mg,Fe

Albite green-brown mottling
Framework silicates $KAlSi_3O_8$ + $NaAlSi_3O_8$ + Ca,Ba,Pb,Fe,H_2O

172

Heulandite
clear, white, yellow, green, red
Framework silicates
$(Ca,Na_2,K_2)_4(Al_8Si_{28}O_{72}) \cdot 24\ H_2O + Ba,Fe,Sr,Mg$

Larvikite
grey with labradorescent inclusions
Framework silicates and others $KAlSi_3O_8 + Ca,Na,Fe + NaAlSi_3O_8/CaAl_2Si_2O_8 + Fe,\ K$ u.a.

Metarhyolite
grey, brown, beige, yellowish, reddish, green
Framework silicates and others $SiO_2 + Fe,Al$ u.a.

Moonstone
white, yellow, green, grey, black, adularescent
Framework silicates
$KAlSi_3O_8/NaAlSi_3O_8 + Fe,Ca,Ba,Sr,Mg$

Orthoclase
white, yellowish, reddish, brown
Framework silicates
$KAlSi_3O_8 + Na,Ca,Mg,Fe,Ba$

Scolecite
white, grey yellowish to brownish
Framework silicates
$Ca[Al_2Si_3O_{10}] \cdot 3\ H_2O + Na,K,Sr$

Stilbite
white, yellowish, reddish or brown
Framework silicates
$NaCa_2Al_2[Al_5Si_{13}O_{36}] \cdot 14\ H_2O + Fe,K,Na,Sr$

◻ Monclinic structure/sedimentary origin (secondary)

Mineral/Rock	Colours
Mineral class	Chemical formulae

Jamesonite
lead grey, brown to grey-black
Sulphides
$Pb_4FeSb_6S_{14} + Ag,Bi,Cu,Zn$

Realgar
glowing red to red-orange
Sulphides
$As_4S_4 + (Ge,Sb,Se,V)$

Cryolite
white, grey, brown
Halogenides
$Na_3AlF_6 + (Ca,Fe)$

Psilomelane
grey to black
Oxides
$(Ba,H_2O)_2Mn_5O_{10} + K,Na,Ca,Mg,Sr,Fe,Ti$

Sonora Sunrise
red, black, green, blue
Oxides and others
$Cu_2O + CuO + Cu_4[(OH)_6\,|\,SO_4] + (Cu,Al)_2[H_2Si_2O_5(OH)_4] \cdot n\ H_2O$

Azurite
light blue, azure blue to blue-black
Carbonates
$Cu_3[(OH)_2\,|\,(CO_3)_2] + (Ca,Fe,Mg,Co,Zn,Mn)$

Azurite malachite
blue and green
Carbonates
$Cu_3[(OH)_2\,|\,(CO_3)_2]+Cu_2[(OH)_2/CO_3]+H_2O+(Ca,Fe,Mg,Co,Zn,Mn)$

Eilat stone
green/turquoise-blue
Carbonates and others
$(Cu,Al)_2[H_2Si_2O_5(OH)_4] \cdot n\ H_2O + Cu_2[(OH)_2\,|\,CO_3] +$
$Cu_3[(OH)_2\,|\,(CO_3)_2]$

Malachite
pale green to a powerful dark green
Carbonates
$Cu_2[(OH)_2\,|\,CO_3] + H_2O + (Zn,Co,Ni)$

Borax
white, grey, yellow
Borates
$Na_2B_4O_7 \cdot 10\ H_2O + K,Li,NH_3$

Lazulite
light blue to dark blue
Phosphates
$(Mg,Fe)Al_2[OH/PO_4]_2 + Ca,Mn$

Vivianite
clear, blue, blue-green, black
Phosphates
$Fe_3(PO_4)_2 \cdot 8\ H_2O + Mg,Mn,Si$

Erythrin
dark pink to peach blossom red
Arsenates
$Co_3[AsO_4]_2 \cdot 8\ H_2O + Fe,Ni,Zn,P$

Alabaster (gypsum)
grey, white, yellow, orange, reddish, brown
Sulphates
$CaSO_4 \cdot 2H_2O + Na,K,Al,Fe,Ba,Sr,C$

Gypsum
grey, white, beige, yellow, orange, reddish, brown
Sulphates
$CaSO_4 \cdot 2H_2O + Na,K,Al,Fe,Ba,Sr,C$

Sand rose
sand-coloured to brown
Sulphates and others
$SiO_2 + CaSO_4$

Selenite (gypsum) clear, white
Sulphates $CaSO_4 \cdot 2H_2O + Na,K,Al,Fe,Ba,Sr,C$
Sonora Sunrise red, black, green, blue
Sulphates and others $Cu_2O + CuO + Cu_4[(OH)_6|SO_4] + (Cu,Al)_2[H_2Si_2O_5(OH)_4] \cdot n\,H_2O$
Crocoite red, yellow-red, orange
Chromates $PbCrO_4 + S,Zn$
Howlite white to beige with brown or grey veins
Nesosilicates $Ca_2(BOOH)_5SiO_4 + Fe,Mn,Na,K,Sr,Ba$
Hawk's eye blue-grey to blue-black, also green-black
Chain silicates and others $SiO_2 + Na_2Mg_3Fe_2(OH/Si_4O_{11})_2 + Al,Ti$
Pietersite blue-black and/or yellow-brown brecciation
Chain silicates and others $SiO_2 + Na_2Mg_3Fe_2(OH/Si_4O_{11})_2 + Al,Ti + FeOOH$
Chrysocolla blue-green, turquoise
Ring silicates $(Cu,Al)_2[H_2Si_2O_5(OH)_4] \cdot n\,H_2O$
Eilat stone green/turquoise blue
Ring silicates and others $(Cu,Al)_2[H_2Si_2O_5(OH)_4] \cdot n\,H_2O + Cu_2[(OH)_2|CO_3] + Cu_3[(OH)_2|(CO_3)_2]$
Gem silica light blue to turquoise
Ring silicates and others $SiO_2 \cdot n\,H_2O + (Cu,Al)_2[H_2Si_2O_5(OH)_4] \cdot n\,H_2O$
Sonora Sunrise red, black, green, blue
Ring silicates and others $Cu_2O + CuO + Cu_4[(OH)_6|SO_4] + (Cu,Al)_2[H_2Si_2O_5(OH)_4] \cdot n\,H_2O$
Printstone beige, red, brown stripes
Sheet silicates and others $SiO_2 + Al_4[(OH)_8/Si_4O_{10}] + Fe_2O_3 + FeOOH$
Snake stone dark brown with yellow-brown fossils
Sheet silicates and others $CaCO_3 + Al_4[(OH)_8/Si_4O_{10}] + FeOOH$
Septarian stone grey to brown with white to yellow filling
Sheet silicates and others $CaCO_3 + Al_4[(OH)_8/Si_4O_{10}] \cdot n\,H_2O + K,Fe,Mg$
Shiva lingam beige/red/brown zones
Sheet silicates and others $SiO_2 + Al_4[(OH)_8/Si_4O_{10}] + FeOOH + Fe_2O_3$
Stichtite serpentinite dark pink to light pink in a green-yellow matrix
Sheet silicates and others $Mg_6[(OH)_8|Si_4O_{10}] + Mg_6Cr_2[(OH)_{16}|(CO_3)] \cdot 4\,H_2O + Al,Fe,Ni$
Stromatolite brown-black stripes
Sheet silicates and others $SiO_2 + CaCO_3 + Al_4[(OH)_8/Si_4O_{10}] \cdot n\,H_2O + FeOOH$
Heulandite clear, white, yellow, green, red
Framework silicates $(Ca,Na_2,K_2)_4(Al_8Si_{28}O_{72}) \cdot 24\,H_2O + Ba,Fe,Sr,Mg$
Klinoptilolite white, light grey, beige
Framework silicates $(K,Na,Ca)_{2-3}[(Si,Al)_{18}O_{36}] \cdot 11\,H_2O$
Scolecite white, grey, yellowish to brownish
Framework silicates $Ca[Al_2Si_3O_{10}] \cdot 3\,H_2O + Na,K,Sr$
Stilbite white, yellowish, reddish or brown
Framework silicates $NaCa_2Al_2[Al_5Si_{13}O_{36}] \cdot 14\,H_20 + Fe,K,Na,Sr$

⬜ Monclinic structure/metamorphic origin (tertiary)

| Mineral/Rock | Colours |
Mineral class	Chemical formulae
Jamesonite lead	grey, brown to grey-black
Sulphides	$Pb_4FeSb_6S_{14} + Ag,Bi,Cu,Zn$
Jamesonite quartz	grey threads in clear quartz
Sulphides and others	$SiO_2 + Pb_4FeSb_6S_{14} + Ag,Bi,Cu,Zn$
Realgar	glowing red to red-orange
Sulphides	$As_4S_4 + (Ge,Sb,Se,V)$

Lazulite light blue to dark blue
Phosphates $(Mg,Fe)Al_2[OH/PO_4]_2$ + Ca,Mn

Euclase clear, sea green, light blue to deep blue
Nesosilicates $AlBe[OH|SiO_4]$ + Fe,Zn,F

Staurolite red-brown to black-brown
Nesosilicates $FeAl_4[O|OH|SiO_4]_2$ + Li,Mg,Cr,Zn,Mn,Ti,Co

Garnet schist staurolite silver-grey with brown and red-brown inclusions
Nesosilicates and others $KAl_2[(OH,F)_2|AlSi_3O_{10}]$ + $(Fe,Mg)_3Al_2(SiO_4)_3$ +
$FeAl_4[O|OH|SiO_4]_2$ + Li,Mg,Cr,Zn,Mn,Ti,Co

Titanite (sphene) yellow, green, brown, black, rarely pink, violet
Nesosilicates $CaTi[O/SiO_4]$ +
Al,Ce,Cl,Cr,F,Fe,K,Mn,Mg,Na,Nb,Sn,Sr,Th,V,Y,Zr,SE

Red aventurine quartz raspberry red to violet-brown (piemontite quartzite)
Group silicates and others SiO_2 + $(Ca,Mn)_2Al_3[O|OH|SiO_4|Si_2O_7]$

Epidote green to brown-black
Group silicates $Ca_2(Fe,Al)Al_2[O|OH|SiO_4|Si_2O_7]$ + Cr,Mg,Mn,Sr,Ti,Pb,V,Th

Snowflake epidote green-white mottling
Group silicates and others $Ca_2(Fe,Al)Al_2[O|OH|SiO_4|Si_2O_7]$ + Cr,Mg,Mn,Sr,Ti,Pb,V,Th +
$KAlSi_3O_8$ + Fe,Na,Ca,Ba,Sr,Mg

Epidote quartz clear with green-black or silvery threads
Group silicates and others SiO_2 + $Ca_2(Fe,Al)Al_2[O|OH|SiO_4|Si_2O_7]$ +
Cr,Mg,Mn,Sr,Ti,Pb,V,Th

Piemontite vintage pink, red to red-brown
Group silicates $(Ca,Mn)_2Al_3[O|OH|SiO_4|Si_2O_7]$ + Na,Ba,Cr,Fe,Mg,Sr

Unakite (epidote granite) green-pink mottling
Group silicates and others $Ca_2(Fe,Al)Al_2[O|OH|SiO_4|Si_2O_7]$ + Cr,Mg,Mn,Sr,Ti,Pb,V,Th +
$KAlSi_3O_8$ + Fe,Na,Ca,Ba,Sr,Mg

Actinolite dark green, grass green, grey-green
Chain silicates $Ca_2(Mg,Fe)_5[(OH)_2|Si_8O_{22}]$ + Na,K,Al,Cr,Cl,F,Mn,H_2O

Actinolite quartz green crystals in clear quartz
Chain silicates and others SiO_2 + $Ca_2(Mg,Fe)_5[(OH)_2|Si_8O_{22}]$ + Na,K,Al,Cr,Cl,F,Mn,H_2O

Amphibolite black-and-white speckles
Chain silicates and others $(Na,K)_{0-1}Ca_2(Mg,Fe,Al)_5[(OH)_2|Si_{6-7.5}Al_{2-0.5}O_{22}]$ +
$NaAlSi_3O_8/CaAl_2Si_2O_8$

Augite black, more rarely dark green or brown
Chain silicates $(Ca,Na)(Mg,Fe,Ti,Al)[(Si,Al)_2O_6]$ + Na,Mn,Zn,Cr,V

Chrome diopside intense green
Chain silicates $Ca(Mg,Cr)[Si_2O_6]$ + Fe,Na,Al,Mn,Zn,Ti

Diopside white, grey, green, light blue, blue-violet, black
Chain silicates $CaMg[Si_2O_6]$ + Cr,Fe,Na,Al,Mn,Zn,Ti

Eclogite grey-green to green with red-brown inclusions
Chain silicates and others $(Na,Ca)(Mg,Fe,Al)[(Si,Al)_2O_6]$ + Cr,Ti,K +
$(Mg,Fe,Ca)_3Al_2[Si_3O_{12}]$ + Mn,Cr,Ti

Glaucophane schist blue-grey with red-brown and other inclusions
Chain silicates and others $Na_2(Mg,Fe)_3(Al,Fe)_2[(OH)_2|Si_8O_{22}]$ + F,Cl,Ti,Mn,Cr,Ca +
$(Mg,Fe)_3Al_2(SiO_4)_3$ u.a.

Amphibolite garnet black-and-white speckles with brown inclusions
Chain silicates and others $(Na,K)_{0-1}Ca_2(Mg,Fe,Al)_5[(OH)_2|Si_{6-7.5}Al_{2-0.5}O_{22}]$ +
$NaAlSi_3O_8/CaAl_2Si_2O_8$ + $(Fe,Mg)_3Al_2(SiO_4)_3$ u.a.

Pyroxenite garnet black, grey to green with red inclusions
Chain silicates and others $CaMg[Si_2O_6]$ + $(Mg,Fe)_2[Si_2O_6]$ + $(Mg,Fe)_2[SiO_4]$ +
$(Mg,Fe)_3Al_2(SiO_4)_3$ u.a.

Hornblende   dark green, dark brown or black
Chain silicates $Ca_2(Na,K)(Mg,Fe)_3(Fe,Al)_2[(O,OH,F)_2/Al_2Si_6O_{22}] + Mn,Ti$

Jadeite   green, yellow, brown, light pink, lilac, black
Chain silicates $NaAl[Si_2O_6] + Ca,Cr,Fe,Mg,Mn$

Lapis lazuli   blue with small white or golden spots
Chain silicates and others $(Na,Ca)_8[(SO_4,S,Cl)_2 | (AlSiO_4)_6] + CaCO_2 + FeS_2 + CaMg[Si_2O_6]$

Lavender jade   lilac to lavender
Chain silicates $Na(Al,Mn)[Si_2O_6] + Ca,Cr,Fe,Mg$

Mawsitsite   intense green with dark sections
Chain silicates and others $Na[AlSi_3O_8] + Ca,K + (Na,K)(Mg,Ca,Sr,Ba)[Al_xSi_yO_z] \cdot n\ H_2O + (Mg,Fe)_5Al[(Si_3Al)O_{10}(OH)_8] + Na(Al,Cr)[Si_2O_6]$

Metagabbro   black-and-white foliation
Chain silicates and others $(Na,K)_{0-1}Ca_2(Mg,Fe,Al)_5[(OH)_2 | Si_{6-7.5}Al_{2-0.5}O_{22}] + NaAlSi_3O_8/CaAl_2Si_2O_8$

Nephrite   green to green-black
Chain silicates $Ca_2(Mg,Fe)_5[(OH,F)_2 | Si_8O_{22}] + Al,Na,Cr$

Prase   grass green to leek green
Chain silicates and others $SiO_2 + Ca_2(Mg,Fe)_5[(OH)_2 | Si_8O_{22}]$

Quartz cat's eye   grey with a silver sheen
Chain silicates and others $SiO_2 + Ca_2(Na,K)(Mg,Fe)_3(Fe,Al)_2[(O,OH,F)_2/Al_2Si_6O_{22}]$

Richterite   blue, green, yellow, brown
Chain silicates $NaCaNaMg_5(Si_8O_{22})(OH)_2 + K,Fe,Mn,Al,Ti$

Tremolite   white, green, brown, blue
Chain silicates $Ca_2Mg_5[(OH)_2 | Si_8O_{22}] + Fe,Al,Mn,Zn,F$

Green aventurine quartz light green to glittering dark green
Sheet silicates and others $SiO_2 + K(Al,Cr)_2[(OH,F)_2 | AlSi_3O_{10}]$

White aventurine quartz white to light grey
Sheet silicates and others $SiO_2 + KAl_2[(OH,F)_2 | AlSi_3O_{10}]$

Biotite   dark grey, brownish, black
Sheet silicates $K(Mg,Fe,Mn)_3[(OH,F)_2 | (Al,Fe)Si_3O_{10}] + Ca,Ba,Li,Na,Rb,Ti$

Budstone   grass green, dark green to black-green
Sheet silicates and others $NaAlSi_3O_8/CaAl_2Si_2O_8 + K(Al,Cr)_2[(OH,F)_2 | AlSi_3O_{10}]$

Charoite   violet to grey-violet
Sheet silicates $(Ca,Na)_4(K,Sr,Ba)_2[(OH,F)_2Si_9O_{22}] \cdot H_2O + Fe,Mn$

Chlorite   light green to dark green
Sheet silicates $Mg_5AlSi_3AlO_{10}(OH)_8 + Fe,Cr,Mn,Ni,Zn,Ti$

Chlorite quartz   clear with green inclusions
Sheet silicates and others $SiO_2 + Mg_5AlSi_3AlO_{10}(OH)_8 + Fe,Cr,Mn,Ni,Zn,Ti$

Fuchsite   green
Sheet silicates $K(Al,Cr)_2[(OH,F)_2 | AlSi_3O_{10}] + Ca,Fe,Mg,Mn,Na,Ti,V$

Fuchsite disthene   green/light blue
Sheet silicates and others $K(Al,Cr)_2[(OH,F)_2 | AlSi_3O_{10}] + Ca,Fe,Mg,Mn,Na,Ti,V + Al_2SiO_5 + Fe,Cr$

Mica schist   silver-grey, rust brown
Sheet silicates and others $KAl_2[(OH,F)_2 | AlSi_3O_{10}]$ und/oder $K(Mg,Fe,Mn)_3[(OH,F)_2 | (Al,Fe)Si_3O_{10}]$ u.a.

Gneiss   white, grey, greenish, yellow, pink, red stripes
Sheet silicates and others $SiO_2 + KAlSi_3O_8 + NaAlSi_3O_8 + KAl_2[(OH,F)_2 | AlSi_3O_{10}]$ und/oder $K(Mg,Fe,Mn)_3[(OH,F)_2 | (Al,Fe)Si_3O_{10}]$ u.a.

Mica schist garnet   silver-grey to brown with red-brown inclusions
Sheet silicates and others $KAl_2[(OH,F)_2 | AlSi_3O_{10}]$ und/oder $K(Mg,Fe,Mn)_3[(OH,F)_2 | (Al,Fe)Si_3O_{10}] + (Fe,Mg)_3Al_2(SiO_4)_3$ u.a.

Green quartz   light green to glittering dark green
Sheet silicates and others $SiO_2 + K(Al,Cr)_2[(OH,F)_2 | AlSi_3O_{10}]$
Hermanov's sphere   silver-grey to dark brown
Sheet silicates and others $KMg_3[(F,OH)_2 | AlSi_3O_{10}] + (Mg,Fe)_7[OH | Si_4O_{11}]_2 +$
$Al,Ca,F,K + (Na,Mn,Ti)$
Mawsitsite   intense green with dark sections
Sheet silicates and others $Na[AlSi_3O_8] + Ca,K + (Na,K)(Mg,Ca,Sr,Ba)[Al_xSi_yO_z] \cdot n\ H_2O$
$+ (Mg,Fe)_5Al[(Si_3Al)O_{10}(OH)_8] + Na(Al,Cr)[Si_2O_6]$
Muscovite   clear, silver-grey, yellow
Sheet silicates $KAl_2[(OH,F)_2 | AlSi_3O_{10}] + Na,Rb,Cs,Ca,Ba,Mg,Fe,Mn,Li,Cr,Ti,V$
Ophicalcite   light green to dark green with white veins
Sheet silicates and others $Mg_6[(OH)_8 | Si_4O_{10}] + Fe,Ni,Al + CaCO_3 +$
Mg,Fe,Sr oder $CaMg(CO_3)_2 + Fe$
Phlogopite   grey to brown
Sheet silicates $KMg_3[(F,OH)_2 | AlSi_3O_{10}) + Ca,Ba,Li,Na,Rb,Ti$
Porcellanite   light grey, grey-green, brown, black
Sheet silicates and others $Al_4[(OH)_8/Si_4O_{10}] + FeOOH + FeS \cdot n\ H_2O + CaCO_3$
Pyrophyllite   white, grey, light green, light blue, brown
Sheet silicates $Al_4[(OH)_4 | (Si_8O_{20})] + Mg,Fe,Ti$
Ruby disthene   fuchsite red/blue/green
Sheet silicates and others $Al_2O_3 + Al_2SiO_5 + K(Al,Cr)_2[(OH,F)_2 | AlSi_3O_{10}] +$
Ca,Fe,Mg,Mn,Na,Ti,V,Cr
Seraphinite (clinochlore) grass to pine green with a fibrous texture
Sheet silicates $(Mg,Fe)_5Al[(Si_3Al)O_{10}(OH)_8] + Cr,Mn,Ni,Zn + (Ti)$
Serpentine antigorite   yellow-green, green, olive green to black
Sheet silicates $Mg_6[(OH)_8 | Si_4O_{10}] + Fe,Ni,Al$
Spanish olivine   brown/grey/green zones
Sheet silicates and others $Mg_6[(OH)_8 | Si_4O_{10}] + (Mg,Fe)_2[SiO_4] + Ni,Al$
Sphalerite magnetite in serpentine greenish-yellow with brown inclusions
Sheet silicates and others $Mg_6[(OH)_8 | Si_4O_{10}] + ZnS + Fe_3O_4$
Garnet schist staurolite silver-grey with brown and red-brown inclusions
Sheet silicates and others $KAl_2[(OH,F)_2 | AlSi_3O_{10}] + (Fe,Mg)_3Al_2(SiO_4)_3 +$
$FeAl_4[O | OH | SiO_4]_2 + Li,Mg,Cr,Zn,Mn,Ti,Co$
Steatite (talc)   greenish, white, grey, yellowish, brownish
Sheet silicates $Mg_3[(OH)_2/Si_4O_{10}] + Al,Fe,Ti,Ni,Mn$
Stichtite serpentinite   dark pink to light pink in a green-yellow matrix
Sheet silicates and others $Mg_6[(OH)_8 | Si_4O_{10}] + Mg_6Cr_2[(OH)_{16} | (CO_3)] \cdot 4\ H_2O + Al,Fe,Ni$
Verdite striped   brown-green or schistose
Sheet silicates and others $K(Al,Cr)_2[(OH,F)_2 | AlSi_3O_{10}] + NaAlSi_3O_8 +$
$(Mg,Fe)_5Al[(Si_3Al)O_{10}(OH)_8]$ and others
Snowflake epidote   green-white mottling
Framework silicates and others $Ca_2(Fe,Al)Al_2[O | OH | SiO_4 | Si_2O_7] + Cr,Mg,Mn,Sr,Ti,$
$Pb,V,Th + KAlSi_3O_8 + Fe,Na,Ca,Ba,Sr,Mg$
Gneiss   white, grey, greenish, yellow, pink, red stripes
Framework silicates and others $SiO_2 + KAlSi_3O_8 + NaAlSi_3O_8 + KAl_2[(OH,F)_2 | AlSi_3O_{10}]$
and/or $K(Mg,Fe,Mn)_3[(OH,F)_2 | (Al,Fe)Si_3O_{10}]$ u.a.
Heulandite   clear, white, yellow, green, red
Framework silicates $(Ca,Na_2,K_2)_4(Al_8Si_{28}O_{72}) \cdot 24\ H_2O + Ba,Fe,Sr,Mg$
Stilbite   white, yellowish, reddish or brown
Framework silicates $NaCa_2Al_2[Al_5Si_{13}O_{36}] \cdot 14\ H_2O + Fe,K,Na,Sr$
Unakite (epidote granite) green-pink mottling
Framework silicates and others $Ca_2(Fe,Al)Al_2[O | OH | SiO_4 | Si_2O_7] + Cr,Mg,Mn,Sr,$
$Ti,Pb,V,Th + KAlSi_3O_8 + Fe,Na,Ca,Ba,Sr,Mg$

Allalin gabbro grey-green mottling
Silicates (diverse) $Ca,Na)(Mg,Fe,Al)[Si_2O_6] + Na(Al,Fe)[Si_2O_6]$ and others

△ Triclinic structure/magmatic origin (primary)

Mineral/Rock	Colours
Mineral class	Chemical formulae

Amblygonite   clear, grey, white, blue, green, yellow, pink, light pink
Phosphates $LiAl[(F,OH)|PO_4] + Na,Fe$
Larimar   light blue-white
Chain silicates $Ca_2Na[HSi_3O_9] + (Cu,Fe,K,Mn,V)$
Rhodonite   pink, rarely raspberry red
Chain silicates $CaMn_4[Si_5O_{15}] + Fe,Zn$
Astrophyllite   bronze brown, golden yellow, orange
Chain/sheet silicates $(K,Na)_3(Fe,Mn)_7Ti_2[(O,OH,F)_7(Si_4O_{12})_2] + Li, Mg,Ca,Cs,Al,Zr,Nb$
Albite   white, grey, yellowish, reddish, pale blue, light green
Framework silicates $Na[AlSi_3O_8] + Ca,K + (Fe,Mn,Mg,Ba,Sr,Pb)$
Amazonite   green to turquoise
Framework silicates $(K,Na)[AlSi_3O_8] + Ca,Ba,Pb,Fe,H_2O$
Basalt   dark grey, greenish, brown to red
Framework silicates and others $Na[AlSi_3O_8] + Ca[Al_2Si_2O_8] + (Ca,Na)(Mg,Fe,Ti,Al)[(Si,Al)_2O_6]$
Bronzite-Gabbro   black with glittering gold-yellow flecks
Tectosilicates and others $NaAlSi_3O_8/CaAl_2Si_2O_8 + (Mg,Fe)_2[Si_2O_6]$
Albite   green-brown mottling
Framework silicates $KAlSi_3O_8 + NaAlSi_3O_8 + Ca,Ba,Pb,Fe,H_2O$
Eldarite   light green-dark green with round aggregates
Framework silicates and others $NaFe[Si_2O_6] + SiO_2 + KAlSi_3O_8 + NaAlSi_3O_8$
Gabbro   brown-black with white inclusions
Framework silicates and others $(Mg,Fe)_2[Si_2O_6] + NaAlSi_3O_8/CaAl_2Si_2O_8 + (Mg,Fe)_2[SiO_4]$
Galaxite   black with labradorescent inclusions
Framework silicates and others $(Mg,Fe)_2[Si_2O_6] + NaAlSi_3O_8/CaAl_2Si_2O_8$
Granite   grey, brown, red, pink, yellow, green, bluish dappling
Framework silicates and others $KAlSi_3O_8 + NaAlSi_3O_8/CaAl_2Si_2O_8 + SiO_2 +$
                           $K(Mg,Fe,Mn)_3[(OH,F)_2|(Al,Fe)Si_3O_{10}]$
Labradorite   white, yellow, green, grey, black, colourful fluorescence
Framework silicates $NaAlSi_3O_8/CaAl_2Si_2O_8 + K,Mg,Sr,Ba,Ti,Fe,Mn$
Larvikite   grey with labradorescent inclusions
Framework silicates and others $KAlSi_3O_8 + Ca,Na,Fe + NaAlSi_3O_8/CaAl_2Si_2O_8 + Fe, K$ u.a.
Metarhyolite   grey, brown, beige, yellowish, reddish, green
Framework silicates and others $SiO_2 + Fe,Al$ u.a.
Microcline   white, grey, bluish, green, yellowish, pink, brown
Framework silicates $K[AlSi_3O_8] + Ca,Ba,Fe,H_2O$
Moonstone   white, yellow, green, grey, black, adularescent
Framework silicates $KAlSi_3O_8/NaAlSi_3O_8 + Fe,Ca,Ba,Sr,Mg$
Porphyrite   dark grey with white or greenish phenocrysts
Group silicates and others $Ca_2(Na,K)(Mg,Fe)_3(Fe,Al)_2[(O,OH,F)_2/Al_2Si_6O_{22}] + (Mg,Fe)_2$
                           $[Si_2O_6] + K(Mg,Fe,Mn)_3[(OH,F)_2|(Al,Fe)Si_3O_{10}] + NaAlSi_3O_8/Ca$
                           $Al_2Si_2O_8 + Ca_2(Fe,Al)Al_2[O|OH|SiO_4|Si_2O_7]$
Sunstone   copper red to glittering orange-brown
Framework silicates $Na[AlSi_3O_8] + Ca[Al_2Si_2O_8] + Fe/Cu,K,Ba,Sr,Mn,Ti$

◻ Triclinic structure/sedimentary origin (secondary)

Mineral/Rock	Colours
Mineral class	Chemical formulae

Ulexite
white
Borates
$NaCa[B_5O_6(OH)_6] \cdot 5\ H_2O + K,Mg$

Turquoise
green, turquoise, light blue
Phosphates
$CuAl_6[(OH)_2 | (PO_4)_4 \cdot 4\ H_2O + Fe,Zn,Ca$

Chalcanthite
green-blue to blue
Sulphates
$CuSO_4 \cdot 5\ H_2O + Fe,Mg,Co$

Printstone
beige, red, brown stripes
Sheet silicates and others $SiO_2 + Al_4[(OH)_8/Si_4O_{10}] + Fe_2O_3 + FeOOH$

Snake stone
dark brown with yellow-brown fossils
Sheet silicates and others $CaCO_3 + Al_4[(OH)_8/Si_4O_{10}] + FeOOH$

Septarian stone
grey to brown with white to yellow filling
Sheet silicates and others $CaCO_3 + Al_4[(OH)_8/Si_4O_{10}] \cdot n\ H_2O + K,Fe,Mg$

Shiva lingam
beige/red/brown zones
Sheet silicates and others $SiO_2 + Al_4[(OH)_8/Si_4O_{10}] + FeOOH + Fe_2O_3$

Stromatolite
brown-black stripes
Sheet silicates and others $SiO_2 + CaCO_3 + Al_4[(OH)_8/Si_4O_{10}] \cdot n\ H_2O + FeOOH$

◻ Triclinic structure/metamorphic origin (tertiary)

Mineral/Rock	Colours
Mineral class	Chemical formulae

Disthene (kyanite)
blue, blue-green, yellow-green, grey, black
Nesosilicates
$Al_2SiO_5 + Fe,Cr$

Fuchsite disthene
green-light blue
Nesosilicates and others $K(Al,Cr)_2[(OH,F)_2 | AlSi_3O_{10}] + Ca,Fe,Mg,Mn,Na,Ti,V + Al_2SiO_5 + Fe,Cr$

Ruby disthene
red to red-violet in a blue coating
Nesosilicates and others $Al_2O_3 + Al_2SiO_5 + Cr,Fe$

Ruby disthene
fuchsite red/blue/green
Nesosilicates and others $Al_2O_3 + Al_2SiO_5 + K(Al,Cr)_2[(OH,F)_2 | AlSi_3O_{10}] + Ca,Fe,Mg,Mn,Na,Ti,V,Cr$

Axinite
clear, grey, yellow, pink, violet-brown
Group silicates
$(Ca,Mn)_2(Fe,Mg,Mn)Al_2[O | OH | B(Si_2O_7)_2]$

Bustamite
pale pink to brown-red
Chain silicates
$(Mn,Ca,Fe)_3[Si_3O_9] + Mg,Zn$

Rhodonite
pink, rarely raspberry red
Chain silicates
$CaMn_4[Si_5O_{15}] + Fe,Zn$

Porcellanite
light grey, grey-green, brown, black
Sheet silicates and others $Al_4[(OH)_8/Si_4O_{10}] + FeOOH + FeS \cdot n\ H_2O + CaCO_3$

Albite
white, grey, yellowish, reddish, pale blue, light green
Framework silicates
$Na[AlSi_3O_8] + Ca,K + (Fe,Mn,Mg,Ba,Sr,Pb)$

Amphibolite
black-and-white speckles
Framework silicates and others $(Na,K)_{0-1}Ca_2(Mg,Fe,Al)_5[(OH)_2 | Si_{6-7.5}Al_{2-0.5}O_{22}] + NaAlSi_3O_8/CaAl_2Si_2O_8$

Budstone
grass green, dark green to black-green
Framework silicates and others $NaAlSi_3O_8/CaAl_2Si_2O_8 + K(Al,Cr)_2[(OH,F)_2 | AlSi_3O_{10}]$

Gneiss
white, grey, greenish, yellow, pink, red stripes
Framework silicates and others $SiO_2 + KAlSi_3O_8 + NaAlSi_3O_8 + KAl_2[(OH,F)_2 | AlSi_3O_{10}]$ and/or $K(Mg,Fe,Mn)_3[(OH,F)_2 | (Al,Fe)Si_3O_{10}]$ and others

Amphibolite garnet   black-and-white speckles with brown inclusions
Framework silicates and others $(Na,K)_{0-1}Ca_2(Mg,Fe,Al)_5[(OH)_2 | Si_{6-7.5}Al_{2-0.5}O_{22}] +$
        $NaAlSi_3O_8/CaAl_2Si_2O_8 + (Fe,Mg)_3Al_2(SiO_4)_3$ u.a.

Mawsitsite   intense green with dark sections
Framework silicates and others $Na[AlSi_3O_8] + Ca,K + (Na,K)(Mg,Ca,Sr,Ba)[Al_xSi_yO_z] \cdot n$
        $H_2O + (Mg,Fe)_5Al[(Si_3Al)O_{10}(OH)_8] + Na(Al,Cr)[Si_2O_6]$

Metagabbro   black-and-white foliation
Framework silicates and others $(Na,K)_{0-1}Ca_2(Mg,Fe,Al)_5[(OH)_2 | Si_{6-7.5}Al_{2-0.5}O_{22}] +$
        $NaAlSi_3O_8/CaAl_2Si_2O_8$

Verdite   striped brown-green or schistose
Framework silicates and others $K(Al,Cr)_2[(OH,F)_2 | AlSi_3O_{10}] + NaAlSi_3O_8 +$
        $(Mg,Fe)_5Al[(Si_3Al)O_{10}(OH)_8]$ u.a.

◯ Amorphous stones/magmatic origin (primary)

Mineral/Rock	Colours
Mineral class	Chemical formulae

Cinnabarite opal   clear-grey with red inclusions
Oxides/silicates and others $SiO_2 \cdot n\,H_2O + HgS + Zn,Sb,Cu$

Girasol opal   clear to cloudy
Oxides/silicates $SiO_2 \cdot n\,H_2O + Al$

Obsidian   black, grey, brown
Oxides/silicates $SiO_2 + Al_2O_3 + K,Na,Fe,Ca + (Mg,Ti)$

Opal, Andean opal   clear, white to light blue
Oxides/silicates $SiO_2 \cdot n\,H_2O + Al,Fe$

Opal, blue   light blue to dark blue
Oxides/silicates $SiO_2 \cdot n\,H_2O + Al,Fe$

Opal, chrysopal   green-turquoise to blue-green
Oxides/silicates $SiO_2 \cdot n\,H_2O + Cu$

Opal, dendritic   white, light blue with black dendrites
Oxides/silicates and others $SiO_2 \cdot n\,H_2O + MnO_2$

Opal, noble opal   clear, white, grey, black with opalescence
Oxides/silicates $SiO_2 \cdot n\,H_2O + Al,Fe$

Opal, fire opal   orange to fiery red
Oxides/silicates $SiO_2 \cdot n\,H_2O + Fe$

Opal, green (chloropal)   yellow-green, grass green to dark green
Oxides/silicates and others $SiO_2 \cdot n\,H_2O + Na_{0.3}Fe_2(Si,Al)_4O_{10}(OH)_2 \cdot 4\,H_2O$

Opal, Honduran opal   black with small opalescent spots
Oxides/silicates and others $SiO_2 \cdot n\,H_2O + Al,Fe,Mn$

Opal, milky opal   white to creamy colours
Oxides/silicates $SiO_2 \cdot n\,H_2O + Al,Fe$

Opal, moss opal   white, yellow, brownish with inclusions
Oxides/silicates $SiO_2 \cdot n\,H_2O + Al,Fe$

Opal, pink opal   pale pink to a powerful pink
Oxides/silicates $SiO_2 \cdot n\,H_2O + Mn$

Opal, pistachio opal   garish green
Oxides/silicates $SiO_2 \cdot n\,H_2O + Ni$

Opal, prase opal   light green to apple green
Oxides/silicates $SiO_2 \cdot n\,H_2O + Ni$

Opal, Veta opal   black with white, opalescent veins
Oxides/silicates and others $SiO_2 \cdot n\,H_2O + Al,Fe,Mn$

Opal, water opal   clear to transparent as water
Oxides/silicates $SiO_2 \cdot n\,H_2O + Al,Fe$

Amorphous stones/sedimentary origin (secondary)

Mineral/Rock Mineral class	Colours Chemical formulae
Flint Oxides/silicates	black, grey, brown, red-brown, bluish $SiO_2 \cdot n\ H_2O + Al,Fe$
Hornstone Oxides/silicates	brown, grey, yellow, red, also colourful/multi-coloured $SiO_2 \cdot n\ H_2O + Al,Fe$
Mookaite Oxides/silicates	white, beige, yellow, red, red-violet $SiO_2 + Fe,O,OH$
Opal, blue Oxides/silicates	light blue to dark blue $SiO_2 \cdot n\ H_2O + Al,Fe$
Opal, boulder opal Oxides/silicates and others	colourful noble opal in a brown matrix $SiO_2 \cdot n\ H_2O + Fe,O,OH$
Opal, dendritic Oxides/silicates and others	white, light blue with black dendrites $SiO_2 \cdot n\ H_2O + MnO_2$
Opal, noble opal Oxides/silicates	clear, white, grey, black with opalescence $SiO_2 \cdot n\ H_2O + Al,Fe$
Opal, matrix opal Oxides/silicates and others	colourful noble opal, finely distributed in a matrix $SiO_2 \cdot n\ H_2O + Fe,O,OH$
Opal, milky opal Oxides/silicates	white to creamy colours $SiO_2 \cdot n\ H_2O + Al,Fe$
Opal, moss opal Oxides/silicates and others	white, yellow, brownish with inclusions $SiO_2 \cdot n\ H_2O + Al,Fe$
Opalite Oxides/silicates	white, yellow, brownish, partially marbled $SiO_2 \cdot n\ H_2O + Fe,O,OH$
Tiffany stone Oxides/silicates and others	beige-violet $CaF_2 + SiO_2 \cdot n\ H_2O$
Fossilized wood Oxides/silicates	yellow-brown, red-brown, brown-grey $SiO_2 \cdot n\ H_2O + Fe,O,OH$
Amber Organic resin	white, yellow, brown, black, bluish, greenish approx. 78% C, 10% H, 11% O
Copal Organic resin	white, yellow, brown approx. 77% C, 13% H, 10% O
Gagat (jet) Organic rock	black approx. 83% C, 5% H, 10% O, 0,1% N

Amorphous stones/metamorphic origin (tertiary)

Mineral/Rock Mineral class	Colours Chemical formulae
Fulgurite Oxides/silicates	sand-coloured, grey $SiO_2 + Al,Fe,Mg,Ti,C$
Libyan Desert glass Oxides/silicates	yellow $SiO_2 + Al,Fe,Mg,Ti$
Moldavite Oxides/silicates	bottle green, more rarely grass green $SiO_2 + Al_2O_3 + Ca,K,Fe,Mg + (Na,Ti,Mn)$
Tektite Oxides/silicates	black, rarely olive green $SiO_2 + Al_2O_3 + Ca,K,Fe,Mg,Na,K,Sr,Ba$
Shungite Organic rock	black C_n

To identify the right healing crystal, first, identify the individual lifestyle (crystal system) and the present general situation (manner of formation) independently of the problems that currently exist. This will immediately and clearly show you the choice of possible healing minerals and crystals.

The fundamental characteristic feature of the present problem will then lead you to the right mineral class. Does something need dissolving, transforming, fortifying or stabilizing? The minerals that are then left to choose from can be further differentiated by looking at the mineral-forming substances from which they are formed. Then, by considering the colour, you will be able to home in on the right choice of mineral.

The mineral selected should be used in an appropriate way (see the Practical applications chapter, page 200) for as long as it takes for a clear change in conditions, lifestyle, a solution to the existing problem, or an improvement in the case of illness to become apparent. There may be some 'initial aggravation' or 'worsening', but this will usually last for no more than one to three days, rarely a week.

If there is no improvement or initial worsening goes beyond an acceptable degree or beyond the specified time limit, the analysis should be rechecked and corrected, if necessary. Here we recommend the basic principle 'success through minimal change', which means working through the tables 'backwards', from right to left.

Will the same mineral, but of a different colour, result in the desired success? Are there varieties or related minerals with a different content of mineral-forming substances? Does the solution of the problem require a basically different characteristic (mineral class)? Was the person's life situation analysed properly (crystal system)? If you are basically satisfied with your analysis, then, as a rule, only minor details will need altering. In extreme cases success can be achieved with the same mineral with a slightly different appearance or from a different location.

This is where we meet the boundaries of the analytical art of healing with crystals and minerals. The basic principles described here should lead to the right mineral, but choosing exactly the right stone is often a matter that is not accessible to rational thought or logic.

Trust in your own 'instinct', or the feeling you have for the person for whom the stone is intended. Choose exactly the one that 'appeals' to you, independently of its shape, beauty or quality. And please note that a strong antipathy for a particular crystal or stone registers a 'response' to it just as much as a strong attraction does.

A 'neutral stone', one that leaves you completely cold, should be ignored, as should those that do not interest you or that you might even overlook. In cases of uncertainty, simply choose the right one with your eyes closed – or use a dowsing procedure or kinesiology if you are familiar with these techniques.

In healing, intuition is just as important as rational thinking and logic. You can only use logic to analyse something on which you already have information and of which you are aware. Intuition will often take you that final step on the way. This is the reason why the next chapter is dedicated to 'intuitive' healing with crystals.

2.3 The intuitive art of healing with crystals

Choosing your healing crystals

Before you start to read this chapter, I should like to invite you to do a little test. All you will need for this is a handful of minerals (about 15–20) and a helper. Once you have both, proceed as follows.

Spread out the minerals in front of you on a table top or on the floor. Now, spontaneously pick one that you like. Do not evaluate, do not think about what you are doing or about its name, simply look and take one.

You have just intuitively chosen your first healing crystal: you chose it with your eyes.

Next, close your eyes and ask your helper to rearrange the stones so that you no longer know where each one is. Now pass your left hand, eyes closed, across the stones spread out before you. Do this for as long as it takes for you to feel an impulse to pick one up. Do not hesitate, just do it!

Now you have chosen your second healing crystal intuitively: you chose it with your hand.

Now ask your helper to call out individual keywords that match any of the stones lying in front of you, words that refer to the properties and healing powers of the stones. There should never be any indication which keyword goes with which stone. If a keyword is called out that spontaneously means something to you, or stirs something within (whether pleasant or unpleasant), say so immediately and let your helper give you the stone to which the keyword fits.

In this way, you will have intuitively chosen your third healing crystal. It was chosen by means of a word.

Next, ask your helper to lay out the stones in a row but invisible to you (for example, behind a screen of some kind). Then let your helper tell you how many stones have been laid in the row, and you then spontaneously name a number between one and the total number of stones. Your helper should then pass you the stone that is lying in the row in the position you have chosen.

In this way, you will have intuitively chosen the fourth crystal: it was chosen 'at random'.

These four crystals will now represent your personal healing crystals at this moment in time. Each of these crystals will, of course, represent a different quality, another facet of yourself as each method of choosing includes or excludes certain areas.

Choosing with your eyes: the soul stone

When we look at things, we also immediately make comparisons. Our subconscious will always compare a visual impression with old memories and experiences. This is done with lightning speed, much faster than you would be able to do consciously.

Just think what is happening when you walk along a path. You are constantly taking in impressions, and you are recognizing things you see: trees, stones, flowers, grasses, birds, and so on. Now imagine you had to walk along the same path and call out by name everything you met. Everything! You would only manage a few metres an hour!

This demonstrates the incredible faculties of our subconscious or our soul. The soul is our inner world of images (our 'inner world') that has stored all impressions and experiences. The soul perceives everything, nothing is lost – something we are made conscious of through unexpected memories of things we had thought we had forgotten long ago. During this process, every new impression is not just simply stored away but is compared, similarities are recorded and assigned. The new impression will be carefully sorted and stored.

This process will also automatically stir up old memories: the feelings and images connected with past experiences will emerge. This is the reason why we feel attractions or antipathies to certain things, people or situations. If there exists an early, similar experience that we felt was positive, this will automatically create sympathy (attraction, affection).

Conversely, if the present experience reminds us of something that was negative, we will experience antipathy (revulsion, disgust). Our subconscious will always compare and find similarities! It will string similar experiences together and then conclude that the outcome of what is happening now will be similar to something that happened in the past.

All of this happens almost exclusively in the subconscious. As already described above, we do not think about all this, merely respond accordingly: we trust the one situation and mistrust the other. We avoid certain people and are attracted by others, sometimes we feel quite safe while at other times our 'inner alarm bells' go off!

The meaning and purpose of this soul quality is simply – survival. We all learn from experience or we are meant to. The collected experiences of the past and that rapid 'intelligence' (or grasp) of the soul increase our chances of survival. We recognize dangers more quickly, make some mistakes only once and, based on our facility for remembering, we have some bearings by which to steer our lives.

Just imagine that you were only able to remember things that happened within the last 24 hours, and everything previous to that time was forgotten. How would you be able to conduct your life at present? There would be no real opportunity for learning anything at all; no social life; you would not possess a real identity. In addition, the soul controls our unconscious bodily functions and actions.

Just think what it would be like to have to drive your car in a fully conscious manner all the time, as you did in your first driving lesson: steering, changing gears, clutch, accelerating, braking, indicating, looking about. You would be continuously occupied and driving would be extremely exhausting. If, however, all these actions are safely 'stored' for further use, you are able to drive 'unconsciously' and your attention is free to concentrate on the traffic.

This means that automatic or instinctive reactions that are not under our conscious control belong to the soul also. The soul is our inner treasure, the sum total of our capabilities that we need to lead our lives. In the soul, all has been collected together that we have brought with us from the past: experiences, events, stories and images that have impressed themselves upon us in one way or another.

This does mean, however, that we have one weak point: some of the images and explanations we have absorbed from others will be wrong, that is, they will not be appropriate to our own experience. As long as we hang on to these, they will keep leading us to wrong conclusions.

This is also true for some of the experiences from our childhood, which may no longer be appropriate for our adult lives. Some of our other inner images will weigh heavily on us. They may represent unpleasant experiences and cause negative manifestations in our lives the moment we are (consciously or unconsciously) reminded of them.

Among these are, in particular, all memories connected with

pain – *traumas* (Greek trauma, 'wound'). Because everything in our inner soul life is treated in the same way, in situations of extreme stress, serious illness, violent pain, shock, unconsciousness (also under anaesthetic!), under the influence of alcohol, drugs, strong medication or during sleep, the same thing happens: the ability of our reasoning side to differentiate and discriminate is greatly diminished or is switched off altogether. This is not, however, the case for the soul's willingness to perceive and absorb; that will always (!) be retained. This means that all sensory perceptions we are subject to in such moments are treated in the same way.

This can lead to tragic consequences: for example, suppose you fall off your bicycle on a wet road and hit your head so that you are unconscious for a few moments (a 'black-out'). Your subconscious will connect all sensory perception during those moments with pain. The accident is stored away in a kind of formula that reads: pain = wet road (touch) = pedestrians in raincoats (visual) = screeching car brakes (hearing) = traffic fumes (smell) = blood in your mouth (taste).

This, in turn, means that all those different perceptions you had during those moments are now connected and perceived as painful. Precisely because you no longer remember all this later on, the 'false' storage process is retained and determines your future life. From now on, wet roads, pedestrians in raincoats, screeching car brakes, traffic fumes and the taste of blood will trigger off the most unpleasant sensations that may even result in spontaneous black-outs – depending on how painful the experience was.

It also means that, in future, you will do everything you can to avoid any of these sensory perceptions: avoiding walking on wet streets, refusing to buy a raincoat, and so on. There may be a useful point in the message 'take care on wet roads', but all the other negatively loaded impressions represent an unnecessary limitation of your actions, and furthermore can produce the risk of making you respond with total panic to similar situations in the future.

The reactive responses are quasi-mechanical, being triggered by something from outside (without will or attention). It is precisely this type of response that can often lead us to repeat negative experiences over and over again.

Our souls are our inner treasure and Pandora's box in one. The soul contains dormant experiences that help and support us when we think of them and others that limit us or stop us from using our capabilities and opportunities; some experiences may even be like 'time bombs' that are dangerous to 'touch'. The soul is both a source of power and a battlefield, depending on what images it is fed with.

The crystal you have chosen for your soul with your eyes (it must have triggered a response to some memory, or you would not have chosen it) may tell you different things:

1. It may awaken a memory in you that is supportive and strengthening and is, therefore, like recovery or leisure for you. You will soon feel this by its beneficial effect. Images and memories may increasingly pop up in your dreams. Many (but not all) dreams are first and foremost the soul's image-processing faculty (sorting process), out of which may come revelations, realizations and creative ideas.

2. The stone may endow you with trust in your own inherent capabilities and bring to light again qualities that have been dormant for a long time. In such a case, simply follow those spontaneously appearing inclinations and interests, especially if you know that you used to carry them out successfully in the past.

3. The stone may respond to an unpleasant memory that you have suppressed and may, therefore, churn things up inside you. Again, you will notice this very quickly and the important thing is to accept what is happening and face the emerging feelings and images without blocking them. In this way, the stone may help you to dissolve a 'falsely' stored event or an old misunderstanding. I should like to give you a little help here: in my own experience, only those things that are 'ripe' will come up, or in other words, we are only confronted with things that we are ready and able to handle.

4. The stone may represent something that would be a beneficial experience for you. It may remind you of that holiday you have been meaning to take for ages, or prompt you to remember something that urgently needs seeing to. Allow your soul to experience new images – the stone will show you which ones.

Whichever one of these four possibilities applies, the crystal or stone will help you find out, or you will find out yourself by simply trying it out. Having chosen it visually, it will be sufficient to lay it somewhere where you will look at it often. Or meditate daily with the stone by quietly contemplating it. Just looking at the stone will have an effect …

Choosing with the hand: the stone for your body

The second stone was chosen by you without your being able to see it. The impulse to pick it up came from your own body. Our bodies possess a very finely tuned sensitivity that is always present, even if we are not consciously aware of it. We are very capable of sensing what is good for us and what is not. Depending on our general state at a given moment we will automatically choose things that will help us balance ourselves – in this case a stone that represents a balancing factor for an inner deficiency or excess.

Our entire body works on a range of systems in equilibrium. We absorb nourishment and fluids when we require them and eliminate excess substances or fluids when there is too much of them. Every breath is calculated to take in the necessary oxygen and exhale excess carbon dioxide. If we require warmth, we release it from stored energy (fuels). If we require cooling, we obtain relief by the evaporation of perspiration.

The characteristic feature of a living system is that it is able to keep what it needs for life in a constant state of balance. This means we possess a large number of regulatory mechanisms that keep energy and substances in equilibrium. The metabolism of nutrients, vitamins, mineral substances, hormones, acids and alkaline levels are all regulated with these mechanisms. You could define physical good health as having an organism in a position to maintain an inner equilibrium of all systems at all times.

The harmful habits in our lives – unbalanced diet, stress, overwork, toxins, negative images and thoughts, or spiritual developments that we push at such a rate that our being is not able to adjust to them at the right pace – all these will often upset our inner equilibrium. This will result in a partial failure of our regulatory mechanisms, leading to deficiencies or excesses in the relevant areas of life.

A more balanced lifestyle can help these imbalances to rectify by themselves during the course of time, except that we do not always have that much time. Sometimes, when we refuse to give ourselves this time, perhaps it is because we have already ended up in a life-threatening situation that requires quick action or because we no longer know how to get back to that balanced way of life.

In those cases, it is a good idea to reach for suitable outside sources of help. However, the precise meaning of the expression 'sources of help' is important here. The source should be something that will help us regain our inner equilibrium and not just represent an outer substitute for what is lacking inside. Only by seeing it in this manner will you be able to distinguish between different medications and therapies and decide whether they make sense or are dubious.

In emergencies – I should like to emphasize this here – any form of help that ensures survival is right! The difference between this and a long-term, proper healing of a problem, however, is great. Therapies that provide information, like homeopathy, the Bach flower remedies, aromatherapy or the art we are dealing with here, offer immense advantages. They do not introduce any substances into the body, but instead provide the information needed to give us the means of finding our own inner equilibrium again, thus activating our own self-healing processes.

For this to happen, the information needs to fit the situation exactly. It has to be exactly the right key to open the locked door. The method of finding the right key with an analytical process by reasoning alone has been provided by the previous chapter, The art of analytical healing with crystals. Here, we shall be encountering a second, equally valid way that is based on simple laws:

We will always look for something 'outside' that is missing 'inside'!

This is why, when your eyes are closed, your hand will find you exactly the right stone that will give your body the information it needs. At the precise moment when your hand is close to the stone, the information radiated by the stone will already begin to have an effect. Your body will already be registering the first indications for regaining that inner equilibrium and will receive the impulse 'Grab this!'

You can trust it. There is no finer instrument than your body, a fact proven by the numerous methods such as radiaesthesia (dowsing) (Latin *radius*, 'ray', Greek *aisthesis*, 'perception') and kinesiology (the knowledge of movement; Greek *kinesis*, 'movement', *logos*, 'knowledge, teaching'), with the help of which we can repeatedly measure or identify qualities for which no physical measuring instruments exist!

Your body has two fundamental functions: it is your instrument of perception and also the means by which you act in this material world. It is perfectly adapted for these two tasks (remember, it has been evolving for millions of years). Just how perfect it is can be appreciated by noting the feeble attempts of modern science at duplicating its capabilities. Most of what we desire and wish to experience is carried out with this body, so the body stone you have chosen will demonstrate the following possibilities:

1. The stone will encourage your body to heal itself as it helps to regulate a disturbed inner equilibrium. In this case, it may initially cause temporary worsening, but will, in the long term, create a sense of well-being. This means that, to begin with, you will be more conscious of the existing imbalance. By continuing to use the stone (perhaps with short breaks) these temporary worsenings will dissolve by themselves.

2. The stone will help you improve the capabilities of your body. Depending on what is involved, this will occur through an improvement in your ability to perceive or by extending the scope of your actions. Your body will be able to accomplish more than you believe at the moment. With this attitude you will support the influence of the stone most effectively.

3. The stone will put you in touch properly with your own body. This alone will have pain-relieving and healing results but will also lead to your being able to gauge your physical needs better and to understand them. Every instrument, including your body, needs looking after but, unfortunately, we are often inclined to spend more effort on the care of our cars than on our bodies. At least you take your car regularly for servicing, and do not drive it into the ground.

To allow your body stone to unfold its full potential, if possible wear it next to your skin. You may lie down in a quiet moment and allow yourself to feel it working inside. Place it wherever it appears to produce the feeling of greatest well-being. Try out two or three positions until you find the right place, and then simply enjoy it!

Choosing via the word : the stone for the intellect
During this process of choosing, you were neither able to see the stone nor touch it, the only connection to it being through the

spoken word that stimulated you to choose it. This is not an unusual way of choosing.

It happens, for example, if you acquire a stone through reading the information in a book. This is your reasoning making the choice, as it is your reasoning that assigns a certain image to a sequence of sounds. Naturally, your reasoning is not entirely free of inner (spiritual) influences as they will automatically emerge whenever an image conjured up by a specific word appears before our mind's eye.

Still, this choice is a conscious one, compared with choosing visually. Whenever we choose a stone with our eyes, we are not in a position to know which feature or characteristic it was that 'spoke' to us. Perhaps the colour, the shape or was it a finer perception, its aura or similar, something that is just below the threshold of conscious perception? Perhaps we believe we know what it was but it remains a belief, a typical function of the soul.

When choosing via a word, we know what qualities of the stone are addressing us, that is the very ones named, and here we touch on the fundamental quality of reason: the urge for knowledge. While the soul believes that a momentary situation represents a previous one, your reason wants to know for sure. For this, it requires a further instrument the soul does not possess: the ability to discriminate.

The soul always draws parallels and sees things as being the same; your reason is able to do that but also discriminates. It is in a position to define what exactly about a situation is similar to another previous one and what is different.

Your reason is the instrument for avoiding 'faulty storage of memories' (as discussed in the section Choosing with your eyes: the soul stone, see page 185) or undoing such a process later by remembering a past experience consciously and analysing it (dissolving, analysing, Greek ana-lyein, 'to dissolve'). Your reasoning power is in a position to dissolve equalizing procedures that were incorrectly carried out.

Your reasoning corresponds to your waking state or consciousness. It is able to communicate via language and works with words, thoughts and images. It is important to emphasize this as we use many words for which we have no real inner images! Do you know what the words 'transformer', 'politics', 'index', 'studio', 'assistant' or 'therapist' really mean? Have a look in your dictionary! It is really quite interesting to see what we are jabbering about daily: for example, the word just used – 'interesting' – is from the Latin interesse, 'being between things', which means that if you find something interesting, something exists between you and the object you are observing. Did you know that?

With the help of our reasoning powers, we think, which means that we understand and interpret whatever is happening. Your reasoning will not simply recreate past experiences, but instead is able to develop something new out of completely different sources, coming partly from your own experiences and partly from external information.

Your reasoning serves to solve problems (Greek *problema*, 'the task, the matter at hand'). Your reason will proceed logically (correct sequence), associatively (spontaneously connecting up different thoughts) or inspirationally (following inspiration). Its thought processes are always perceived, that is, we are conscious of them. It serves as a conscious control over our bodies and our lives.

The problem of reasoning lies in the fact that it has a far lesser capacity to absorb than has our soul and also works much more slowly (think of the example above with the walk along a path). Obviously, the ability to discriminate takes up more time. This makes sense, as different things really do need to be understood first (all the details and connections) before they can be compared with each other. Identifying and sorting by similarities is a much faster process.

If our reasoning does not understand a particular thing it becomes 'hung up'. This means it will focus all its attention on this thing it does not understand, until we either consciously leave it be or define the thing we do not understand for ourselves (Latin *definire*, 'to delimit'), in this way finding an explanation that helps us to distinguish this 'thing' from other things.

The more we collect things we have not understood, the more our attention becomes distracted and the more the ability of our reasoning to assimilate is reduced. The best example for this state is that of the 'absent-minded professor'.

This problem can get so out of hand that our reasoning is almost totally switched off, as it is constantly occupied with puzzles it has not solved and is, therefore, unable to pay attention to the present We also start to become 'reactive', which means we act according to the dictates of our subconscious.

Then we have no other option but to deal with these unresolved problems one after the other. Every problem solved, even if it is only the clear definition of a word, helps us regain a piece of consciousness.

Unanswered questions also tend to lead to doubts. As long as two contradictory pieces of information are present, our reasoning will not find peace until it is able to distinguish which piece is correct and which is not. Doubt, therefore, stimulates decision making: either through a logical process of balancing arguments or by trying out. This is the only way to free our reasoning again.

Our reasoning is the instrument for further development of our being. It is, therefore, very important to keep it free for present experiences and also for expanding our consciousness as well as we can. Every form of learning belongs in this category, as learning increases our ability to think and understand.

Bearing all this in mind, the reasoning stone you chose by means of a word can have the following meanings:

1. It can serve to increase your consciousness and guide your attention to present matters. The type of stone will show what you need to pay particular attention to. The stone will help you to control your life or your body more consciously. You will find that certain mechanisms and routines can now be changed if you so wish.

2. The stone reflects the way you think and communicate. It also represents your world view, your ideals and your ideas. Often, we are inclined to turn something into an ideal that is particularly distanced from our own reality. The stone you chose will help you to turn your ideal into reality but will, initially, confront you with reality. All this follows the motto: 'Knowing yourself is the first step towards improvement'.

3. The stone can represent a current problem and can help you develop a creative solution. In this case, depending on the stone involved, logical conclusions, chains of ideas or sudden impulsive actions may emerge. In all cases, it will serve to help you understand your situation or it may simply show you which project or possible course of action to embark on consciously.

The reasoning stone serves the flow of information. The best way to encourage its effect is by interacting with it: carry it around with you, gaze at it, meditate with it and – very important – obtain information on its mythological, mineralogical and healing nature.

Always approach any information you gather with the following question: 'What do these statements (whether symbolic or real) have to do with my situation, the current problem, my task or my imminent projects?' Use Part 1 of this book, in particular, for this process. You will be inundated with ideas!

Choosing at random: the stone for the spirit

The question is, of course, whether it really is at random, or rather, how does the stone become chosen? To begin with, it is certain that neither the soul (you were unable to see it), nor your body (you did not touch it), nor your reasoning (you were given no clues) interfered with the choosing of this stone. So, it had to be a higher authority that dealt you this stone. This higher authority could be nobody other than yourself!

As you may have already noticed when reading the explanations for the soul, body and reasoning, you are neither your soul (that merely represents your memory store, your world of images), nor are you your body (which is your tool in the material world), nor your reasoning (representing your manner of thinking). So, who are you then?

Like all of us you are a free spirit being, which means that you have a soul, a body and reasoning facilities, but you are in actual fact spirit! You are a creative, non-material being that uses an earthly body in order to be able to act in a material world and have experiences in it. However, your perception and your circle of action and effectiveness go far beyond the framework of your physical body.

Just think about how often you knew things in advance: for example, you knew at the first shrill ring of the telephone who would be at the other end, or you suddenly drove more slowly just before you reached a dangerous spot in heavy traffic, or you suddenly thought intensely of a certain person and did not find out until later what was happening to that person at that precise moment. How often did you ignore a feeling or inner warning and then later said, 'I just knew it!'

We do, in fact, perceive a great deal more than would be possible merely through our physical senses. We have many small experiences that confirm again and again that, as spiritual beings, we are not tied to space and time. When I was about sixteen years old, my mother had the embarrassing knack of catching me out whenever I tried to sneak into the house late at night. No matter what time it was, she always woke up when I got home, and this in spite of the fact that I was a master at opening doors silently, and negotiating creaking stairs …

Further proof of our creative faculties as spiritual beings are those statements, or postulates, we are in the habit of making that inevitably come true. A postulate is a firm decision that we sometimes just 'happen' to voice in a certain situation: 'That is bound to work/not work!', 'That's unlucky/lucky!' and so on.

Among these are counted all the statements we make about ourselves: 'I'm going to do it!', 'I'm far too clumsy to do that!', 'I'll always be poor!', 'I am a lucky devil!', and many others. If you check these events carefully, you will find you always made a relevant postulate just before any kind of success or supposed failure. A 'supposed' failure, because even a negative postulate is successful in the sense that it does happen (so success or failure is that which follows a postulate).

Further indications of our spiritual nature are the many recorded 'out of body experiences' in which the people who experienced them report unanimously that they found themselves outside their bodies and were even able to see their own bodies from a detached viewpoint.

I have twice had such an experience in my life, the first occasion being when I had my tonsils removed as a child of two. I found myself slightly to one side, just above my body, and was able to follow the entire operation in all its details. Of course, nobody believed what a small child had to say after waking up from the anaesthetic but, although I was only two at the time, I can still remember all of it clearly to this day.

The second incident was when I was climbing in the mountains, aged seventeen. During a school trip, I was climbing rather precariously on rocks with a friend. Suddenly I slipped off with both feet simultaneously – at the same moment I found myself outside my own body.

I can still remember exactly how I calmly considered what to do to control my body hanging there on the rock face, while I was no longer 'in' my body. I was positioned about 3 metres (3 yards) behind myself, and from this position my 'detached' self was able to see where there were firm footholds for my feet. At the moment that I made the decision where to place my feet, my body carried out the thought. I was still watching this from 'outside', however.

The moment I felt firm rock under my feet, I was suddenly back 'inside' again. I calmly carried on climbing and it was not until a few minutes later, when I had reached the top of the rock, that panic overcame me and I realized I could have fallen. Then I found it an effort to shake off the fear.

It need not be that dramatic. You can convince yourself of your spiritual capabilities in quite a safe way by simply crossing out the words 'coincidence' and 'chance' from your vocabulary. Belief in 'coincidences' is nothing other than a feature of our modern materialist religion, which can be truly given the term 'opiate of the people'.

Reducing ourselves to mere physical existence contradicts all daily experiences of life and you would really require quite a stubborn strength of belief in the 'god of chance'. Think of how many strange experiences occur daily to help us progress further with our lives. Surely, they are too conspicuous to be chance!

Simply accept that, as a spiritual being, you are able to be effective and perceive, even over great distances, that you are not tied to space and time and that you yourself are the cause of what you experience. Perhaps you will feel some opposition to this way of viewing things, as it is often easier to make others responsible for your fate.

But even if you have consciously cheated or were cheated – it always takes two to do it: one who cheats and one who allows him/ herself to be cheated. What is your inner voice telling you at any given moment?

Please understand me correctly here: I am not interested in standing a sense of justice on its head. A cheat remains a cheat and should be tried. I merely wish to show that we always have the opportunity to change ourselves and our lives. Just as we may have postulated something in the past that we have to suffer from today, we are always in a position to change this postulate again and to make a new decision. We are not passively subject to fate – we create our own fate!

As spiritual beings, we have two basic capabilities: we can postulate something, that is, decide what is to happen, and we can perceive something or experience the thing (that we postulated). Once we perceive what we wished to experience, the postulate dissolves again and we are content. As long as the experience has not yet taken place, however, something is left open. Seen from this angle, life becomes a game: we can either plunge into new experiences or placidly allow things to happen to us.

This is exactly where the true fulfilment of a spiritual being lies: in play. Just observe children absorbed in their game – to them it is totally real. We grown-ups are not really doing anything different, while we are earnestly occupied with our games in our homes, at work and in our leisure time.

Just think about how happy we grown-ups can be when we have been offered a new 'game' and how much enthusiasm and energy are bound up in it. If we approach a thing playfully, it works effortlessly. Playing is in our nature!

Your spirit stone that came to you through an oracle game will, therefore, reveal three things to you.

1. It represents a postulate, a decision you have made and the result of which you will experience now or in the future. You can dissolve this postulate if you no longer like it or begin happily to look forward to success. If you keep the message of the stone in your consciousness, you will experience how you actually determine your own life.

2. The stone will improve your means of perception and will make you conscious of your spiritual capabilities. Depending on which stone you have chosen, certain characteristics will be encouraged. The important thing is that you recognize the resulting phenomena as your own spiritual qualities and leave 'chance' out of the game. You will experience ever more clearly who you really are.

3. Your stone will simply show you what game you are playing at the moment or what game you want to play. Depending on where you stand now, your stone will make it clear to you how you begin your game, how you carry it on, or how you can bring it to a successful conclusion.

How you use your spirit stone is up to you. There are no rules, anything is possible. Make it into your own game!

Please read the next chapter with that last thought in mind. Chapter 2.4 deals with the 'practical application' of the art of healing with crystals. All possibilities described there are just that: possibilities. You can use them, you can change them, or you can invent new ones. Play the game according to your own rules!

2.4 Practical applications

Real skill at healing (the art of healing) requires no rules or laws but will always, and at every moment, do what is right and necessary. However, the fear of doing something wrong is apparently very great because the teaching of the art of healing is studded with advice and recipes that purport to give it an aura of general applicability.

The more competent this advice appears, the more gratefully it is received by the student. Yet the danger here is that advice or rules are blindly followed without the student really seeing the sense or meaning of them.

The literature on gem therapy, for example, abounds with rules and dogmas (most of which are not clearly described or explained) about what one can and cannot do. If you took all these rules together seriously, you would end up doing nothing at all!

One 'expert' recommends using rough stones, the other prefers spherical gems. In one volume you are forbidden to drill holes in anything, while in another you are advised to do so in all cases, and in yet another you are told that no metal should be attached to or surround a gem. For cleansing purposes, you are advised to bury your gems for weeks on end and bathe and anoint them thrice daily....

All your own valuable intuition is disregarded along with sound common sense, both of which are really our most valuable assets for healing. Yet, all the time, there is one very simple basic principle that is helpful not only in healing but also for one's entire life: 'Everyone would act the right way in a given situation if he/she knew how!'

For this reason, in all the following suggestions for use I will concentrate on explaining how certain methods work, as this understanding will leave you free to decide what you will use and when. You are then also free to vary things and invent your own new uses – which is exactly what the art of healing is!

Remembering what was said in the previous chapter, take a playful approach towards the art of healing with crystals. In this way, you will benefit from a great expansion of innovation and creative energy as well as ultimately achieving success in healing.

The 'right' crystal

I am very tempted to reduce this section to a single sentence: 'Follow your own feelings!' But perhaps that would be a little too simple.

It is a fact that not every individual stone of the same type will have exactly the same effect. You can use three different criteria in order to assess the effect and healing power of a particular stone: its quality, its size and the manner in which it has been shaped.

Quality: A stone is defined as qualitatively better if it displays the typical characteristics and qualities of the mineral in the most obvious and clear manner. For example, a dark green emerald is qualitatively better than a light green-grey one, a clear rock crystal is better than a milky, cloudy one, and a transparent ruby is better than an opaque one. As the healing effect of a mineral can be traced back to the mineralogical facts, as described in Part 1, it seems obvious that a qualitatively better stone has a more intense effect than a qualitatively mediocre one.

Size: Large stones have a stronger effect than small ones. This is obviously connected with the fact that the power of its radiation increases with its mass. Its effectiveness at a distance also increases. A small amethyst crystal has a radius of effectiveness of a few centimetres (a few inches), a large druse, on the other hand, may 'irradiate' an entire hall.

Form: The effect of form can also be traced back to one basic principle: crystals emit their greatest effective radiation along their edges. A crystal will, therefore, radiate its greatest effect from its tip. An irregular splinter will cast its rays in all directions and a sphere will emit a weaker, more regular radiation in all directions. Stones with facets are seen as more powerful, while round, polished stones, as for example tumbled stones, are felt to be gentler and more harmonious.

The effect of a crystal can, therefore, be based roughly on these three criteria. Yet the three criteria do not make any statement about which stone might objectively be more suitable because such a generally applicable criterion (good/bad) does not exist!

The stone that is suitable for the purpose is exactly the right stone! Depending on the application or the person, it might be a precious stone one time, a larger one another time, or a faceted stone or a round, polished one. For example, if you use a deep violet coloured amethyst to illuminate dreams, you may well find yourself bouncing about wide awake in bed at night! In this case, a lighter coloured, clearer one would be better.

For cleansing the skin, however, an amethyst cannot be deep violet enough. Again, it is really only your own 'feeling' or instinct that will help. If you have understood the three criteria discussed above, you should know or sense, in any situation, which is the right stone.

And please, just forget those standard dogmas! In principle, you can use any stone for healing purposes. Only if the stone is so minute that you can hardly see it, or if it is of such bad quality that it can barely be identified as a specific mineral, will it be unlikely to have any healing effect.

Variations and possibilities

Healing crystals are available nowadays in many different forms, either as a rough stone or polished, as a 'touchstone' (to fondle in one's hand) or as jewellery. The forms and colours of minerals are very often both beautiful and unique and, in addition to their healing powers, they also have an aesthetic value.

This means that the art of healing and decoration or the art of healing and use as jewellery can be combined quite easily. In the following, I will briefly elaborate on the most important ways of effectively employing your healing crystal.

Rough stones: A rough stone left in its natural state will, in many cases, display the real character of the mineral most clearly and will, therefore, also most clearly demonstrate its qualities and healing effects. Depending on their size, rough stones can be used to change the 'climate' of a room (for example, rose quartz), as a touchstone (for example amber, pop rocks, garnet), for laying on certain parts of the body (for example biotite lenses, chalcedony rosettes, lepidolites, zoisites), or as meditation stones (for example azurite, moldavite, pyrite).

Crystals: Naturally grown crystals possess the ability to channel energy from the base to the tip of the crystal and are, therefore, used for energy treatments (rock crystal, smoky quartz, tourmaline), for gem acupuncture (rock crystal, tourmaline), or can be used like other rough stones for laying on the body (hyacinth, kunzite, topaz, tourmaline).

Groups, geodes and druses: Several crystals that have grown together are referred to as 'groups'. If such a group of crystals fills a small hollow or cyst in rock it is called a geode, in the case of a large hollow we speak of a druse (examples are groups of rock crystal, an agate geode, an amethyst druse). Where small crystals completely fill up a cyst (for example, agate) we speak of an 'almond'.

Groups and druses radiate very powerfully and can, therefore, also be used to alter the 'climate' in a room (for example amethyst, rock crystal, fluorite, smoky quartz). Very small groups and geodes are very suitable for treatment by laying on, particularly if an intense, powerful effect is desired (for example agate, apophyllite, rock crystal).

Slices and sections: Almonds and crystals that often hide the most beautiful or characteristic part of the stone inside (agate, tourmaline) are often cut into slices. The representation obtained in this way, the 'signature' (Latin *signum*, 'sign') will enable one to 'read off' the healing effects (see Agate, Part 3, page 222). These slices or sections are also very good for laying on, or they can be worked into pendants.

Tumbled or polished stones: To obtain polished stones, the rough stones are polished by tumbling them in large rotating drums full of water. Gradually ever-finer sand is added for finer grinding. This process, which takes several weeks, imitates the formation process of natural pebbles in rivers and other waters. The inner structure of the stones will then determine their outer shape; irregular, 'baroque' shapes are created that have given these stones their name.

Polishing all the rough edges makes the stone radiate more evenly and with a more limited spatial distribution. This means they are excellent for laying on certain parts of the body as well as for fondling in your hand. The most popular place, in your trouser pocket, is particularly advantageous as you will then (unconsciously) touch the stone whenever you need it. The effect on your entire body is also ensured because your hand, like your feet, possesses reflexology zones.

Massage stones: Flat stone discs, teardrop-shaped crystal wands and other special shapes are manufactured especially for gemstone massage and many massage techniques may be intensified and enhanced with healing crystals.

Pendants and pierced stones: This is probably one of the simplest ways to utilize a crystal for healing as the object can be worn directly on the skin. Whether you prefer a pendant with a metal ringlet or pierced stones is merely a matter of taste.

In spite of any assertions to the contrary, the stone is in no way interfered with in its effect by the presence of the metal, providing skin contact is maintained. Personally, I would recommend using only pure sterling silver (925.000), gilded sterling silver or high-quality gold alloys of at least 14 carat (585.000). Non-precious metals and alloys may irritate the skin and react with perspiration from the skin. Even silver can tarnish and irritate certain sensitive humans.

Many different shapes can now be found among the pierced stones: the classical 'caboche' and medallion shapes, baroque or free shapes, or geometrical and symbolic shapes of all kinds. Here, again, the first approach should be to make a decision based on your own feeling. The important thing is that you like the stone and enjoy wearing it. A healing crystal can quite easily be a decorative stone or piece of jewellery.

Doughnuts: Doughnuts are flat, round stone discs with a central hole, a name derived from the pastry of the same name, widely distributed in the USA and Asia. The name is modern but the shape is extremely ancient: turquoise, in particular, has been worked into this shape for centuries in India, Nepal and China and amber doughnuts have been found in Palaeolithic graves. The shape may well have been created after the model of natural 'holed stones' that were looked upon as lucky in almost all cultures. Doughnuts can be used in the same way as the pendants described above.

Pyramids, spheres and healing wands: The effect of their special shape has long been considered in the case of these specially polished stones. Pyramids are used as 'storage' objects or for concentrating energy, spheres are used for meditation and healing, while wands are used for acupuncture or acupressure massage. The preferred types of mineral for healing wands are amethyst, rock crystal, citrine, fluorite, obsidian, smoky quartz and rutile quartz.

Necklaces: Necklaces are really the classic way to wear healing crystals. The healing effect of the stone will be very strong and the closed 'stone circle' around the head has a stronger radiative effect than a single pendant or touchstone. Among necklaces, those with round beads are considered to be 'mild' in their effect, whereas necklaces made of random, rough pieces are seen as 'strong'; faceted stone beads are seen as the most intense.

Jewellery: Rings, bracelets, necklaces – here, too, the stones that have been incorporated unfold their full effect if direct contact with the skin is established.

If you are just as interested in the healing properties as in the decorative effect, make sure that the ring is worked with an open setting underneath the stone. The ideal is found in a piece of jewellery in which the minerals have been combined according to principles of healing or alchemy. Such pieces do indeed unfold the magic of a classic talisman. Unfortunately, nowadays only very few goldsmiths and jewellers are familiar with this ancient side of their craft.

Precious gem essences and gemstone elixirs: Immersing healing crystals in clear water or similar methods will transfer the stones' information to the liquid. This transference becomes particularly intense if the glass containing the water and the stones is left in the sun for a few hours – ideally at dawn or dusk, as sunlight has charging properties at these hours. Gemstone water and gemstone elixirs may be consumed internally, applied topically or added to poultices, showers or baths. They have a similar effect to the stones themselves and are often even faster and more intense, as the effect spreads through the whole body when they are drunk.

Unfortunately, the information stored in the water soon dissipates, though alcohol can be added to fix it. Ready-made gemstone elixirs are available in stores and these are manufactured using a variety of methods: either through the transmission of information in sunlight, as with Bach flowers, using crystals to instigate the process or by steeping crystals for months in alcohol. They have a very intense effect and will keep for years.

The shape of stone you use will, therefore, depend on the desired purpose or on your personal preference. In principle, however, stones can be used in all sorts of ways. Perhaps a present or heirloom may acquire a new value when viewed from this angle.

Practical applications

In Part 3 you will find short suggestions for application among the descriptions of the individual healing crystals. Once the right stone has been chosen through the analytical or intuitive path, basically, only two more questions need to be asked:

1. In what manner is the stone to be used: wearing it, laying on, massage, in a circle, in meditation, as a precious gem essence/ elixir, positioned in a room?

2. Over what amount of time should it be used: starting time, duration, rhythm, end of treatment?

As a rule, there are several possibilities of which you can choose whichever you prefer: if you have a choice between sticking the crystal to your forehead or drinking a gemstone elixir, and you would find it embarrassing to appear in your workplace with a stone stuck to your head, then it would be better to opt for the elixir.

Wearing or carrying healing crystals
By 'wearing' and 'carrying' I mean all manners of application that include the stone being close to your body for a longish period. This can mean carrying a pendant, pierced stones, wearing a chain of stones, or even carrying a touchstone or rough stone in your trouser pocket. If you have been given exact instructions for carrying the stone, you may not get around sticking it to a part of your body with a piece of plaster. In any case, when wearing or carrying a stone it should, if possible, come into direct contact with your skin. Clothes, even if made of natural fibres, tend to have a screening effect.

Basically, healing crystals should be carried or worn until a clear improvement of the situation or symptoms has occurred or until the desired result has been obtained. In many cases, there may be an initial 'worsening' of the symptoms that merely shows that the situation or illness has been addressed; this should be seen as a symptom of healing. These initial 'worsenings' can last from a few hours to about three days, in rare cases up to a week. If still no improvement has occurred after that, the choice of stone should be checked.

Also, if an initial 'worsening' seems unbearable, it may be better to wear the crystal intermittently rather than constantly, perhaps wearing it only two or three times for about half an hour each time. The effect will be more bearable at the beginning, but during the course of time it will be just as intense as if you were to wear it permanently. A general statement is difficult to make about the right time sequence to adopt for wearing the crystal, as every human being will react differently. When in doubt, it is always better to increase the number of occasions gradually: begin with once daily, then twice, three times, etc. At the same time, the duration should be increased: start with half an hour at a time, then increase to an hour, one and a half hours, and so on. In this way, you will gradually reach a state of permanent application.

Laying on healing crystals

'Laying on' includes all temporary applications in which the stone is brought into direct contact with the body. As a rule, clear indications for the position on the body will be given in terms of where the afflicted organ, the pain or the area with an energy deficiency is located. When laying the stone on, you will notice that the crystal is almost 'sucked' to your skin if it is laid on the correct spot. When applying the stone, hold it to your body, applying light pressure for about a minute, and then carefully let go: even in spots it ought to drop off, it will usually remain stationary (unless it is too heavy).

Treatment by laying on a stone can end as soon as a definite improvement is noticed. Here, it is particularly important not to extend the period unnecessarily. Rejoice in the relief you have gained, even if it is not complete, end the treatment at this point and enjoy the result. You can always resume the treatment again at a later time. Impatience is a trait that generally has an unfavourable effect in healing! You cannot force anything, even healing has to 'grow', just as the illness gradually 'grew'.

Another point to be considered, regarding the right time of treatment, is that the organs in our bodies are not active to the same degree at all times of the day or night. This is particularly noticeable with respect to activity in the brain which controls at what times of day we go to sleep and wake up again. Phases of activity and phases of rest, phases of high output and phases of regeneration are quite familiar to us.

The same goes for all the other organs, each of which has its own individual 'morning', a time when its activity increases, its 'midday' when it reaches a peak, its 'evening' when activity begins to decrease and its 'night-time' when it has a rest phase.

In most cases, the organs are influenced more positively whenever their activity is just on the increase or is almost at its peak. This means that the best point in time to lay on a stone is, as a rule, before or during the phase of greatest activity. These points of time have been shown in the form of an 'organ clock' below so you can see at a glance at which time a certain treatment might

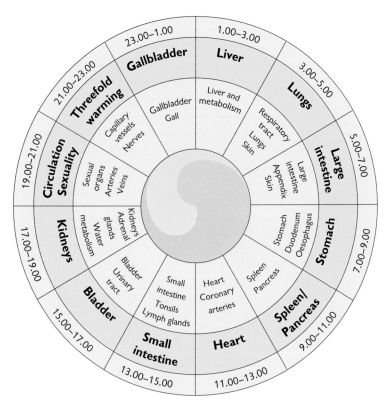

The organ clock

promise to be most successful. Please note here that our bodies are not interested in 'political time': it will always be the real local time that counts, disregarding any displacements through 'summer time' and so on.

The stone circle

Stones radiate, so spending time in a stone circle will have a noticeable effect. 'Stone circle' is defined generously here and you will not have to travel to Stonehenge as, in this volume, stone circles are simply stones or crystals laid in a circle. Whereas laying crystals on the body means the entire organism is being influenced, spending time in a stone circle works on the most subtle planes of your being and its effects will be noticed first in spiritual, emotional and mental changes.

You can sit or lie down in a stone circle, but in all cases it is important to find the correct radius. Should you experience feelings of restriction or claustrophobia while in the circle, you will need to increase the area of the circle; if you feel distracted or uncomfortable in some way, the circle may well be too large.

You will experience the optimal sense of well-being in a circle with the correct radius. Frequently repeating treatments with a stone circle will lead to your experiencing a variation in your own 'personal' radius, depending on the situation and your mood. During the course of time, your feeling for the circle will improve, so you will be able to determine the right radius from the start.

Remain sitting or lying in your stone circle as long as it takes to feel distinctly better or until you receive a strong impulse to leave the circle. Follow this impulse, whether it occurs after ten minutes or three hours. You can leave the stone circle where it is in order to continue on another occasion.

It has been proved to be advantageous to use it when you are well rested, particularly if you are going to lie down in the circle, otherwise you may well sleep though all the most beautiful experiences.

Provided you have chosen your four personal healing crystals described in Chapter 2.3, The intuitive art of healing with crystals (see page 184), you may lay these four stones in their own circle. Seen from the centre of the circle, lay your soul stone towards the south, the body stone in the west, the reasoning stone in the north, and the spirit stone in the east. Now sit down in the circle, first facing south, then after 10–15 minutes change to facing west, then north, and finally east. In this way, you will be able to experience the meanings of the soul, body, intellect and spirit thoroughly and you will also feel the effects of the healing crystals in these areas.

You can use this circle as a recovery island in your daily life. Even after a few minutes in the circle, either lying down with your head to the north, or sitting facing south, you will find it relaxing and regenerating.

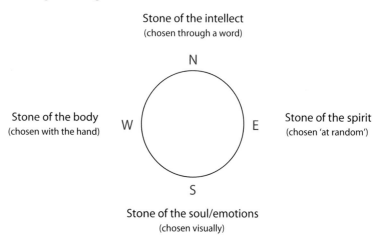

Stone of the intellect
(chosen through a word)

N

Stone of the body
(chosen with the hand)

W

E

Stone of the spirit
(chosen 'at random')

S

Stone of the soul/emotions
(chosen visually)

The circle of personal healing crystals

Meditating with healing crystals

It is difficult to write about meditation as the phenomenon can really only be understood through actually doing it. If our eyes were only able to see black and white we would find it impossible to conceive of colour. For this reason, I can only think of two ways you might experience meditation with the help of stones. You will have to see for yourself what happens.

Contemplation: Give yourself enough time, unplug the telephone, explain to everyone living with you that you do not wish to be disturbed for a while and sit down in a quiet spot. You can sit on the floor or equally well on a chair. The important thing is to be absolutely upright with a straight spine. A bent back will lead to tiredness and prevent meditation. Now, if possible, lay the stone in front of you so you can look down upon it and observe it without strain or effort. You will have found the right distance if you are able to direct your gaze at the stone in a fully relaxed manner for a long time.

It will be advantageous not to have a source of light in your range of vision: no candle, no lamp, no window, no sun. Sources of light would simply distract your attention. The same goes for the background, which should be as neutral as possible so the stone can really stand out. Your entire attention should now be directed towards the stone lying in front of you. However, do not fixate on it, just let your gaze come to rest a little above it, into infinity.

Remain sitting in this manner quietly without moving. Every movement represents a new start and prevents meditation. If you become as slow as the stone in front of you, you will suddenly see it, understand it and experience it as a living being. Allow yourself to be surprised.

Meditating with laid-on stones: Equipped with enough time and a calm atmosphere and, above all, having slept well (!), you will be able to experience the effect of healing crystals by lying down and placing the stone on your body.

Here, again, skin contact is particularly advantageous. Favoured positions on the body for laying on the stone are the forehead (between the eyebrows), the heart, the solar plexus or the lower edge of the pubic bone. Then, consciously relax, by 'thinking' your way through from head to toe, that is, consciously relaxing each part of your body in turn and letting go of all tension.

Observe your own breathing as it becomes calmer and slower until you are just as 'slow' as the stone resting on you. Now, allow yourself to be filled right up with the stone; identify with it, which means becoming like the stone, or better, become the stone itself as then the memory of the stone will open itself to you and you will see the world with its 'eyes'.

'Meditation' means complete spiritual awareness at one moment in time and space. You will recognize the state instantly and understand it once you have experienced meditation. You will also immediately know what aim meditation can have in your life. Again, allow yourself to be surprised …

Precious gem essences and gemstone elixirs
Precious gem essences and gemstone elixirs demonstrate similar properties and reactions on our personalities and our bodies as the

appropriate precious gem. Their advantages, however, lie in their application – taking them internally.

Where precious gems have been laid on the body and only have a limited, localized effect, the effect of a precious gem essence or elixir taken internally will be distributed through all body fluids in the entire organism. You are 'filling' yourself with the gem. In this way, better results are achieved, particularly with generalized complaints (affecting the whole body).

Where a gem may only help a blockage caused by stress locally, a precious gem essence or elixir is able to help with inner tension and stress (both physical and psychological) and will thereby improve all existing tensions and stress as well as any tendency towards being tense.

If for practical reasons it is not possible to wear or carry a gem or to apply it externally (for example, if the movement of your joints would be restricted or – as already said – you might not wish to appear in the office with a gem or crystal strapped to your forehead), consuming a precious gem essence or elixir will be preferable.

Precious gem essences and elixirs have an automatic effect on the body in exactly the place where they are applied. Treatment with a precious gem essence or elixir also constitutes information therapy and the information will only be effective where your body 'understands' it, that is where the information is missing (principle of resonance).

Precious gemstone elixirs in particular are very powerful in their effect. In order to achieve a comparable effect, a precious gem would have to be very large and very precious. Even leaving aside the problem of obtaining such a gem (often very difficult) and using it (how would you wear a gem weighing 2 kilograms (4.5 lb)?), there would still be the problem of price, which would be many times more than that of the elixir (diamond, emerald). An elixir is, therefore, also good for your wallet.

With an elixir the cleansing that has to be undertaken when treating someone with precious gems is eliminated. Also, the amount of elixir taken internally can be dosed very exactly.

Of course, the wearing and laying on of precious gems also has advantages over the use of elixirs. In particular, experiments with gems are less binding as the gem can quickly be removed again and its effect will fade comparatively more quickly. Even if, for certain reasons, a targeted local treatment of a particular point, for example, an acupuncture point, is desired, gemstones are preferable to elixirs.

However, in most cases, the gem and the precious gem essence or elixir will complement each other well because, used simultaneously, they strengthen each other. Using a precious gem essence or elixir is just as simple as wearing a gem.

Taking internally: Ideally a good hour before eating, or two hours afterwards. Precious gemstone essences you have made yourself may be taken in sips, but just a few drops will be enough for the more intense elixirs! As a rule of thumb for dosage: sensitive natures should tend to take less (1–2 drops), more robust people more (5–10 drops). Also, once swallowed, an essence is absorbed more quickly if needed more by the body. In such cases, the daily cycle of doses can be accelerated; i.e. several small doses instead of a few larger ones. Gem essences and elxirs can be taken over several weeks.

External application: Precious gemstone essences may be applied directly to the skin; gemstone elixirs should be diluted with water in such cases. They will assist in treating skin complaints, inflammation and wounds. Mixing them into ointments is also possible. A further possibility is adding them to your bath, although the bathwater should not be too warm as this will cause the effect to disperse too quickly.

Combinations: In principle, different precious gemstone essences and gemstone elixirs may be mixed together for special purposes. Producing mixtures with balanced and harmonious effects is an art, however.

 A number of gems like rock crystal, diamond, white topaz etc. will enhance the effect of others and can, therefore, be added if necessary. Certain mixtures for particular applications can be obtained in the specialist trade. Compared with old herb tea recipes, these are the result of years of research, have been carefully measured and are in tune with each other, both with respect to the combination of gems as well as the quantitative composition.

Storage: Precious gemstone essences and gemstone elixirs should be stored in cool, dark places. In order to prevent them from influencing one another, they should be kept apart or wrapped in aluminium foil. Elixirs of neutral healing crystals in particular (for example rock crystal/crystal quartz) will easily absorb the qualities of other gemstone elixirs.

They should not be kept near sources of energy, such as electric power lines or cables, wifi routers, DECT telephones, television or computer screens or neon lights.

Positioning healing crystals in a room

The atmosphere in which we live and work will have a lasting effect on our health and on the results of what we do. This means that we can even use healing crystals in our daily environment to obtain fast, positive results. The important thing here is that the stones we place in certain positions are effective across a sufficient radius. Rough stones, crystals and druses are, therefore, preferable.

Whenever you are within the radius of influence of the crystal or stone, you will always feel physically better. If you also want enrichment on the level of the soul, the crystal should be placed in such a way that you can see it, even if only out of the corner of your eye. Aesthetics is also an important consideration here, so choose a crystal or stone that you love unconditionally!

The exchange between the crystal and the human being occurs in both directions. This means that the crystals also receive information from us, especially if we lay them directly on our bodies or against our skin.

This is the reason why, after using a crystal for a while, it may suddenly feel unpleasant. This happens at the moment when the information received becomes so powerful that the crystal begins to reflect it back at us. At that moment, the point has been reached when the crystal should be cleansed.

Cleansing and care

There is a great deal of confusion in the literature that currently exists with respect to energy cleansing of crystals, and this is obviously based on the fact that the meaning of the different processes has not been understood properly. It is the case that very often three different procedures have been combined under the heading 'cleansing': discharging, cleansing and charging of healing crystals, gems and stones.

Discharging: Particularly when crystals come into direct contact with the body, they will become statically charged. The most extreme example is amber, which may become quite hot in a few minutes. This static charge can be discharged again under running water.

Cleansing: The information received will, however, remain stored even after the stone has been discharged and it will recharge again. In order to wipe this information, a more intense action is required. Complete wiping of stored information can be achieved with two simple procedures, by laying the crystal on an amethyst druse or by laying it in salt.

The amethyst druse represents the gentler procedure. The finely distributed iron atoms and the energy concentration of quartz give amethyst a powerful, fiery radiation. Healing crystals 'irradiated' in this way are stripped of the information they have stored. The time required is generally one day, or if the stone was only used briefly, an hour will be sufficient. You can, however, allow the crystal to lie in the druse for longer; it will not come to any harm.

Salt needs more careful handling. In particular, direct contact with salt may produce chemical reactions with some crystals, making the stone lose its polished finish or change colour. Laying an opal in dry salt would be detrimental, as the salt will extract water from the opal and it will lose its refractive colours. It will still be a healing crystal, but will generally be worth a great deal less!

We recommend, therefore, laying the crystal in a small glass dish that is embedded in a larger glass dish full of salt. The energy cleansing process is still maintained, but the stone itself is not affected. You can add mineral-poor water to the crystal where there are chains or necklaces attached to it whose threads might be damaged. This procedure will extract information even more quickly. The water should be changed each time you do this, but the salt can be used for months. The cleansing power of salt is very quick. If the stone has been worn for weeks, four to six hours of cleansing will be enough; if the crystal was only briefly laid on, ten minutes of cleansing will be sufficient. Carrying out cleansing for too long may 'leach' out the energy of the stone and its effectiveness will be decreased!

Other methods that have been recommended, such as laying the stone in salt water, burying it in soil or cleansing it in fire, are definitely to be avoided, as many crystals will be severely damaged by this: salt water will penetrate pores and cracks and make the stone cloudy, some secondary minerals will be attacked by acids in the soil and transformed, and fire will obviously tend to disperse too efficiently!

Charging: The intensity of radiation from a crystal is connected with the absorbed energy, so its healing effect can be increased and fortified through targeted charging. The most gentle method consists of laying the stone in sunlight at sunrise and sunset. The period of time during which we can dare to look almost into the sun without damage to our eyes is when the sun possesses a charging quality. Never at midday, however! At this time the sun's energy tends to be discharging rather than charging.

Immediately before using a crystal for treatment, the stones used can be warmed up in your hand or near a radiator. This, too, will intensify its effect. In many cases, charging is not necessary as the stone will be warmed up and stimulated by body contact.

Care: Physical cleansing should be restricted to eliminating dust from mineral groups and mineral druses. Use a fine paintbrush for the purpose. If you are cleaning a druse, for example with water, only use mineral-poor water in order to avoid obtaining ugly calcium deposits on the crystals.

Please never use any strong abrasive household cleaning agents on your crystals. Some of them are almost impervious to such substances, while others extremely sensitive. By the time you have noticed the difference, it will already be too late!

Storage: It is, of course, very natural to want to display beautiful stones so you can see them most of the time. However, if you do not want regular dusting to become your main hobby, I definitely recommend keeping them in a lockable display cabinet. I would also like to recommend you do not use a windowsill, with the exception of agate sections (which actually look rather good hanging in a window) and light-insensitive crystals (such as rock crystal, hematite, jasper, lapis lazuli, tiger's eye, black tourmaline), as many of them will lose their colour in direct sunlight (amethyst, kunzite, rose quartz).

Please do not stand any rock crystal spheres in sunlight. They will work like extremely good lenses, as I have experienced to my cost through burn holes in boxes and car seats!

You can seek out more information on the background, effects and possible uses of a range of purification methods in specialist handbooks devoted to the subject.

Healing crystals as aids

To end this section of 'practical applications', here are a few thoughts that are important to me personally: there is life without healing crystals! These objects should never become a substitute for your own creativity and ability to solve problems.

Healing crystals are aids. Every aid also has the possibility of becoming superfluous at some time. This is why I would like to point out here again something that should be considered along with the treatment with crystals.

The overall effect of healing crystals is enhanced and supported by consciously dealing with the particular problem: asking yourself 'why?' and 'wherefore?' the problem or illness exists and working out possible solutions. Every illness conceals a potential gain, so the question that has to be asked is, how can I rid myself of the problem or illness without losing the gain? Healing crystals will encourage this conscious effort but will not do it for you.

The effect of healing stones will only remain stable after you have stopped using them, if the insight gained is then transformed into action. We ourselves are the causes of our problems and we ourselves can change them. Crystals, precious gems and elixirs are merely aids in the process – nothing more.

The listing of qualities and symptoms in Part 3 of this volume, therefore, serves mainly to provide information, to give a brief characterization of the healing crystals, gems and stones, and specifically to stimulate the intuitive side of using the art. Wherever an illness is present, or for the solution of soul-spiritual problems, you should always pay attention to the entire situation, your character, the whole range of symptoms and your ideas, desires and goals in the art of healing with crystals.

This holistic approach may lead you to an entirely different healing crystal than perhaps one isolated symptom would lead you to suppose. For this reason, I would like to point out again that this volume serves to provide information about the art of healing with crystals and will not replace a doctor, complementary medical practitioner or therapist. In cases of severe illness or serious problems, do not fail to seek expert advice.

3.1 Healing Crystals

The healing properties of precious stones

It is important to establish that in the descriptions that follow of the healing powers and effects of precious gems, only those effects that have been tested and confirmed for many years have been recorded. Suppositions and phenomena that have been observed only in isolated cases have been left out or are clearly stated to be such. This has been done in order to offer security and certainty, something that is greatly needed in view of the contradictory and confusing information currently being offered in various publications.

However, this also means that none of the crystals or stones has been exhaustively and comprehensively described. At present nobody can offer this information, simply because research and development of the entire subject has only been carried out since the mid-1980s. This is still an extremely short period of time compared with the time other healing methods have been practised, some based on traditions centuries or millennia old. The main work with healing crystals and stones is still in fundamental research, with every year bringing new insights.

When choosing a particular healing crystal, please rely mainly on the analytical or intuitive paths described in Part 2. The descriptions in Part 3 are primarily meant to confirm the choice you have made. Still, trust your own choice, even if the information that follows in the book does not appear to offer a connection between your desire and the stone you have chosen. Perhaps you are on the brink of discovering something completely new and unknown. If this is the case, I would be very glad to hear about it.

Such an exchange of information is also possible through the various crystal healing associations. The work of these associations consists, among other things, in collecting and evaluating reports on the healing effects of minerals and precious stones and in publishing the results after checking them. All contributions will be much appreciated.

Descriptions of the healing crystals

Many healing crystals have one or more trade names in addition to their mineralogical designation. Using a specific name in order to be precise about exactly which stone is meant (such as with the many members of the quartz group) can be useful.

However, some trade names are unnecessary or even misleading, such as those that suggest a quite different mineralogical composition (e.g. onyx marble). But it is impossible to avoid using trade names if they are more commonly used than the appropriate mineralogical description (e.g. ocean chalcedony). For this reason, they are also included in the headings in the following list of crystals.

The names used in this book have also been chosen for providing the most correct and clear descriptions (of the minerals and gemstones) as a reference for both the general public and the gemstone trade alike.

In addition, and in order to clarify their connection with the first part of this book, the descriptions of the healing properties of each particular mineral include the most important mineralogical facts. The crystal system, the manner of formation, the mineral class, the colour and the mineral-forming substances contained are listed first, followed by the (extended) chemical formula.

This information allows you to take into account the descriptions of Part 1 when studying the healing crystal, thus providing a considerably deeper and more comprehensive understanding of its healing effects. Refer back to the table on page 91 if you need help in identifying the chemical abbreviations of the mineral-forming substances.

The important elements of the formation of the mineralogical qualities of the healing crystals are emphasized in the section headed '**mineralogy**'.

Wherever traditions and mythological anecdotes about a certain stone exist, these have been briefly sketched under the heading '**mythology**'. Frequently, this will include the name of the crystal and – very importantly – an indication that, during the Middle Ages, often quite different minerals were designated by a name that is used nowadays! This is why many old traditions cannot be transferred to present-day minerals. A definite identification of modern minerals in ancient texts is often very difficult, but I hope to have eliminated 'translation errors' for the main part.

Under the heading '**healing**' are listed the currently known and tested healing effects of the mineral. They are divided up into the

spiritual effect, which describes how the crystal can affect the transient state of the spirit, or what motivations and stimulation it will offer. Then follows the **emotional** effect, which comprises the influence on the subconscious, the inner images, feelings and moods. The **mental** effect describes changes in understanding, thoughts and conscious action, and finally the **physical** effect refers to the organism and the energy system of our bodies.

This structuring makes clear the interplay on all four levels and the special effects of the crystal with regard to the intuitive side of the art. The final notes on '**application**' of the crystal offer uses that have been shown to lead to good results (based on experience). Here too, the underlying principles suggest that much more may be possible! Make it your own game …

Agate

Crystal system: trigonal
Manner of formation: primary or secondary
Mineral class: oxides/tectosilicates, quartz group
Colour: clear, white, grey, light blue, yellow, orange, red, brown, black
Chemical formula, mineral-forming substances: SiO_2 + Al,Fe

Mineralogy

Agate is formed in gaps and cracks in a range of rocks, as well as often appearing in hollows formed by gas bubbles in volcanic rocks. Hydrothermal silicic acid solutions of post-volcanic (primary) or sedimentary (secondary) origin may form layers of different quartzes, generally chalcedonies (chalcedony, cornelian, onyx) and crystal quartzes (rock crystal, amethyst), although occasionally also jasper or opal. Trapped layers of other substances lend the agate's characteristic banded appearance a wide range of different colours. If agate fills a void entirely, it is called an agate amygdule, while if there's a hollow centre, it is known as an agate geode.

Mythology

Agate enjoyed a high reputation as a protective and good luck stone in the ancient world, as well as in India, Nepal and Tibet. Amulets were carved out of agates with straight, parallel bands and the continuation of this art has resulted in the present-day gem cutting art. Agates whose central hollow was filled with water ('water agates', 'enhydros' or 'eagle stones') were particularly popular and were considered to be charms for pregnancy.

Healing

Spiritually Agate supports retreat and spiritualization. It encourages a calm and contemplative view of life and helps with a concentrated, positive regulation of our affairs. Agate encourages the conscious 'digesting' of our life's experiences and leads to spiritual maturity and growth, inner stability and a sense of reality.

Emotionally Agate gives protection, security and safety by dissolving internal tensions, and also makes us better able to resist external influences. Examples that consist of regularly shaped, concentric banding are particularly effective for this. Agates that contain rock crystal at their core stimulate the ability to remember things, even as far back as prenatal memories (past lives).

Agate, Brazil;
Actinolite in matrix, Corsica

Mentally Agate strengthens logical/rational thought that we use to help ourselves analyse problems back to their causes. Agate helps find simple, pragmatic solutions that are put into action, calmly but without delay. Agate also enhances concentration on that which is essential and avoids distractions.

Physically Agate balances our auras and the energy body. On this level, it has, therefore, a protective effect, is harmonizing and stabilizes health. Agate encourages regeneration and growth and is the pregnancy stone for both mother and child. Because of its layered structure made of different quartzes, agate works on those organs that are built up of different layers of skin and tissue. It helps with diseases of the eyes (conjunctivitis), gastritis and stomach ulcers, bladder and intestinal inflammation, as well as diseases of the uterus. It protects from prolapse of the uterus and encourages normal shrinkage of the uterus after childbirth. Agate stimulates the digestion and elimination, strengthens the blood vessels and helps with skin diseases.

Application

When using agate for specific physical complaints, the agate chosen should always carry the 'signature' (Latin *signum*, 'sign') of the respective organ. When in doubt, I recommend consulting a book on anatomy. This mineral should be worn with direct skin contact and laid on the respective part of the body shortly before or during the 'organ peak' (see the organ clock, Chapter 2.4 page 208). It will be sufficient to place the agate somewhere where it can be seen for much of the time, in order to obtain an effect on the emotional/spiritual level; for example hang it up in the window. Meditating in a circle of agate pieces is particularly powerful.

Actinolite

Crystal system: monoclinic
Manner of formation: tertiary
Mineral class: chain silicates, amphibole group
Colour: green
Chemical formula, mineral-forming substances: $Ca_2(Mg,Fe)_5[(OH)_2 \,|\, Si_8O_{22}]$
$+ \, Na,K,Al,Cr,Cl,F,Mn,H_2O$

Mineralogy

Actinolite is an alkaline calcium magnesium iron silicate that forms crystals that radiate outwards or broad, stalk-like fibrous aggregates. It is formed metamorphically at temperatures between 300 and 400 degrees Celsius in actinolite, green, talc and serpentine slates.

Mythology

Actinolite has been known as a 'ray stone' for centuries but there are no extant traditions on its healing powers.

Healing

Spiritually Actinolite is supportive when taking new directions. It helps with setting new goals and will help initiate the requisite action. Actinolite encourages straightforwardness.

Emotionally Actinolite helps us to recognize our own capabilities. It strengthens our sense of self-worth and encourages inner balance, patience and a sense of timing.

Mentally Actinolite helps us to obtain an awareness of when and where we have diverged from our original, real goals. This will help us to correct our course.

Physically Actinolite stimulates the functioning of the liver and kidneys, as well as all building and growth processes. In the form of actinolite quartz (actinolite in rock crystal) it stimulates all elimination of toxins, etc.

Application

Actinolite is slow to unfold its effects, so it should be used over a longer period of time as a touchstone or as a pendant worn against the skin.

Alexandrite

Crystal system: rhombic
Manner of formation: tertiary
Mineral class: oxides, chrysoberyl family
Colour: green in sunlight, in artificial light red to violet
Chemical formula, mineral-forming substances: $Al_2BeO_4 + Cr,Fe,V$

Mineralogy

Alexandrite is a metamorphic chrysoberyl containing chromium. It is created in the contact zone between aluminium- and beryl-rich pegmatites as well as chromium-rich basalt or peridotite.

The chromium content causes a fascinating change of colour: alexandrite looks green in sunlight and red or violet under artificial light.

Mythology

Alexandrite was discovered in the Ural mountains of Russia in 1833 and was the Russian Czar Alexander II's favourite stone. It rapidly became the national stone of Russia owing to the colour change from red to green, which corresponded to Russia's military colours.

Healing

Spiritually Alexandrite combines stark contrasts: intuition, clairvoyance and mediumistic tendencies are encouraged, as are a strong will, spiritual greatness and personal magic.

Emotionally Alexandrite intensifies our experience of imagery. This helps make not only dreams and inner images but also feelings and desires clearer. It also refines our perception of imagination and visualization.

Mentally Alexandrite, like chrysoberyl, encourages strategic thinking and planning, but also enhances the willingness to take risks and to trust our inner voice more than logic.

Physically Alexandrite increases the power of self-healing and helps particularly with inflammations of all kinds. It has a detoxifying effect and stimulates the regenerative powers of the liver.

Application

I recommend meditating with alexandrite for spiritual and emotional effects, used alternately in sunlight and by candlelight. Otherwise, it will be sufficient to carry it about your person.

Alexandrite, Russia;
Amazonite, Namibia

Amazonite

Crystal system: triclinic or monoclinic
Manner of formation: primary
Mineral class: lattice silicate, feldspar family
Colour: green to turquoise
Chemical formula, mineral-forming substances: $(K,Na)[AlSi_3O_8]$ +
Ca,Ba,Pb,Fe,H_2O

Mineralogy

Amazonite is a feldspar whose green colour is the result of lead traces. It is mostly created magmatically and is differentiated according to its crystal structure and chemistry – microcline amazonite (triclin, potassium), orthoclase amazonite (monoclin, potassium) and albite amazonite (triclin, sodium).

Mythology

Amazonite was used as a precious gemstone as far back as the Neolithic era, while 7000 years ago, in Egypt, it served as an amulet. In Ecuador, jewellery made of amazonite has been dated back 2000 years and amazonite artefacts have been discovered in northern India.

Healing

Spiritually Amazonite encourages self-determination. It helps us discard the notion of being the victim of all-powerful fate and encourages us to take charge of our own life.

Emotionally Amazonite balances extremes of moods and has a calming effect. It dissolves sadness and feelings of apprehension and encourages a healthy trust in God.

Mentally Amazonite helps solve problems through encouraging a proper interaction between rational thought and intuition.

Physically Amazonite regulates metabolic disturbances (liver) and has a relaxing, cramp-dissolving effect. It is also helpful during childbirth by helping the birth canal to expand naturally. It strengthens the nerves and helps with brain disorders. It harmonizes the pituitary gland and thymus gland as well as the autonomic nervous system and the inner organs. Amazonite also helps with heart complaints due to grief.

Application

Amazonite is best used by wearing it or laying it on the body or taking it internally as a gem essence or elixir.

Amethyst

Crystal system: trigonal
Manner of formation: primary or secondary
Mineral class: oxides/tectosilicates, quartz group
Colour: mauve, violet to deep purple
Chemical formula, mineral-forming substances: SiO_2 + (Fe,Al,Ti,Na,Li)

Mineralogy

Amethyst is a crystal quartz, part of the group that form large visible crystals. Its colour is due to the traces of quadrivalent iron (Fe^{4+}) that it contains, which are lodged in the crystal lattice. It is formed hydrothermally from silicic acid solutions of magmatic or sedimentary origin, mainly in hollows formed by gas bubbles in volcanic rock, but occasionally also in clefts and rocks with cracks and passages running through them. A hollow cavity in a rock lined on the inside with amethyst crystals is called an amethyst druse.

Mythology

The name of the amethyst is derived from Greece and means 'non-inebriated' (*amethustos*). Its sober, clearing effect was already known in antiquity and the crystal itself was, therefore, highly prized. In the Middle Ages, Konrad of Megenberg quite aptly defined the amethyst as a mineral that 'makes a person better, disperses bad thoughts, brings good commonsense and makes one mild and gentle'.

Hildegard of Bingen left us information on its healing effects on skin diseases and swellings, and in Arabic countries we know that amethyst was put under the pillow to prevent nightmares.

Healing

Spiritually Amethyst encourages constant spiritual wakefulness, a sense of spirituality and insight into the reality of the spirit. It imbues a sense of justice and the ability to judge and provokes honesty and uprightness. As a meditation stone it helps quieten the mind and is an aid to finding deep inner peace and discovering the wisdom within us.

Emotionally Amethyst will help in sadness and grief and lend support in coming to terms with loss. It clarifies the inner world of images and also our dream lives. If you put amethyst under your pillow, you will find that, initially, it will strongly stimulate dreaming until all undigested impressions have been clarified. After a few days, however, sleep will suddenly become calmer, deeper and more refreshing. During waking consciousness, amethyst stimulates inspiration and intuition.

Mentally Amethyst encourages sobriety and awareness. It helps us face up to all experiences, even unpleasant ones, and encourages consciously dealing with perception. This heightens concentration and effectiveness in thinking and acting and encourages the overcoming of blocks, uncontrolled mechanisms and addictive behaviour.

Physically Amethyst helps to get rid of pain and release tension, especially tense headaches. It also assists with injuries, bruises and swelling, which will reduce rapidly. It is useful for eyestrain, nervous complaints, high blood pressure, bronchial and lung complaints, itching, rashes, spots and other skin complaints, as well as for diarrhoea and bowel disorders. It regulates the intestinal flora of the large intestine, even in cases of parasitical infection.

Application

An amethyst should be worn – for an extended period of time – either as a chain or a pendant next to the skin, or it can be contemplated in (regular) meditation. For applying to the body in healing, placing the crystal directly on the area close to the relevant organ is recommended. A stone circle of amethyst crystal tips is extremely powerful. To help understand your dreams, simply place a light-coloured, clear (!) crystal under your pillow. For further effects on your mind and thoughts, place amethyst druses or pieces of druse around the room. Their energy field is so strong that the entire (spiritual) climate of the room will be transformed. Amethyst can also be consumed as a precious gem essence and/or elixir (e.g. for nervous disorders and bowel complaints) or applied externally (e.g. for skin conditions).

Amethyst on chalcedony, Uruguay;
Amethyst, Vera Cruz, Mexico;
Amethyst, Brazil

Ametrine

Crystal system: trigonal
Manner of formation: primary, secondary or tertiary
Mineral class: oxides/tectosilicates, quartz group
Colour: violet and yellow in clearly delimited colour zones
Chemical formula, mineral-forming substances: SiO_2 + (Fe,Al,Ti,Na,Li)

Mineralogy

Ametrine is an unusual crystalline quartz that combines amethyst and citrine colour zones; the colours are clearly divided within the crystal. It may be formed from ferrous hydrothermal silicic acid solutions in all kinds of rock.

Mythology

Ametrine is believed to have been known since the seventeenth century, although there is no recorded tradition of its healing properties.

Healing

Spiritually Ametrine makes a connection between the wakefulness of amethyst and the dynamic energy of citrine and thus provides a crystal of considered and deliberate action. It helps connect apparent contradictions and helps give the wearer luck, that intuitive means of success on all levels.

Emotionally Ametrine encourages optimism and *joie de vivre*. It brings harmony and an inner feeling of well-being that will not disperse even when there is great stress from outside.

Mentally Ametrine harmonizes perceptions and conscious action. It stimulates the extraordinary creativity that goes hand in hand with great energy. Ametrine improves our control over our own lives.

Physically Ametrine has a strong cleansing effect on the metabolism and in the tissues. It enhances the activity of the autonomic nervous system and harmonizes the interplay between the inner organs.

Application

In all applications, ametrine should be worn directly on the body for long periods of time. Spiritual and mental aspects are also fortified in meditation, and the mind strengthened through laying a crystal on the solar plexus.

Ametrine, Bolivia;
Amphibolite, Graubünden, Switzerland

Amphibolite

Crystal system: monoclinic (hornblende) + triclinic (feldspar)
Manner of formation: tertiary
Mineral classes: chain silicates, amphibole group (hornblende)
+ tectosilicates, feldspar family (plagioclase)
Colour: black/white flecks
Chemical formula, mineral-forming substances: hornblende
$(Na,K)_{0-1}Ca_2(Mg,Fe,Al)_5[(OH)_2|Si_{6-7.5}Al_{2-0.5}O_{22}]$ +
plagioclase $NaAlSi_3O_8$ / $CaAl_2Si_2O_8$

Mineralogy

Amphibolite is a metamorphic rock composed of hornblende (amphibole) and plagioclase (feldspar). It is created through the metamorphic transformation of magmatic gabbro or volcanic basalt and, on occasion, of sedimentary dolomite and limestone marl.

Mythology

Amphibolite was being worked into tools as early as the Neolithic period, although there is no evidence of any tradition of its use in healing. It wasn't until the twenty-first century that it was recognized as a healing crystal. It is sometimes known as the 'yin and yang' stone because of its appearance and effects.

Healing

Spiritually Amphibolite promotes mental balance, stability and inner peace. It brings the will, thoughts, feelings and actions into balance and promotes a good relationship with the environment.

Emotionally Amphibolite helps with fatigue, exhaustion, tension, dissatisfaction, inner turmoil, growing frustration and unpleasant feelings in general.

Mentally Amphibolite promotes alertness and observation, as well as the objective contemplation of internal images and memories. It brings vitality and helps us to let go of unrealistic expectations.

Physically Amphibolite stabilises the autonomic nervous system. It is helpful for digestive problems, boosts the kidneys and soothes complaints affecting the ears (hearing difficulties and noises in the ear such as tinnitus), vocal cords and larynx.

Application

Amphibolite may be worn on the body, applied to the skin and can be taken internally as a precious gem essence. Time spent in an amphibolite gemstone circle will have extremely beneficial results.

Antimonite

Crystal system: rhombic
Manner of formation: tertiary
Mineral class: sulphides
Colour: grey
Chemical formula, mineral-forming substances: Sb_2S_3 + As,Bi,Se + (Au)

Mineralogy

Antimony is formed in quartz and ore passages, where in hollows and cysts it forms beautiful, grey silvery crystals that radiate from one point.

Mythology

In antiquity, antimonite was used as a healing medium for the sexual organs, the throat and eyes, and was also applied in a pulverized form as eye shadow. The ray form of the crystal caused it to be seen as a symbol of the Sun.

Healing

Spiritually Antimonite encourages creative energy, general creativity and the aesthetics of form. It helps bring our personal interests and higher ideals into harmony so that our lives become joyful and full of meaning.

Emotionally Antimonite helps us to control our feelings as well as give up habits, replace gratification (for example, eating out of frustration) and reduce excessive sexual desire.

Mentally Antimonite enhances objective, sober thought and helps us to overcome limiting views ('I can't ...') and oppressive feelings. It makes it easier to follow our inner voice.

Physically Antimonite regulates digestive processes and helps with stomach problems, particularly acid indigestion, nausea and vomiting. It helps with skin diseases, dry, cracked skin, skin eruptions of all kinds, eczema and constant itching.

Application

Solid antimonite crystals can be applied to the skin or worn. Meditative contemplation, especially of beautifully formed mineral layers, is recommended for its emotional and mental benefits.

Apatite

Crystal system: hexagonal
Manner of formation: primary or tertiary
Mineral class: phosphates
Colour: black, blue, green, yellow, more rarely pink or red
Chemical formula, mineral-forming substances: $Ca_5[(F,Cl,OH)|(PO_4)_3]$ +
Na,Mg, Mn,Sr,Y,SE,CO_3,SO_4

Mineralogy

Apatite is usually created magmatically, or more rarely metamorphically, and is the most common phosphate mineral. It generally forms crude nodules, while crystals tend to be rare.

Mythology

Apatite was often confused with other minerals (beryl, calcite) and was not named until 1786 (from the Greek *apatao*, 'to delude'). In anthroposophical medicine, pulverised apatite is used as a powdered preparation to promote bone growth.

Healing

Spiritually Apatite provides openness and social ease. It makes us extroverted and instils motivation and drive, helping us to live a life full of variety.

Emotionally Apatite helps with apathy. It encourages liveliness, helps with exhaustion, particularly if periods of extreme activity are followed by complete lack of activity, and also reduces irritability and aggression.

Mentally Apatite eases apathy, sorrow, anger and lack of incentive and helps to turn our attention to happier circumstances.

Physically Apatite stimulates healthy eating habits. It mobilizes energy reserves, encourages the formation of new cells, as well as the growth of cartilage, bone and teeth. It ameliorates damage to posture, rickets, arthritis and joint problems, and promotes the healing of broken bones.

Application

Apatite can be worn directly on the body or applied to the affected areas. Apatite stone circles are extremely effective, as is consuming the stone as a precious gem essence or elixir.

Antimonite, Romania;
Apatite, both Mexico

Apophyllite

Crystal system: tetragonal
Manner of formation: secondary
Mineral class: phyllo or sheet silicates
Colour: clear, light green to blue-green
Chemical formula, mineral-forming substances: $(K,Na)Ca_4[(F,OH)|(Si_4O_{10})_2]$
$\cdot\ 8\ H_2O\ +\ Al,V$

Mineralogy

Apophyllite is a phyllo or sheet silicate containing water that is formed hydrothermally or in sedimentary rocks. Because of its water content, it conducts energy much more effectively than sheet silicates.

Mythology

Apophyllite has only been known since the end of the eighteenth century. There are no known traditions regarding its effectiveness. Any fractured surfaces shine like mother-of-pearl.

Healing

Spiritually Apophyllite encourages a calm attitude, tranquillity and honesty. It helps us to be open, as we really are, without hiding things; it gets rid of pretence, reserve or a bad conscience.

Emotionally Apophyllite helps reduce fears, inner pressure and feelings of apprehension and helps overcome anxieties, worry and uncertainty. It helps us to be in control and to release suppressed emotions.

Mentally Apophyllite provides that saving light in times of great pressure and stress. It helps us get rid of blocks and negative thought patterns and, above all, helps us get rid of the thought habit of 'wanting' things.

Physically Apophyllite heals respiratory problems, particularly asthma. It stimulates regeneration of the skin and mucous membranes, the activity of the nerves and helps with allergies.

Application

The spiritual effect of apophyllite becomes very apparent during the meditative contemplation of small groups of crystals. Wearing or carrying some crystals with you is also recommended and, in the case of an asthma attack, hold them directly against your chest. Taking the crystals internally as a precious gem essence or an elixir is also recommended.

Apophyllite, India

Aquamarine

Crystal system: hexagonal
Manner of formation: primary
Mineral class: ring silicates, beryl family
Colour: blue-green to sky blue
Chemical formula, mineral-forming substances: $Be_3Al_2[Si_6O_{18}]$ +
Na,K,Li,Cs,Mg,Fe,Ti,Sc,H_2O

Mineralogy

Aquamarine is a blue-green to blue beryl. It is created as a late formation in granite druses and granite pegmatites when the magmatic solution is enriched with beryllium. It obtains its blue colour from traces of iron.

Mythology

The name aquamarine (Latin/Italian *aqua marina*, 'seawater') was coined in the Renaissance period, but the blue-green beryl has been known for a long time. Old legends tell of how it changes colour to reveal true and false, friend and foe. According to tradition, it brings well-being, a good memory and clairvoyance.

Healing

Spiritually Aquamarine encourages spiritual growth, foresight, far-sightedness, mediumistic qualities and clairvoyance. It makes us upright and honest, goal-oriented, dynamic, persistent and successful.

Emotionally Aquamarine bestows light-heartedness and a happy, relaxed disposition that is due to all things undertaken developing quickly and smoothly.

Mentally Aquamarine clears up confusion and stimulates orderliness, bringing unfinished business to a conclusion.

Physically Aquamarine harmonizes the pituitary gland and the thyroid gland, thereby regulating growth and the hormone balance. It improves the sight in cases of short- or long-sightedness and calms overreactions of the immune system, autoimmune diseases and allergies, in particular hayfever.

Application

Aquamarine can be worn on the body on a continuous basis or taken internally as an elixir or precious gem essence. For eye complaints, it can also be laid directly on the closed eyelids in the evening.

Aquamarine, Pakistan

Aragonite

Crystal system: rhombic
Manner of formation: secondary
Mineral class: carbonates
Colour: white, yellow, brown, greenish, blue
Chemical formula, mineral-forming substances: $CaCO_3$ + Sr,Pb,Ba

Mineralogy

Aragonite is generally created as the sediment of a chemical deposit from limestone-rich water, such as in tropical seas, near warm springs or as a sinter formation in caves. More rarely, it may be found as a secondary formation in ore lodes and pockets in volcanic rocks. Aragonite will often transform into calcite over a long period of time.

Mythology

Aragonite received its name in 1788 after a source on the Rio Aragon in Spain. No traditions about its effects are known.

Healing

Spiritually Aragonite stabilizes spiritual developments that are moving too fast, that lead to excessive demands or to a decrease in interest.

Emotionally Aragonite is calming in cases of oversensitivity, inner restlessness and nervous twitching. Aragonite makes us feel physically well in our own body.

Mentally Aragonite brings flexibility and tolerance; however, if our behaviour tends to be erratic, aragonite helps us to keep our concentration focused on the matter in hand.

Physically Aragonite also stabilizes developments that are proceeding too fast. It regulates the metabolism of calcium, stimulates muscle activity and encourages the build-up and elasticity of the intervertebral discs. Aragonite strengthens the immune system and helps with digestive complaints.

Application

Aragonite can be used constantly as a touchstone or worn as a pendant.

Aragonite, Spain;
Aventurine quartz, Zimbabwe

Green aventurine quartz

Crystal system: trigonal
Manner of formation: tertiary
Mineral classes: oxides/tectosilicates (quartz) + phyllo or sheet silicates (fuchsite)
Colour: light green to glittering dark green
Chemical formula, mineral-forming substances: SiO_2 (quartz) +
$K(Al,Cr)_2[(OH,F)_2 | AlSi_3O_{10}]$ (fuchsite)

Mineralogy

Green aventurine quartz is a quartzite with inclusions of glittering green fuchsite (muscovite chromium). It is created during the metamorphosis of sandstones containing chromium and with a high quartz content.

Mythology

In the seventeenth century, 'aventurine' was a term used for glass that glittered due to the interspersed copper (from the Italian *a ventura*, 'randomly'). The name was not used for aventurine quartz until the nineteenth century.

Healing

Spiritually Green aventurine quartz reveals what makes us happy or unhappy. It fortifies our self-determination and individuality and stimulates dreaming and making dreams come true.

Emotionally Green aventurine quartz enhances relaxation, regeneration and recovery. It helps with difficulty getting to sleep, makes us more patient and calms anger and annoyance.

Mentally Green aventurine quartz promotes versatile thought and enthusiasm, but at the same time encourages tolerance and acceptance of the suggestions of others.

Physically Green aventurine quartz encourages regeneration of the heart. It stimulates the metabolism of fat and lowers cholesterol levels, and helps to prevent arteriosclerosis and heart attack. Green aventurine quartz also has an anti-inflammatory effect, soothes pain, helps ease eruptions of the skin, skin disease and allergies, and fortifies the connective tissues.

Application

Green aventurine quartz may be applied to the part of the body affected, worn as a chain or pendant or carried as a touchstone. It may also be placed under the pillow or consumed as a precious gem essence.

Azurite

Crystal system: monoclinic
Manner of formation: primary or secondary
Mineral class: carbonates
Colour: light blue, azure blue to blue-black
Chemical formula, mineral-forming substances: $Cu_3[(OH)_2|(CO_3)_2]$ + (Ca,Fe,Mg,Co,Zn,Mn)

Mineralogy

Azurite is a basic copper carbonate that can be created primarily through the contact of magmatic solutions with carbonate rocks, or secondarily through the reaction of surface water containing carbon dioxide with copper ore.

Mythology

Azurite was used in copper mining in ancient times and has been used as a pigment for paint since the Middle Ages. Unlike other copper minerals, there is no tradition of using azurite for healing purposes.

Healing

Spiritually Azurite represents a drive towards enlightenment. It awakens a hunger for our own experiences so that we are not satisfied with explanations given to us that we are unable to prove for ourselves.

Emotionally Azurite reveals and dissolves imprints from the past, in particular, those ideas and inner images that we have taken on unconsciously and believed to be true.

Mentally Azurite makes us very critical. It reveals our own thought patterns and allows us to think through apparently obvious circumstances in depth, thereby encouraging awareness and self-knowledge.

Physically Azurite is primarily a liver stimulant and aids detoxification. It stimulates the activity of the brain and nerves. Azurite also stimulates the activity of the thyroid gland, thereby encouraging growth.

Application

Azurite unfolds its emotional and spiritual effects as a meditation crystal that can be either contemplated calmly or laid on the forehead. When used on the body, it should be laid directly on the skin of the relevant part.

Azurite-malachite

Crystal system: monoclinic
Manner of formation: primary or secondary
Mineral class: carbonates
Colour: blue and green
Chemical formula, mineral-forming substances: $Cu_3[(OH)_2|(CO_3)_2]$ +
$Cu_2[(OH)_2/CO_3]$ + H_2O + (Ca,Fe,Mg,Co,Zn,Mn)

Mineralogy

Azurite-malachite is a basic copper carbonate that may be formed primarily through the contact of magmatic solutions with carbonate rocks or secondarily through the reaction of surface water containing carbon dioxide with copper ore, or else through the partial transformation of azurite into malachite.

Mythology

Azurite-malachite is far more rare than azurite and there are no known traditions concerning its healing effects.

Healing

Spiritually Azurite-malachite encourages an interest in our surroundings and fellow human beings. It makes us open, honest and helpful, and leads to well-being on all levels.

Emotionally Azurite-malachite brings harmony, particularly in conditions of inner conflict and disunity. It helps with overcoming pain and sadness as well as releasing suppressed emotions.

Mentally Azurite-malachite encourages harmony between the intellect and feelings. It helps us listen to our feelings and be able to put them into words as well as arriving at a positive view of life.

Physically Azurite-malachite stimulates the liver and detoxifies and releases cramps. It also stimulates the immune system and dissolves disharmonious cell growth (tumours, etc.).

Application

Azurite-malachite can be worn on the body either as a rough stone or hand touchstone or it may be taken internally in the form of a gem essence. The stone itself should be placed directly on the skin of the area of the body affected.

Azurite, USA;
Azurite-malachite, USA

Barite (heavy spar)

Crystal system: rhombic
Manner of formation: primary, secondary or tertiary
Mineral class: sulphates
Colour: clear, brown, yellow, greenish, more rarely red, grey and blueish
Chemical formula, mineral-forming substances: $BaSO_4$ + Ca,Pb,Sr

Mineralogy

Barite is an anhydrous barium sulphate that may be formed primarily from magmatic hydrothermal solutions, secondarily through the weathering of other minerals containing barium or occasionally as a tertiary formation from metamorphic hydrothermal solutions.

Mythology

Barite was long regarded as nothing more than a heavy variant of gypsum. Its great weight was puzzling and it was even thought to contain gold. Barite is used in homeopathy as barium sulfuricum, but is principally known for its radiation-shielding properties.

Healing

Spiritually Barite promotes a striving for stability and security. It helps us to concentrate on what is essential, to find a solid point of view and to defend it with determination.

Emotionally Barite promotes independence. It strengthens performance, brings inner strength and helps to combat uncertainty, shyness, depression and feelings of inadequacy.

Mentally Barite helps you to concretise thoughts and ideas and to express yourself. It boosts the memory, clears confusion and enables concentration when you are mentally fatigued.

Physically Barite helps to fight fatigue, muscle weakness, numb limbs, digestive problems and bronchial complaints. It improves posture, helps to combat diseases of the skin or glands, and reduces the effects of radiation.

Application

Barite has a very intense effect when worn on the body or placed in your environment. If taken internally as a precious gem essence, it should be a small dose only.

Barite, Black Forest;
Barite, Wölsendorf, Germany

Tree agate

Crystal system: trigonal (quartz/chalcedony) + monoclinic (chlorite)
Manner of formation: primary
Mineral class: oxides/tectosilicates (quartz) + phyllo or sheet silicates (chlorite)
Colour: white with green inclusions
Chemical formula, mineral-forming substances: SiO_2 (quartz/chalcedony) +
$(Mg,Fe,Al)_{12}[(Si,Al)_8O_{20}(OH)_{16}]$ (chlorite)

Mineralogy

Tree agate is either white, coarse quartz with deposits of green chlorite in cracks, gaps and crevices, or white chalcedony with fibres or streaks of green chlorite inclusions. Both are created from magmatic silicic acid solutions. Higher temperatures promote the formation of coarse quartz, which is why this kind of tree agate is most often found in pegmatites. Chalcedony formation is more likely to occur in hydrothermal areas at lower temperatures. As tree agate has no striations, the use of the term 'agate' is actually incorrect.

Healing

Spiritually Tree agate encourages inner peace and certainty. It makes us aware of our own strength and thus gives security and stability.

Emotionally Tree agate strengthens endurance and constancy. It gives courage in situations in which we feel unprotected and bereft of power.

Mentally Tree agate helps see difficulties as challenges and how to deal with them. It awakens the warrior in us and the urge to strive and conquer.

Physically Tree agate ensures vitality, stable good health and a well-functioning immune system. It makes us more resistant to frequent bouts of infection.

Application

Tree agate should be worn for long periods of time in order to be effective. It is not a stone to be used for rapid effects but will work on 'building up' slowly, inconspicuously but persistently.

Tree agate, India

Rock crystal

Crystal system: trigonal
Manner of formation: primary, secondary or tertiary
Mineral class: oxides/tectosilicates, quartz group
Colour: clear (clear as glass)
Chemical formula, mineral-forming substances: SiO_2 + (Al,Li,Na,H)

Mineralogy

Rock crystal is clear, pure quartz crystal. It arises in cracks, gaps and druses, created by hydrothermal solutions of magmatic, sedimentary or metamorphic origin. Crystals whose early forms are still visible as a series of layered deposits are known as phantom quartzes.

Mythology

The Greeks believed rock crystal to be deeply frozen ice (Greek *krystallos*). In all cultures it was thought to be a healing and magical crystal. Rock crystal was thought to be able to drive away demons and disease and was used as a strength and energy supplier. Crystal balls were used for predicting the future.

Healing

Spiritually Rock crystal encourages clarity and neutrality and thus improves perception and understanding. It strengthens our conviction in own point of view and encourages development that is appropriate to our own inner nature.

Emotionally Rock crystal recalls forgotten memories and brings them into conscious awareness. It helps with solving problems in simple ways and in revitalizing capabilities we thought we had lost.

Mentally Rock crystal brings self-knowledge and, in the form of phantom quartz, helps us to overcome what we believe are mental limits.

Physically Rock crystal revitalizes parts of the body that have lost feeling, are cold, numb or paralysed. It balances the working of both halves of the brain, fortifies the nerves and stimulates glandular activity. Rock crystal supplies energy but can still reduce fever and alleviate pain, swelling, nausea and diarrhoea.

Application

Rock crystal can be used as a single crystal, a group, or a cut stone, or in the form of a gem essence or gemstone elixir. It also enhances the effectiveness of other crystals.

Rock crystal, Brazil;
Phantom crystals, Brazil

Amber

Crystal system: amorphous
Manner of formation: secondary
Mineral class: organic resin
Colour: white, yellow, brown to dark brown, rarely black, blueish or greenish
Mineral-forming substances: approx. 78% C, 10% H, 11% O,
some S (mixture of various hydrocarbons)

Mineralogy

Amber is fossilized tree resin that has 'aged' during the course of millions of years by losing water, and has hardened gradually. It is found mainly in brown coal deposits.

Mythology

Amber was the first precious stone in human history. It has been used as a healing stone and amulet since the Stone Age.

Healing

Spiritually Amber encourages a sunny nature, which appears gentle and pliable, but is actually very self-confident. It makes us spontaneous and open but respectful of tradition at the same time.
Emotionally Amber bestows freedom from care, good luck and happiness. It makes us peace-loving and trusting and strengthens self-belief. It is the source of easily obtained success.
Mentally Amber dissolves oppositions, making us more flexible, and encourages creativity. Motivation arises from personal wish fulfilment that will often become the main drive in our lives.
Physically Amber helps with stomach, spleen and kidney complaints as well as with liver, gallbladder and metabolically based skin complaints. Amber helps joint problems (build up of cartilage), fortifies the mucous membranes, enhances healing of wounds and alleviates teething pain in small children.

Application

Amber works best if it is worn frequently and for long periods of time. Chains of amber for babies work better if they are worn by the mother for a while first (they absorb relevant information).

Beryl

Crystal system: hexagonal
Manner of formation: primary
Mineral class: ring silicates
Colour: clear, yellow, yellow-green, green, light blue, pink, red, black
Chemical formula, mineral-forming substances: $Be_3Al_2[Si_6O_{18}]$ +
$Na,K,Li,Cs,Mg,Ca,Rb,Mn,Sc,H_2O$ + (Cr,Fe,N,U,Ti,V)

Mineralogy

Most beryl arises in druses and cracks in granite pegmatites, created as a late formation in the crystallization of magma that is rich in silicic acid. Pure beryl is clear (goshenite), while traces of iron colour it green to blue (aquamarine) or green to yellow (heliodor); manganese lends it a pink hue (morganite) and lithium makes it red (bixbite), while chromium (emerald) and vanadium colour it green (vanadium beryl).

Mythology

Beryl has been used as a detoxifying crystal that strengthens the eyes since ancient times. It was polished to make lenses and visual aids.

Healing

Spiritually Beryl makes us goal-oriented and effective but at the same time, versatile, far-sighted and full of *joie de vivre*. Golden beryl and heliodor both have a very harmonious effect and bixbite makes us dynamic.

Emotionally Beryl (better still golden beryl) helps nervousness and emotional eruptions caused by excessive stress. Bixbite helps with apathy and lack of drive.

Mentally All types of beryl encourage a feeling of security and self-confidence. They stimulate a thoughtful manner and a gradual but determined development in carrying out all plans.

Physically Beryl has a detoxifying, liver-stimulating effect and has a balancing effect on the autonomous nervous system. It helps with short-sightedness and long-sightedness (best with heliodor) and any symptoms typical of constant stress.

Application

The best way to use beryl is to wear it on the body or use it in meditation. As a healing stone for the eyes, place it on the closed eyelids in the evenings or consume it as a precious gem essence and/or gemstone elixir.

Beryl, USA;
Golden beryl, South Africa; Heliodor, South Africa

Biotite lenses

Crystal system: monoclinic
Manner of formation: tertiary
Mineral class: phyllo or sheet silicates, mica family
Colour: dark grey, brownish, black
Chemical formula, mineral-forming substances:
$K(Mg,Fe,Mn)_3[(OH,F)_2|(Al,Fe)Si_3O_{10}]$ + Ca,Ba,Li,Na,Rb,Ti

Mineralogy

Biotite lenses are metamorphic mica aggregates from northern Portugal that were produced during the formation of mountains. In the summer, when the rocks heat up, they expand into lens shapes, breaking open the rock and coming to the surface.

Mythology

Owing to their manner of formation and their use in childbirth, biotite lenses are called 'birthing stones' in the area they come from. They are also used as protective stones in Portugal.

Healing

Spiritually Biotite lenses stimulate individual self-fulfilment. They allow flexibility and adaptation as long as the wearer does not become untrue to him/herself.

Emotionally Biotite lenses protect us from outer influences. They help us to free ourselves from other people's influences and demands whenever they contradict our innermost convictions.

Mentally Biotite lenses enhance the ability to make clear-cut decisions. They amplify creativity and intuition and help turn decisions and ideas into reality much more quickly and easily.

Physically Biotite lenses are used as aids during the birth process. They speed up the birth as they trigger labour, while simultaneously softening the neck of the womb. Furthermore, they have a detoxifying effect and are helpful with constipation, kidney problems, excess acid, sciatica, rheumatism and gout.

Application

Biotite lenses work best when carried close to the body. They can be laid on the lower abdomen (pubic area) to start labour or alleviate labour pains.

Biotite lens (birthing stone), Portugal;
Bronzite, Brazil

Bronzite

Crystal system: rhombic
Manner of formation: primary or tertiary
Mineral class: chain silicates, pyroxene family
Colour: bronze, brown to black-brown with glittering gold-yellow flecks
Chemical formula, mineral-forming substances: $(Mg,Fe)_2(S_2O_6)$ +
Al,Ca,Mn,Ti,Cr,Na.

Mineralogy

Bronzite is a chain silicate in the pyroxene group containing iron and magnesium. It may be formed magmatically in abyssal rocks (plutonites) and volcanic rocks, or metamorphically in granulites. Bronzite deposit sites of both kinds can be found all over the world.

Mythology

There are no records of traditions involving bronzite. It was only recognized by modern crystal healing when it was nicknamed 'the parents' friend', thanks to its content of iron (stimulating, strengthening) and magnesium (calming, relaxing).

Healing

Spiritually Bronzite promotes an inner serenity that can withstand great pressure. It helps us to face life with confidence and to maintain a positive mental attitude.

Emotionally Bronzite helps with stress, everyday fatigue and exhaustion. It promotes relaxation and regeneration, even when external circumstances make it impossible to 'switch off'.

Mentally Bronzite provides support in difficult situations and helps us to keep a cool head and maintain control. In doing so, it makes dealing with conflict and extreme situations easier. *Physically* Bronzite boosts the nerves and the digestion (especially in stress-related conditions). It also soothes cramps, eases pain and, in combination with apatite, promotes bone strength.

Application

Bronzite should be worn on the body for an extended period of time. Its uses in gemstone massage, precious gem essences and as a gemstone circle are also highly effective.

Budstone

Crystal system: triclinic (plagioclase feldspar) + monoclinic (fuchsite)
Manner of formation: tertiary
Mineral classes: tectosilicates (plagioclase feldspar) + phyllo
or sheet silicates (fuchsite)
Colour: grass green, dark green to black-green
Chemical formulae: $NaAlSi_3O_8/CaAl_2Si_2O_8$ (plagioclase-feldspar) +
$K(Al,Cr)_2[(OH,F)_2|AlSi_3O_{10}]$ (fuchsite)

Mineralogy

Budstone is a 3.2 billion-year-old metamorphic verdite, with elements of plagioclase feldspar and chromium-rich mica (mostly fuchsite). Rutile (titanium oxide), eskolaite (a chromium oxide in the corundum group) and quartz may be found as host rocks. Budstone was sold for years as 'prase' or 'prasem quartz', although both terms are misleading for this stone (see Prase, page 373).

Mythology

The name budstone is a modern trade name deriving from the way a tumbled budstone looks a little like a closed bud.

Healing

Spiritually Budstone brings decisiveness and vitality. It promotes mental growth, strengthens self-control and enables you to take conscious control of your own life.

Emotionally Budstone soothes hot temper, anger and outbursts of rage. It rebuilds the body's strength at times of extreme exhaustion, helping you to stay abreast of things and to overcome difficulties.

Mentally Budstone helps us to take conscious control of our own actions, even in the most fraught emotional situations. It promotes creativity, inventiveness and dynamism.

Physically Budstone soothes inflammation and pain. It helps with mobility, eases joints and relieves the effects of radiation, sunburn, heatstroke and insect bites.

Application

Budstone can be worn on affected areas of the body as a chain or pendant, or carried as a touchstone. It may also be laid out in a stone circle or taken internally as a precious gem essence.

Calcite

Crystal system: trigonal
Manner of formation: secondary
Mineral class: carbonates
Colour: clear, white, grey, black, red, orange, yellow, green, blue, violet
Chemical formula, mineral-forming substances: $CaCO_3$ + Mn,Fe,Mg + (Sr,Ba,Co,Zn)

Mineralogy

Calcite is created secondarily during the formation of limestones. Well-formed crystals of calcite may be created from sedimentary hydrothermal solutions in pockets and cracks in such rocks.

Mythology

Calcite has been used for thousands of years as lime in folk medicine. It was used as a poultice mainly for skin diseases, ulcers, warts and suppurating wounds.

Healing

Spiritually Calcite has a strong effect in speeding up development. This is particularly noticeable in small children but also in adults who no longer believe in a positive turn in their lives.

Emotionally Calcite bestows stability, trust in ourselves and constancy. It is effective against laziness and strengthens the ability to overcome difficulties.

Mentally Calcite encourages the ability to transform ideas into actions. It increases our power to discriminate and differentiate, also enhances memory and makes us more energetic, industrious and successful.

Physically Calcite stimulates the metabolism, fortifies the immune system and encourages growth in small children. It alleviates skin and intestinal complaints, stimulates blood-clotting and encourages healing of tissue and bone. Calcite normalizes the rhythm of the heart and strengthens the heart.

Application

Calcite may be carried as a touchstone or worn as a pendant for extended periods of time. When it is consumed as a precious gem essence or gemstone elixir, its effects are noticed sooner.

Budstone, South Africa;
Calcite, Brazil

Blue chalcedony

Crystal system: trigonal
Manner of formation: primary or secondary
Mineral class: oxides/tectosilicates, quartz group
Colour: pale blue to light blue, partly striated
Chemical formula, mineral-forming substances: $SiO_2 \cdot H_2O$

Mineralogy

Blue chalcedony is a pure, fibrous microcrystalline quartz formed at temperatures of below 100 degrees Celsius out of solutions rich in silicic acid, usually of magmatic origins and rarely of sedimentary origin. These solutions percolate through fine cracks and veins in rock and collect in larger clefts and cysts, where they solidify and crystallize. Chalcedony obtains its light blue colour by the refraction of light through its microscopically fine crystals (the 'Tyndall effect'), in which the red part of the light is absorbed and the blue part is reflected.

Mythology

In antiquity, chalcedony was already known to represent the elements of air and water. As such, it was employed for weather magic and for healing illnesses that were connected with the weather, such as colds, sensitivity to changes in the weather or circulatory problems. It is also used for the spiritual aspect of the element air, in communication. It has always been considered to be the crystal of orators.

Healing

Spiritually Blue chalcedony represents both aspects of communication: the ability to listen and to understand, as well as the ability to communicate effectively. It encourages the pleasure of contact with other humans, with animals, plants and beings from all worlds. Just as the mineral itself is able to form itself into any given spaces during its formation, chalcedony also helps us to accept new situations and to overcome resistance without at the same time losing our own character.

Emotionally Blue chalcedony bestows a light-heartedness, a carefree, elated feeling for life with an optimistic *joie de vivre*. It enhances conscious self-awareness through improving perception.

Banded chalcedony, Namibia;
Chalcedony rosette, Brazil; Blue chalcedony, Turkey;
Dendritic chalcedony, Brazil

of our feelings, emotions, desires and needs. This is how we learn about the true motives for our actions and are able to change them. In addition, blue chalcedony improves memory, has a calming effect and dissolves stress (touchstone).

Mentally Blue chalcedony improves powers of oratory, verbal dexterity and the ability to speak foreign languages. For this reason, chalcedony is also the crystal of diplomats. With this crystal, we remain mentally open to new ideas; it generally eases understanding and helps us to translate ideas we agree with into action. This increases creativity and openness to inspiration.

Physically Blue chalcedony alleviates problems of the respiratory tract such as colds or the effects of smoking. Banded chalcedony, in particular, encourages regeneration of the mucous membranes. Blue chalcedony also helps with complaints caused by extreme sensitivity to changes in the weather, problems with the eyes that relate to pressure (glaucoma), the ears, and our sense of balance. It has an anti-inflammatory effect, lowers the blood pressure and has a cooling effect in raised temperatures. It stimulates the flow of the lymphatic fluids and body fluids, abolishes water retention in the tissues (oedema) and enhances the immune system and the secretions of the glands. By stimulating insulin production, it can help with the early stages of diabetes.

Clear blue, white or rose-coloured chalcedony, owing to its manner of formation, encourages the formation of milk in nursing mothers. Mother's milk too is formed in spaces between the cells of the breast and then flows through tiny channels to be collected in the gland of the breast.

Application

Chalcedony may be consumed internally as a precious gem essence or gemstone elixir or used as a touchstone. It may also be worn as a chain or a pendant, or as an item of jewellery for extended periods, or placed directly on the diseased part of the body. When used for healing specific organs, chalcedony rosettes are recommended that have the 'signature' of the relevant organ. For example, rosettes with a 'signature' of female sexual organs help to encourage a healthy flora in the vagina and prevent fungal infections as blue chalcedony produces a slightly acid milieu in fluids.

Dendritic chalcedony

Crystal system: trigonal
Manner of formation: primary or secondary
Mineral class: oxides/tectosilicates, quartz group
Colour: white, light blue with black dendrites
Chemical formula, mineral-forming substances: $SiO_2 \cdot H_2O + MnO_2$

Mineralogy

Dendritic chalcedony is formed from solidified silicic acid into which liquid containing manganese has penetrated without creating a mixture. This forms the black dendrites (Greek *dendron*, 'tree') that give the stone its name.

Mythology

In the Middle Ages, the manganese contained in this chalcedony was assigned to the cleansing aspect of the element fire; coloured, impure glass did indeed become clear and pure through melting it together with manganese dioxide.

Healing

Spiritually Dendritic chalcedony represents an affable, sociable nature which is, however, still able to discriminate clearly between its own goals and the opinions and influences of others.

Emotionally Dendritic chalcedony encourages clear thinking, systematic research, the art of unravelling confusion as well as the ability to identify precisely what motives and values really lie behind a piece of information.

Mentally Dendritic chalcedony encourages precise thinking, systematic enquiry, the ability to clarify confusion, as well as the ability to comprehend the real meaning and motives behind information received.

Physically The effects of dendritic chalcedony are similar to those of blue chalcedony. Its effects are even stronger in the case of chronic illnesses and the physical problems associated with smoking.

Application

Dendritic chalcedony can be used as a touchstone, a pendant or a piece of jewellery worn close to the body. It can also be applied directly to the part of the body affected or consumed as a precious gem essence or gemstone elixir.

Copper chalcedony

Crystal system: trigonal
Manner of formation: secondary
Mineral class: oxides/tectosilicates, quartz group
Colour: blue-green with copper inclusions
Chemical formula, mineral-forming substances: $SiO_2 \cdot H_2O$ + Cu + (Cu)

Mineralogy

Copper chalcedony is formed in the cementation zone of rock that contains copper. The copper, which is initially dissolved by the silicic acid, is then partially reduced and is, therefore, preserved as metallic copper in the chalcedony.

Mythology

There are no known traditions for copper chalcedony itself, although copper has always been considered a metal of Venus. It represents love, beauty, sensuality and harmony, and also balance and neutrality.

Healing

Spiritually Copper chalcedony helps us live in the present in full awareness, to face unpleasant things, to communicate calmly when attacked, and to remain relaxed. It helps reveal the true meaning of life and awakens a sense for aesthetics and harmony. It helps us enjoy life.

Emotionally Copper chalcedony stimulates proper processing of inner images and memories. It helps us develop an open, friendly attitude towards fellow human beings and the environment.

Mentally Copper chalcedony helps us preserve neutrality and see situations, other humans and experiences without judging. It encourages both a proper sense of judgement and tolerance.

Physically Copper chalcedony stimulates the metabolism of copper in the body and the detoxification of the liver. It hinders inflammations of the female sexual organs and prevents fungal infections (thrush) in the vagina. Copper chalcedony strengthens the immune system.

Application

Copper chalcedony can be worn for long periods of time on the body or laid directly on the relevant part. Taking copper chalcedony internally as a precious gem essence may also be helpful.

Pink chalcedony

Crystal system: trigonal
Manner of formation: primary or secondary
Mineral class: oxides/tectosilicates, quartz group
Colour: pink to pink-violet
Chemical formula, mineral-forming substances: $SiO_2 \cdot H_2O + (Mn)$

Mineralogy

Pink chalcedony is created in the oxidation zone of rocks containing manganese from silicic acid solutions of magmatic or sedimentary origin.

Mythology

Pink chalcedony has no known traditions of usage, although there are some for manganese, which is the mineral that gives this stone its pink colour. It represents sustaining warmth, inner fire and liveliness.

Healing

Spiritually Pink chalcedony represents liveliness, understanding and helpfulness. It enhances the ability to listen, to understand and to help others deal with their problems and sorrows.

Emotionally Pink chalcedony encourages goodness, kindness and warm-heartedness. It bestows a carefree attitude, inner peace and deep trust, particularly in the case of conflicts and psychosomatic illnesses, such as anxiety about the heart (heart neuroses).

Mentally Pink chalcedony teaches us to view the world with a sense of wonder. It bestows a child-like curiosity, the willingness to learn new things and encourages the gift for story telling.

Physically Pink chalcedony bestows liveliness and warmth. It fortifies the heart so it can function strongly without effort. Pink chalcedony eases breastfeeding and provides the inner tranquillity for the task. Just like blue chalcedony, it enhances the immune system and the flow of lymphatic fluids.

Application

Pink chalcedony can be consumed as gem essence and worn close to the body for longer periods of time or placed directly on the relevant part of the body. For heart problems or for helping breastfeeding, it should, if possible, be in contact with the skin.

Red chalcedony

Crystal system: trigonal
Manner of formation: primary or secondary
Mineral class: oxides/tectosilicates, quartz group
Colour: dark red
Chemical formula, mineral-forming substances: $SiO_2 \cdot H_2O + Fe$

Mineralogy

Red chalcedony is created from a viscous, ferrous silicic acid solution of magmatic or sedimentary origin, in which the iron content is not dissolved in the solution but is retained in the form of a flaky iron oxide.

Mythology

No traditions about red chalcedony have been handed down. The iron that gives it its red colour has, however, been assigned to Mars, and represents willpower, activity, dynamism and the joy of undertaking tasks.

Healing

Spiritually Red chalcedony bestows strength, persistence and the energy to overcome difficulties and attain set goals. It helps us select the right strategy – to give in, fight or remain still – and keeps the mind flexible without at the same time sacrificing our own point of view.

Emotionally Red chalcedony bestows strength and confidence. It makes us aware of our own life's dreams and helps to prove them and realize them without letting a fixation upon them arise.

Mentally Red chalcedony encourages the ability to design strategies. It encourages openness and inspiration and fortifies our intentions, which makes it easier for one's voice to be heard.

Physically Red chalcedony encourages clotting of the blood and stimulates the blood circulation without allowing the blood pressure to become high. It inhibits the absorption of nutrients in the small intestine and reduces hunger pangs.

Application

Red chalcedony should only be used continuously for about two to three weeks. As it inhibits the absorption of nutrients, longer use may induce temporary nausea.

Pink chalcedony, USA;
(Group clockwise from left:) Red chalcedony, Russia;
Blue chalcedony, South Africa; Pink chalcedony;
Copper chalcedony, Turkey

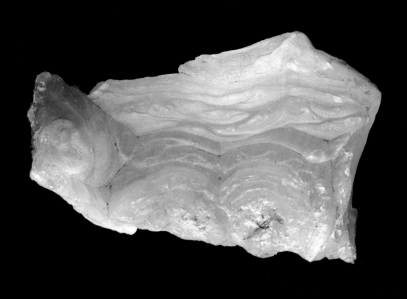

Chalcopyrite

Crystal system: tetragonal
Manner of formation: primary, secondary or tertiary
Mineral class: sulphides
Colour: brass yellow to gold-yellow, with colourful tinting on its oxidised surface
Chemical formula, mineral-forming substances: $CuFeS_2$ + Ag,Au,In,Tl,Se,Te,Zn

Mineralogy

Chalcopyrite is found in all areas of rock formation and is one of the most common minerals worldwide. Beautiful crystals are created in hydrothermal solutions of magmatic and sedimentary origin in particular. Tumbled stones are often made from coarse amygdules of metamorphic origin.

Mythology

Chalcopyrite is one of the few minerals to contain considerable amounts of both copper and iron, in equal quantities. The characteristics of both Venus (copper) and Mars (iron) are therefore to be found in equal proportions in chalcopyrite.

Healing

Spiritually Chalcopyrite excites curiosity and the spirit of research. It awakens a desire to understand the secrets of life.

Emotionally Chalcopyrite inspires us to seek new experiences. It reveals the causes of problems and illnesses and helps us to accept who we are.

Mentally Chalcopyrite helps us to develop systematic thinking and learn from mistakes. In this respect, it promotes powers of observation for even the smallest details.

Physically Chalcopyrite stimulates purification processes. It strengthens the release and excretion of toxins and may therefore cause initial negative symptoms such as drowsiness or nausea, but for a short time only.

Application

Chalcopyrite should be left in direct contact with the skin for only short periods of time, as it exudes a black sulphide upon longer contact, which may irritate the skin. Chalcopyrite is better used for meditation or placed in a position where it can be regularly observed.

Skeletal chalcopyrite growth, China;
Chalcopyrite with tinting, France

Charoite

Crystal system: monoclinic
Manner of formation: tertiary
Mineral class: phyllo or sheet silicates
Colour: intense violet to grey-violet
Chemical formula, mineral-forming substances: $(Ca,Na)_4(K,Sr,Ba)_2[(OH,F)_2Si_9O_{22}] \cdot H_2O + Fe,Mn$

Mineralogy

Charoite is created metasomatically at temperatures around 200 degrees Celsius in the contact zone between limestone and a nepheline syenite with a high content of alkaline or alkaline-earth metals (potassium, sodium, lithium, calcium, barium, strontium). Charoite is always found ingrown in the surrounding rock (charoitite).

Mythology

Charoite is found in the Murunsk Massif between the Chara and Tokko rivers to the south of Olekminsk, in Siberia, Russia. Unfortunately, there is no known tradition for its healing effects.

Healing

Spiritually Charoite helps us cope with profound changes in our lives. It bestows determination, spontaneity, vigour and drive, whenever tasks that have not been dealt with threaten to assume unmanageable proportions, and also helps overcome resistance.

Emotionally Charoite imparts a relaxed attitude towards things and makes us impervious to stress and worry. It bestows quiet, refreshing sleep with intense, creative dreams.

Mentally Charoite helps us make decisions in a thoughtful but unhesitating fashion. It encourages perceptive observation, including self-observation, and counteracts heteronomy (feeling subjected to orders by others) and compulsions.

Physically Charoite helps relieve cramps and encourages an alkaline metabolism. It calms the nerves, alleviates pain and helps with problems of the autonomous nervous system, particularly if they affect the heart.

Application

Charoite should be worn on the body, making contact with the skin, or consumed as a precious gem essence or gemstone elixir. Spending time in a circle of charoite stones also has a very intense effect.

Chiastolite

Crystal system: rhombic
Manner of formation: tertiary
Mineral class: island silicates, andalusite
Colour: white, yellowish, light grey, grey-brown to reddish-brown with a black cross
Chemical formula, mineral-forming substances: Al_2SiO_5 + Fe,Mn,Cr + C

Mineralogy

Chiastolite is an andalusite formed in carbonaceous clayey slates. Carbon is deposited along the crystal edges of this mineral. Because the growth process of the crystal occurs in layers, carbonaceous diagonal cruciform shapes are formed as it grows.

Mythology

The cross with equal sized 'arms' as displayed in chiastolite is an ancient symbol for multiplication (hence the 'x' symbol for multiplying). The meaning of the symbol has, therefore, also been transferred to this mineral.

Healing

Spiritually Chiastolite gives us persistence in realizing our own identity and our life's task. It encourages a proper sense of reality, sobriety and alertness and dissolves illusions.

Emotionally Chiastolite is extremely calming in cases of nervousness, fears and feelings of guilt. It centres, stabilizes and helps us, particularly against the fear of madness.

Mentally Chiastolite fortifies the analytical capabilities of the intellect. It enhances conscious awareness and helps us discard the behavioural patterns of holding on and holding back.

Physically Chiastolite alleviates excess acidification and its consequences, for example, rheumatism and gout. It fortifies the nerves and helps in states of weakness, slowed perception and movement, even in cases of paralysis.

Application

The best application for chiastolite is in daily meditation, for its spiritual, emotional and mental effects. It can also be worn or placed on the body. Consuming chiastolite as precious gem essence or gemstone elixir for physical problems is also recommended.

Chrysoberyl

Crystal system: rhombic
Manner of formation: primary or tertiary
Mineral class: oxides
Colour: white, yellowish, light grey, grey-brown to reddish-brown with a black cross
Chemical formula, mineral-forming substances: Al_2BeO_4 + Cr,Fe,Ti,V

Mineralogy

Chrysoberyl is formed magmatically, mainly in pegmatites, or metamorphically during the formation of mica slates. Its crystals are, as a rule, only a few millimetres long (25.4 mm = 1 inch).

Mythology

In ancient times, no distinction was made between chrysoberyl and golden beryl. The stone we now know as chrysoberyl was not named as such until the eighteenth century. Chrysoberyl is therefore known only today as the stone of rulers and commanders.

Healing

Spiritually Chrysoberyl bestows severity, authority and leadership qualities. It encourages (self) discipline, self-control, ambition and independence and brings to light hidden talents.

Emotionally Chrysoberyl helps with fears, feelings of apprehension and nightmares. It enables us to complete necessary tasks without becoming overwhelmed by our feelings and moods.

Mentally Chrysoberyl encourages strategic thinking and planning, as well as becoming conscious of and recognizing thought, behavioural and social structures.

Physically Chrysoberyl enhances the self-healing properties of the body and helps with illnesses and inflammations in the area of the chest. Chrysoberyl fortifies the liver.

Application

Chrysoberyl produces its effects simply when worn on the body but it should not be in permanent contact with the skin. Just holding it in the hand occasionally is sufficient. Precious gem essences and elixirs are usually very strong and should therefore be taken in small doses only.

Charoite, Russia; Chiastolith, Chile;
Chrysoberyl, Zimbabwe; Chrysoberyl Drilling, Brazil

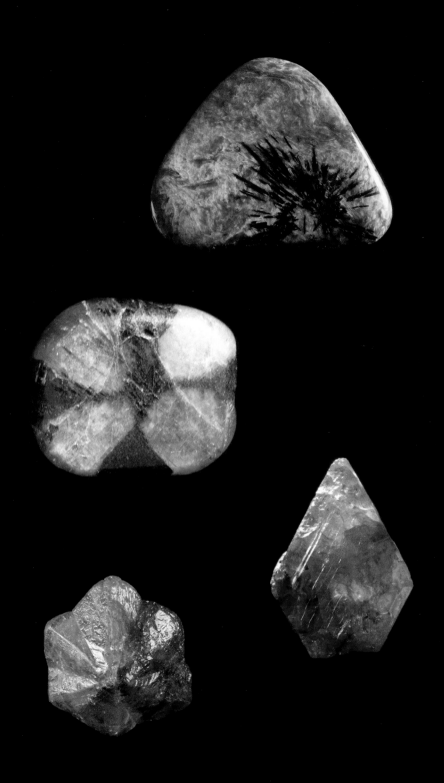

Chrysocolla

Crystal system: monoclinic
Manner of formation: primary or secondary
Mineral class: ring silicates
Colour: blue-green, turquoise
Chemical formula, mineral-forming substances: $(Cu,Al)_2[H_2Si_2O_5(OH)_4] \cdot n\ H_2O$

Mineralogy

Chrysocolla is created in the oxidation zone of copper ore deposits, under the influence of hydrothermal silicic acid solutions of magmatic or sedimentary origin.

Mythology

Chrysocolla was known as healing stone mainly among the Native American cultures, where it was used for strengthening the body's resistance and for calming upset feelings.

Healing

Spiritually Chrysocolla encourages a balanced nature and self-awareness. It helps us accept situations that are constantly changing and to pursue our own goals in spite of ups and downs.

Emotionally Chrysocolla bestows drive in cases of laziness but, at the same time, improves nervousness and irritability.

Mentally Chrysocolla helps us keep a 'cool head'. It encourages neutrality and clarity.

Physically Chrysocolla helps with infections, particularly those of the tonsils and throat area. It detoxifies and fortifies the liver functions. Chrysocolla has a cooling effect, lowers the blood pressure and speeds up healing of burns. It regulates the functioning of the thyroid gland and helps in cases of stress-related digestive disturbances. Chrysocolla also has fever-reducing properties and alleviates cramps, particularly in menstruation.

Application

For physical complaints, chrysocolla produces the best results when placed directly on the part of the body affected or consumed as a precious gem essence or elixir. Wearing chrysocolla produces a spiritual and emotional effect, and laying it on the forehead (as a 'third eye') a spiritual effect.

Chrysocolla, USA;
Chrysocolla, Peru

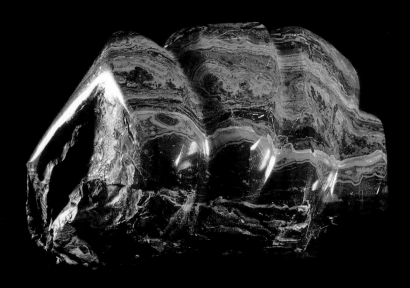

Chrysoprase

Crystal system: trigonal
Manner of formation: secondary
Mineral class: oxides/tectosilicates, quartz group
Colour: apple green
Chemical formula, mineral-forming substances: $SiO_2 \cdot H_2O$ + Ni,Fe,Cr

Mineralogy

Chrysoprase is an apple green chalcedony that obtains its colour from nickel traces. It is formed through a secondary process from solutions of silicic acid in the oxidation zone of nickel deposits. The nickel that is dissolved out of the surrounding rock by silicic acid will only give the mineral its colour as long as water is also present in the crystal lattice of the mineral. During the intermediate stage, prase opal is created, which looks so similar to chrysoprase it could almost be mistaken for it. This, in turn, is transformed into chrysoprase through loss of water. When it dries out completely, it loses its characteristic green colour and turns pale.

Mythology

In antiquity, chrysoprase was assigned to Venus. It does not, however, represent physical sensuality or love for the other sex but the 'very divine love of truth', as later summarized by the seer Emmanuel Swedenborg. This aims at a sense of justice that is also an attribute of the goddess Venus. Hildegard of Bingen assigned a detoxifying effect to chrysoprase and mentions its healing power particularly with gout. She also recommended it for calming anger and even for preventing speaking thoughtlessly in anger. This also demonstrates its relation to chalcedony.

Healing

Spiritually Chrysoprase endows us with the experience of being part of a greater whole. It makes us alert and quick-witted and draws our attention to seemingly random coincidences in which we can perceive the activity of the spiritual realm. Chrysoprase encourages a simple, child-like world view in which guardian angels and spirit guides are not in conflict with logical or rational considerations. Chrysoprase combines a search for truth with patience so we can become happy even if we only understand a tiny fraction of the universe. It encourages an appreciation of aesthetics, art and beauty.

Chrysoprase, Australia;
Citrine, Brazil

Emotionally Chrysoprase bestows trust and a feeling of security. It helps us become independent of others and be content with ourselves. This reduces jealousy and heartache and also helps with sexual problems. Just as it physically detoxifies, chrysoprase also relieves us of oppressive images, or helps us deal with them. It puts an end to recurring nightmares, particularly in children who wake up crying at night without recognizing their surroundings.

Mentally Chrysoprase helps us recognize egotistical motives in actions and encourages us to examine whether our real actions are in harmony with our own inner ideals. It helps us to avoid compulsive actions, behaviour and thought patterns. In cases of negative attitudes, chrysoprase draws the attention to positive events and thus alters the 'perception filter' with which we normally try to confirm our own inner attitude through selective perception.

Physically Chrysoprase stimulates detoxification and elimination. Even heavy metals and other substances that are difficult to dissolve are eliminated from the body. In addition, the liver's functions are strongly stimulated. Illnesses that have occurred as a result of toxification (including through taking strong medicines) can be healed in this way. Chrysoprase also helps many skin diseases, even some forms of neurodermititis, and helps in combination with smoky quartz for fungal infections. It also stimulates fertility in women, particularly if infections have led to infertility.

Application

Chrysoprase may be worn as a chain or pendant, or carried as a touchstone for extended periods of time, or be laid directly on affected areas of the body. Its eliminating properties may be supported by a fasting cure. The strongest effect in acute cases is achieved by taking chrysoprase in the form of a precious gem essence or elixir.

Citrine

Crystal system: trigonal
Manner of formation: primary, secondary or tertiary
Mineral class: oxides/tectosilicates, quartz group
Colour: light yellow, gold-yellow to brownish yellow (cognac),
more rarely greenish yellow
Chemical formula, mineral-forming substances: SiO_2 + (Al,Fe)

Mineralogy

Citrine is a yellow crystal quartz whose colour is produced by tiny deposits of iron or slight doses of ionising irradiation. It is created in hydrothermal solutions of magmatic, sedimentary or metamorphic origin.

Mythology

The term 'citrine' was used until the sixteenth century for many different yellow coloured stones (beryl, zircon, etc.). It was not until 1546 that the term was first clearly assigned to yellow quartz. Modern citrine was then said to be able to strengthen the intellect and provoke a sunny disposition.

Healing

Spiritually Citrine encourages individuality, self-confidence and the courage to face and enjoy life. It makes us dynamic and encourages a desire for variety, new experiences and self-realization.

Emotionally Citrine bestows *joie de vivre*. It helps us overcome depression and free ourselves from oppressive influences. Citrine makes us extroverted and encourages self-expression.

Mentally Citrine helps us digest impressions we have received. It stimulates the ability to confront and help ourselves, to draw conclusions rapidly and to understand them.

Physically Citrine stimulates the digestion. It promotes the working of the stomach, spleen and pancreas and will even alleviate diabetes in its early stages. Citrine fortifies the nerves and has a warming effect.

Application

Citrine should be worn in contact with the skin or used, for example, as a sphere or crystal for meditation. Internal consumption as a precious gem essence or gemstone elixir is also extremely beneficial.

Diamond

Crystal system: cubic
Manner of formation: tertiary
Mineral class: native elements
Colour: clear, grey, yellow, brown, black, more rarely blue, red, green
Chemical formula, mineral-forming substances: C_n + (N,B)

Mineralogy

Diamonds are formed in peridotite and eclogite rock at depths of approximately 150–200 kilometres (90–125 miles). The pressure at these depths of around 40,000 atmospheres and temperatures of more than 2,000 degrees Celsius are such that carbon that is present in the form of hexagonal graphite is transformed into diamond in a metamorphosis. The mineral is then brought to the surface from the inside of the Earth through volcanic eruptions, when rising lava rips entire pieces of rock from the deep rock and takes them up with it. This mixture of lava and rock in the volcanic chimney then forms rocks called kimberlite and lamproite, in which diamonds are later found.

Because of its material purity (pure carbon), diamond can be completely clear and transparent. Its ability to bend/refract light is very pronounced (its 'fire') and it is the hardest known mineral. Trace deposits of other elements can lend diamonds a variety of colours. Nitrogen produces yellow, brown and green, while boron creates blues and greys. Other colours are caused by faults in the crystal lattice.

Mythology

The name 'diamond' is derived from the Greek *adamas*, 'invincible'. This is precisely the theme that runs through the entire mythology of the diamond. In many cultures, the diamond was assigned to Venus. It was seen as a liberator from demonic influences and represented justice and virtue. In the Middle Ages, it symbolized strength, courage and invulnerability. The diamond was thought to protect whoever carried it from the threat of danger and also to encourage the development of a noble character. Woe betide anyone, however, who dared to steal it or obtain it by foul or unjust means. Then it appeared to bring bad luck, as demonstrated by the history of all the great and famous diamonds. The tradition that the diamond is helpful with mental illnesses and nervous complaints has been upheld to the present day.

Diamond, South Africa;
Dioptas, Namibia

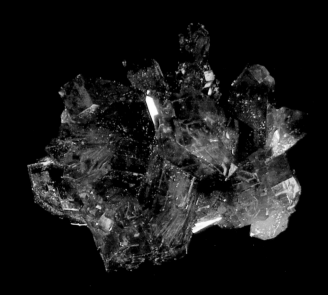

Healing

Spiritually The diamond endows us with a clear insight into our own life's situation. It helps us cope with life's trials and tests and serves to ennoble the character. Diamonds bring order into our life and help us get rid of both poor compromises and unnecessary rules and restrictions. It encourages spiritual freedom and helps us to develop integrity, that is, to be true to ourselves. It fortifies our sense of ethics and inner justice. Thus, it creates objectivity, the ability to do what is right without prejudice.

Emotionally Diamond helps us overcome fear, depression and a feeling of a lack of meaning in our lives. It helps overcome crises that have arisen through the failure of plans and goals. Diamonds make us aware of the causes of problems or illnesses and also make it possible to examine them without bias. This enables us to achieve better control of our inner images, our feelings and moods, and ultimately of our entire lives.

Mentally Diamonds help us gain a complete overview of the consequences of our own actions. They encourage logical thinking and make it possible for us to observe broader connections between things. Diamond bestows the ability to learn easily, making immediate connections between new impressions and familiar experiences. This means that things we have learned can be applied quickly. Diamond encourages the ability to make clear decisions and solve problems.

Physically Diamond can be employed whenever insight or long overdue change in our life become necessary. In particular, it heals diseases of those organs that have a direct bearing on mental activities, for example the brain, nervous system, sensory organs and hormonal glands. Just as it is able to improve the mental control of our lives, it also fortifies control of our body.

Application

Diamond can be either worn on the body or placed on the forehead during meditation ('third eye'). Powerful effects are also produced by drinking diamond as gem essence. Diamond also enhances the effects of other crystals.

Dioptase

Crystal system: trigonal
Manner of formation: primary or secondary
Mineral class: ring silicates
Colour: intense emerald green to dark green
Chemical formula, mineral-forming substances: $Cu_6(Si_6O_{18}) \cdot 6\ H_2O + (Zn)$

Mineralogy

Dioptase is formed primarily in the sedimentary process out of silicic acid solutions containing copper in clefts of limestone and sandstone rock, or secondarily in the oxidation zone of copper ore deposits.

Mythology

Dioptase (also called 'copper emerald' in German) was always considered to be a stone of abundance and riches. It was assigned to Venus and represents a sense of beauty.

Healing

Spiritually Dioptase makes us aware of our inner riches. It helps shed light on our own capabilities and realize our ambitions.

Emotionally Dioptase encourages self-awareness. It bestows vivid dreams, hope and depth of feeling and stimulates us to place ourselves at the centre of general interest.

Mentally Dioptase enlivens the imagination and the ability to use the imagination creatively. It stimulates creativity, engenders abundance of ideas and makes it easier for them to be translated into action.

Physically Dioptase stimulates the regenerative power of the liver. It has a pain alleviating effect, loosens cramp, and helps with chronic headaches.

Application

Dioptase forms only very tiny crystals and in fragile small groups, so it can only very rarely be worn. For its effects on the mind and spirit, using dioptase as a focus for meditation or laying it on the forehead is recommended. For healing the body, place it carefully on the affected area or take it internally as a precious gem essence and gemstone elixir.

Disthene (kyanite)

Crystal system: triclinic
Manner of formation: tertiary
Mineral class: island silicates
Colour: blue, blue-green, yellow-green, grey, black
Chemical formula, mineral-forming substances: Al_2SiO_5 + Fe,Cr

Mineralogy

Disthene, or kyanite, is one of the characteristic principal minerals formed during the metamorphosis of crystalline slates (indicating a particular relationship between temperature and pressure in their metamorphosis).

Mythology

In ancient times, kyanos was a collective term for blue minerals (azurite, lapis lazuli). The mineral discussed here was not named until the eighteenth century, which is why there are no existing traditions as to the effects of disthene/kyanite. The name disthene originated in the nineteenth century and has only recently been used as an alternative to kyanite.

Healing

Spiritually Disthene helps us to detach ourselves from a belief in fate and to recognize when and where we have created the causes that have certain effects later on. Disthene also gives us determination.

Emotionally Disthene leads to a calming effect on the inner world of images and stirred-up emotions. It encourages a pleasant, peaceful nature and liberates us from frustrations and stress.

Mentally Disthene encourages logical, rational thought and spontaneous action whenever necessary. Disthene also encourages conscious self-awareness.

Physically Disthene fortifies the functions of the cerebellum and of the motor nervous system, thus improving mobility and dexterity.

Application

Although for a long time disthene was only available as crystals or aggregates, it is now also available as tumbled stones. Disthene is best worn on the body, applied to the affected areas or consumed as a precious gem essence.

Disthene, Brazil

Dolomite

Crystal system: trigonal
Manner of formation: secondary or tertiary
Mineral class: carbonates
Colour: white, grey, beige, yellow, brown, orange, pink, red, pink-violet
Chemical formula, mineral-forming substances: $CaMg(CO_3)_2$ + Fe,Mn + (Co,Pb,Zn)

Mineralogy

Dolomite forms rocks in sediments and metamorphites (dolomite marble), where beautiful crystals are created from hydrothermal solutions of sedimentary or metamorphic origin.

Mythology

In 1791, during his journeys through the Alps, a man called Dolomieu discovered limestones that differed in their properties from the usual limestone. Following this, the composition of dolomite was investigated for the first time. This is why there are no traditions regarding dolomite as it was previously always identified with calcite.

Healing

Spiritually Dolomite encourages self-realization. It makes it easier to be ourselves without pretending otherwise. At the same time, it fortifies a sense of tradition and helps us fit into developing communities.

Emotionally Dolomite ensures stability. It has a balancing effect in cases of sudden, violent emotional outbursts and bestows contentment.

Mentally Dolomite encourages simple, pragmatic thought and helps with the easy, uncomplicated realization of goals we have set for ourselves. Dolomite also stimulates healthy commonsense.

Physically Dolomite stimulates the metabolism of calcium and magnesium and keeps the balance between these two 'opponents'. This means it stabilizes health, particularly blood, the heart and the circulation, and has a relaxing, cramp-dissolving effect.

Application

Dolomite can be worn, placed on the body or consumed as gemstone essence or elixir. The most powerful effect is achieved by spending time close to dolomite rock or in a stone circle of dolomite.

Dolomite, Brazil;
Dolomite, pyrite, Switzerland

Dumortierite

Crystal system: rhombic
Manner of formation: primary and tertiary
Mineral class: island silicates
Colour: blue, grey, green, brown
Chemical formula, mineral-forming substances: $(Al,Fe)_7[O_3|BO_3|(SiO_4)_3] + Mn,Ti$

Mineralogy

Dumortierite is created either magmatically in pegmatites, or through the pneumatolytic process (the action of boracic acid on aluminium silicate rocks), or alternatively through contact or regional metamorphic conditions.

Mythology

Dumortierite was not discovered until the end of the nineteenth century and named after the French palaeontologist Eugène Dumortier. This is why there are no existing traditions about its effects.

Healing

Spiritually Dumortierite bestows a positive attitude towards life. It provides courage and trust in difficult situations and helps us gain control over our own life or preserve it.

Emotionally Dumortierite confers an easy, cheerful outlook on life and is, therefore, often termed the 'take-it-easy' stone. Dumortierite helps us cope with panic and fear and encourages harmony and trust.

Mentally Dumortierite helps us recognize compulsive behavioural patterns and dissolve them. It is, therefore, also used as a supportive aid in addiction therapy.

Physically Dumortierite helps with nausea, vomiting, cramp, colic and diarrhoea. It alleviates skin irritation caused by toxins or radiation (UV light) and helps with nervous problems, for example with severe headaches, epilepsy or disturbances of perception.

Application

Dumortierite can be worn for long periods of time or, in acute cases, directly on the part of the body affected. Consuming dumortierite in precious gem essence or gemstone elixirs also produces good results.

Epidote

Crystal system: monoclinic
Manner of formation: tertiary
Mineral class: sorosilicates
Colour: green to brown-black
Chemical formula, mineral-forming substances: $Ca_2(Fe,Al)$
$Al_2[O|OH|SiO_4|Si_2O_7] + Cr,Mg,Mn,Sr,Ti,Pb,V,Th$

Mineralogy

While epidote may be created at great depths of crystallization in magmatic rocks, it has not yet been of great importance in crystal healing. Epidote is often created through contact or regional metamorphosis if the transformed rocks are basic and rich in calcium and aluminium. When mixed with red feldspar, it forms a rock that is available under the trade name 'unakite'. Epidote crystals are formed in metamorphic hydrothermal crevices.

Mythology

Epidote was not identified as a separate mineral until the beginning of the nineteenth century, by the French crystallographer Rene-Just Haüy (see also Part 1, Chapter 1.2, page 43). Before that, it was always considered to be the same mineral as actinolite. Epidote also received its name from Haüy. It means something like 'addition' (Latin) as epidote, unlike actinolite, has two 'extended' sides. Unfortunately, there are no traditions about the healing effects of epidote.

Healing

Spiritually Epidote bestows patience. It dissolves false self-images, makes us aware of reality and highlights the weaknesses and strengths of the true self-image. This results in desires for change that are, however, realistic so they can be realized and success can then build on success. In this manner, epidote takes us back to the original positive inner images of a healthy, happy existence. This is exactly the meaning of 're-generate' (*re*, 'back, again, anew'; *generere*, 'to form').

Emotionally Epidote encourages recovery and regeneration after severe illnesses or in cases of great exhaustion caused by overwork, stress and painful experiences. It lifts the emotions and dissolves sadness, sorrow, self-pity and grief. Epidote also helps overcome frustration caused by failure and teaches us not to devalue ourselves because of mistakes we have made.

Mentally Epidote improves our capabilities. It helps us live up to our own demands in an appropriate fashion, with due consideration of our own strength and ability, and in this way saves us from failure. By gradually increasing these demands, our own capabilities can then be harmoniously expanded and developed. Epidote also helps us accept and admit to our weaknesses.

Physically Epidote strengthens the constitution and our general condition, stimulates the immune system and generally supports all healing processes. It can, therefore, be added to other appropriate minerals but the effect cannot be felt fully in the presence of a major weakness. Along with all this, epidote also stimulates the liver in its function as our central organ of regeneration, encourages the production of gall, and improves the digestive processes in the small intestine. This means that more nutrients are absorbed into the bloodstream, which, in turn, has a building up, fortifying effect.

Application

The spiritual effect of epidote is most obvious in meditation. In this case, an epidote crystal can be either laid on the forehead or on the solar plexus. A similar effect is achieved by spending time inside an epidote circle (or double circle) that will, at the same time, noticeably stimulate the regeneration of mind and body. Otherwise, this mineral can be worn for a long period of time as a chain or pendant, or carried as touchstone, and in cases of acute illness may be laid on the affected part of the body or taken internally as a precious gem essence and gemstone elixir.

Dumortierite, Mozambique;
Epidote (unakite), South Africa

Falcon's eye

Crystal system: trigonal (quartz) + monoclinic (crocidolite)
Manner of formation: secondary
Mineral class: oxides/tectosilicates (quartz) + chain silicates, amphibole (crocidolite)
Colour: blue-grey to blue-black, also green-black
Chemical formula, mineral-forming substances: SiO_2 (quartz) + $Na_2Mg_3Fe_2(OH/Si_4O_{11})_2$ + Al,Ti (crocidolite)

Mineralogy
Falcon's eye is created secondarily through the silicification of crocidolite (black-blue riebeckite asbestos) when the asbestos fibres of the crocidolite are firmly enclosed in quartz.

Mythology
The silky gleam created by the asbestos fibres in the quartz makes light play in the polished stone so that it resembles an eye. This is how the stone got its name, and also explains the belief that falcon's eye can cure eye complaints and give protection.

Healing
Spiritually Falcon's eye helps us see the seemingly random events of everyday life in a broader context. It bestows an understanding of our own life plan.

Emotionally Falcon's eye brings proper distance to our own feelings and emotions and, thereby, helps us be less influenced by mood fluctuations.

Mentally Falcon's eye helps us gain a better overview in complicated situations and assists in making difficult decisions.

Physically Falcon's eye has a pain-alleviating effect. It tones down the flow of energies in the body, thereby helping with nervousness and trembling, as well as with an excitability of the glands that govern hormone production.

Application
If there is already a blockage in the body, falcon's eye can inhibit the flow of energy within it, which may be experienced as numbness of the limbs. In such cases, it should never be worn continually for periods longer than a week. Otherwise, falcon's eye may be worn, applied or consumed as a gem essence or gemstone elixir. Meditation is recommended for its emotional and spiritual effects.

Fluorite

Crystal system: cubic
Manner of formation: primary, secondary or tertiary
Mineral class: halogenides
Colour: clear, blue, green, yellow, pink, violet, also multicoloured
Chemical formula, mineral-forming substances: CaF_2 + C, Ce, Cl, Fe, Mn, Y

Mineralogy

Fluorite may be formed magmatically and hydrothermally (China, Mexico, Germany), sedimentarily and hydrothermally (England, Spain and Illinois, Missouri, Tennessee/USA) or metamorphically and hydrothermally (pink fluorite from the Alps). The largest deposits are of magmatic origin, where it is created through the action of solutions of fluorine on rocks containing calcium.

Mythology

Fluorite has been known as fluorspar since the eighteenth century. Before that, it was not recognized as a separate mineral but simply belonged among the 'spars', a general term for minerals that break in 'leaves' (related to 'cleaving', from the German *spalten*). It was also classed among substances called by the German name Fluss ('flow'), an equally general term denoting additives that enable ore to reach a melting point more quickly (German *fliessen*, 'to flow, melt'), or even among the German *Glasflusse* ('molten glasses'), products that arise during the production of glass. Fluorite, like glass and coloured quartzes, can be used for the production of imitation gems. As a result, it is not possible to establish now whether the old names 'ruby glass', 'topaz glass', etc. actually refer to fluorite or to quartz and glass. This makes it equally difficult to establish any definite traditions concerning its healing properties!

Healing

Spiritually Fluorite stimulates the 'free spirit' that wishes to determine and shape our lives. It makes us aware of where we are being controlled by outside influences and 'not playing our own game', and helps us rapidly dissolve these undesirable influences. Fluorite can make us radical and uncompromising whenever we come across injustice or oppressive structures. At the same time, it helps us structure our own existence and enables us to find systems that are stable but dynamic. Generally speaking, fluorite makes us creative and inventive, with the dominant theme being 'free decision-making'.

Fluorite, Switzerland;
Fluorite, USA

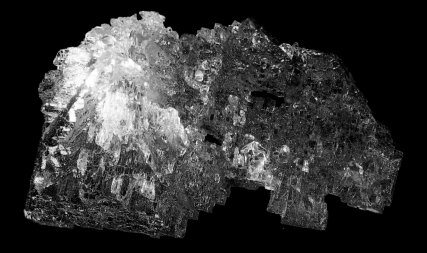

Emotionally Fluorite makes us aware of suppressed feelings. It does not, however, emphasize their expression, but helps them 'happen gradually'. Fluorite opens the gateway to the subconscious, but as a rule an external event will have to trigger this before we suddenly recognize the depth of feeling we have achieved. Overall, fluorite has an emotionally stabilizing effect, gives us self-confidence, and clears up confusion.

Mentally Fluorite helps dissolve blocks, fixed ideas, 'small thinking', narrow-mindedness and constricting thought and behavioural patterns. It also helps with organization and the rapid processing of information. This makes it an excellent learning aid as it helps us to use our existing knowledge and experiences and grasp elusive concepts. Fluorite stimulates rapid absorption of information and quick thinking.

Physically Fluorite stimulates the regeneration of the skin and mucous membranes, particularly in the respiratory tract and the lungs, and helps with ulcers and suppurating wounds. It fortifies the bones and teeth, decreases adhesions and helps with posture problems. Fluorite makes us physically mobile and improves stiffness and joint problems, including cases of arthritis (inflammation of the joints). The activity of the nervous system, particularly the cerebrum, is encouraged and psychosomatic allergies are alleviated.

Application

The spiritual effect of fluorite is felt most through meditating with banded Chinese fluorite (expression of creativity) or with fluorite octahedrons (expression of order). For a better sense of order, fluorite groups or octahedrons can be placed in the personal environment, or as a learning support on a desk. Otherwise, fluorite can be worn, laid directly on the body or consumed as a precious gem essence or gemstone elixir.

Fluorite octahedra, USA

Jet (lignite, brown coal)

Crystal system: amorphous
Manner of formation: secondary
Mineral class: organic rocks
Colour: black
Mineral-forming substances: approx. 83% C, 5% H, 10% O, 0,1% N
(mixture of various hydrocarbons)

Mineralogy

Jet is a sedimentary carbonaceous rock. It is created through the pressure decomposition of wood in swamp areas, when lignite is suffused with bitumen (oily hydrocarbons). Jet is thus particularly commonly found in lignite deposits or clay sediments.

Mythology

Jet was worn in the Bronze Age in armbands, necklaces and rings, as goods found in graves have demonstrated. It was used in ancient times for stomach complaints and its smoke was said to protect against demons. For many of the Native American peoples of North America, jet was considered one of the four holy stones (along with turquoise, abalone and white mussel abalone). It was a popular stone for jewellery in nineteenth-century Europe and was later worn in particular during times of mourning or crisis (such as after the Second World War).

Healing

Spiritually Jet helps us to overcome pessimism and inner emptiness, to develop confidence and trust and to respect our own dignity.

Emotionally Jet enables us to overcome grief, despair, depression and disappointment, to let things go and to accept the inevitable.

Mentally Jet helps us to strive continually and determinedly towards an improvement in life circumstances and always to remain open to new things.

Physically Jet promotes purification and excretion. It is an aid for complaints of the mouth, gums, bowels (diarrhoea), skin, joints and spine.

Application

Jet can be worn for longer periods, placed directly on affected areas of the body or consumed as a precious gem essence or gemstone elixir.

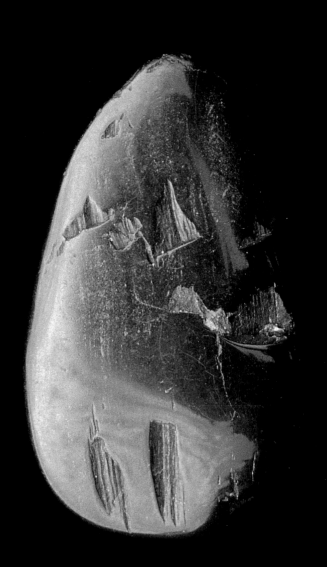

Garnet

Crystal system: cubic
Manner of formation: tertiary
Mineral class: island silicate
Colour: red, pink, orange, yellow, green-brown to black
Chemical formula, mineral-forming substances:
$Me^{2+}_3Me^{3+}_2(SiO_4)_3$ + Al,Ca,Fe,Mg,Mn,Ti

Mineralogy

Garnet is a mineral group made up of a number of stones that are so different in their chemical composition that they should be discussed as minerals in their own right. In practice, however, this creates difficulties, as the pure form is practically never encountered in nature and the various garnets appear as mixed crystals. In addition, the characteristics of the stones are very similar as they are almost all formed in metamorphic rocks, all have the same cubic structure, are all island silicates and all retain a very particular proportion of elements in their chemical composition, even though the particular substances are different: every garnet consists of divalent metal ions, trivalent metal ions and island silicate molecules in invariable 3 : 2 : 3 proportions (the general formula is: $Me^{2+}_3Me^{3+}_2(SiO_4)_3$). The similarity of their properties is understandable when the similarity of the various members of the group is taken into account. The following garnets are currently known and used as healing crystals.

Variety	Formula, minerla-forming substances	Colour
Almandine	$Fe_3Al_2(SiO_4)_3$ + Ca,Mg,Mn,Ti	red, brown through black
Andradite	$Ca_3Fe_2(SiO_4)_3$ + Al	khaki, brown, blackish
Grossularite	$Ca_3Al_2(SiO_4)_3$ + Fe,Mn	grey, green through pink
Hessonite	$Ca_3(Al,Fe)_2(SiO_4)_3$	red, yellow, orange, brown
Melanite	$(Ca,Na)_3(Fe,Ti)_2(SiO_4)_3$	black
Pyrope	$Mg_3Al_2(SiO_4)_3$ + Fe,Ti	dark red
Rhodolithe	$(Mg,Fe)_3Al_2(SiO_4)_3$ + Ti	dark red to reddish violet
Spessartite	$Mn_3Al_2(SiO_4)_3$ + Fe	yellow, red-brown, brown
Uvarovite	$Ca_3Cr_2(SiO_4)_3$	emerald green

*Almandine in slate, Austria;
Andradite, USA; Hessonite, Italy*

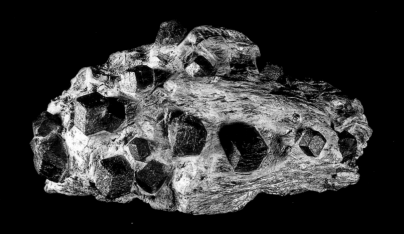

Mythology

Garnet corresponds to the carbuncle in medieval times. It is the stone that was reputed to glow in the dark. Even in the Middle Ages, however, this was considered to be on a spiritual level: the carbuncle that illuminates the darkened soul and brings light and hope where the path (of life) seems to have no end. It was the stone of heroes who had to deal with difficult tasks and trials in order to prove their courage. This is demonstrated by how a rough garnet often looks very inconspicuous before its hidden inner colour and fire are brought to light by polishing. Correspondingly, life's trials and difficulties were seen as a spiritual 'polishing process' that ennobled the character. Warriors in the Middle Ages often had garnets set into their shields and sword hilts to protect themselves against injury in battle and garnet amulets were thought to bring luck, wealth and blessings.

Healing

In general, garnet does the following:

Spiritually Garnet helps in situations with no way out. It is the classical stone of crises, whenever our world view collapses or general life circumstances become extremely difficult. It is a fact that it has always been in fashion in times of crisis (for example, after the First and Second World Wars). Garnet also helps us cope with and surmount everyday problems in extreme situations. It fortifies that inner flame, the desire for self-realization and encourages the basic dynamics of shared survival: mutual help. Garnet also helps us see further than our own narrow horizon and to be committed to the good of the community.

Emotionally Garnet promotes self-confidence, strength of character and *joie de vivre*. It bestows courage, hope and trust; obstacles are seen as challenges that have to be dealt with. In difficult situations, garnet displays an endurance that will surprise its wearer. Garnet eliminates unnecessary inhibitions and taboos, ensures active, balanced sexuality, and helps with potency problems.

Mentally Garnet helps us reject unusable or worn-out ideas, views, agreements and correspondences and to begin a new life. It dissolves behavioural patterns and habits that hinder us from achieving freedom in our lives. Garnet bestows a wealth of new ideas and the necessary dynamic to realize them in spite of resistance, enmity or conscious sabotage.

Grossularite, Russia;
Grossularite, Mexico; Pyrope, Alaska

Physically Garnet fortifies the power of regeneration in the body. It eliminates blocks, stimulates the metabolism and harmonizes the composition of body fluids, particularly of the blood. Garnet stabilizes the circulation and fortifies the immune system, encourages absorption of nutrients in the intestines and accelerates healing of inner and external wounds.

Application

Garnet may be worn as a chain (only a few types of garnet) or pendant, or carried as a touchstone or rough stone. It may be laid directly on the affected part of the body, where direct contact with the skin is essential. It can also be consumed in the form of a precious gem essence or gemstone elixir. Special varieties are recommended for certain applications:

Almandine: Thirst for action, capacity for work, gift for imagination, absorption of iron in the intestine, wound healing.
Andradite: Dynamic, flexibility, creative thoughts, stimulates liver, encourages formation of blood.
Grossularite: Relaxation, fortifies the kidneys, good for skin and mucous membranes, good against rheumatism and arthritis.
Hessonite: Self-respect, spiritual growth, regulates hormone production.
Melanite: Honesty, resistance, strengthens the spine and bones.
Pyrope: Courage, good quality of life, charisma, fortifies the circulation, improves the quality of the blood.
Rhodolite: *Joie de vivre*, warmth, sincerity, trust, healthy sexuality, stimulates the metabolism.
Spessartite: Willingness to help others, strengthens the heart, antidepressive, helps with nightmares and sexual problems.
Uvarovite: Individuality, enthusiasm, detoxification, anti-inflammatory, helps with fever.

Melanite, USA;
Spessartite, Madagascar;
Uvarovite, Russia

Halite (rock salt, salt stone)

Crystal system: cubic
Manner of formation: secondary
Mineral class: halogenides
Colour: clear, white, pink, orange, blue, blue-violet, brown to black
Chemical formula, mineral-forming substances: NaCl + K,F,Br,J

Mineralogy

Rock salt is created sedimentarily as an evaporite in shallow salt lakes and seas. When horizontal deposits are covered over by ever heavier layers of sediment, the slicker, lighter salt begins to force its way into cracks and crevices under the pressure and rises; this is how vertical salt pillars are formed.

Mythology

Rock salt (halite) is an ancient resource and medicine with a rich tradition of use. Three of its properties have long been valued all over the world: the power to protect, to purify and to heal.

Healing

Spiritually Halite has a purifying and liberating effect. It promotes consciousness and protects us against subtle influence and manipulation.

Emotionally Halite brings inner balance. It helps to break habits and unconscious behaviour patterns and relieves melancholy moods.

Mentally Halite helps us to break habitual patterns of thinking. It promotes concentration and boosts decisiveness.

Physically Halite regulates the nervous system, metabolism and the body's water balance. It clears blockages, detoxifies and clears the airways, bowels and skin.

Application

Halite may used as a focus in contemplative meditation, or it can be arranged as a stone circle or set up in the user's immediate environment (e.g. as a rock salt lamp). For physical complaints, it can be applied externally as a crystal or rough stone and worn on the body. Halite is also used in a 1.5% solution as a spa drink, for rinsing, inhalations, bathing and poultices.

Halite crystal, Germany

Hematite

Crystal system: trigonal
Manner of formation: primary, secondary or tertiary
Mineral class: oxides
Colour: iron-grey, red-brown
Chemical formula, mineral-forming substances: Fe_2O_3 + Al,Mg,Ti

Mineralogy

Hematite is generally a secondary or tertiary formation. The largest hematite deposits were created 3.8 to 1.8 billion years ago from iron that found its way into the sea through volcanic activity or weathering and remained there due to sedimentary processes. Other deposits resulted as iron solutions, which were released from rock lying near the surface by weathering and then collected in deeper strata. Large masses may also be created through the metamorphic transformation of magnetite, siderite and limonite if sufficient oxygen is present. Magmatic hydrothermal formation is comparatively rare, however.

Mythology

Hematite was used in ancient Egypt and Mesopotamia as a healing stone for the formation of blood and for staunching the blood flow from wounds. In the Middle Ages it was called 'bloodstone'.

Healing

Spiritually Hematite encourages the ability to survive, in the sense of a permanent further development towards better conditions.
Emotionally Hematite strengthens the will and makes us aware of unfulfilled desires. It bestows vitality and dynamism in our life.
Mentally Hematite draws our attention to our elementary basic needs and physical well-being. It helps fight for this in emergencies.
Physically Hematite stimulates the absorption of iron in the small intestine and the formation of red blood corpuscles. This improves the oxygen supply to the body and stabilizes health.

Application

Hematite is best placed on the skin or worn in contact with it; it can also be consumed as a precious gem essence or gemstone elixir. Care should be taken in cases of inflammation, as it has an irritating effect.

Hematite (red glass head), United Kingdom;
Hematite rosette, Brazil

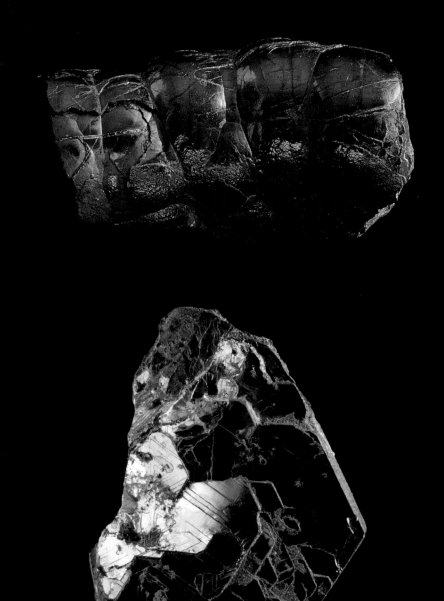

Heliotrope

Crystal system: trigonal
Manner of formation: primary
Mineral class: oxides/tectosilicates, quartz group
Colour: moss green to dark green with red flecks
Chemical formula, mineral-forming substances: $SiO_2 \cdot H_2O + Al, Fe$

Mineralogy

Heliotrope forms the connecting link between the quartz families of chalcedony and jasper. Chalcedony coloured green by iron silicate (related to moss agate) forms its basis, but as in jasper, small, grainy quartz crystals are found, also hematite and other iron oxides may be present, appearing as yellow and red spots.

Mythology

Heliotrope is Greek and means 'solstice', which is thought to refer to its powerful healing properties. This tradition has been documented since antiquity. In medieval texts it is referred to as green jasper or blood jasper and recommended for healing infections, inflammations and poisoning.

Healing

Spiritually Heliotrope helps us protect ourselves, limiting and fending off undesirable influences.

Emotionally Heliotrope is calming in cases of irritability, aggressiveness and impatience and it revitalizes in cases of exhaustion and tiredness. It stimulates dream activity.

Mentally Heliotrope helps us adjust quickly to unexpected occurrences, so that we keep control in any situation.

Physically Heliotrope is the best immune-boosting mineral for acute infections. It stimulates the flow of lymph fluid and the metabolic processes, reduces the formation of pus, detoxifies and neutralizes overacidification.

Application

For strengthening the immune response, as soon as an infection appears, place the heliotrope on the thymus gland above the heart. Otherwise, it can be worn on the body or consumed as a precious gem essence or gemstone elixir.

Heliotrope, India

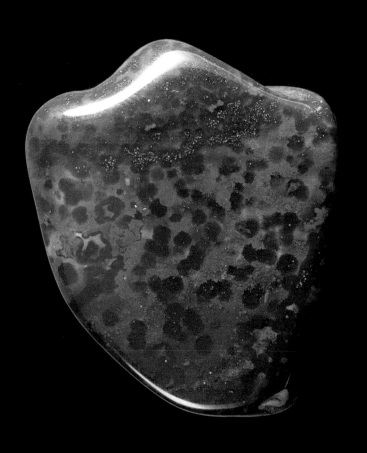

Jadeite

Crystal system: monoclinic
Manner of formation: tertiary
Mineral class: chain silicates, pyroxene family
Colour: green, yellow, brown, mauve to lilac
Chemical formula, mineral-forming substances: $NaAl[Si_2O_6]$ + Ca,Cr,Fe,Mg,Mn

Mineralogy

Both jadeite and nephrite are often sold as 'jade', and there are historical reasons for this; both minerals have very similar properties. They are very different chemically, however (see Nephrite, page 348). Jadeite is created in the pressurised metamorphosis of rocks containing albite (granite, greywacke, etc.) at depths of more than 40 kilometres (25 miles). Traces of chromium colour the stones green to lilac, iron hydroxide produces yellow to brown colouration, while substances containing manganese create pinks and mauves (lavender jade).

Mythology

Jadeite has been looked upon as a good luck charm for thousands of years, especially in the Far East. It was worked into amulets and was known as a kidney healing stone in the ancient cultures of the Americas and Asia.

Healing

Spiritually Jadeite encourages self-realization. It helps us recognize ourselves as spiritual beings and to handle our lives in a playfully spontaneous manner. Lavender jade bestows inner peace.

Emotionally Jadeite enlivens inner images and dreams and awakens hidden inner knowledge. It creates a balance: activity for laziness, calm for irritability. Lavender jade helps us to set clear boundaries.

Mentally Jadeite stimulates ideas and promotes a readiness for action. Physical rest periods are employed for spiritual activities, and decisions are transformed into action without hesitation.

Physically Jadeite stimulates the functioning of the kidneys and balances the metabolism of water, salts, and acid and alkali ratios. It stimulates the nervous system and suprarenal glands, thus improving and accelerating response and reaction times.

Application

Jadeite can be worn, applied to the skin or taken internally as a precious gem essence and gemstone elixir.

Jade, China;
Lavender jade, Turkey

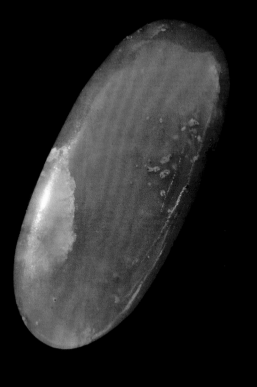

Jasper

Crystal system: trigonal
Manner of formation: primary, secondary, rarely also tertiary
Mineral class: oxides/tectosilicates, hornstone group
Colour: beige, brown, grey, red, yellow, sandy, green, often multicoloured
Chemical formula, mineral-forming substances: SiO_2 + Al,Fe

Mineralogy

Jasper is a fine-grained, microcrystalline quartz with a range of substances occurring as inclusions. It may be formed primarily or secondarily when silicic acid solutions seep into clay or sandy rocks and solidify. If it is encountered as a filling in a gap or a pocket in rock, it will be the result of hydrothermal solutions that are rich in other substances. In either case, the silicic acid solutions may be of both sedimentary or (more rarely) magmatic origin. Jasper is a mineral that can occur almost anywhere, and appears in a wide variety of forms. The different markings on these different forms of jasper have led to them being traded under a plethora of imaginative names, but to classify jasper, the three basic colours (the only certain criteria) are used: red, yellow and green.

Variety	Formula, mineral-forming substances	Colour
Yellow jasper:	SiO_2 + Fe,O,OH	yellow, sandy, brown
Green jasper:	SiO_2 + Fe,Si	light to dark green
Red jasper:	SiO_2 + Fe,O	brick red to brown-red

Yellow jasper is available in the gem trade, named as such, but it also includes beige and sandy coloured varieties. Brown 'turritella jasper' is actually a chalcedony and contains fossilized snail shells. Yellow jasper obtains its colour from the iron oxide it contains, the iron being present mainly in its bivalent form (Fe^{2+}).

Green jasper is also available under its own name and, in some cases heliotrope (see Heliotrope, page 314) is also included in the same group. The green colour is caused by the presence of iron silicate compounds (chlorite, etc.). Most red jasper sold in the trade is known as 'silex' or 'radiolarite'; red brecciated jasper is also included in this group, created sedimentarily from dead diatoms. The colour is due to iron oxide, mainly from trivalent iron (Fe^{3+}).

Buntjaspis, India;
Yellow jasper, South Africa; Breccia jasper, South Africa

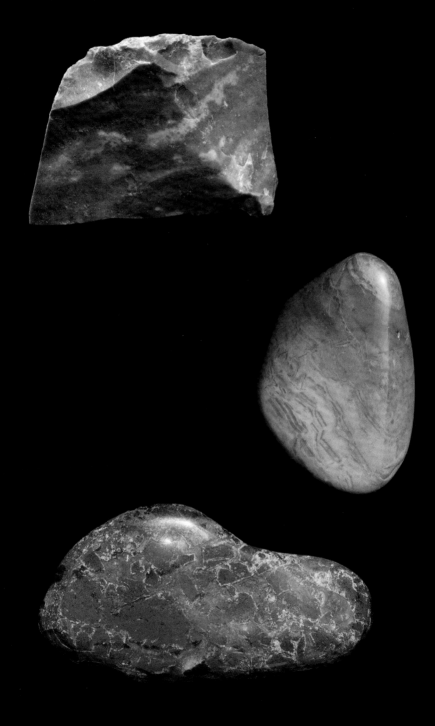

Mythology

The term jasper originates from the orient, and in the Middle Ages it meant the same as our present word quartz. The clear jasper mentioned in the Bible was probably rock crystal/crystal quartz, the transparent green 'jasper' mentioned by Pliny was probably chrysoprase, and the jasper associated with Orpheus was most likely heliotrope, also mentioned by Hildegard of Bingen. Today, things are not much different: colourful minerals that are hard to identify are often termed 'jasper': 'silver eye' serpentine is called 'zebra jasper', epidote (unakite) is sometimes called 'flower jasper'. Rhyolite is also known as 'leopard skin jasper', 'eye jasper' and 'rainforest jasper'. The only thing we know today about the real jasper is that it was used for making amulets in ancient Egypt; scarab amulets were carved from it, and in the Middle Ages it was considered to be the stone of warriors. According to legend, jasper was set in the hilt of Siegfried's legendary sword, Balmung.

Healing

Spiritually Jasper stimulates a war-like nature. It helps us pursue and achieve goals with determination. Red jasper is supposed to be the most dynamic for this, yellow jasper the calmest, and green jasper the most balanced.

Emotionally Jasper imbues courage, readiness for conflict, aggression (in the sense of dealing with things forthrightly), willpower (red), endurance (yellow) amd the ability to protect ourselves (green).

Mentally Jasper stimulates uprightness and honesty (also towards ourselves). It delivers the courage to get to grips with even unpleasant tasks. Jasper stimulates the imagination and helps transform ideas into actions.

Physically Jasper stimulates the circulation and energy flow (red). It fortifies the immune system (yellow) and has a detoxifying and anti-inflammatory effect (green). It helps with diseases of the sexual organs, and with digestive and intestinal problems. Jasper, in particular turitella jasper, increases resistance to environmental stress (pollution, toxins, radiation).

Application

Jasper should be worn in contact with the skin or laid on it. Internal consumption as a precious gem essence or elixir is also effective, as is arranging as a stone circle or placing larger jasper objects in your immediate environment.

Red jasper, South Africa; Green jasper, India;
Turritella jasper, Wyoming, USA

Calcoolite (margarita stone)

Crystal system: trigonal (calcite, dolomite) or rhombic (aragonite)
Manner of formation: secondary
Mineral classes: carbonates
Colour: brown with reddish or beige grains
Chemical formula, mineral-forming substances: $CaCO_3$ +
Fe (aragonite, calcite) or $CaMg(CO_3)_2$ + Fe (dolomite)

Mineralogy

Calcoolite is a rock made of aragonite, calcite or dolomite pebbles around 1–5 mm in length, in a tight, fine-grained matrix. It is created as a sediment in shallow, warm oceanic areas where a layer of precipitated limestone forms around suspended particles to form pearl-like pebbles (ooides). Depending on the size of the ooides, these are known as roestone (1–2 mm) or peastone (up to 5 mm).

Mythology

Hildegard of Bingen describes the creation of inorganic pearls in certain bodies of water in which 'the salt and grease content come out of the sand (…) and together form Margarites (pearls).' Calcoolite is therefore also sometimes known as margarita stone.

Healing

Spiritually Calcoolite promotes purification and clarity. It frees usfrom inner 'baggage' and protects us from being weighed down by too many internal and external conflicts.

Emotionally Calcoolite relieves hypersensitivity. It brings relief gently, stabilises the emotions and helps you to sleep better at night.

Mentally Calcoolite frees us from troublesome thoughts and headaches. It also makes it easier to recognize and work through repressed insights and memories.

Physically Calcoolite reduces fever, detoxifies and clears blockages. It relieves metabolism-related headaches, strengthens the liver, stomach and bowels and promotes excretion.

Application

Calcoolite may be worn for extended periods of time or placed directly on the affected areas of the body. Taking calcoolite as a precious gem essence (also known to Hildegard of Bingen) is highly effective, too.

Calcoolite (roestone), Harz, Germany;
Calcoolite (peastone), Bohemia, Czech Republic;
Carnelian, Botswana; Kunzite, Pakistan

Carnelian

Crystal system: trigonal
Manner of formation: primary or secondary
Mineral class: oxides/tectosilicates, quartz group
Colour: red-brown, orange to meaty red
Chemical formula, mineral-forming substances: $SiO_2 \cdot H_2O$ + (Fe,O,OH)

Mineralogy

Carnelian is chalcedony that contains iron. It is formed in areas of magmatic or sedimentary rock from magmatic silicic acid solutions containing iron. Red-brown carnelian is also called sard.

Mythology

In antiquity, carnelian was known generally as sard. Hildegard of Bingen was the first person known to make a distinction between the orange and brown varieties. In the Middle Ages, it was assigned a blood-staunching and anger-calming effect. Hildegard of Bingen recommended it for headaches and as a birthing aid. Tomb offerings in Egypt prove its importance as a protective stone for the dead.

Healing

Spiritually Carnelian promotes steadfastness and encourages a spirit of community. It makes us willing to help, be idealistic, and stand up for a good cause with zeal.

Emotionally Carnelian bestows steadfastness and courage – not the risky heroic courage but everyday courage to overcome and stand up to difficulties. It lifts the emotions.

Mentally Carnelian encourages the facility to solve problems quickly and pragmatically. It helps bring actions embarked upon come to a proper conclusion and a sense of reality to times of confusion.

Physically Carnelian stimulates the absorption of vitamins, nutrients and minerals in the small intestine, thereby improving the quality of the blood. It ensures a good blood supply to the organs and tissues. Carnelian alleviates rheumatism and stimulates the metabolism.

Application

Carnelian should be laid on the skin or worn in contact with it, or consumed as a precious gem essence or gemstone elixir.

Kunzite

Crystal system: monoclinic
Manner of formation: primary
Mineral class: chain silicates, pyroxene family
Colour: pale to intense pink or pink-violet
Chemical formula, mineral-forming substances: $LiAl[Si_2O_6] + Fe,Mn$

Mineralogy

Kunzite is a differently coloured variety of the mineral spodumene. It is formed in pegmatites exclusively from acid, magmatic solutions containing lithium.

Mythology

Kunzite was not discovered until 1902, in California, and it was described by the gemologist G.F. Kunz and named after him. Consequently, no traditions about its effects are known.

Healing

Spiritually Kunzite enourages dedication and humility, also devotion to a task that needs to be carried out with all the energy we have. It teaches us to give way without being untrue to ourselves and encourages the willingness to serve.

Emotionally Kunzite gets rid of resistances. It helps us be compromising and fit in with the needs of others. Kunzite enhances memory, has a mood-lifting effect and helps with depression.

Mentally Kunzite helps us take constructive criticism. It encourages introspection about the self as well as tolerance towards ourselves and others. Kunzite combines logic with inspiration and intuition.

Physically Kunzite alleviates nervous complaints, for example the pain of trapped nerves, sciatica, neuralgia, and also epilepsy and disorders of the sensory organs and nerves. It dissolves tension in the area of the heart and helps with joint complaints.

Application

Kunzite should be worn in direct contact with the body and in serious cases, such as when pain is present, it should be laid directly on the affected area. Taking kunzite internally as a precious gem essence or gemstone elixir is also helpful.

Labradorite

Crystal system: triclinic
Manner of formation: primary
Mineral class: tectosilicates, feldspar family
Colour: white, yellow, grey-green, grey, black with white, blue or a colourful surface iridescence
Chemical formula, mineral-forming substances: $NaAlSi_3O_8/CaAl_2Si_2O_8$ + K,Mg,Sr,Ba,Ti,Fe,Mn

Mineralogy

Labradorite is a mixed crystal of the feldspars albite and anorthite (plagioclase mixed crystal group) that is formed in pegmatites and basic magmatites. Its scintillating colours are the result of very fine veins that catch the light entering the stone. Black labradorite that breaks up the light into different colours is also known as spectrolite.

Mythology

Labradorite was found for the first time in 1770 on the Labrador peninsula; spectrolite was not found until the twentiethth century in Finland. Neither of these minerals is associated with any traditions.

Healing

Spiritually Labradorite is an outstanding 'illusion killer'. Like its colourful display of iridescence, it clearly shows us our goals and intentions – so we suddenly see their real shape. Labradorite fortifies intuition and mediumistic abilities.

Emotionally Labradorite throws up forgotten memories and bestows depth of feeling. It stimulates the imagination, making us contemplative and introverted.

Mentally Labradorite helps us develop a child-like enthusiasm and a host of new ideas. It bestows a lively although sometimes rather erratic creativity.

Physically Labradorite alleviates feeling cold, colds, rheumatic illnesses and gout. Labradorite also has a blood pressure lowering effect and is calming.

Application

Labradorite's spiritual effects are best experienced through meditation, while its physical effects can be accessed when it is worn or consumed as a precious gem essence or elixir.

Labradorite, Madagascar;
Spectrolite, Finland

Lapis lazuli

Crystal system: cubic (lazurite, pyrite), trigonal (calcite), monoclinic (diopside)
Manner of formation: tertiary
Mineral class: tectosilicates (lazurite), chain silicates (diopside),
sulphides (pyrite), carbonates (calcite)
Colour: azure blue to ultramarine blue (lazurite),
gold-yellow (pyrite), white (calcite, diopside)
Chemical formula, mineral-forming substances:
$(Na,Ca)_8[(SO_4,S,Cl)_2 | (AlSiO_4)_6]$ (lazurite)

Mineralogy

Lapis lazuli is created metamorphically through the contact of limestone or dolomite with silicic magma that is rich in acid. This forms blue lazurite, which frequently features white calcite and diopside or golden pyrite inclusions.

Mythology

Lapis lazuli derives its name from the Persian 'lazur' and roughly means 'blue stone', although other blue stones were also given this name. The only certainty is that it was already known in India as the 'Stone of Rulers' and in Egypt as the 'Stone of Truth'.

Healing

Spiritually Lapis lazuli bestows wisdom and honesty and reveals our own inner truth. It helps us be ourselves and liberates us from compromises and holding back. With lapis lazuli, you can be the 'ruler in your own (spiritual) kingdom'. It was also considered to be the stone of friendship.

Emotionally Lapis lazuli encourages self-awareness, dignity, honesty and uprightness. It makes us enjoy contact with others and helps us convey feelings and emotions clearly.

Mentally Lapis lazuli helps us face and accept the truth that we are confronted with, while at the same time allowing us to also express our own opinion. It also helps us to contain conflicts.

Physically Lapis lazuli heals problems affecting the neck, larynx and vocal chords, particularly if they originate in reserve or repressed anger. Lapis lazuli lowers the blood pressure, regulates the functioning of the thyroid gland and lengthens the menstruation cycle.

Application

Lapis lazuli may be placed on the forehead in meditation, worn around the neck, or it may be consumed internally as a precious gem essence.

Lazurite crystal, Afghanistan;
Lapis lazuli with pyrite, Afghanistan

Larimar

Crystal system: triclinic
Manner of formation: primary
Mineral class: chain silicates, pectolite
Colour: light blue-white
Chemical formula, mineral-forming substances: $Ca_2Na[HSi_3O_9]$ + (Cu,Fe,K,Mn,V)

Mineralogy

Larimar is a light-blue colour variant of the mineral pectolite. It is created magmatically and hydrothermally in crevices in basic volcanic rocks.

Mythology

Larimar was not known until very recently (the last few years). Even in its country of origin, the Dominican Republic, no early uses as a healing crystal are known.

Healing

Spiritually Larimar stimulates us to take proper control of our lives. It eliminates sacrificial behaviour and philosophies that encourage suffering. Larimar makes us aware of the extent of effectivity of our personal spiritual spectrum and shows us that the spirit only has boundaries wherever it believes in them.

Emotionally Larimar helps dissolve fear, suffering and excessive emotions. It bestows inner peace and helps us remain calm and relaxed when dramatic changes take place.

Mentally Larimar makes constructive thinking easier and stimulates creative activity. It helps us refrain from manipulating things and events unnecessarily, instead just allowing them to happen.

Physically Larimar stimulates the self-healing properties by strengthening our certainty of being able to decide about our own health or illness. Generally, it dissolves energy blocks, particularly in the chest, neck and head areas and stimulates brain activity.

Application

Larimar may be placed on the solar plexus, chest or forehead for meditation. It can be arranged as a stone circle or used simply as a stone to be contemplated quietly. Physically, it breaks up blockages in the location where it is placed. It also has a strong effect when taken internally as a precious gem essence or gemstone elixir.

Larimar, Dominican Republic;
Lepidolite, USA

Lepidolite

Crystal system: monoclinic
Manner of formation: primary
Mineral class: phyllo or sheet silicates, mica family
Colour: red-violet to blue-violet
Chemical formula, mineral-forming substances: $K(Li,Al)_3[(OH,F)_2 | AlSi_3O_{10}]$
+ Na,Rb,Cs,Fe,Mn,Mg,Ca,Ba,Sr,Nb,Ti

Mineralogy

Lepidolite is a mica containing lithium. It is formed in the primary process in pegmatites or in pneumolytically transformed granites (gneiss).

Mythology

Lepidolite was discovered in the eighteenth century and initially was given the name lilalite by Abbé Poda, who was trying to create wordplay both on its colour and the Hindu word *lila*, meaning 'play, game'. This appeared to be insufficiently serious for scientists, and the mineralogist Klaproth later renamed it lepidolite ('scale stone').

Healing

Spiritually Lepidolite encourages independence. It helps us to set our own goals and to realize them without outside help. Lepidolite allows developments to take their course quietly and inconspicuously.

Emotionally Lepidolite protects us from outer influences and helps us preserve our own space in crowds. Lepidolite bestows calm and inner peace and helps with sleep disturbances.

Mentally Lepidolite encourages objective evaluation and targeted decision-making. It helps us concentrate on what is essential, to stick to our intentions and neutralize distractions.

Physically Lepidolite helps with nerve pain, sciatica, neuralgia and problems with the joints. It has a detoxifying effect and stimulates purification processes in the skin and connective tissues.

Application

Lepidolite can be worn on the body and laid directly on painful areas. For sleep disturbance and to access its spiritual effects, simply place it under your pillow. Internal consumption as a precious gem essence or elixir is also effective.

Magnesite

Crystal system: trigonal
Manner of formation: secondary or tertiary
Mineral class: carbonates
Colour: white to beige
Chemical formula, mineral-forming substances: $MgCO_3$ + Ca,Fe,Mn

Mineralogy

Magnesite is generally formed sedimentarily through the weathering of rocks containing magnesium. It may also result from the metamorphosis of limestone to marble or in the metasomatic replacement of calcium with dolomite.

Mythology

Magnesite was discovered in the eighteenth century and was initially called 'pure talc earth', as the magnesium contained in it was not yet chemically recognized. Once magnesium was identified, the mineral was renamed magnesite. There are no traditions on its effects.

Healing

Spiritually Magnesite encourages a positive attitude towards life. It helps us accept and love ourselves.

Emotionally Magnesite has a calming, relaxing effect, helps with nervousness, fearfulness and irritability. It increases tolerance for emotional stress and makes us more patient.

Mentally Magnesite encourages the ability to listen and to stay a little more in the background.

Physically Magnesite is the most important healing crystal for magnesium deficiency. It has a detoxifying, antispasmodic, muscle-relaxing effect and helps with migraines, headaches, vascular, stomach and intestinal cramp as well as with gallbladder colic. It slows blood clotting, stimulates the metabolism of fat and the dispersal of cholesterol, thus preventing arteriosclerosis, and it expands the coronary blood vessels. This makes magnesite a prophylactic aid to combat heart attacks.

Application

Magnesite should be worn in contact with the skin or consumed as a precious gem essence or elixir.

Malachite

Crystal system: monoclinic
Manner of formation: primary or secondary
Mineral class: carbonates
Colour: pale green to deep dark green
Chemical formula, mineral-forming substances: $Cu_2[(OH)_2|CO_3]$ +
H_2O + (Zn,Co,Ni)

Mineralogy

Malachite is a basic copper carbonate, which is formed primarily through the contact of magmatic solutions with carbonate rocks, or secondarily through the reaction of surface water containing carbon dioxide with copper ore. Malachite is related to azurite but contains more water than the latter.

Mythology

Malachite is one of the minerals surrounded by myths and legends. In the Ural Mountains (central Russia), it was dedicated to the Lady of the Copper Mountain, a personification of Venus whose rather ambiguous favours brought either bad or good luck to the malachite miners. Nobody was quite sure whether it was right to accept the gifts of this goddess, as in many cases wealth brings nothing but unhappiness. Some of those who declined to accept her gift went away happy and contented. This is probably an indication of the balancing justice of creation. Malachite was always a women's mineral and was always dedicated to a goddess in whatever culture: in Egypt to Hathor, in classical times to Aphrodite/Venus, in northern Europe to Freya. Malachite represented seduction, sensuality, beauty, curiosity, aesthetics and the arts of the Muses. It was considered to be the stone of Paradise, and later signified that we mortals ought to avoid it. It still has a scent of Lucifer about it to this day. Since the Middle Ages, it has been known that malachite alleviates menstrual problems and eases labour. For this reason it is still called the 'midwife stone' in folklore.

Healing

Spiritually Malachite encourages an appreciation of aesthetics, sensuality and beauty, friendship and justice. It helps us imagine ourselves in the position of others and to empathize with them (sense their thoughts and feelings). Malachite gets rid of shyness and awakens the desire for knowledge. Life is experienced more

Magnesite, Zimbabwe;
Malachite, Zaire

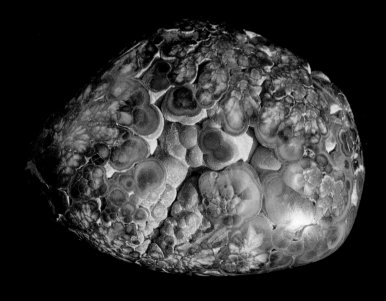

intensely and is more adventurous. Inspired by malachite, we learn to love risks and to rely on luck. Malachite helps make us more aware: desires, needs and ideals become visible but the realization of them remains up to us.

Emotionally Malachite stimulates inner imagery. Dreams, imagination and memories become alive and real. Suppressed feelings are suddenly brought out into the open. Malachite takes away inhibitions and encourages the expression of feelings. Moods are experienced more intensely and then rapidly dropped again as fast as they arose. Old pain and traumas may surface and be dissolved if we are in a position to face them. This is one of the weaknesses of malachite: it makes many things conscious but does not help much with changing what it has given us an insight into.

Mentally Malachite strengthens the understanding of concepts. We are in a position to absorb information more quickly as the imagination makes us strong and aware of how to handle it. Thoughts flow very fast and decisions are made without having to think a great deal. Malachite fortifies the capacity to observe; even tiny things are perceived much more rapidly and their meaning is recognized. This also increases the ability to criticize and confront and the willingness to do so.

Physically Malachite dissolves cramp. It helps with menstruation problems and facilitates labour. In addition, malachite encourages the development of the female sexual organs and heals their ailments. It also helps with sexual problems, particularly if bad experiences were the cause. Malachite stimulates liver activity, has a detoxifying effect, alleviates rheumatism and helps reduce acidification of the tissues. It stimulates the nerves and brain activity.

Application

Malachite's effects can be experienced by simply wearing it or laying it directly on the body. Malachite gem essences and elixirs have a very pronounced effect and should be taken in very low doses to begin with.

Marble, Ticino, Switzerland;
Metarhyolite (rainforest stone), Australia;
Metarhyolite (leopard stone), Mexico

336

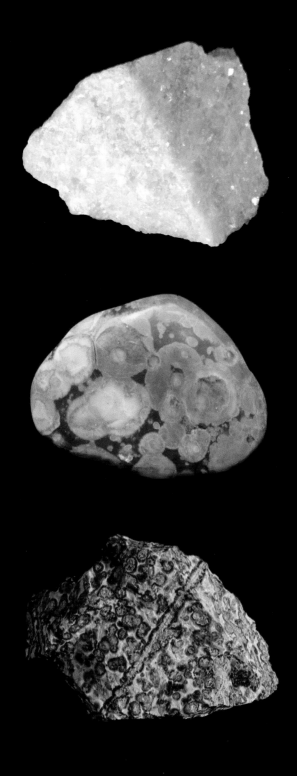

Marble

Crystal system: trigonal
Manner of formation: tertiary
Mineral class: carbonates
Colour: white, cream, yellow-green, reddish, brown to black
Chemical formula, mineral-forming substances: $CaCO_3$ + Mg,Fe,Sr (calcite)
+ $CaMg(CO_3)_2$ + Fe (dolomite)

Mineralogy

Marble is a metamorphic, monomineralic rock formed from calcite or dolomite through the transformation of sedimentary limestone or dolomite under pressure at high temperatures. This metamorphosis squeezes the calcite of the sediment into larger crystals, which give the marble its transparency and typical grainy appearance. NB All limestones that can be polished are referred to as 'marble' by stonemasons, even when not metamorphic.

Mythology

Marble (Greek *marmaros*, 'white stone') was a collective term in antiquity for 'special stones that appeal through their marking and patterning' (Isidorus). Not much is therefore known that relates specifically to what we now call marble. However, there are traditions about the transforming power of the stones the Greeks and Romans understood by this name, and how they turned sorrow into joy, and their symbolism for wealth, splendour and glory.

Healing

Spiritually Marble transforms unhappy circumstances. It helps change dynamically things we believed we had to put up with.

Emotionally Marble brings the repressed contents of our consciousness to the surface. It helps us rid ourselves of all emotional dissatisfaction.

Mentally Marble opens up new perspectives and stimulates creative solving of problems that we would previously have resigned ourselves to.

Physically Marble improves the processing of calcium in the body. In this, its effect is similar to that of calcite.

Application

Marble soon reveals its constructive properties, which are intensified by wearing it for long periods of time or taking it internally as precious gem essence and elixirs.

Metarhyolite

Crystal system: trigonal (mainly)
Manner of formation: primary
Mineral classes: oxides/tectosilicates, quartz group (mainly)
Colour: grey, brown, beige, yellowish, reddish, green with inclusions and filled pockets
Chemical formula, mineral-forming substances: SiO_2 + Fe,Al (mainly quartz)

Mineralogy

Metarhyolites are the fossilized remains of volcanic rocks (rhyolites). The action of magmatic silicic acid solutions forces out most of the original minerals – lavas, tuff and layers of ash – and replaces them with quartz. More recent voids have also been filled in in the same way, e.g. with chalcedony. Depending on their appearance, metarhyolites are sold as leopard stone (sandy-brown), rainforest stone (green-brown) or Dr. Liesegang stone (beige-red striped).

Mythology

The name rhyolite originates from the Greek *rhyx*, meaning 'stream of lava'. No traditions for its healing properties are known.

Healing

Spiritually Rhyolite has the interesting effect of strengthening the existing spiritual state and clarifying it without, however, effecting any changes.

Emotionally Rhyolite fortifies our self-respect and feeling of self-value. It helps us accept ourselves as we are and has an emotionally balancing effect.

Mentally Rhyolite helps us deal with strenuous life situations in a calm, concentrated manner and with awareness of our own strength.

Physically Rhyolite fortifies our natural resistance. 'Leopard skin jasper', due to its signature, helps with skin diseases, hardened tissues and the formation of stones, 'orbicular jasper' helps with influenza, colds and infections.

Application

Physically spending time on metarhyolite rocks is of course the most effective method, otherwise they can be worn on the body placed on the skin or consumed as a precious gem essence.

Moldavite

Crystal system: amorphous
Manner of formation: tertiary
Mineral classes: oxides/silicates, igneous glass
Colour: bottle green, more rarely grass green
Chemical formula, mineral-forming substances: $SiO_2 + Al_2O_3 + Ca,K,Fe,Mg + (Na,Ti,Mn)$

Mineralogy

Moldavite was formed approximately 15 million years after the impact of a giant meteorite in present day Nordlinger Ries (Bavaria). Splatters of rocks that were melted by the impact were propelled over a radius of about 400 kilometres (250 miles). These cooled while they were airborne and many fell to the ground in the general area of the present day Moldavia. Moldavite is now found along the banks of the river Moldau, hence its name.

Mythology

Archeological discoveries from the Stone Age have proved that moldavite was used as an amulet stone. Its reputation as a magical stone for luck, the fulfilment of wishes and fertility magic has survived to this day.

Healing

Spiritually Moldavite allows us to experience intensely spiritual dimensions, enhances clairvoyance and gives us inklings of what actual spiritual greatness humans could be capable of.

Emotionally Moldavite brings memories and dream images that allow an insight into the meaning and duties of our lives. Moldavite also encourages sympathy and compassion.

Mentally Moldavite helps us detach our attention and awareness from strongly materialistic leanings and blocks, as well as from money problems and worries about the future. Moldavite encourages spontaneous, unconventional ideas and solutions to problems.

Physically Moldavite supports healing processes by making us aware of the cause of the illness and the gain that can be had from experiencing the illness.

Application

Moldavite exerts a strong effect when placed on the forehead ('third eye'), but it is usually sufficient to simply wear or carry some with you. It has a very intensive effect when consumed as precious gem essences and elixirs.

Moldavite, Czech Republic;
Moonstone, Tanzania; Mookaite, Australia

Moonstone

Crystal system: monoclinic/triclinic
Manner of formation: primary
Mineral class: tectosilicates, feldspar family
Colour: white, yellow, grey-green, grey, black with white, blue or with a colourful surface iridescence
Chemical formula, mineral-forming substances: $KAlSi_3O_8/NaAlSi_3O_8$ + Fe,Ca,Ba,Sr,Mg

Mineralogy

Moonstone is a magmatic alkali feldspar in which fine layers of orthoclase (potassium feldspar) or albite (sodium feldspar) are formed as it cools. Light refracting through the stone causes a blue or white shimmer.

Mythology

Moonstone is associated with the moon and is therefore traditionally linked to intuition, the emotions, the heart and fertility. In the Far East, the orient and Europe it was thought to be a lucky stone and was used for love magic.

Healing

Spiritually Moonstone increases mediumistic abilities and clairvoyance. It encourages lucid dreaming, particularly at the time of a full moon.

Emotionally Moonstone refines our (subconscious) perception of light, thereby enhancing intuition. It bestows depth of feeling, improves the remembering of dreams and diminishes any tendencies to sleepwalking.

Mentally Moonstone makes us more open to sudden, irrational impulses. This means that it encourages 'happy coincidences', but can just as easily let us trip up on our own illusions.

Physically Moonstone stimulates the functioning of the pineal gland and, via this gland's sensitivity to light, balances the internal hormone cycles with nature's rhythms. In this way, the moonstone also enhances women's fertility and helps with menstrual problems, after childbirth and during the menopause.

Application

To experience moonstone's spiritual effects place it on the forehead or over the heart for the emotions. For all other purposes, it can simply be worn or carried, or consumed as gem essence or an elixir.

Mookaite

Crystal system: trigonal (quartz) + amorphous (opal)
Manner of formation: secondary
Mineral class: oxides/silicates, hornstone group
Colour: white, beige, yellow, red, red-violet
Chemical formula, mineral-forming substances: SiO_2 + Fe,O,OH

Mineralogy

Mookaite is a colourful radiolarite hornstone from Western Australia that is mostly made up of quartz, although small amounts are a quartz/opal mixture. It was formed from 2-billion-year-old radiolarite sediment. The intrusion of later solutions introduced the iron oxides that produce its beautiful colours.

Mythology

Mookaite was used for blades and spear tips by the aboriginal inhabitants of Australia as it forms a sharp edge when it breaks. It was also used to heal wounds.

Healing

Spiritually Mookaite encourages the desire for variety and new experiences. It helps keep a harmonious balance between the external activities and internal processing of the impressions derived from such experiences.

Emotionally Mookaite simultaneously bestows both a deep inner calm and a desire for adventure. It helps us experience the possibility that meditation is actually possible during any activity.

Mentally Mookaite makes us mobile and flexible. It helps us recognize several possibilities at the same time and still choose the most suitable solution without any problems.

Physically Mookaite stabilizes health. It fortifies the immune system and stimulates the purification of the blood in the liver and spleen. Mookaite encourages wounds to heal and alleviates suppuration.

Application

Mookaite should be worn on the body for long periods of time as its effects take time to build up gradually. It also has a gentle effect when consumed as a precious gem essence or elixir.

Green moss agate

Crystal system: trigonal
Manner of formation: primary
Mineral class: oxides/tectosilicates, quartz group
Colour: clear to light blue with dark green inclusions
Chemical formula, mineral-forming substances: $SiO_2 \cdot H_2O$ + Al,Fe + green silicates

Mineralogy

Green moss agate belongs to the chalcedony family and is created from viscous silicic acid gel that has been formed magmatically and hydrothermally and into which green silicate solutions have found their way without mixing. This creates chalcedony that contains moss-green inclusions in the form of layers or streaks.

Mythology

Throughout literature, it has been suggested that green moss agate enhances a love for nature because of its plant-like signature. There are, however, no other indications as to its healing properties.

Healing

Spiritually Green moss agate liberates us from spiritual fetters and blocks. It encourages new initiatives after long periods of hesitation or holding back. Green moss agate bestows inspiration and makes it possible to begin anew again and again.

Emotionally Green moss agate liberates us from pressure and stress. It helps loosen deep fear and encourages trust and hope. Green moss agate brings recovery and refreshes the soul.

Mentally Green moss agate encourages the ability to communicate. It enhances certainty, helps us understand even the most difficult set of circumstances, and enlivens the intellect.

Physically Green moss agate encourages the flow of lymphatic fluid, alleviates swellings of the lymph nodes and, in cases of stubborn infections, has an immune-boosting effect, lowers fevers, is anti-inflammatory, mucous-forming (in cases of a dry cough) and tones down oversensitivity to changes in the weather.

Application

For all applications, green moss agate should be placed on the skin or worn in contact with it. It also has a strong effect when consumed as a precious gem essence or elixir.

Green moss agate, India;
Pink moss agate, India

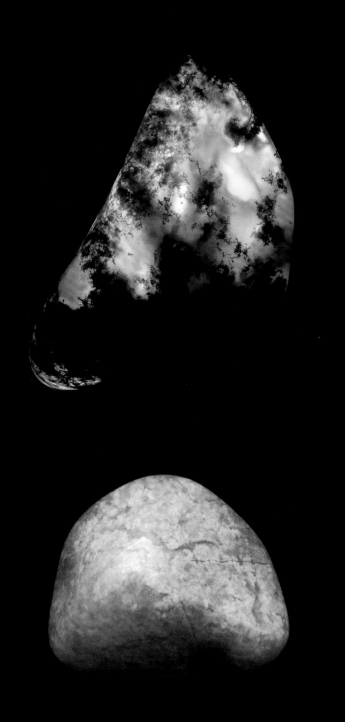

Pink moss agate

Crystal system: trigonal
Manner of formation: primary
Mineral class: oxides/tectosilicates, quartz group
Colour: clear-brownish with orange-pink to orange-brown inclusions
Chemical formula, mineral-forming substances: $SiO_2 \cdot H_2O + Al, Fe$

Mineralogy
Pink moss agate is a chalcedony formed magmatically and hydrothermally from silicic acid solutions containing chlorite minerals. These are replaced by quartz and the brown inclusions are an example of pseudomorphosis from quartz to chlorite.

Mythology
Pink moss agate did not reach the market in large amounts until the 1990s. There are no traditions of its healing properties.

Healing
Spiritually Pink moss agate helps us to work through previous life experiences, to let go of obsessions and to gain openness and freedom.

Emotionally Pink moss agate enables us to overcome sensations of disgust, repulsion, resentment and belligerence. It brings inner stability and security, banishing shyness and the need for protection.

Mentally Pink moss agate eliminates thoughts of revenge and recrimination. It helps us take responsibility for our own well-being and to experiment playfully with new life strategies.

Physically Pink moss agate stimulates digestion and excretion. It promotes the secretion of digestive enzymes, helps combat nausea, promotes bowel movement, improves bowel flora and soothes inflammation in the digestive tract. It provides rapid relief of constipation and longer applications are useful against diarrhoea.

Application
Pink moss agate should be placed on the stomach against the skin. Short immersion of the crystal creates a precious gem essence that helps with many digestive complaints. If the stone is left in water for three days, it will create a powerful laxative.

Morganite

Crystal system: hexagonal
Manner of formation: primary
Mineral class: ring silicates, beryl family
Colour: pale pink, pink to apricot
Chemical formula, mineral-forming substances: $Be_3Al_2[Si_6O_{18}]$ + Li,Mn + (Cs,Fe)

Mineralogy

Morganite is a type of beryl that has been coloured pink by traces of lithium, caesium or manganese. It is formed in pegmatites whenever the magmatic solution is sufficiently enriched with these trace elements.

Mythology

Morganite was not discovered until this century, and was named after the mineral collector, banker and secret society member John Pierpoint Morgan. This is why there are no extant traditions on its effects.

Healing

Spiritually Morganite helps us recognize self-importance, fanaticism, blinkered views and habitual escapism as such, and instead inclines us to devote ourselves to a more contemplative lifestyle. Morganite awakens a love of life itself, and with it a love of all living things.

Emotionally Morganite helps reduce stress and the pressure to succeed. Morganite brings an awareness of the ignored needs of the soul and helps us become aware of feelings and to live them out.

Mentally Morganite helps us let go of ambition and to experience the joy of engaging in spiritual activities that serve neither gain nor success. Morganite creates space for leisure.

Physically Morganite alleviates illnesses caused by stress such as heart problems, nervous complaints, vertigo and impotence.

Application

Morganite can be placed over the heart as a meditation stone. Spending time in a morganite stone circle will rapidly alleviate stress symptoms, after which the stone should be worn directly on the body for long periods of time. Consuming morganite as precious gem essences and elixirs is also effective.

Nephrite

Crystal system: monoclinic
Manner of formation: tertiary
Mineral class: chain silicates, amphibole group
Colour: green to green-black
Chemical formula, mineral-forming substances: $Ca_2(Mg,Fe)_5[(OH,F)_2|Si_8O_{22}]$
+ Al,Na,Cr

Mineralogy

Nephrite is a fine-grained variety of actinolite. It is created metamorphically during the formation of verdites and in the vicinity of basic (gabbro, basalt) and ultrabasic rocks (serpentine).

Mythology

The name nephrite is derived from the Greek word *nephron*, meaning 'kidney'. Even in antiquity and in the early cultures of South America and New Zealand, nephrite was known as a healing stone. In addition, it was used as an amulet and for the manufacture of images of the gods.

Healing

Spiritually Nephrite is numbered among the stones that protect against hostile influences. It renders us unable to be influenced by means of applying pressure (blackmail) and helps us preserve our identity.

Emotionally Nephrite brings certainty. It helps to reduce tension and worries, to discharge violent emotions, to soothe aggression and will lead to inner peace over the long term.

Mentally Nephrite encourages neutrality and tolerance. It helps with indecisiveness and dissolves doubt and senseless brooding. Nephrite makes us creative and ready for action.

Physically Nephrite improves the functioning of the kidneys, alleviates kidney infections and prevents deposits in the urinary tract and kidney stones. In this way, it also encourages detoxification of the body fluids and of the tissues.

Application

Nephrite should be worn on the body for long periods of time until an inner equilibrium has been attained. In serious cases, it can be laid directly over the kidneys, applied to the skin with a plaster or consumed as a precious gem essence or elixir.

Morganite, Brazil;
Nephrite, Russia

Obsidian

Crystal system: amorphous
Manner of formation: primary
Mineral classes: oxides/silicates, igneous glass
Colour: black, grey, brown
Chemical formula, mineral-forming substances: $SiO_2 + Al_2O_3 +$
$K,Na,Fe,Ca + (Mg,Ti)$

Mineralogy

Obsidian is created volcanically through the rapid cooling of silicic lava that is rich in acids and that has largely vented its gas; this solidifies so quickly that no crystalline structures form ('thermal shock'). It creates an amorphous 'frozen liquid rock' containing numerous mineral, water and gas inclusions. Obsidian is therefore known as 'volcanic glass'. The basic colour of obsidian is black and it is generally opaque; obsidian can be transparent if few other substances are present in its glassy composition (smoky obsidian or Apache tears). The variant with alternating opaque and transparent layers is known as striped obsidian. A distribution of fine bubbles of gas and glass lend obsidian a silvery or golden sheen (silver or gold obsidian), as well as tiny brightly coloured crystalline inclusions (rainbow obsidian) through refraction. When sanidine, cristobalite or tridymite crystallise out in obsidian, radiating inclusions are formed (snowflake obsidian). A high content of iron oxides sometimes gives rise to brown flecks (mahogany obsidian).

Mythology

Obsidian was used for some of man's oldest cultural artefacts. As early as in Palaeolithic times, obsidian blades were used for cult purposes as burial finds reveal. In antiquity, it was regarded as a stone that would drive out demons and in the Middle Ages, as an aid for magical rituals. The Mayan priests of the god Tetzcatlipoca ('Smoking Mirror') employed obsidian mirrors for predicting the future. According to very ancient traditions, obsidian was also used for healing wounds and alleviating pain – an interesting connection since as it also supplied the material for some of the first blades and also weapons made by man. Obsidian is supposed to derive its name from the Roman Obsius who, according to Pliny's reports, found the stone in present day Ethiopia.

Obsidian, Mexico;
Mahogany obsidian, Mexico

Healing

Spiritually Obsidian helps us attain integrity through helping us to see our shadow sides in their true nature, so they can once more become part of the self. This is how to attain the 'unimpeachability of the warrior', a spiritual invulnerability and freedom (liberty). In this manner, forgotten capabilities may be retrieved and our perception refined to the point of clairvoyance.

Emotionally Obsidian dissolves shocks, fear, blocks and traumatization. It has an enlivening effect and brings hidden inner images to light. Obsidian bestows an unimagined depth on our emotional nature and helps with any type of obsession. It purifies the atmosphere of negative, spiritual influences and serves as a protection against psychic attacks.

Mentally Obsidian expands the consciousness and helps change restricting beliefs, communication and behavioural patters. It sharpens the senses and helps the intellect penetrate mysterious phenomena, experiences and accounts.

Physically Obsidian dissolves pain, tensions, energy blocks and vascular contraction. Shock sustained through injury is dissolved on a cellular level and it thus helps staunch bleeding and accelerate the healing of wounds. Obsidian improves the circulation, even in extreme cases such as hardening of the arteries in the legs caused by smoking, and also ensures warming of the extremities, for example, chronically cold hands and feet.

Application

For effects on the emotions/soul, obsidian should be used as a meditation stone in the form of a mirror or a sphere and contemplated quietly. For a final 'clearing', it is recommended to end the meditation every time with rock crystal. Black, rainbow and silver obsidian are best suited to meditation. Smoky obsidian worn next to the skin will rapidly alleviate pain, while the circulation will be best improved with mahogony or snowflake obsidian (worn on the body).

Silver obsidian, Mexico;
Rainbow obsidian, Mexico;
Snowflake obsidian, USA

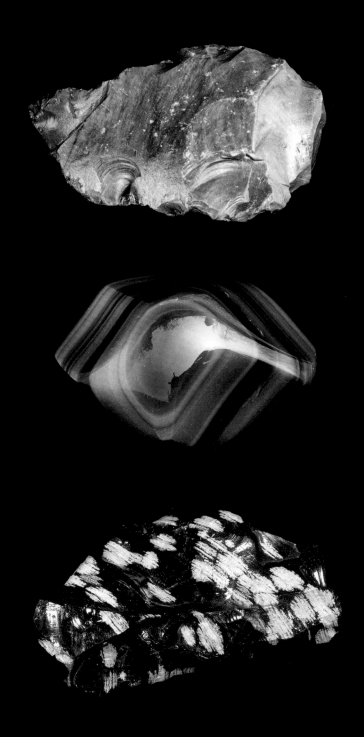

Olivine (peridot, chrysolite)

Crystal system: rhombic
Manner of formation: primary
Mineral class: island silicates
Colour: yellow-green, bottle green, olive green
Chemical formula, mineral-forming substances: $(Mg,Fe)_2[SiO_4]$ + Mn,Ni,Ca

Mineralogy

Olivine is the most important mineral in the Earth's upper mantle, where, combined with pyroxenes and chromite, it it is found as the rock peridot. On occasion it may be caught up in deep volcanic eruptions and is then found as an inclusion in basalt.

Mythology

Olivine was used in jewellery and for healing two thousand years before the birth of Christ. In ancient writings it is often referred to as topaz, so it is thought that the 'topaz' in the breastplate of the high priest mentioned in the Old Testament might actually be an olivine. In the Middle Ages, it was employed for warding off evil spirits and to bestow wisdom and friendship.

Healing

Spiritually Olivine helps us disassociate ourselves from outside influences, to live our own lives and to draw wisdom from the abundance of experience.

Emotionally Olivine gets rid of oppressive feelings that arise from self-blame and a guilty conscience. It helps with pent-up anger and fury.

Mentally Olivine helps us to admit our mistakes and to forgive ourselves. It makes us aware of things we have neglected to do and stimulates us to make up for any harm done.

Physically Olivine has a strong detoxifying effect and stimulates the liver. It enhances the liver and gallbladder, stimulates the metabolism and helps with skin problems, even warts.

Application

Olivine should be worn next to the skin, placed over the liver or taken internally as a precious gem essence and/or elixir. To detoxify fatty tissue in particular, olivine is soaked in sunflower oil for four weeks and is then added to food as a salad dressing or similar.

Olivine (beryl), USA;
Olivine (peridot), Lanzarote

Onyx

Crystal system: trigonal
Manner of formation: primary or secondary
Mineral class: oxides/tectosilicates, quartz group
Colour: black
Chemical formula, mineral-forming substances: $SiO_2 \cdot H_2O + Mn, Fe$

Mineralogy

Onyx is a chalcedony that is coloured black through the presence of iron and manganese. It is formed in pockets from magmatic or sedimentary silicic acid solutions.

Mythology

In the Middle Ages onyx was thought to bring bad luck, sadness, fear and images of madness during sleep, as well as inciting discord and dispute. To this day, it has a bad reputation as the 'stone of egotists'.

Healing

Spiritually Onyx encourages self-realization. It helps us to pursue our own goals with determination and is, therefore, particularly suited to people who are easily influenced and led.

Emotionally Onyx fortifies our self-confidence and sense of responsibility. It encourages a healthy egotism and the willingness to get involved in a dispute if necessary.

Mentally Onyx improves the ability to assert ourselves. It stimulates analytical thought and logic, improves concentration and helps us to argue in a conclusive and determined manner. Onyx makes us sober and realistic and improves our control over our own actions.

Physically Onyx sharpens our sense of hearing and heals diseases of the inner ear. It promotes purification and removes blockages in connective tissue. It also improves the functioning of the sensory and motor nervous system, helps with poor eyesight, and strengthens the immune system against infection.

Application

Onyx should be worn for extended periods as it takes some time for its power to take effect. Consuming onyx internally as precious gem essence or an elixir works much more quickly, while spending time in a stone circle has a powerful effect.

Onyx, Brazil

Onyx marble

Crystal system: rhombic (aragonite) or trigonal (calcite)
Manner of formation: secondary
Mineral classes: carbonates
Colour: white, yellow, brown and greenish, always striped
Chemical formula, mineral-forming substances: $CaCO_3$ +
Fe (aragonite, calcite) or $CaMg(CO_3)_2$ + Fe (Dolomite)

Mineralogy

Onyx marble is a limestone rock formed through the rhythmic deposition of alternating layers of aragonite and calcite in warm springs. The usual trade name is doubly misleading: although according to longstanding stonemason tradition, striped stones are called 'onyx' and polishable limestones are known as 'marble', in mineralogy, 'onyx' has since become a term for black or black/ white chalcedony and marble is now a term for metamorphic limestone. Neither of these applies to onyx marble.

Mythology

Onyx marble was used in ancient times in the manufacture of containers, vases, sculptures and idols; similar uses were also known in the Aztec culture.

Healing

Spiritually Onyx marble promotes rhythmic spiritual development adapted to the cycles of nature, bringing relief in stressful phases of life.

Emotionally Onyx marble has a liberating effect, making us more relaxed and sensitive. It promotes a healthy balance between activity and rest and so helps recovery in times of continual stress and strain.

Mentally Onyx marble promotes flexibility and creativity. It encourages us to seize the moment.

Physically Onyx marble helps to combat complaints of the liver, gall bladder, bones, cartilage, joints, intervertebral discs and meniscus.

Application

Onyx marble may be worn for longer periods, applied directly to affected areas of the body, arranged as a stone circle or placed in your immediate surroundings. Precious gem essences and elixirs are also extremely effective.

Onyx marble, Pakistan

Noble opal

Crystal system: amorphous
Manner of formation: primary or secondary
Mineral class: oxides/silicates
Colour: clear, white, grey or black coloration with colourful, opalising light reflexes
Chemical formula, mineral-forming substances: $SiO_2 \cdot n\ H_2O + Al,Fe$

Mineralogy

Noble opal is formed from silicic acid gel of magmatic or sedimentary origin that solidifies as it loses water. The teardrop-shaped silicic acid formations in the gel create nodules of silicon dioxide in which a fluid content of up to 20% is enclosed. The refraction of light across these grains is what gives noble opal its characteristic coloration. Depending on the base colour, it may be known as crystal opal (clear), light opal (white) or black opal (black). Flat layers of noble opal are also known as veta opal or seam opal, and stones with veins of noble opal running through them are known as boulder opals.

Mythology

Noble opal is known both as a lucky and an unlucky stone. According to Greek mythology it was formed out of the tears of joy of Zeus after his victory over the Titans, while in India it was thought to be the Goddess of Rainbows, turned to stone when fleeing from the unwanted advances of other gods.

Healing

Spiritually Noble opal brings joy to our worldly life. It draws our attention to the more colourful sides of life and awakens the desire for variety and distraction.

Emotionally Noble opal strengthens desire, eroticism and sexuality. It makes us emotional, seductive, unconventional, in love with life and enhances optimism.

Mentally Noble opal makes us light-hearted, sometimes even a little light-headed. It encourages spontaneity, poetry and an interest in the arts of the Muses.

Physically Noble opal has a generally health-enhancing effect because it strengthens the will to live.

Application

Noble opal is effective when carried, worn or placed on the body, when consumed as precious gem essence or water and through meditative contemplation.

Boulder opal and light opal, Australia;
Black opal and veta opal, Honduras

Chrysopal

Crystal system: amorphous
Manner of formation: primary
Mineral class: oxides/silicates
Colour: green-turquoise to blue-green
Chemical formula, mineral-forming substances: $SiO_2 \cdot n\ H_2O + Cu$

Mineralogy

Chrysopal is created from silicic acid gel containing copper of magmatic origin that solidifies as it loses its water content. It is sometimes found where chrysocolla occurs.

Mythology

Chrysopal is considered to be the stone assigned to oceans, great distances and to the yearning for a (spiritual) home. In South America it is used, to this day, as a magical stone for matters of the heart.

Healing

Spiritually Chrysopal makes us open to new impressions. It makes us open towards other people and encourages community experiences. Chrysopal also imparts enthusiasm.

Emotionally Chrysopal liberates the feelings. It helps allow grief to run its normal course and to release emotional burdens through crying. Chrysopal has a mood-lifting effect and transmits a pleasant exciting-melancholic feeling for life. It helps with lack of courage and stimulates a child-like curiosity that sees the whole world as a huge adventure.

Mentally Chrysopal stimulates us to observe the world with astonished eyes and to appreciate the wonder of life.

Physically Chrysopal encourages the regenerative power of the liver, has a detoxifying effect and lowers temperatures. It liberates the heart and chest of feelings of constriction.

Application

Chrysopal should be worn or laid near the heart. It may also be consumed as a precious gem essence or elixir, arranged as a stone circle or contemplated in meditation.

Chrysopal, Peru;
Fire opal, Mexico

Fire opal

Crystal system: amorphous
Manner of formation: primary
Mineral class: oxides/silicates
Colour: orange to fiery red
Chemical formula, mineral-forming substances: $SiO_2 \cdot n\, H_2O + Fe$

Mineralogy
Fire opal is formed from silicic acid gel of volcanic origin that solidifies as it loses its water content. Its red-orange colour is due to iron.

Mythology
Fire opal is a Mars stone. It is considered to be the stone of discoverers and conquerors and will bestow good outcomes, success and the overcoming of all danger on the wearer.

Healing
Spiritually Fire opal bestows dynamism, initiative and new ideas. It awakens the inner fire, helping us to accomplish much more in a short time and to fire others with enthusiasm. Fire opal makes us spontaneous and impulsive.

Emotionally Fire opal makes us lively, open and ready to take risks. It wakens us up, lifts the spirits, and brings cheerfulness, enthusiasm, *joie de vivre* and enjoyment of sexuality. Occasionally, fire opal makes us a little explosive, so that bottled up emotions are suddenly and violently discharged.

Mentally Fire opal helps us to initiate things. It shakes us out of the habit of thinking too long, makes us quick on the uptake, and stimulates action. With fire opal our thought processes are determined by emotions, and outbursts may occur when we are challenged.

Physically Fire opal gets rid of all energy deficiencies. It stimulates the sexual organs and activates the adrenal glands.

Application
Fire opal has a very strong effect when taken as a precious gem essence and elixir, when worn in the pubic area or when carried in a trouser pocket. Contemplation of the stone is recommended for meditation, (in as calm a manner as possible…).

Green opal (chloropal)

Crystal system: amorphous (opal) + monoclinic (nontronite)
Manner of formation: primary
Mineral class: oxides/silicates (opal) + phyllo or sheet silicates (nontronite)
Colour: yellow-green, grass green to dark green
Chemical formula, mineral-forming substances: $SiO_2 \cdot n\ H_2O$ (opal) +
$Na_{0,3}Fe_2(Si,Al)_4O_{10}(OH)_2 \cdot 4\ H_2O$ (nontronite)

Mineralogy

Green opal is created from silicic acid gel of magmatic origin that solidifies as it loses its water content. Its green colour is the result of inclusions of nontronite. The name chloropal refers to its colour (Greek *chloros*, 'green').

Mythology

Green opal originates in Mexico and has only been available in Europe since the 1990s. Unfortunately, there are no known traditions for its use as a healing mineral.

Healing

Spiritually Green opal helps us to find new perspectives on life. It makes it possible to see a meaning in everyday life or to give life a meaning.

Emotionally Green opal encourages recovery, relaxation and regeneration following exhaustion brought on by strenuous mental activity. It liberates us from fear and feelings of guilt and helps us sleep peacefully.

Mentally Green opal helps with orientation problems. It encourages the ability to select and to filter out intuitively the most important facts from a confusing profusion of information.

Physically Green opal is a strong detoxifying agent. It stimulates the body fluids, the liver and kidneys and the functioning of the gonads and ovaries.

Application

Green opal should be worn on the body or in the general area of the liver. Its liberating and regenerating effects rapidly become apparent if it is used in meditation. Spending time in a circle of opal stones has a very powerful effect, as has consumption of the stone as precious gem essence and elixirs.

Pink opal

Crystal system: amorphous
Manner of formation: primary
Mineral class: oxides/silicates
Colour: pale pink to strong pink
Chemical formula, mineral-forming substances: $SiO_2 \cdot n\, H_2O + Mn$

Mineralogy

Pink opal is created from silicic acid gel containing manganese of magmatic origin that solidifies as it loses its water content. It is found in deposits of manganese ore.

Mythology

Pink opal has only been available in Europe since the 1990s. Unfortunately, there are no known traditions for its use as a healing stone.

Healing

Spiritually Pink opal encourages generosity towards guests and commitment to idealized communities. It helps us submit to a higher ideal and to act in unselfish ways.

Emotionally Pink opal bestows an unhibited, easy manner and lightness. It dissolves worries and a downcast mood and encourages warmth towards our fellow human beings. Pink opal helps us express ourselves openly as our true nature and liberates from shyness, shame and inhibitions. Pink opal helps with the enjoyment of sexuality.

Mentally Pink opal stimulates dreamy introspection in which a mixture of memories and desirable images are spun into new ideas and concepts.

Physically Pink opal alleviates heart problems. It is particularly helpful with heart neuroses, that is, symptoms that only arise due to worry about the heart without there being a physical diagnosis.

Application

Pink opal should be laid or worn near the heart. It may also be consumed as a precious gem essence or elixir, arranged as a stone circle or contemplated in meditation.

Pink opal, Peru;
Green opal, Mexico

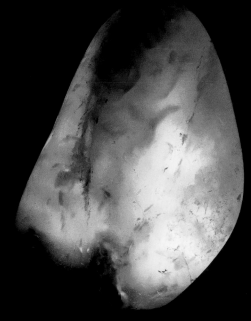

Ocean chalcedony (ocean agate, ocean jasper)

Crystal system: trigonal
Manner of formation: primary
Mineral class: oxides/tectosilicates, quartz group
Colour: white, yellow, orange, reddish, brown, green, light blue
Chemical formula, mineral-forming substances: $SiO_2 \cdot H_2O + Al,Fe$

Mineralogy

Ocean chalcedony is a chalcedony with inclusions of spherulites (spheroid formations). It is created from hydrothermal silicic acid solutions of volcanic origin. It was first named 'ocean jasper' and then 'ocean agate' after the coastal location on Madagascar where it was discovered. As it is up to 99% composed of chalcedony, mineralogists know it as spherulitic chalcedony.

Mythology

Ocean chalcedony was not available on the market in large quantities until the 1990s. There is no pre-existing recorded tradition of its healing properties.

Healing

Spiritually Ocean chalcedony promotes renewal and regeneration. It encourages an awareness of scope and unlimited possibilities and stimulates users to improve their lives.

Emotionally Ocean chalcedony makes users positive, resilient and relaxed. It brings hope, helps exhaustion and promotes good sleep.

Mentally Ocean chalcedony helps to resolve conflicts. It brings creativity, dynamism and healthy interaction with the environment.

Physically Ocean chalcedony promotes digestion, detoxification, regeneration and the immune system. It reduces fever, soothes inflammation, infections and allergies, improves lymphatic flow and helps with migraine, diabetes, oedema, venous ulcers, cysts, myomas and tumours. It is good for the skin, mucous membranes, airways, thyroid gland, ears, eyes and the hollow organs (stomach, bowels, bladder, prostate, womb), kidneys, liver, gall bladder, gonads (testicles and ovaries).

Application

Ocean chalcedony may be worn on the body or applied to the skin. Spending time in a stone circle has a highly beneficial effect, as does internal consumption of the stone as a precious gem essence and elixirs.

Ocean chalcedony, Madagascar

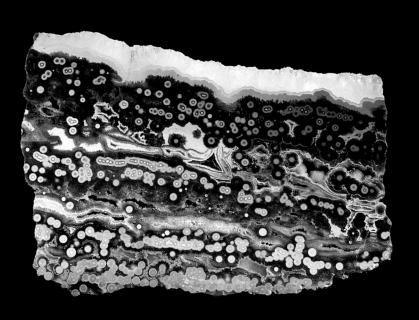

Pietersite

Crystal system: trigonal (quartz) + monoclinic (crocidolite)
+ rhombic (limonite)
Manner of formation: secondary
Mineral class: oxides/tectosilicates (quartz) + chain silicates (crocidolite)
+ oxides (limonite)
Colour: blue-black and yellow-brown debris in clear quartz
Chemical formula, mineral-forming substances: SiO_2 (Quartz) +
$Na_2Mg_3Fe_2(OH/Si_4O_{11})_2$ + Al,Ti (Crocidolite) + FeOOH (Limonite)

Mineralogy

Pietersite is a breccia composed of falcon's eye and tiger's eye
cemented with quartz and has inclusions of blue-black crocidolite
and yellow-brown limonite fibres.

Mythology

Pietersite wasn't discovered until the end of the twentieth century,
in the Namib Desert, and was named after its discoverer, Sid
Pieters. At the gemstone therapy school run by Jane Ann Dow in
New Mexico, it is known as the 'stormstone', a stone that offers
help during times of chaos.

Healing

Spiritually Pietersite helps us to master periods of fast and stormy
(personal or collective) changes and to build a new order out of
chaos. It loosens stubborn blocks and clears up confusion.

Emotionally Pietersite helps us cope with unprocessed images and
inner conflict and, connected with this, all kinds of unpleasant
feelings. Pietersite helps us remain distanced, if necessary, without
lacking feelings.

Mentally Pietersite helps us process impressions faster and to remain
open to absorb spiritual content. It enables us to remain concentrated
and collected, even when there are a multitude of distractions and
diversions.

Physically Pietersite supports the healing of illnesses that arise
through confusion or lack of rest. It is particularly effective with all
respiratory problems.

Application

Pietersite can be worn or laid on the solar plexus. Spending time in
a stone circle has a strongly centering effect. Internal consumption
as a precious gem essence and elixir is also effective.

Pietersite, Namibia;
Pop rocks, USA

Pop rocks (boji stones, spherical pyrites)

Crystal system: cubic (pyrite) + rhombic (limonite)
Manner of formation: secondary
Mineral class: sulphides (pyrite) + oxides (limonite)
Colour: dark grey to rust brown
Chemical formula, mineral-forming substances: FeS_2 (pyrite) + $FeOOH \cdot n$ H_2O (limonite)

Mineralogy

Pop rocks are spherical pyrites formed in ocean sediment by a secondary process and subsequently weathered on the Earth's surface where they obtained a coating of limonite. Depending on how far the weathering has progressed, the cubic crystals are still visible (so-called 'male pop rocks') or have disappeared ('female pop rocks').

Mythology

A number of modern myths have been spun around pop rocks as 'Boji stones', none of which has any real foundation. In fact, there is no tradition of their healing properties.

Healing

Spiritually Pop rocks encourage awareness and draw our attention to the present moment. They encourage all spiritual processes without judging them.

Emotionally Pop rocks make us aware of blocked emotions, images and memories. They enhance emotions and moods and confront us with our dark side.

Mentally Pop rocks encourage the acknowledgement of the kinds of thoughts and behaviours that hinder us and make us ill. They help us recognize inhibiting patterns of the past.

Physically Pop rocks stimulate the flow of energy in the meridians and make it easier to get rid of blockages painlessly. They highlight more severe blockages. Pop rocks are ideally suited for general preventative treatments, but less so for the treatment of acute illnesses.

Application

Take a pair of pop rocks and hold one stone in each hand simultaneously for between ten and thirty minutes. This produces a battery-like charge that boosts the inner flow of energy.

Prase

Crystal system: trigonal (quartz) + monoclinic (actinolite)
Manner of formation: tertiary
Mineral class: oxides/tectosilicates (quartz) + chain silicates (actinolite)
Colour: grass green to leek green
Chemical formula, mineral-forming substances: SiO_2 (quartz) +
$Ca_2(Mg,Fe)_5[(OH)_2 | Si_8O_{22}]$ (actinolite)

Mineralogy

Prase is a ferrous green silicate (generally actinolite) that owes its green colour to quartz. It is created from metamorphic hydrothermal solutions and forms crystals with sides that sometimes taper to sharp points.

Mythology

The name prase can be traced back to Pliny the Elder, who described a stone named 'Prasius'. Hildegard of Bingen later mentions prase as a healing crystal for eye complaints, fever and contusions. However, it is not certain that the green stones described by Pliny and Hildegard are the same as modern-day prase.

Healing

Spiritually Prase brings patience and meekness. It helps us to steer our lives into calm waters and to follow our own goals intuitively. It also promotes balance and equanimity.

Emotionally Prase makes it easier to cope with burdens and worries and to resolve conflicts. It has a calming effect and in particular helps resentful people to 'bury the hatchet'.

Mentally Prase makes it possible to remain reasonable and level headed during difficulties and conflicts and to find simple and pragmatic solutions that suit all those involved.

Physically Prase has a cooling effect, easing pain and reducing fever. It reduces swelling and bruises, helps with bladder conditions and soothes heatstroke, sunstroke and sunburn.

Application

Prase should be worn for longer periods of time as it takes effect quite slowly. The stone may be warmed up first in order to soothe pain and swelling more quickly.

Prehnite

Crystal system: rhombic
Manner of formation: primary or tertiary
Mineral class: sorosilicates
Colour: clear, pale green, yellow
Chemical formula, mineral-forming substances: $Ca_2Al[(OH)_2|AlSi_3O_{10}]$ +
Fe, Na, H_2O

Mineralogy

Prehnite is more likely to form rocks at lower temperatures in regional and contact metamorphosis. However, the most beautiful specimens are created in hydrothermal solutions of magmatic or metamorphic origin.

Healing

Spiritually Prehnite helps counteract avoidance and substitution mechanisms. It also helps us to accept unpleasant truths, helping us to understand our own identities.

Emotionally Prehnite helps us face up to avoided images and memories and to reject unpleasant feelings connected with them. Prehnite does not itself throw up many memories, but it helps when they are activated and become acute as a result of new experiences.

Mentally Prehnite encourages analytical thinking and accelerates the processing of sensory perceptions. Prehnite imperceptibly but continuously increases our perception levels.

Physically Prehnite stimulates the metabolism of fat and accelerates the removal of toxins stored in it. Prehnite stimulates all regeneration processes of the body.

Application

Prehnite may be applied directly to the skin or consumed as a precious gem essence or elixir. Its effects on the metabolism of fat are most pronounced when several prehnite stones are placed together over the liver and pancreas and in the general area of the small intestine.

Prase, Serifos, Greece;
Prehnite, India

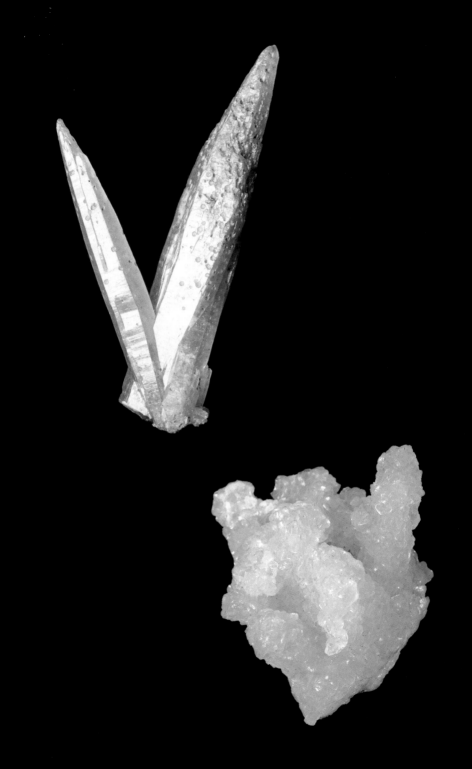

Purpurite

Crystal system: rhombic
Manner of formation: secondary
Mineral class: phosphates
Colour: deep pink to red-violet
Chemical formula, mineral-forming substances: $(Mn,Fe)PO_4 + Li,Na,Ca,H_2O$

Mineralogy

Purpurite is a rare manganese iron phosphate created secondarily when phosphorus-rich pegmatites are oxidised and leached out. This forms crusts or large sections of purpurite, often mixed with the closely related heterosite.

Mythology

Purpurite was only discovered at the beginning of the twentieth century and was named by the mineralologist Graton in 1905 for its colour (Latin *purpureus*, 'purple red'). There is therefore no recorded tradition of its healing properties.

Healing

Spiritually Purpurite promotes alertness, awareness and inspiration. It allows users the time and space to pursue their own life goals and to strive courageously for worthwhile undertakings.

Emotionally Purpurite lightens the mood and reinvigorates the user when faced with tiredness, depression, exhaustion and burn out. It restores *joie de vivre* and strengthens you emotionally.

Mentally Purpurite brings light to dark thoughts. It promotes the resolution of conflicts, helps us to see situations clearly and to implement solutions with energy.

Physically Purpurite mobilises energy reserves while also promoting better sleep for good recovery after exertion. This strengthens the immune system as well as the heart, circulation, nerves and kidneys. Purpurite also boosts the motor functions, senses and sexuality.

Application

Purpurite may be worn on the body or applied to the skin (careful, it can sometimes leave a mark!). Spending time in a circle of purpurite may have a very intense effect.

Purpurite, Namibia

Pyrite

Crystal system: cubic
Manner of formation: primary, secondary or tertiary
Mineral class: sulphides
Colour: brass yellow, greenish-yellow, grey
Chemical formula, mineral-forming substances: FeS_2 + Mn,Ni,Co + (Pb,Zn,Cu,As)

Mineralogy

Pyrite can be created anywhere where rock is formed: the small clumps of pyrites that are commonly found are mainly created magmatically, while pyrite cuboids, framboids and precise pyrite cubes (found in Spain) are created sedimentarily in clay minerals. Large masses are also found in metamorphic rocks.

Mythology

The name pyrite means 'fire stone' as it forms sparks when struck and was used, as far as the Stone Age, to light fires. As 'fire lives in it' it was worked into amulets as a magic stone, and was used in healing as a 'warming stone'.

Healing

Spiritually Pyrite encourages self-realization. It confronts us with our own character and shows up its light and dark sides.

Emotionally Pyrite uncovers secrets and memories that were held back and thus provides an opportunity for openness and honesty.

Mentally Pyrite clarifies the causes of certain life circumstances and illnesses and thus enables us to intitiate necessary changes.

Physically Pyrite clarifies confusing presentations of diseases and unclear symptoms. It shows up the causal symptoms of an illness. Special pyrite 'suns' have a pain-alleviating effect.

Application

Pyrite should only be worn in contact with the skin for a short time, as longer contact (particularly when sweating) makes it secrete black iron sulphide that irritates the skin and stains clothing. Pyrite is better used for meditation or when positioned where it can be contemplated on a regular basis.

Pyrite, Peru;
Pyrite cubes, Spain

Smoky quartz

Crystal system: trigonal
Manner of formation: primary or tertiary
Mineral class: oxides/tectosilicates, quartz group
Colour: yellowish brown to dark brown, blackish grey or black
Chemical formula, mineral-forming substances: SiO_2 + (Al,Li,Na,Fe,Mn,Ti)

Mineralogy

Smoky quartz is a brown crystal quartz whose colour is the result of ionising radiation. It is created in pegmatites and in hydrothermal solutions of magmatic or metamorphic origin.

Mythology

Smoky quartz is believed to protect against bad luck in Alpine regions, and for this reason crucifixes are still made out of it. It was therefore once worn or carried by soldiers in battle.

Healing

Spiritually Smoky quartz increases our tolerance of stress. It helps us bear sorrow and strive hard, to cope more easily with hard times and complete tasks.

Emotionally Smoky quartz has a relaxing effect. It is the classic 'antistress stone' that, in the long term, also takes away the tendency to allow ourselves to be 'stressed' and makes us more resistant to stress factors.

Mentally Smoky quartz encourages sober, realistic and pragmatic considerations. It encourages concentration and helps dissolve contradictions, as well as separate feelings and thoughts.

Physically Smoky quartz has a pain-alleviating effect and dissolves cramps. It is especially helpful with back problems. Smoky quartz fortifies the nerves, protects us against the effects of radiation and helps alleviate the damage caused by radiation.

Application

Smoky quartz should be worn for longer periods of time as a chain or pendant to make use of its strengthening effects. In stressful situations it is helpful to hold two polished or rough crystals, one in each hand. To ease pain, place smoky quartz directly on the part of the body affected. It can generally also be consumed as a precious gem essence or elixir.

Smoky quartz, Switzerland;
Smoky quartz, Gwindel, Switzerland

Rhodochrosite

Crystal system: trigonal
Manner of formation: primary, secondary or tertiary
Mineral class: carbonates
Colour: pink to raspberry red
Chemical formula, mineral-forming substances: $MnCO_3$ + Ca,Mg,Fe

Mineralogy

Rhodochrosite is mainly created secondarily through the intrusion of carbonated water into the oxidation zone of manganese ore deposits. It is also created in small amounts in magmatic hydrothermal solutions or through contact metamorphosis in conjuction with rhodonite.

Mythology

Rhodochrosite (Greek for 'rose coloured') has been known for a long time as manganese spar or raspberry spar. However, there are no indications as to a traditional use of it as a healing stone.

Healing

Spiritually Rhodochrosite bestows a positive, enthusiastic attitude towards life. It stimulates an impersonal, all-encompassing love.

Emotionally Rhodochrosite encourages activity, liveliness, eroticism and spontaneous expressions of feeling. It has a mood-lifting effect, bestows energy and makes us lighthearted and cheerful.

Mentally Rhodochrosite imparts wakefulness and dynamism: it causes us to be busy, fills us with ideas and helps make work appear easy, so that we can succeed.

Physically Rhodochrosite stimulates the circulation, blood pressure, kidneys and sexual organs of reproduction. It makes the blood vessels more elastic, thus helping with migraines.

Application

During a migraine attack, place rhodochrosite on the medulla oblongata – a pressure-sensitive point directly under the cranium (back of the head) where the back of the neck joins the skull. Otherwise, it can simply be worn on the body or consumed as a precious gem essence or elixir.

Rhodochrosite, Argentina;
Rhodonite, Australia

Rhodonite

Crystal system: triclinic
Manner of formation: tertiary, rarely primary
Mineral class: chain silicates
Colour: pink, rarely raspberry red
Chemical formula, mineral-forming substances: $CaMn_4[Si_5O_{15}] + Fe,Zn$

Mineralogy

Rhodonite is very rarely created from magmatically-hydrothermal solutions – it is more frequently formed from the metamorphosis of sedimentary manganese ores or amygdules of oceanic manganese that have become part of mountain formations. This creates coarse, grainy or solid masses that are often still suffused with black manganese oxide. These metamorphic deposits sometimes occur as such large masses that rhodonite can also be used in stonemasonry and architectural work.

Mythology

Rhodonite (Greek *rhodon*, 'rose') has been known by this name for about 200 years. Unfortunately, no traditions on its healing effects have been found.

Healing

Spiritually Rhodonite helps us to forgive and thereby brings about reconciliation between people who have been hurting each other for some time. It helps us realize that strife is very often caused by a lack of self-love and that the triggering 'misdeeds' of the other person are not the real cause. This facilitates mutual understanding, strengthens friendships and helps solve conflicts in a constructive manner. Rhodonite stimulates learning from experience and bestows spiritual maturity.

Emotionally Rhodonite helps heal old 'wounds' and 'scars'. It enables us to forgive harm and injustice received and liberates us from deep mental pain as well as festering anger and persistent annoyance. Rhodonite also helps with renewed injury: it dissolves shock and helps with fear, confusion and panic. Rhodonite can be looked upon as a 'rescue' or 'first aid' stone that can prevent traumatization if used immediately.

Mentally Rhodonite makes it possible to remain clear and conscious even in extreme situations, when in danger, when threatened or under great pressure. It helps us understand that revenge has a mainly self-destructive effect and makes it easier to deal calmly with provocation and insults and to remain prudent and level-headed in all our actions. Rhodonite elucidates the meaning or gain in any experience, even if it is unpleasant, thus showing the way out of seemingly hopeless situations.

Physically Rhodonite is the best wound-healing stone of all. Minor injuries like small cuts, for example, will heal in a matter of minutes. It heals suppurating wounds, helps eliminate toxins out of the tissues (also insect stings) and makes sure that healthy tissue without scar tissue is formed during the healing of a wound. To a lesser degree it will even enable later transformation of scars in the case of healed wounds. Rhodonite will also heal internal injuries and stimulates regeneration during illnesses that involve processes of self-dissolution, for example autoimmune diseases, stomach ulcers, even multiple sclerosis. Rhodonite strengthens the heart and circulation and encourages fertility in both sexes.

Application

Rhodonite should be worn near the heart to heal emotional pain. Daily meditation inside a rhodonite stone circle also has a strong spiritual, emotional and mental effect. For minor injuries, place a moistened piece of rhodonite on the wound as soon as possible, press down and keep the pressure applied for five to ten minutes. Alternatively, in more serious cases, gem essence or a diluted rhodonite elixir may be applied to the injury (approximately ten drops to 0.2 litres (7 fluid ounces) of water). Consuming rhodonite as a precious gem essence and elixir in particular will help with accidents or similar events, counteract the effects of shock and prevent trauma. Talking about what happened to a calm listener is also helpful as it aids the mind to deal with what has happened.

Rose quartz

Crystal system: trigonal (quartz) + rhombic (dumortierite)
Manner of formation: primary
Mineral class: oxides/tectosilicates (quartz) + island silicates (dumortierite)
Colour: pink, rarely with a hint of lilac
Chemical formula, mineral-forming substances: SiO_2 (quarz) +
$(Al,Fe)_7[O_3 | BO_3 | (SiO_4)_3]$ (dumortierite)

Mineralogy

Rose quartz is created magmatically and forms large masses in pegmatites. Its colour is the result of fibrious dumortierite inclusions. Asterism ('star formation') may arise when dumortierite or rutile fibres are orientated and grown within a quartz crystal lattice.

Mythology

For centuries, rose quartz has been considered to be a fertility crystal. It has been used for healing heart problems and female disorders, but also for love magic, therefore, in 'matters of the heart'.

Healing

Spiritually Rose quartz makes us gentle yet firm. There is no question of pliability or giving in, rather there is an awareness of the 'gentle, soft nature overcoming the hard, strong one'. Rose quartz encourages helpfulness, openness and the desire for a pleasant ambience.

Emotionally Rose quartz imparts empathy, sensitivity and sometimes over-sensitiveness. It encourages proper self-love, a strong heart, romance and the ability to love.

Mentally Rose quartz liberates us from worry and helps us discriminate (sympathy/antipathy). Rose quartz draws attention to the fulfilment of elementary needs.

Physically Rose quartz stimulates the blood circulation in the tissues. It fortifies the heart and sexual organs, helps with sexual problems and encourages fertility.

Application

Rose quartz is effective even as a rough stone situated nearby. It can be used in any manner.

Rose quartz, Madagascar;
Rutilated quartz, Brazil

Rutilated quartz

Crystal system: trigonal (quartz) + tetragonal (rutile)
Manner of formation: primary or tertiary
Mineral class: oxides/tectosilicates (quartz) + oxides (rutile)
Colour: clear to smoky brown with yellow to red-brown fibres
Chemical formula, mineral-forming substances: SiO_2 (quartz) + TiO_2 +
Fe,Sn,V,Cr,Nb,Ta (rutile)

Mineralogy

Rutilated quartz is created from silicic acid solutions that contain titanium in which rutile fibres are first formed and then enclosed in quartz. It is generally created magmatically in pegmatites and more rarely from metamorphic hydrothermal solutions.

Mythology

Rutilated quartz was known as 'Venus hair' in ancient times, but was later named sagenite. It was thought to be captured sunlight and to be helpful for dark moods and coughs.

Healing

Spiritually Rutilated quartz gives us new hope and transmits uprightness, independence and spiritual greatness. It helps us to defend ourselves without losing sight of our goals.

Emotionally Rutilated quartz has a mood-lifting and antidepressive effect. It dissolves hidden, unacknowledged fear and liberates us from feelings of anxiety and constriction. Rutilated quartz also helps with sexual problems caused by severe tension, such as potency problems and premature ejaculation.

Mentally Rutilated quartz helps develop vision. It helps us to think big and not to limit our visions and horizons because of supposed pressure of circumstances.

Physically Rutilated quartz helps with diseases of the respiratory tract, particularly with chronic bronchitis. It stimulates the regenerating power of all cells and the flow of energy and body growth. Rutilated quartz encourages an upright posture.

Application

Rutilated quartz may be used in meditation and for a stone circle. It may also be worn or laid on the chest or solar plexus, or consumed as a precious gem essence or elixir.

Ruby

Crystal system: trigonal
Manner of formation: tertiary, more rarely primary
Mineral class: oxides, corundum variety
Colour: red to red-violet
Chemical formula, mineral-forming substances: Al_2O_3 + Cr,Fe

Mineralogy

Ruby is mostly created through contact or regional metamorphosis in gneisses, crystalline slates, marble or dolomite marble, and more rarely also from liquid magma in aluminium-rich rocks such as syenite or related pegmatites. It obtains its red colour from inclusions of chromium. Orientated inclusions of rutile needles cause asterism (star-formation).

Mythology

Ruby (Latin *rubeus*, 'red') was unanimously considered to be the stone of the Sun in all the old cultures of Europe and India. It represents the life force, inner fire, love and passion.

Healing

Spiritually Ruby lends style and vigour to life. It bestows passion as a driving force, but still prevents tendencies towards self-destruction in its role as a life-loving stone.

Emotionally Ruby brings healthy tension and dynamism. It is enlivening, rejuvenates, fires us with enthusiasm, and lifts us out of lethargy and exhaustion; it has a balancing effect on hyperactivity. Ruby stimulates sexual activity.

Mentally Ruby leads to joyful commitment to all social tasks. It makes us awake and aware in thought and action, able to perform well, active, courageous, impulsive and spontaneous.

Physically Ruby stimulates the spleen, adrenal glands and the circulation. It helps with infectious diseases, for example intestinal infections, and encourages fever in its function as resistance.

Application

Ruby can be worn on the body as a chain or pendant, carried as a touchstone or it can be placed on the pubic bone. The latter will activate a great deal of 'power'. Internal consumption as a precious gem essence or elixir also produces intense effects.

Sapphire

Crystal system: trigonal
Manner of formation: primary or tertiary
Mineral class: oxides, corundum variety
Colour: blue, black, clear, green, yellow, pink
Chemical formula, mineral-forming substances: Al_2O_3 + Cr,Fe,Ti,V

Mineralogy

Sapphire is created either from from liquid magma in basalt, syenite and related pegmatites or in the metamorphosis of gneisses, crystalline slates, marble or dolomite marble. It obtains its colours from elements of titanium (blue), iron (yellow) or vanadium (green). Orientated inclusions of rutile needles cause asterism (star-formation).

Mythology

Sapphire (Sanskrit *Sani*, 'Saturn') was always considered to be the stone of Saturn in all the old cultures of Europe and India. It represents the heavens, the sphere of the angels, magic, fidelity and friendship.

Healing

Spiritually Sapphire bestows straightforwardness and the ability to direct scattered spiritual energies towards a single goal. By using sapphire, we are made to look at our own lives in a critical way and reject anything that does not stand up to scrutiny. Sapphire encourages the desire for knowledge and wisdom.

Emotionally Sapphire has a calming effect. It helps with depression, psychic illnesses and delusions. Sapphire strengthens the power of belief and the love of truth.

Mentally Sapphire encourages sobriety, the ability to criticize and the organization of thoughts. Our intentions and will become so clear that both ideas and thoughts are realized very rapidly.

Physically Sapphire encourages all healing processes through a mental decision to get well. It alleviates pain, lowers fevers and is particularly helpful with intestinal, brain and nervous diseases.

Application

Sapphire can be worn, laid on the stomach and forehead, or consumed internally as a precious gem essence and/or elixir.

Ruby, India;
Sapphire, Sri Lanka

Sardonyx

Crystal system: trigonal
Manner of formation: primary or secondary
Mineral class: oxides/tectosilicates, quartz group
Colour: black, white, red-brown
Chemical formula, mineral-forming substances: $SiO_2 \cdot H_2O$ + Mn,Fe

Mineralogy

Sardonyx is a chalcedony that is coloured black and white, sometimes also red-brown due to iron and carbon inclusions. It is formed in voids in rock from magmatic or sedimentary silicic acid solutions.

Mythology

Sardonyx has been known since antiquity and until the Middle Ages was considered to be a stone of abundance, virtue, fearlessness and eloquence. It was thought to bestow a high intellect and common sense. Its name is a composite of the reddish brown sard it contains (carnelian) and onyx.

Healing

Spiritually Sardonyx stimulates the striving for a meaningful existence. It increases willpower and strengthens a virtuous character, making us friendly and helpful.

Emotionally Sardonyx bestows stability, self-confidence and a hopeful attitude. It helps overcome sadness and brings joy that is easily transferred to others.

Mentally Sardonyx strengthens the perceptions and the absorption of information and intensifies perceptions. It helps us understand daily events more easily.

Physically Sardonyx invigorates all the sensory organs and improves all perceptions of the senses. It regulates all body fluids, the immune system, cell metabolism and the activity of the intestines and encourages absorption of nutrients and elimination of wastes.

Application

Sardonyx may be worn as a pendant, carried as a touchstone or consumed as a precious gem essence or elixir. Physically it is very effective when laid on the stomach.

Sardonyx (three-colored agate), Brazil

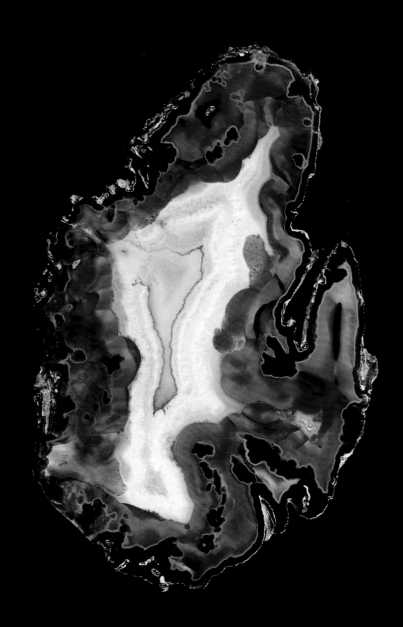

Schalenblende

Crystal system: cubic (sphalerite, galenite, pyrite), hexagonal (wurtzite),
rhombic (markasite)
Manner of formation: secondary
Mineral class: sulphides
Colour: yellow and grey strata
Chemical formula, mineral-forming substances: ZnS (sphalerite, wurtzite) +
PbS (galenite) + FeS_2 (pyrite, markasite)

Mineralogy
Schalenblende is mainly composed of zinc sulphide (cubic sphalerite and hexagonal wurtzite) with additional amounts of lead sulphide (galenite) and iron sulphide (pyrite, markasite). It is created sedimentarily and hydrothermally from a sulphide gel, resulting in its structure of rippled stripes.

Mythology
Schalenblende has been known as 'blende' in mines since the Middle Ages. There are, however, no traditions about its healing effects.

Healing
Spiritually Schalenblende breaks up outworn structures and bestows idealism. It helps one survive dramatic changes in life and uses them for the meaningful creation of better cicumstances.
Emotionally Schalenblende helps combat exhaustion, weakness, lack of courage and fear. It balances inner unrest and helps us get to sleep whenever thoughts are keeping us awake.
Mentally Schalenblende encourages concentration, abstract thinking, spontaneity and intuition as well as the ability to communicate. It helps end fruitless brooding.
Physically Schalenblende encourages the development of the brain as well as of the senses of smell and taste. It stimulates the retina (enhancing vision in half-light), assists regeneration and wound-healing, supports the immune system and alleviates diabetes. It helps with prostate trouble and stimulates the gonads and ovaries. Schalenblende protects the organism from harmful substances and radiation.

Application
Schalenblende works best when it is worn on the body.

Schalenblende, Poland;
Shungite, Carelia, Russia

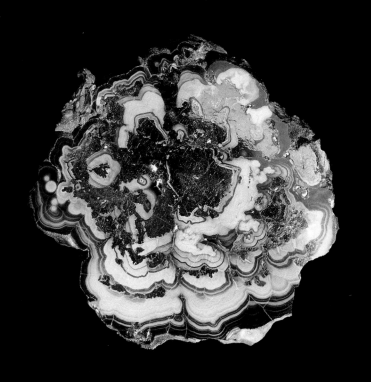

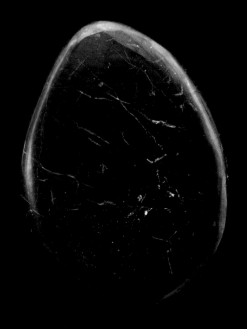

Shungite (black coal)

Crystal system: amorphous + hexagonal
Manner of formation: tertiary
Mineral class: organic rocks
Colour: black
Chemical formula, mineral-forming substances: C_n

Mineralogy

Shungite is an amorphous coal formed from algal sludge and is found in metamorphic oil shale deposits near the village of Shun'ga, in Karelia, Russia, among other places. Shungite always contains additional amounts of hexagonal graphite. It is also believed to contain fullerene, ball-shaped molecules composed of 60 carbon atoms, although it is difficult to prove. The same term is used to sell both pure shungite and an argillaceous slate that contains up to 15% shungite.

Mythology

Shungite is a modern 'cult stone' about which many stories have been spun and which the trade likes to sell as the 'best healing crystal of all'. It is said, for example, that the armies of the Russian Empire used to purify their drinking water with shungite – an assertion that does not stand up to historical enquiry. It is a fact, however, that shungite only became a fashionable healing crystal in Russia in the 1990s, a trend that spread to the West in the twenty-first century.

Healing

Spiritually Shungite supports the fulfilment of personal wishes and the creation of a stable material basis for life.
Emotionally Shungite helps us to overcome fear of loss, isolation and material harm and to strengthen a sense of inner security.
Mentally Shungite enables us to let go of old habits and destructive thoughts and to consolidate successful ideas and concepts.
Physically Shungite promotes digestion, metabolism and excretion. It has a cleansing effect on the bowels and therefore also helps with skin complaints.

Application

Shungite may be worn on the body, applied directly to affected areas or placed in the user's immediate environment. Contrary to common belief, however, it has no purifying effect on drinking water.

Seraphinite (clinochlore)

Crystal system: monoclinic
Manner of formation: tertiary
Mineral class: phyllo or sheet silicates, chlorite
Colour: grass to pine green with a fibrous texture
Chemical formula, mineral-forming substances: $(Mg,Fe)_5Al[(Si_3Al)O_{10}(OH)_8]$
$+ Cr,Mn,Ni,Zn + (Ti)$

Mineralogy

Seraphinite is a trade name for clinochlore that has grown dendritically to form leaves or scales, and which reveals a striking fibrous texture when polished. Seraphinite is a skarn, a contact metamorphic rock created in volcanic regions and in the contact zone of chemically unrelated rocks.

Mythology

Seraphinite was sold as clinochlore for a long time, attracting little attention because of its unappealing name. It wasn't until it began to appear in esoteric circles at the end of the 1990s that it started to attract more interest, this time named after the seraphim (six-winged angels).

Healing

Spiritually Seraphinite promotes attentiveness and being open to contact with people, as well as inner composure and creativity. It strengthens decisiveness and self-assertion and opens the user up to new experiences.

Emotionally Seraphinite helps to break down old behavioural patterns and destructive behaviour. It relieves stress, readies the user for change and emotional development and brings balance, a sense of security and inner peace.

Mentally Seraphinite improves our ability to resolve conflicts by promoting both a capacity for confrontation and a readiness for compromise and reconciliation.

Physically Seraphinite has a reinforcing and detoxifying effect on the liver and kidneys, reducing acidity and boosting the metabolism. It helps us to unwind, while also strengthening our physical capabilities and brings a great sense of well-being. It also promotes weight loss.

Application

Seraphinite may be worn on the body or applied to the skin. Good effects have also been achieved with gemstone massage, consuming as a precious gem essence and using seraphinite for a stone circle.

Serpentine

Crystal system: monoclinic (antigorite), rhombic (chrysotile), trigonal (lizardite)
Manner of formation: tertiary
Mineral class: phyllo or sheet silicates, serpentine group
Colour: yellow-green, green, olive green to black
Chemical formula, mineral-forming substances: $Mg_6[(OH)_8|Si_4O_{10}]$ + Fe,Ni,Al

Mineralogy

Serpentine is created through the metamorphosis of magnesium-rich silicates and often occurs petrogenetically. The serpentine minerals antigorite and lizardite occur as masses or blanket veins while chrysotile occurs as cross veins. Transparent antigorite is sold as 'noble serpentine', yellow-green antigorite as 'Chytha'. Dark lizardite with light veins of chrysotile is known as 'silver eye'.

Mythology

Serpentine ('serpent stone') is so called because it resembles snakeskin. Up until the Middle Ages, serpentine was believed to protect against disease and witchcraft. 'Fright stones' were carved out of this mineral in the shape of ugly-faced amulets that were supposed to drive away 'frightening things'.

Healing

Spiritually Serpentine helps us to establish boundaries and find inner peace. It is an outstanding meditation stone.

Emotionally Serpentine balances mood swings, is calming in cases of nervousness and stress and protects from negative energy effects. It helps women who are unable to reach orgasm because of tension.

Mentally Serpentine stimulates the urge to solve conflicts in a peaceful way; however, it can sometimes make us too eager to compromise for the sake of peace.

Physically Serpentine helps with disturbances to the heart rhythm, kidney and stomach complaints, and also when diarrhoea and constipation keep alternating. It balances over-acidification and stimulates the magnesium metabolism, relaxes cramps and alleviates menstrual pain.

Application

Serpentine can be worn or applied directly to the skin, or consumed as a precious gem essence/ or elixir.

Seraphinite, Urals, Russia;
Silver eye (lizardite with chrysotile), Australia; Antigorite, Austria

Emerald

Crystal system: hexagonal
Manner of formation: primary, secondary or tertiary
Mineral class: ring silicates, beryl family
Colour: grey-green to intense emerald green
Chemical formula, mineral-forming substances: $Be_3Al_2[Si_6O_{18}]$ + K,Li,Na,Cr,V

Mineralogy

Most emerald is created metamorphically through the contact of rocks containing chromium with those containing aluminium and beryllium. It is more rarely formed sedimentarily and hydrothermally in argillaceous schale and magmatically in pegmatites.

Mythology

Emerald was once associated with Mercury, the messenger of the gods, as well as the god of pathways and roads and of sleep and dreams, and so was considered the stone of divine inspiration. In ancient times, it was used to heal the eyes, while in the Middle Ages it was used to combat all 'weaknesses and illnesses in mankind' (Hildegard of Bingen).

Healing

Spiritually Emerald encourages spiritual growth, clairvoyance and a sense of beauty, harmony and justice. It makes us upright, goal-orientated and life-affirming. Emerald enhances friendship, love and unity between partners. It keeps us mentally young.

Emotionally Emerald helps overcome misfortunes and blows dealt by fate. It bestows a balanced nature, openness, recovery and regeneration. Emerald also stimulates us to live intensely and enjoy life.

Mentally Emerald bestows clarity, wakefulness and a broad vision. It improves cooperation in groups, as it enhances mutual understanding.

Physically Emerald improves the ability to see and heals inflammations of the sinuses and upper respiratory tract. It fortifies the heart, stimulates the liver, has a detoxifying effect and alleviates rheumatic complaints. Emerald strengthens the immune system and encourages recovery after infectious illnesses.

Application

Emerald can be worn, laid on the body or used in meditation. It has a very powerful effect when used as a precious gem essence and elixir.

Emerald, Brazil

Sodalite

Crystal system: cubic
Manner of formation: primary, rarely also tertiary
Mineral class: tectosilicates
Colour: dark blue
Chemical formula, mineral-forming substances: $NaAlSi_3O_8/CaAl_2Si_2O_8$ +
$K,OH,Ca,Mg,Fe,Mn,CO_3,SO_4,H_2O$

Mineralogy

Sodalite is formed in magmatites low in silicic acid and in pegmatites in particular; it also occurs more rarely in metamorphic marble.

Mythology

Sodalite was named in 1811 for the sodium it contains. There are no known traditions of its use.

Healing

Spiritually Sodalite encourages idealism and the drive for truth. It makes it possible to observe suppressed parts of our nature non-judgementally and to accept them. Sodalite makes space for living the life we have chosen freely and consciously. It helps us remain true to ourselves.

Emotionally Sodalite transmits a clear sense of who we are and creates a strong antipathy against everything that does not correspond to this identity. It helps us avoid unconscious mechanisms and behavioural patterns, once we have recognized them as being a hindrance to our development. Sodalite dissolves feelings of guilt and makes it possible to stand up for our own feelings and to live them out.

Mentally Sodalite increases awareness and helps us to create order and lend expression to our own convictions, either verbally or through actions. It stimulates a departure from restrictive ideas, dogmas, rules and laws. Sodalite increases a yearning for freedom.

Physically Sodalite heals complaints that afflict the throat, larynx and vocal chords, in particular, long-lasting hoarseness. It has a cooling effect, lowers the blood pressure and stimulates absorption of fluids in the body.

Application

Sodalite should be worn as a chain or pendant, or carried as a touchstone for extended periods of time, or consumed as a precious gem essence or elixir.

*Sodalite, Brazil; Sunstone, Norway;
Sugilite, South Africa*

Sunstone

Crystal system: triclinic
Manner of formation: primary
Mineral class: tectosilicates, feldspar family
Colour: copper red to glittering orange-brown
Chemical formula, mineral-forming substances: $Na[AlSi_3O_8]$ + $Ca[Al_2Si_2O_8]$
+ Fe/Cu,K,Ba,Sr,Mn,Ti

Mineralogy

Sunstone is a plagioclase, a mixed crystal composed of sodium and calcium feldspar, with glittering red-brown (aventurising) inclusions. These may be formed with pegmatites rich in silicic acid and with inclusions of brown hematite flakes or volcanically formed plagioclase with inclusions of solid copper.

Mythology

Sunstone, as the name indicates, is assigned to the Sun. There are no traditions about its use for healing purposes, however.

Healing

Spiritually Sunstone helps us discover and live out our own inner nature. It helps us to affirm our lives and to allow our strong points and 'sunny sides' to shine. Sunstone brings back the belief in luck and happiness and the 'benevolent gods'.

Emotionally Sunstone bestows *joie de vivre*. It has a mood-lifting, antidepressive effect and helps us detach ourselves from feelings of disadvantage, discrimination and failure, as well as images of a 'bad world'. Sunstone increases a sense of self-worth and self-confidence.

Mentally Sunstone encourages optimism and a desire for action. It helps switch our perception filters to the positive events and gives new perspectives even to stubborn pessimists.

Physically Sunstone stimulates self-healing powers. It stimulates the autonomous nervous system and ensures harmonious functioning between all the organs.

Application

Sunstone may be worn on the body, consumed as a precious gem essence or used for meditation.

Sugilite

Crystal system: hexagonal
Manner of formation: secondary or tertiary, rarely primary
Mineral class: ring silicates
Colour: pale violet to intense violet
Chemical formula, mineral-forming substances: $KNa_2(Fe,Mn,Al)_2Li_3[Si_{12}O_{30}]$ + Ba,Ca

Mineralogy

Sugilite is mostly created through the influence of sedimentary or metamorphic hydrothermal solutions (unexplained!) on sedimentary manganese ores. Much more rarely, it is formed from magmatic solutions.

Mythology

Sugilite was discovered in Japan in 1944 and named after its discoverer, Dr. Kenichi Sugi. At the beginning of the 1980s, it was soon adopted as a sought-after 'new age' stone that was supposed to represent the Age of Aquarius. It also has the trade names luvulite and royal azel.

Healing

Spiritually Sugilite helps us maintain our own point of view. It encourages us to live in accordance with our inner truth and not to allow ourselves to be deflected from it, either through pressure or persuasion.

Emotionally Sugilite improves the ability to face up to unpleasant things. It dissolves tension in the soul, alleviates sorrow and grief and helps with fears, paranoia and schizophrenia.

Mentally Sugilite allows us to deal with and overcome conflicts without entering into compromise. It helps find solutions that are based on agreement and do not put any party at a disadvantage.

Physically Sugilite has a harmonizing effect on the nerves and brain and alleviates severe pain. It helps with epilepsy, dyslexia and motor disturbances.

Application

Sugilite should be worn on the body or taken internally as a precious gem essence and/or elixir. To ease pain, it can be applied directly or held in the hand. Its spiritual effects can be experienced through regular meditation with the stone.

Tektite

Crystal system: amorphous
Manner of formation: tertiary
Mineral classes: oxides/silicates, igneous glass
Colour: black, rarely olive green
Chemical formula, mineral-forming substances: SiO_2 + Al_2O_3 +
Ca,K,Fe,Mg,Na,K,Sr,Ba

Mineralogy

Tektite is rock that has been melted by the impact of giant meteorites and has cooled to form igneous glass as it was ejected through the atmosphere.

Mythology

Tektite (Greek *tektos*, 'melted') was named in 1900 by the Viennese geologist F.E. Suess. Stone Age finds have shown that tektite was used as a stone tool and also served as a fertility symbol, thanks to its phallic shape. In Thailand, tektites are even now still prized as stones to bring good fortune and are used in amulets for journeys and pilgrimages.

Healing

Spiritually Tektite helps us to let go. It boosts clearsightedness and has a freeing effect when you are involved in too many things and life becomes too narrow and constricted.

Emotionally Tektite helps to reduce fears about the future and ongoing cares about money and possessions. It induces a strong feeling of freedom and release and promotes compassion.

Mentally Tektite helps us to recognize ourselves as spiritual beings, changing our view of life and helping us to see situations and events from a wider perspective.

Physically Tektite accelerates healing processes, particularly for infectious illnesses. It also helps to offset the effects of radiation and electrosmog.

Application

Tektite has a very strong effect as a precious gem essence or when placed on the forehead. It can additionally be worn as a pendant or carried in the pocket.

Tektite, Thailand;
Thulite (top) and piemontite (bottom), Norway

Thulite

Crystal system: rhombic
Manner of formation: tertiary
Mineral class: sorosilicates, zoisite group
Colour: aged pink, red to blackberry red
Chemical formula, mineral-forming substances:
$(Ca,Mn)_2Al_3[O|OH|SiO_4|Si_2O_7]$ + Na,Ba,Cr,Fe,Mg,Sr

Mineralogy

Thulite is zoisite that contains manganese. It is created through contact metamorphic transformation of rocks containing manganese into limestone silicate bedrock and crystalline shales. It is chemically identical to monoclinic piemontite, which demonstrates similar properties.

Mythology

Thulite received its name after the legendary island 'Thule' of Germanic lore that is supposed to form the northernmost rim of the world, probably because the mineral was first found in Norway. Unfortunately, there are no traditions about its healing properties or use.

Healing

Spiritually Thulite stimulates the life force. It bestows strength and courage for all undertakings and encourages creativity inspired by resistance and challenge.

Emotionally Thulite encourages lust, sensuality and sexuality. It helps us to live life to the full and to immerse ourselves in our feelings. Beauty, adventure, melancholy, romance and eerie atmospheres are all of equal inspiration.

Mentally Thulite fortifies curiosity and the gift for inventions. It stimulates us to search for new ways to solve personal and collective problems.

Physically Thulite enhances fertility. It helps with diseases of the ovaries, testicles and sexual organs. Thulite stimulates regeneration, fortifies the entire nervous system and prevents fainting fits when the body is severely weakened.

Application

Thulite may be consumed as a precious gem essence or elixir, worn on the body or laid on the pubic bone. Spending time in a thulite stone circle has a very interesting effect … (I will say no more!).

Tiger's eye

Crystal system: trigonal (quartz) + rhombic (limonite)
Manner of formation: secondary
Mineral class: oxides/tectosilicates (quartz) + oxides (limonite)
Colour: blue-black and yellow-brown inclusions in clear quartz
Chemical formula, mineral-forming substances: SiO_2 (quartz) + FeOOH (limonite)

Mineralogy

When tiger's eye is cut en cabochon, light refracting in the stone causes the limonite fibres to shimmer like a cat's eye, hence the name. It is also the basis for the belief in the stone's powers to protect and heal the eyes.

Mythology

The silken sheen produced by limonite fibres causes an interesting light effect when the mineral is polished into a round shape, and looks like an eye. This is how the stone gets its name and this is also the origin of the ancient belief that tiger's eye heals eye problems and is a protective stone. In the Middle Ages, it was used to make amulets that protected the wearer against spells, demons and the evil eye.

Healing

Spiritually Tiger's eye helps us get through difficult phases in life without losing courage. It helps preserve that spark of trust in God that leads us on in dark moments.

Emotionally Tiger's eye helps us to distance ourselves from external influences that may come storming in on us; it also mitigates the influence of moods and stressful situations.

Mentally Tiger's eye helps us retain an overall view in complicated, difficult situations and also helps with doubts and difficulties in making decisions.

Physically Tiger's eye has a pain-alleviating effect. It slows down the flow of energy in the body and dampens overexcitation of the nerves and overstimulation of the adrenal glands.

Application

If you are already suffering from blockages, tiger's eye can inhibit the body's energy flow and lead to feelings of numbness in the limbs; in such cases, it should never be used for more than a week at a time. Tiger's eye can otherwise by worn, applied to the skin or consumed as a gem essence or elixir. Meditation is recommended to access the stone's emotional and spiritual effects.

Tiger iron

Crystal system: trigonal (jasper, tiger's eye, hematite)
+ rhombic (limonite in tiger's eye)
Manner of formation: secondary-tertiary
Mineral classes: oxides/tectosilicates (jasper, tiger's eye)
+ oxides (hematite, limonite)
Colour: grey (hematite), yellow-brown (tiger's eye), red to yellow (jasper) striped
Chemical formula, mineral-forming substances: SiO_2 (jasper) +
SiO_2/FeOOH (tiger's eye) + Fe_2O_3 (hematite)

Mineralogy
Tiger iron is composed of jasper, tiger's eye and hematite, with a rippled, striped texture arising from the metamorphic intrusion of sediments containing iron oxide and quartz

Mythology
Tiger iron (a trade name) has only been known since the 1980s and there are no existing traditions for its healing effects.

Healing
Spiritually Tiger iron inspires new impulses when our lives have craved change for a very long time. It clarifies those areas in which we have long since moved on spiritually and actively helps these cycles to be closed, if necessary, and a new start to be made.

Emotionally Tiger iron imparts the kind of endurance that is necessary in order to overcome typical difficulties at the beginning of an undertaking or phase. It lends strength and dynamism to tackle all obstacles (a 'tiger in your tank'). Tiger iron helps with tiredness and exhaustion.

Mentally Tiger iron helps us to find very simple, pragmatic solutions. It clarifies thought according to the notion that 'truth lies in simplicity' and thus helps us act quickly and with determination.

Physically Tiger iron heightens vitality by accelerating the formation of red blood corpuscles and the transportation of oxygen by the blood. Tiger iron eliminates any kind of energy deficiency.

Application
Tiger iron works very quickly if it is worn in contact with the skin. It is a good idea to carry it in your pocket and to hold it in your hand whenever you need extra energy.

Tiger's eye, South Africa;
Tiger iron, Australia

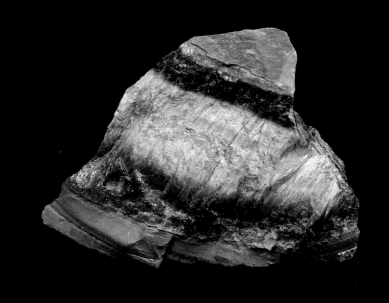

Topaz

Crystal system: rhombic
Manner of formation: primary
Mineral class: island silicates
Colour: clear, light blue, light brown, light yellow
Chemical formula, mineral-forming substances: $Al_2[(F,OH)_2 | SiO_4]$ +
Fe,Ca,Mg + (Cr,Mn)

Mineralogy

Topaz is created pneumatolytically in crevices and veins in acidic plutonite through the action of gases containing fluorine on aluminium silicates. Its colours are the result of trace elements: chromium produces yellow, iron light blue and manganese creates brownish shades.

Mythology

In all the old cultures of Europe and India, topaz was considered the stone of Jupiter. It represented rule over one's own life, self-realization and wisdom. In Mexico, it was used for finding out the truth in cases of disagreement.

Healing

Spiritually Topaz encourages self-realization and the shaping of our lives according to our own wishes. It can enable a breakthrough in spiritual development whenever things have been very laborious and difficult for a long time. Topaz helps us to gain wisdom from of the vagaries of fate.

Emotionally Topaz helps us discover our own inner riches of soul images, abilities and knowledge. It encourages openness, honesty and a fulfilled emotional life.

Mentally Topaz helps us become fully aware of our own influence based on ability and real knowledge gained through hard work, and then to use this meaningfully.

Physically Topaz fortifies the nerves and stimulates the energy flow in the meridians. It improves the digestion and even helps with anorexia. Topaz stimulates the metabolism and the combustion processes of the organism.

Application

Topaz may be worn, placed on the head, or alternatively used in contemplative meditation. Consuming the stone as precious gem essences or elixirs is also effective.

Gold topaz, imperial topaz, pink topaz

Crystal system: rhombic
Manner of formation: primary
Mineral class: island silicates
Colour: gold-yellow (gold topaz), pink-yellow (imperial topaz), pink (pink topaz)
Chemical formula, mineral-forming substances: $Al_2[(F,OH)_2|SiO_4]$ +
Fe,Ca,Mg + (Cr)

Mineralogy

This topaz is created in crevices and veins in acidic plutonite, pneumatolytically through the action of gases containing fluorine on aluminium silicates. Gold-yellow colouration results from traces of chromium, while its natural pink colour is caused by traces of phosphorus.

Mythology

Gold topaz and imperial topaz were known as 'sun stones', bringing light to darkness, while pink-coloured topaz is the 'heart stone'.

Healing

Spiritually Topaz promotes self-fulfillment. These stones help to show our abilities in the right light and in so doing make them visible to others. They reinforce self-esteem (gold topaz), self-assurance (imperial topaz) and self-love (pink topaz).

Emotionally These stones strengthen our self-confidence and awareness of our own personal uniqueness. Gold topaz and imperial topaz make us generous and magnanimous, while pink topaz brings charisma and warm-heartedness.

Mentally These stones encourage the development of grand plans and ideas. They help us overcome apparent obstacles while keeping our feet firmly on the ground.

Physically These stones assist in conditions of nervous exhaustion. They strengthen and activate the nerves, making the entire body more responsive. They stimulate the appetite and are even helpful with anorexia. As topaz contain chromium and phosphorus, they activate vital energy, the body's calorie-burning systems and the entire metabolism.

Application

Gold topaz and imperial topaz should be worn over the solar plexus, while pink topaz should be worn over the heart or applied to the skin. Precious gem essences and elixirs are also effective.

Turquoise

Crystal system: triclinic
Manner of formation: secondary
Mineral class: phosphates
Colour: green, turquoise, light blue
Chemical formula, mineral-forming substances: $CuAl_6[(OH)_2|(PO_4]_4 \cdot 4\ H_2O$
$+ Fe,Zn,Ca$

Mineralogy

Turquoise is created in the oxidation zone of copper deposits through the seepage of water containing phosphate, or in rocks containing aluminium and phosphate through the action of copper solutions.

Mythology

Turquoise derives its name from the country Turkey, where it was first encountered by the Crusaders. For many cultures it was a stone that offered protection against black magic and was worn as an amulet on journeys. Turquoise is said to change colour to warn those who carry it of impending danger.

Healing

Spiritually Turquoise helps us recognize the self-imposed causes of our own fate and their subsequent consequences. This means turquoise makes us aware that we really are the creators of our own luck.

Emotionally Turquoise balances extreme fluctuations of mood and dissolves a tendency to apathy and self-pity. It also refreshes us when tired, downcast or exhausted, and protects us from sensitivity to outside influences.

Mentally Turquoise bestows inner calm but still enables us to be wide awake, lively and ready to act. It encourages good intuition and foresight.

Physically Turquoise neutralizes overacidity and alleviates rheumatism, gout, stomach problems and viral infections. It increases growth, muscular strength, creation of warmth, the ability to regenerate, brain activity and sensory perception and also alleviates pain, relaxes cramps, and has anti-inflammatory and detoxifying effects.

Application

Turquoise should be worn over the thymus gland or solar plexus and/or applied near the affected areas of the body.

Topaz, Pakistan;
Imperial Topaz, Brazil; Turquoise, Arizona, USA

Tourmaline

Crystal system: trigonal
Manner of formation: primary or tertiary
Mineral class: ring silicates
Colour: clear, blue, turquoise, green, yellow, pink, red, violet, brown, black,
also multicoloured
Chemical formula, mineral-forming substances:
$Me^+Me^{2+}_3Me^{3+}_6[(OH,F)_4(BO_3)_2Si_6O_{18}]$

Mineralogy

Tourmalines may be formed in magma containing boron and with a high silicic acid content. Schorl, dravite and uvite are found in plutonites and their pegmatites in particular, due to the presence of large quantities of iron (schorl) and magnesium (dravite, uvite). Colourful elbaites and liddicoatites are formed in pneumatolytic and hydrothermal regions if there is a sufficient additional presence of lithium. The metamorphosis of sedimentary rock containing boron may also create tourmalines such as schorl, dravite and uvite.

Tourmaline invariably consists of monovalent, divalent and trivalent metal ions in the proportions 1 : 3 : 6 as well as basic groups (hydroxide or fluoride), borate groups and silicate rings in the proportions 4 : 2 : 1 – with the simplified chemical formula: $Me^+Me^{2+}_3Me^{3+}_6[(OH,F)_4(BO_3)_2Si_6O_{18}]$ (Me = metal ion). Classified by their chemical composition, there are five tourmalines that are important in crystal healing:

Tourmalines	Chemical Formula	Colour
Dravite	$NaMg_3(Al,Fe,Cr)_6[(OH)_4 \mid (BO_3)_3 \mid Si_6O_{18}]$	brown to black
Elbaite	$Na(Li,Al)_3Al_6[(OH,F)(OH)_3 \mid (BO_3)_3 \mid Si_6O_{18}]$	any colour
Liddicoatite	$Ca(Li,Al)_3Al_6[FO(OH)_2 \mid (BO_3)_3 \mid Si_6O_{18}]$	any colour
Schorl	$NaFe_3(Al,Fe)_6[(OH,F)_4 \mid (BO_3)_3 \mid Si_6O_{18}]$	black
Uvite	$CaMg_3(Al_5Mg)[(OH)_4 \mid (BO_3)_3 \mid Si_6O_{18}]$	brown to olive green

Given this structure, it is the differing metal contents that lend tourmalines their beautiful colours. In the case of elbaites and liddicoatites (which are generally found as mixed crystals), four colour variants in particular are of importance to crystal healing:

Polychrome tourmaline (elbaite) with rubellite and verdelite, Brazil;
Indigolite (elbaite), Brazil

Tourmalines	Chemical Formula	Colour
Indigolite	$(Na,Ca)(Li,Al,Fe)_3(Al,Fe)_6[(OH,O,F)_4 \mid (BO_3)_3 \mid Si_6O_{18}]$	blue
Rubellite	$(Na,Ca)(Li,Al,Mn)_3(Al,Mn)_6[(OH,O,F)_4 \mid (BO_3)_3 \mid Si_6O_{18}]$	red, pink
Verdelite	$(Na,Ca)(Li,Al,Fe)_3(Al,Cr,V)_6[(OH,O,F)_4 \mid (BO_3)_3 \mid Si_6O_{18}]$	green
Paraiba	$(Na,Ca)(Li,Al,Cu)_3(Al,Mn)_6[(OH)_4 \mid (BO_3)_3 \mid Si_6O_{18}]$	green to turquoise

Multicoloured 'polychrome tourmalines' may be either different kinds of tourmaline or colour variations within a crystal.

Mythology

Tourmaline was probably already known in antiquity, but was always equated with other precious stones depending on its colour. It was not until the eighteenth century that it appeared as the 'stone of wisdom, that is clear and resistant to all vagaries of fate ...' (Bernardus Caesius). According to Arabic traditions, tourmaline is a stone of the Sun that strengthens the heart and protects from nightmares.

Healing

Thanks to their great variety, all the tourmalines possess a wide spectrum of healing properties. The list below matches these individual effects with the different varieties that in principle are best suited to achieve them, although other tourmalines can be used in an emergency. Multicoloured tourmalines combine their various qualities.

Blue tourmaline (indigolite)

Spiritually Indigolite strengthens a striving for spiritual freedom and personal development. It promotes loyalty, ethics and a love of truth and inspires great vision.

Emotionally Indigolite breaks the hold of despair and blocked feelings. It helps tears to flow and brings relief. Indigolite frees us emotionally, easing nervousness and helping with hyperactivity.

Mentally Indigolite broadens our intellectual horizons. It encourages ideas, makes us open and tolerant and promotes a sense of responsibility.

Physically Indigolite stimulates the body's water balance and excretion via the kidneys and bladder. It helps burns to heal more quickly (in the best cases, without leaving a scar), helps sensitivity to temperature, eases tension and boosts the function of eyes, ears and all the senses.

Dravite and uvite tourmaline

Spiritually Dravite and uvite promote openness, a sense of community, welfare, helpfulness and social involvement. They help users to feel spiritually relaxed and yet to be involved in life.

Emotionally Dravite and uvite strengthen our ability to empathise with others. They provide help for family problems and in situations of anxiety and conflict in large groups.

Mentally Dravite and uvite stimulate pragmatic, uncomplicated creativity. They help us recognize immediately what is needed and promote manual dexterity.

Physically Dravite and uvite encourage the regeneration of cells, tissue and skin. They help combat cellulite and skin conditions, promote the healing of wounds, soothe cramps and chronic tension and are helpful with growth disorders and bowel complaints.

Green tourmaline (verdelite)

Spiritually Verdelite brings relaxation and *joie de vivre*. It helps us to find a new direction, rediscover lost goals and ideas and be grateful for the miracles of life.

Emotionally Verdelite makes us patient and open. It helps us to express feeling and promotes an interest in other people and the environment. Verdelite eases stress and helps with hyperactivity.

Mentally Verdelite helps us to see a range of possible solutions in any situation and to select the most appropriate, (according to the best of our knowledge and belief).

Physically Verdelite has a detoxifying effect and reduces inflammation. It strengthens the nerves, the heart, the bowels and the functional tissue (parenchyma) of many organs. Verdelite helps with complaints affecting the tendons and joints (carpal tunnel syndrome, tendosynovitis, tennis elbow) and is useful in combating rheumatism, degenerative processes and tumours. It promotes excretion and is effective against constipation and diarrhoea.

Paraiba tourmaline

Spiritually Paraiba tourmaline helps us to see the world and life with kindly, well-meaning eyes and to see the beauty in all things.
Emotionally Paraiba tourmaline allows us to experience an all-encompassing love for the world and for life during meditation. It promotes vivid dreams and a rich emotional world.
Mentally Paraiba tourmaline brings wisdom and justice to difficult decisions. It promotes deeper understanding, clears confusion and stimulates the imagination.
Physically Paraiba tourmaline stimulates hormone production and for this reason should not be used for too long or too often. It energises the activity of the liver, nerves and brain.

Polychrome tourmaline

Spiritually Polychrome tourmaline helps to bring mind, soul, intellect and body together as one harmonious unit. Experiencing this feeling of 'wholeness' gives rise to wisdom and creativity.
Emotionally Polychrome tourmaline stimulates the imagination and visual creativity, and promotes both creative day- and night-time dreaming. It helps feelings to flow freely and to be expressed.
Mentally Polychrome tourmaline promotes visual thinking, receptiveness and imagination. It helps us to recognize progress and developments, to understand them fully and to use them for everyone's benefit.
Physically Polychrome tourmaline harmonises the nerves, metabolism, hormonal glands and immune system. It is therefore good for tension, problems with coordination, sensations of numbness in the limbs, general weakness, susceptibility to infection and sluggish digestion or excretion.

Dravite, Namibia;
Paraiba tourmaline (elbaite), Brazil

Red tourmaline (rubellite)

Spiritually Rubellite promotes vitality and involvement. It makes us dynamic and goal-orientated, and yet flexible enough to examine our own objectives and to correct them if necessary.

Emotionally Rubellite makes us seek human contact and be enterprising and charming. It promotes a powerful sense of well-being as well as an enjoyment of life and sexuality.

Mentally Rubellite helps us to devote ourselves actively to a task, making it easier to coordinate and progress with activities.

Physically Rubellite improves energy flow and conductivity in the nerves and so helps with nerve pain (neuralgia, sciatic conditions, lumbago), motor function impairments and sensory disturbances. It strengthens the function of the reproductive organs and boosts blood flow and blood purification in the spleen and liver. Rubellite also helps to break up blood clots (thrombosis). Dark red rubellite stimulates the circulation without raising the blood pressure too high, while pink varieties are good for the heart.

Schorl tourmaline

Spiritually Schorl improves perception and also enables us to retain self-control while maintaining a neutral, distanced and impartial position.

Emotionally Schorl promotes serenity and inner peace. It diverts tension, helps with stress and emotional overload, protects against negative influence and improves sleep.

Mentally Schorl stimulates sober, clear, logical and rational thinking. It helps us to recognize and analyse our mistakes and to develop and implement solutions.

Physically Schorl has a general analgesic effect and reduces tension. It helps combat strains, back conditions and sensations of numbness in the limbs, clears blockages and stimulates vital energy to flow. Schorl neutralises the effects of radiation and may be used to reduce scarring. It stimulates bowel movements, eases bloating and stomach ache and helps against constipation. Schorl also strengthens the kidneys and soothes ear complaints.

Schorl, Brazil;
Watermelon tourmaline (elbaite), Afghanistan;
Tourmaline quartz, Brazil

Watermelon tourmaline

Spiritually Watermelon tourmaline promotes understanding, love and friendship. It helps to create an atmosphere where everyone feels at ease.

Emotionally Watermelon tourmaline makes us patient, loving and tender. It eases depression and fear while helping us to protect ourselves, encouraging us to develop a sense of security and well-being from within.

Mentally Watermelon tourmaline helps us to express our intentions clearly, keeping our own goals in mind, while also respecting the wishes and needs of others.

Physically Watermelon tourmaline strengthens the heart and all the senses (sight, sound, smell, taste and touch). It helps with growth disorders and sensations of numbness in the limbs, soothes nerve pain and inflammation, promotes nerve regeneration and helps combat paralysis and multiple sclerosis.

Application

Tourmaline may be worn on the body or applied to the skin on specific regions of the body as required. To stimulate energy flow, crystals should be applied to the skin with their points in the direction of meridian flow. Precious gem essence and elixirs also work extremely powerfully and rapidly.

Tourmaline quartz

Crystal system: trigonal
Manner of formation: primary or tertiary
Mineral class: oxides/tectosilicates (quartz) + ring silicates (schorl)
Colour: black tourmaline crystals in clear quartz
Chemical formula, mineral-forming substances: SiO_2 (Quartz) +
$NaFe_3(Al,Fe)_6[(OH,F)_4 \,|\, (BO_3)_3 \,|\, Si_6O_{18}]$ (Schorl)

Mineralogy

Tourmaline quartz (tourmalinated quartz) is generally formed magmatically in pegmatites but may also be created metamorphically or hydrothermally. During its formation, tourmaline is created first (generally black schorl) and the tourmaline needles are then embedded in the subsequent quartz.

Mythology

Inclusions of black tourmaline in quartz were once viewed as contaminating the stone and it was not until the twentieth century that attention began to be paid to tourmaline quartz. There are no known traditions for its healing properties.

Healing

Spiritually Tourmaline quartz makes it possible to reconcile opposites. It helps us both to accept ourselves as we are and to fulfil our own ideals.

Emotionally Tourmaline quartz helps to settle inner struggles and to resolve conflicts. It helps us to resolve impossible dilemmas and to develop emotional balance and serenity.

Mentally Tourmaline quartz helps us to recognize the causes of mishaps and failures and the reasons for our strengths and successes.

Physically Tourmaline quartz strikes the right balance between tension and relaxation. It eases pain, tension and breathing blockages, reinvigorates fatigue and listlessness, stimulates digestion and excretion, promotes regeneration and keeps us looking young and vital.

Application

Tourmaline quartz may be used as a crystal, a crystal group, a polished stone, precious gem essence or elixir. It is also very pleasant used in gemstone massage.

Variscite

Crystal system: rhombic
Manner of formation: secondary
Mineral class: phosphates
Colour: pale green to grass green
Chemical formula, mineral-forming substances: $AlPO_4 \cdot 2\ H_2O$ + Fe,As,Cr,V

Mineralogy

Variscite is created secondarily near the Earth's surface in the oxidation zone of rocks containing aluminium, through the action of liquids containing phosphates. It may either form rocks or fill crevices.

Mythology

Variscite is named after the place where it was found, 'Variscia', the Latin name for Vogtland. No traditions about its healing properties are known.

Healing

Spiritually Variscite encourages authenticity and truthfulness. As long as we carry variscite, it will be difficult for us to indulge in pretence; we just reveal ourselves as we are. Variscite also helps us develop interests and remain spiritually aware.

Emotionally Variscite has an enlivening effect and lifts the spirit. It helps with chronic tiredness, for example in the spring, but also has a calming effect on nervousness and inner unrest.

Mentally Variscite promotes wakefulness, sobriety and clear, rational thinking. It helps us to express ourselves clearly and in a fashion that can be easily understood. It also increases our level of perception.

Physically Variscite stimulates energy reserves. It neutralizes an excess of acid and helps with acid indigestion, gastritis, stomach ulcers, rheumatism and gout. Variscite helps loosen cramp and calms the nerves.

Application

Variscite should be worn as a pendant or carried as a touchstone for a longer period of time and be held in the hand when needed. Variscite precious gem essences and elixirs are also very effective.

Variscite, USA;
Fossilized wood, Australia

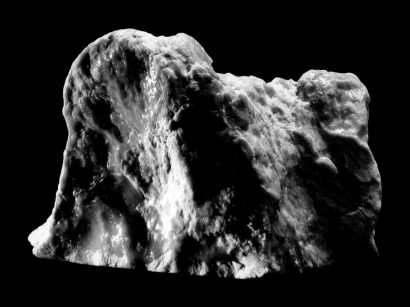

Fossilized wood

Crystal system: trigonal (quartz) and/or amorphous (opal)
Manner of formation: secondary
Mineral class: oxides/silicates
Colour: yellow-brown, red-brown, brown-grey
Chemical formula, mineral-forming substances: SiO_2 + Fe,O,OH

Mineralogy

Fossilized wood is formed when dead wood is saturated with silicic acid in the absence of oxygen and then solidifies through loss of water. Depending on the exact circumstances of formation, the substance of the wood is replaced either by quartz or, more rarely, by opal.

Mythology

Cult objects fashioned from fossilized wood were discovered in an Etruscan temple dating back 4,300 years. Over the centuries, the wood was believed to be the bones of giants or the tools of the gods by some peoples and was, therefore, used in magic as an object of power.

Healing

Spiritually Fossilized wood promotes a sense of ease with the planet we live on and the feeling of being in the right place at the right time.

Emotionally Fossilized wood stimulates inner imagery. It stimulates recovery, is calming, helps us collect ourselves and helps us keep our feet firmly planted in reality.

Mentally Fossilized wood stimulates us to create a pleasant atmosphere, live a simple life and grant ourselves enough time for leisure and reflection.

Physically Fossilized wood stabilizes our health. It stimulates the metabolism, calms the nerves, creates a feeling of well-being and helps with obesity, which is often caused by 'inadequate earthing'.

Application

Fossilized wood should be worn, consumed as a precious gem essence or elixir, or arranged as a stone circle. A disc large enough to sit on is ideal for meditation.

Zircon

Crystal system: tetragonal
Manner of formation: primary
Mineral class: island silicates
Colour: brown, red-brown, red-orange
Chemical formula, mineral-forming substances: $ZrSiO_4$ + Al,Fe,P,Hf,Th,U,Y

Mineralogy

Zircon is formed as a liquid out of acid magmas and is, therefore, found as a component of granites and seyenites. It forms larger, usually double-ended crystals in pegamatites. Some types of zircon may be slightly radioactive due to deposits of approx 2% hafnium, thorium and uranium.

Mythology

Zircon was known in antiquity as hyacinth and was used for healing. It was reputed to heal madness, make us resistant to temptations and strengthen the intellect. Nowadays, only the red-brown variety of zircon is called hyacinth.

Healing

Spiritually Zircon helps us become detached from materialism and experience spiritual reality. Zircon stimulates dealing with the meaning of existence.

Emotionally Zircon helps us overcome loss. It also helps us to let go of pain, sadness and fear, as well as all kinds of 'hanging on to' things. Zircon encourages lucid dreaming.

Mentally Zircon makes us aware of the ephemeral nature of all things. It stimulates us to re-evaluate the 'important things in life' from this viewpoint and to shed our adherence to material things.

Physically Zircon has a liver-stimulating, pain-alleviating and cramp-dissolving effect. It helps with menstrual pains that are caused by delayed menstruation.

Application

Zircon should be worn or laid on only for a maximum of one hour daily (except in cases of pain or menstrual complaints).

Zoisite

Crystal system: rhombic
Manner of formation: tertiary
Mineral class: sorosilicates
Colour: brown, grey, green
Chemical formula, mineral-forming substances: $Ca_2Al_3[O|OH|SiO_4|Si_2O_7]$ +
Ba,Cr,Fe,Mg,Mn,Sr,V

Mineralogy

Zoisite is created through the regional metamorphosis of basic magmatite to limestone silicate bedrock, verdites and eclogites. In crystal healing, it is generally used as anyolite, a zoisite with green coloration from chromium, which also contains ruby.

Mythology

Zoisite was first found in Carinthia (Karnten, Austria) towards the end of the eighteenth century and named after the mineral collector Freiherr von Zois. There are no traditions about its healing powers.

Healing

Spiritually Zoisite helps us to avoid conforming to the instruction of others and being affected by outside influences, and helps us to realize our own ideas and desires. It makes it possible to transform destructive attitudes into a constructive way of life.

Emotionally Zoisite encourages recovery after illnesses or heavy stress. It helps us rediscover suppressed feelings and gradually live through them and express them.

Mentally Zoisite makes us creative. After a short or longer interruption, it will always help us to find our way back to the point of departure, to our real intentions.

Physically Zoisite helps with diseases of the testicles and ovaries. It stimulates fertility and, in combination with ruby, will increase potency. Zoisite detoxifies the tissues, neutralizes overacidification and stimulates regeneration of the cells. It hinders inflammation and strengthens the immune system.

Application

Zoisite should be worn on the body for longer periods or applied directly to the skin near the affected regions of the body. Consuming zoisite as a precious gem essence or elixir will also have a powerful effect.

Zircon (hyacinth), Brazil;
Zoisite with Ruby, Tanzania

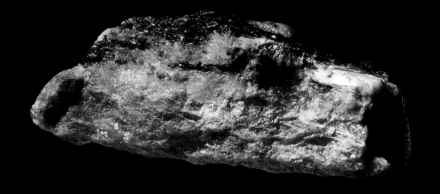

Therapeutic Index

The following index is intended to give an overview, in alphabetical order, of the beneficial qualities and healing properties attributed to crystals. Please, only use this index for reference and not to choose your crystal! Selecting a stone for particular symptoms according to a list of key words may seem nice and simple, but will too often result in error. You would be ignoring your general situation, your lifestyle, the mineral-forming substance and its colour, all described in Part 1 of this book, with the result that you would not be making an informed decision. The entries here should be checked against the detailed descriptions of the minerals (Part 3), and you should also consult the information on the mineralogical and therapeutic background (Part 1). Only by proceeding this way will you be able to get the information necessary for a sound, reliable choice.

A

abilities, realizing actinolite, dioptase, Imperial topaz, obsidian, rock crystal, topaz
ability to take things in pietersite, prehnite, sardonyx, tourmaline, variscite
abundance dioptase, sardonyx
acceptance aventurine, chalcedony (blue), kunzite, lapis lazuli, rutilated quartz
accomplishment, ease of (see success)
achieve, ability to epidote, fire opal, hematite, ruby, tiger iron
acid indigestion antimonite, turquoise, variscite
acid/alkaline metabolism/balance jade, nephrite
action, readiness for/joy of amethyst, ametrine, chrysoberyl, disthene, fire opal, nephrite, onyx, prase, rhodonite, tiger iron, turquoise
action, urge for/energy for ametrine, charoite, garnet (almandine), jade, jasper, sodalite, sunstone
activity (see also over-activity) Imperial topaz, jade, mookaite, rhodochrosite, ruby, tourmaline (rubellite)
adapting biotite lenses, zoisite
addiction amethyst, dumortierite
admiration chrysopal, tourmaline (verdelite)
adrenal glands jade, fire opal, ruby, tiger's eye

adrenalin (see also adrenal glands) fire opal
adventure, urge for chrysopal, malachite, mookaite, thulite
aesthetics antimonite, chrysoprase, copper chalcedony, malachite
aggression apatite, heliotrope, jasper, nephrite
allergies apophyllite, aquamarine, aventurine, fluorite
ambition chrysoberyl, morganite
ambitions dioptase
anger chrysoprase, peridot, prase
annoyance apatite, aventurine, lapis lazuli, peridot, rhodonite
anorexia Imperial topaz, topaz
anxiety chalcedony (pink), opal
apathy apatite, turquoise
appetite apatite, Imperial topaz
argumentativeness (see also communication) onyx
arteriosclerosis (see also blood vessels/fat metabolism) aventurine, magnesite
arthritis fluorite, garnet (grossular)
arthrosis (see also cartilage) apatite
assertiveness onyx
asthma apophyllite
atmosphere fossilized wood, obsidian (black), thulite
attentiveness chrysoprase, copper chalcedony, dendritic chalcedony, pop rocks, variscite

authority chrysoberyl, topaz
autoimmune diseases (*see also* immune system) aquamarine, rhodonite
avoidance mechanisms prehnite

B

back problems smoky obsidian, smoky quartz
bad luck azurite-malachite, aventurine, marble, opal
bad conscience (*see* conscience)
balance chalcedony (blue), copper chalcedony, dendritic chalcedony, dolomite, jade, mookaite, morganite, rhyolite
balance, consistency actinolite, chrysocolla, emerald, jasper (green)
beauty copper chalcedony, chrysoprase, dioptase, emerald, malachite, thulite
beginnings, new garnet, rutilated quartz, tiger iron
behavioural patterns chiastolite, chrysoberyl, chrysoprase, dumortierite, fluorite, garnet, obsidian (black), pop rocks, rainbow obsidian, silver obsidian, sodalite
belief/faith amber, larimar, black obsidian, larimar, rainbow obsidian, silver obsidian, sapphire, sunstone
birth amazonite, biotite lenses, malachite, moonstone
bladder agate, chalcedony, citrine, tourmaline (indicolite)
blinkered attitudes aquamarine, beryl, morganite
blocks, energy garnet, larimar, obsidian, pop rocks, tourmaline (indicolite)
blood clotting calcite, chalcedony (red), marble, magnesite
blood pressure (*see also* circulation) – raising: jasper, rhodochrosite, ruby; lowering: chalcedony (blue), chrysocolla, labradorite, lapis lazuli, sodalite; stabilizing: chalcedony (red)
blood purification mookaite, tourmaline (rubellite)
blood sugar (*see* diabetes)
blood vessels agate, aventurine, hematite, carnelian, magnesite, mahogany obsidian, obsidian, snowflake obsidian, rhodochrosite
blood, formation of garnet (andradite), hematite, tiger Iron
blood, quality of carnelian, dolomite, garnet (pyrope)
body fluids chalcedony (blue), dendritic chalcedony, garnet, jade, nephrite, onyx, opal (green), sardonyx

bones apatite, calcite, fluorite, garnet (melanite), marble
boundlessness moldavite
brain amazonite, azurite, diamond, disthene, fluorite, larimar, malachite, rock crystal, sapphire, schalenblende, sugilite, turquoise
breastfeeding chalcedony (blue and pink)
bronchitis, chronic rutilated quartz
brooding nephrite, schalenblende
bruises amethyst, prase
building up actinolite, dendritic agate, epidote
burns chrysocolla, tourmaline (indicolite)

C

calcium metabolism apatite, aragonite, calcite, dolomite, marble
calming amazonite, charoite, chiastolite, chrysopal, disthene, fossilized wood, labradorite, magnesite, prase, sapphire, serpentine, variscite
carefree attitude chalcedony (blue), pink opal
cartilage apatite, amber
cells, growth of apatite, azurite-malachite, calcite, tourmaline (dravite), zoisite
cellular metabolism ametrine, sardonyx
centring chiastolite
certainty rose quartz
challenge dendritic agate, garnet, fire opal, thulite
changes charoite, chrysocolla, diamond, epidote, larimar, marble, pietersite, pyrite, schalenblende, tiger iron
chaos pietersite
character chalcedony (blue), diamond, pyrite, sardonyx
charisma garnet (pyrope), Imperial topaz
charm tourmaline (rubellite)
cheerfulness amber, fire opal
cholesterol (*see also* fat metabolism) aventurine, magnesite
chronic feeling of coldness chrysopal, emerald, obsidian, mahogany obsidian, snowflake obsidian, opal (green), rhodonite, rutilated quartz, schalenblende, thulite, tourmaline (dravite), turquoise, watermelon tourmaline, zoisite
circulation (blood supply) carnelian, obsidian, mahogony obsidian, snowflake obsidian, rose quartz, tourmaline (rubellite)
circulation (*see also* blood pressure) – stimulating: chalcedony (red), garnet (pyrope), hematite, jasper (red), rhodochrosite, ruby, tiger iron; calming: chalcedony (blue), lapis lazuli, sodalite; stabilizing: dolomite, garnet, rhodonite

clairvoyance aquamarine, alexandrite, emerald, moldavite, moonstone, obsidian, zircon

clarity chrysocolla, diamond, emerald, rhodonite, rock crystal, watermelon tourmaline

clearness amethyst, dendritic chalcedony, fluorite, obsidian, pietersite, pyrite, rock crystal

coldness, feelings of labradorite, mahogany obsidian, obsidian, rock crystal, snowflake obsidian

colds chalcedony (blue), dendritic chalcedony, labradorite, rhyolite (orbicular jasper)

colic dumortierite

commitment ruby, tourmaline (rubellite)

communication chalcedony (blue and pink,) copper chalcedony, lapis lazuli, moss agate, obsidian (black), onyx, rainbow obsidian, sardonyx, schalenblende, silver obsidian, variscite

community, sense of carnelian, chalcedony (blue), chrysopal, dendritic chalcedony, dolomite, garnet, pink opal, tourmaline (dravite)

competence calcite

composure, inner agate, fossilized wood, pietersite

compromise, readiness for serpentine

compromise, unwillingness to diamond, fluorite, lapis lazuli, sugilite

compulsions charoite, chrysoprase, dumortierite concentration agate, amethyst, aragonite, lepidolite, onyx, pietersite, smoky quartz, rhyolite, sapphire, schalenblende

confidence (faith, trust) chalcedony (red), dumortierite, garnet, moss agate, sardonyx

conflicts chalcedony (pink), jasper, lapis lazuli, pietersite, rhodonite, serpentine, sugilite

confrontation, readiness for amethyst, carnelian, citrine, copper chalcedony, diamond, malachite, onyx, prehnite, pyrite, sugilite

confusion aquamarine, carnelian, dendritic chalcedony, fluorite, pietersite, pyrite, rhodonite

conjunctiva agate

conscience apophyllite, peridot, tourmaline (verdelite)

consciousness amethyst, ametrine, azurite, chalcedony (blue), copper chalcedony, chiastolite, disthene, fluorite, larimar, malachite, moldavite, moss agate, obsidian (black), rainbow obsidian, silver obsidian, rhodonite, rhyolite, sodalite, topaz, turquoise, zircon

consistency actinolite, aquamarine, beryl, chiastolite, chrysocolla, emerald, onyx, sugilite, zoisite

constipation (*see also* elimination, intestines, large intestine) biotite lenses, serpentine, tourmaline (verdelite)

constitution epidote

contemplation labradorite

contentment chrysoprase, dolomite

control ametrine, apophyllite, chrysoprase, dumortierite, heliotrope, onyx, prase, tourmaline

contusions prase

conversion calcite, carnelian, chalcedony (blue), chalcedony (red), chiastolite, diamond, dioptase, dolomite, epidote, garnet, jade, jasper, lepidolite, zoisite

coolness chalcedony (blue), chrysocolla, sodalite

cooperation emerald

copper metabolism azurite, azurite-malachite, dioptase, chrysocolla, copper chalcedony, malachite, turquoise

coronary blood vessels magnesite

coughs moss agate, rutilated quartz

courage carnelian, dendritic agate, diamond, dumortierite,garnet (general), garnet (pyrope), jasper, ruby, thulite, tiger's eye

courage, lack of chrysopal, marble, schalenblende

cramps amazonite, azurite-malachite, charoite, chrysocolla, dioptase, dolomite, dumortierite, magnesite, malachite, smoky quartz, serpentine, turquoise, varscite, zircon

creativity ametrine, antimonite, amber, biotite lenses, chalcedony (blue), dioptase, garnet (andradite), labradorite, larimar, marble, nephrite, thulite, tourmaline, zoisite

crises diamond, garnet

criticism, ability to criticize (*see also* self-criticism) azurite, malachite, sapphire, tourmaline (rubellite)

cuts rhodonite

cycles, unfinished business aquamarine, carnelian, tiger iron

D

danger fire opal, rhodonite

daydreams tourmaline, labradorite

decisions, power to make biotite lenses, charoite, diamond, falcon's eye, jade,

lepidolite, nephrite, tiger's eye, tourmaline (verdelite)
delimiting/boundaries dendritic chalcedony, heliotrope, lavender jade, lepidolite, serpentine
depression citrine, diamond, garnet (spessartite), kunzite, rutilated quartz, sapphire, sunstone, watermelon tourmaline
depth obsidian (black), rainbow obsidian, silver obsidian
desires/wishes, fulfilment of alexandrite, amber, chalcedony (blue), hematite, malachite, moldavite (pink), opal, zoisite
determination biotite lenses, charoite, disthene, jade, malachite, sapphire, tiger iron
detoxification actinolite, azurite, azurite-malachite, beryl, biotite lenses, chrysocolla, chrysopal, chrysoprase, emerald, heliotrope, jasper (green), magnesite, malachite, opal (green), peridot, prehnite, rhodonite, tourmaline (verdelite), turquoise, zoisite
devaluation/debasement epidote
development, physical aragonite, calcite, tourmaline
development, spiritual aragonite, rock crystal, beryl, calcite, epidote, hematite, lepidolite, schalenblende, sodalite, topaz
devotion kunzite, tourmaline (rubellite)
dexterity disthene
diabetes chalcedony (blue), citrine, schalenblende
dialogue, inner amethyst
diarrhoea amethyst, dumortierite, rock crystal, serpentine, tourmaline (verdelite)
difficulties, solving carnelian, chalcedony (red), dumortierite, garnet, moss agate, smoky quartz, tiger's eye, tree agate
digestion agate, antimonite, aragonite, chrysocolla, citrine, epidote, jasper, topaz
dignity lapis lazuli
dimensions, spiritual moldavite
diplomacy chalcedony (blue)
discipline chrysoberyl
discrimination sunstone
discs, intervertebral aragonite
displacement/repression/suppression, mechanisms prehnite
distance disthene, falcon's eye, malachite, pietersite, tiger's eye
distinction/discrimination aquamarine, calcite, lepidolite, opal (green), rose quartz, tourmaline (verdelite), garnet, sardonyx
distraction agate, lepidolite, pietersite
disunity, inner conflict azurite-malachite

doubts falcon's eye, nephrite, tiger's eye
downheartedness pink opal, turquoise
dreams alexandrite, amethyst, aventurine, charoite, dioptase, emerald, heliotrope, jade, malachite, moldavite, moonstone (pink), opal, tourmaline
drive/lack of drive apatite, beryl (bixbite), chrysocolla, ruby
dynamism aquamarine, beryl (bixbite), citrine, fire opal, fluorite, garnet in general, garnet (andradite), hematite, jasper (red), marble, rhodochrosite, ruby, tiger iron
dyslexia chalcedony (blue), sugilite

E

ears chalcedony (blue), dendritic chalcedony, onyx
Earth, connection with fossilized wood
eczema (*see also* skin) antimonite
effect, increasing diamond, rock crystal, topaz (clear)
effectivity amethyst, beryl, rhodochrosite
egotism chrysoprase, onyx
ejaculation, premature rutilated quartz
elation/exhilaration chalcedony (blue), dumortierite, rhodochrosite
elimination (see also kidneys, intestines, large intestine) agate, actinolite, sardonyx, tourmaline (indicolite), tourmaline (verdelite)
eloquence sardonyx
embryo (see pregnancy)
emotions (see also moods) azurite-malachite, beryl, carnelian, epidote, fire opal, larimar, nephrite, opal, prase, pop rocks, rhyolite
empathy kunzite, malachite, moldavite, rose quartz, tourmaline (dravite)
energy apatite, fire opal, rhodochrosite, rock crystal, tiger iron, variscite
energy flow – stimulating: pop rocks, jasper (red), rutilated quartz, tiger eye, topaz, tourmaline; slowing: falcon's eye, tiger eye
enlivening turquoise, variscite
enterprise, spirit of thulite, tourmaline (rubellite)
enthusiasm aventurine, chrysopal, fire opal, garnet (uvarovite), labradorite, rhodochrosite
environment azurite-malachite, copper chalcedony, turitella jasper
epilepsy dumortierite, kunzite, sugilite
erratic behaviour aragonite
eroticism fire opal, opal, rhodochrosite, ruby, thulite
eruptions, skin (see also skin) antimonite, aventurine

escape, habits morganite
ethics diamond, tourmaline (indicolite)
evaluation copper chalcedony, sodalite
excessive demanding aragonite
excitement (see calming)
exertion opal (green), smoky quartz, rhyolite, rose quartz
exhaustion apatite, epidote, heliotrope, Imperial topaz, opal (green), ruby, schalenblende, tiger iron, turquoise
existence, meaning of (see life, meaning of)
expansion, feeling of moldavite
experiences, new azurite, citrine, malachite, mookaite, peridot
extreme situations, ability to handle garnet, rhodonite
extrovertedness apatite, citrine, dioptase, Imperial topaz
eyes (see also seeing, sight) agate, aquamarine, beryl, chalcedony (blue), emerald, prase, schalenblende

F

failure sunstone
fainting emerald, thulite
faith in God amazonite, chrysoprase, tiger's eye
fame dioptase, Imperial topaz
family tourmaline (dravite)
fanaticism beryl, morganite
farsightedness (see also eyes, seeing, sharp sight) aquamarine, beryl (heliodor)
fat metabolism aventurine, magnesite, prehnite
fate/belief in fate amazonite, disthene, emerald, topaz, turquoise
fear/fears/anxiety/apprehension apophyllite, chiastolite, chrysoberyl, diamond, dumortierite, larimar, magnesite, moss agate, obsidian, onyx, opal (green), rhodonite, rutilated quartz, schalenblende, sugilite, watermelon tourmaline, zircon
feelings alexandrite, apophyllite, azurite-malachite, chrysocolla, chrysopal, citrine, dolomiote, labradorite, malachite, moonstone, morganite, chrysopal, pietersite, rhodochrosite, sodalite, thulite, tourmaline (indicolite), zoisite
feelings of being oppressed, apprehension or trepidation amazonite, apophyllite, chrysoberyl, chrysopal, rutilated quartz, tourmaline (dravite)
feelings, depth of chrysopal, dioptase, labradorite, malachite, moonstone, emerald
feelings, expression of azurite-malachite, lapis lazuli, malachite, rhodochrosite, zoisite

feelings, lack of pietersite, rock crystal, tourmaline, tourmaline quartz
fertility chrysoprase, Imperial topaz, moldavite, moonstone, rhodonite, rose quartz, thulite, zoisite
fever – lowering: chalcedony (blue), chrysocolla, chrysopal, moss agate, prase, rock crystal, sapphire; bringing on: garnet (uvarovite), rhodochrosite, ruby
fiery temper fire opal, prase, ruby
fire, inner chalcedony (pink), fire opal, garnet, ruby
first aid stone rhodonite
flawlessness obsidian
flexibility aragonite, amber, biotite lenses, chalcedony (red), garnet (andradite), heliotrope, mookaite, tourmaline (verdelite, rubellite)
fluid intake and absorption sodalite, tourmaline (indicolite)
foolishness/thoughtlessness opal
foresight, view of future aquamarine, turquoise
formation of stones (in organs) nephrite, rhyolite (leopard skin jasper)
free will/free spirit fluorite, sodalite
freedom diamond, fluorite, garnet, lapis lazuli, obsidian, sodalite, tourmaline (indicolite)
friendship emerald, lapis lazuli, malachite, peridot, rhodonite, sapphire, sardonyx, watermelon tourmaline
frugality fossilized wood
frustration disthene, epidote
fufilment sardonyx, topaz
fun fire opal
fungal infections chalcedony (blue), combination of chrysoprase and smoky quartz, copper chalcedony
fury aventurine, peridot, prase, rhodonite

G

gallbladder amber, epidote, magnesite, peridot
gastritis (see also stomach) agate, variscite
generosity/generousness of spirit Imperial topaz
generosity towards guests pink opal
gentleness amethyst, amber, rose quartz
glands (see also hormones) chalcedony (blue), dendritic chalcedony, diamond, rock crystal, tourmaline
glaucoma chalcedony (blue)
goal orientedness aquamarine, beryl, emerald, rutilated quartz, tourmaline (rubellite)
goals, setting of actinolite, diamond,

labradorite, lepidolite, sapphire, tourmaline, watermelon

gonads opal (green), rhodochrosite, schalenblende, thulite, zoisite

gout biotite lenses, chiastolite, chrysoprase, labradorite, turquoise, variscite

gratification, substitute antimonite

greatness, spiritual alexandrite, moldavite, rutilated quartz

gregariousness apatite, azurite-malachite, chalcedony (blue), copper chalcedony, lapis lazuli, pink opal, tourmaline (rubellite, verdelite)

grief epidote, sugilite

groups, shyness in tourmaline (dravite)

goodness chalcedon (pink)

growth, physical agate, actinolite, aquamarine, azurite, calcite, rutilated quartz, turquoise

growth, spiritual agate, aquamarine, emerald, garnet (hessonite)

grudges prase

guilt, feelings of chiastolite, opal (green), peridot, sodalite

H

habits antimonite, dendritic chalcedony, fluorite, garnet

hardening of skin (also lumps, knots) rhyolite (leopard skin jasper)

harmony agate, ametrine, azurite-malachite, beryl (golden beryl, heliodor), copper chalcedony, chrysocolla, dumortierite, emerald, mookaite, sunstone, sugilite, tourmaline

hayfever (*see also* allergies) aquamarine

head/headache amethyst, dioptase, dumortierite, emerald, larimar, magnesite, smoky obsidian

healing epidote, garnet, rhodonite, sapphire

health, preventive/ stabilizing agate, dendritic agate, dolomite, fossilized wood, hematite, mookaite, opal, sapphire

hearing, sense onyx, sardonyx

heart amazonite, aventurine, calcite, chalcedony (pink), charoite, chrysopal, dolomite, emerald, garnet (spessartite), heliotrope, kunzite, magnesite, marble, moonstone, morganite, pink opal, rhodonite, rose quartz, tourmaline (verdelite)

heart attack, prophylactic aventurine, magnesite

heart rhythm calcite, rose quartz, serpentine

heartiness copper chalcedony, chalcedony, chalcedony (pink), garnet (rhodolite), pink opal, rose quartz

heat stroke prase

heavy metal poisoning chrysoprase, emerald, peridot

helper, spiritual chrysoprase

helpfulness azurite-malachite, carnelian, chalcedony (pink), garnet, garnet (spessartite), rose quartz, sardonyx, tourmaline (dravite)

hesitation charoite, moss agate

hiding/covering up apophyllite, rutilated quartz

hoarseness lapis lazuli, sodalite

holding back/suppressing amethyst, apophyllite, fluorite, malachite, moldavite, moss agate, pietersite, tourmaline (indicolite), zircon

holding on apophyllite, chiastolite, zircon

home chrysopal, fossilized wood

honesty amethyst, apophyllite, jasper, lapis lazuli, pyrite, sodalite, topaz, variscite

honesty/sincerity amethyst, aquamarine, emerald, garnet (melanite), jasper, lapis lazuli, rutilated quartz

hope dioptase, garnet, moss agate, rutilated quartz

horizons, broadening of fluorite, garnet, lapis lazuli, tourmaline (indicolite)

hormones (*see also* glands) aquamarine, diamond, falcon's eye, garnet (hessonite), moonstone, tourmaline

hostility/attacks, spiritual copper chalcedony, garnet, obsidian (black), rhodonite

humility kunzite

hunger pangs chalcedony (red)

I

ideals/idealism antimonite, carnelian, chrysoprase, malachite, pink opal, schalenblende, sodalite

ideas/abundance of ideas aventurine, fire opal, garnet, Imperial topaz, jade, labradorite, moldavite, pink opal, rhodochrosite, sapphire, zoisite

idées fixes fluorite

identity, finding/keeping chiastolite, dolomite, lapis lazuli, nephrite, prehnite, sodalite, variscite

illness, gain from/causes moldavite, pop rocks, pyrite

illnesses, prophylaxis pop rocks

illusions chiastolite, labradorite, moonstone

images, inner alexandrite, amethyst, azurite, chrysoprase, copper chalcedony, dendritic chalcedony, fossilized wood, jade, malachite, obsidian (black), rainbow obsidian, silver obsidian, sunstone, topaz, tourmaline

imagination/power of imagination
alexandrite, antimonite, azurite, dioptase, garnet (almandine), jasper, labradorite, malachite, sodalite, tourmaline
immune system aquamarine, aragonite, azurite-malachite, calcite, chalcedony (blue), dendritic chalcedony, copper chalcedony, chalcedony (pink), emerald, epidote, garnet, heliotrope, jasper (yellow), marble, mookaite, moss agate, onyx, sardonyx, schalenblende, tourmaline, tree agate, zoisite
impartiality/uninhibitedness pink opal
importance zircon
impotence (*see also* potency) morganite, rutilated quartz
impressions (*see* processing, spiritual)
impulsiveness fire opal, moonstone, rhodochrosite, ruby
independence chrysoberyl, chrysoprase, lepidolite, rutilated quartz
individuality aventurine, biotite lenses, citrine, garnet (uvarovite), tourmaline
indulgence copper chalcedony, emerald, pink opal, thulite
industriousness rhodochrosite
infections dendritic agate, chalcedony (blue), chrysocolla, chrysoprase, emerald, heliotrope, moss agate, onyx, rhyolite (orbicular jasper), ruby, turquoise
infertility (*see* fertility)
inflammation of joints (*see* arthritis)
inflammations aventurine, alexandrite, chalcedony (blue), copper chalcedony, chrysoberyl, dendritic chalcedony, emerald, garnet (uvarovite), heliotrope, jasper (green), moss agate, turquoise, zoisite
influences, external biotite lenses, charoite, fluorite, peridot, topaz, zoisite
influencing people/ability to be influenced lepidolite, nephrite, obsidian, onyx, serpentine
influenza chalcedony (blue), heliotrope, jasper (green), moss agate, rhyolite (orbicular jasper)
inhibitions garnet, malachite, pink opal
initial difficulties tiger iron
initiative fire opal, moss agate
injuries amethyst, obsidian, rhodonite
injustice fluorite, rhodonite
inner ear onyx
inner voice alexandrite, anitmonite
inquisitiveness/curiosity chalcedony (pink), chrysopal, thulite
insect bites rhodonite

insight tiger's eye
inspiration amethyst, chalcedony (blue), chalcedony (red), emerald, kunzite, moss agate, thulite
insult rhodonite
integrity biotite lenses, obsidian, sodalite
intelligence/mental grasp fire opal, fluorite
intentions chalcedony (red), labradorite, lepidolite, sapphire, watermelon tourmaline, zoisite
interest antimonite, aragonite, azurite-malachite, tourmaline (verdelite), variscite
intestine, large (*see also* elimination, diarrhoea, constipation) agate, amethyst, hematite (kidney)
intestine, small (*see also* iron absorption, nutrient absorption, etc.) carnelian, chalcedony (red), epidote, hematite, prehnite
intestines agate, amethyst, calcite, garnet, jasper, magnesite, marble, ruby, sapphire, sardonyx
intoxication amethyst
intuition alexandrite, amazonite, amethyst, ametrine, biotite lenses, fossilized wood, kunzite, labradorite, moonstone, schalenblende, turquoise
inventiveness fluorite, thulite
invincibility diamond
iron, absorption of garnet (almandine), hematite, tiger iron
irritability heliotrope, jade, magnesite
itching antimonite, emerald, rhodonite

J
jealousy chrysoprase
joie de vivre/life force ametrine, beryl, citrine, emerald, fire opal, garnet, opal, ruby, sunstone, thulite, tourmaline (verdelite)
joints apatite, amber, fluorite, kunzite, lepidolite
joy morganite, opal, rhodochrosite, sardonyx
judge, ability to amethyst, copper chalcedony
justice amethyst, azurite, chrysoprase, diamond, emerald, malachite, sugilite

K
kidneys actinolite, amber, biotite lenses, garnet (grossular), hematite (kidney), jade, nephrite, opal (green), rhodochrosite, serpentine, tourmaline (indicolite)
knowledge jade, lapis lazuli, malachite, sapphire, topaz

L

labour pains (*see also* birth) biotite lenses
laissez faire larimar
language chalcedony (blue)
larynx chalcedony (blue), lapis lazuli, sodalite
laws diamond, sodalite
laziness calcite, chrysocolla, jade
leadership qualities chrysoberyl
learning/ability to learn amethyst, chalcedony (blue), diamond, fluorite, rhodonite, rock crystal, sapphire
lethargy fire opal, rhodochrosite, ruby, tiger iron
letting go (*see* blocks)
level-headedness/calm charoite, rhodonite
liberation diamond, moss agate, opal (green)
life, affirming azurite-malachite, chrysoprase, dumortierite, Imperial topaz, magnesite, rhodochrosite, sunstone, zoisite
life, liveliness apatite, chalcedony (pink), fire opal, morganite, rhodochrosite
life, meaning of antimonite, copper chalcedony, chiastolite, moldavite, opal (green), sardonyx, topaz, zircon
life, perspectives on marble, opal (green), sunstone, zircon
life, quality of garnet (pyrope)
life, trials and tests azurite, chalcedony (blue), diamond, garnet, sapphire
life's will for jasper, opal
life's work (*see* meaning of life)
light, insight apophyllite, garnet
light, sensitivity to/perception of light moonstone aquamarine, chalcedony (blue), dumortierite, opal, rhodochrosite
limitations, boundaries (overcoming) Imperial topaz, larimar, rock crystal (phantom quartz)
listening chalcedony (blue and pink), dendritic chalcedony, magnesite
liver actinolite, amazonite, azurite, azurite-malachite, copper chalcedony, chrysoberyl, alexandrite, chrysocolla, chrysoprase, emerald, epidote, garnet, malachite, opal (green), peridot, tourmaline (rubellite), zircon
logic (*see* thinking, logical)
loss amethyst, zircon
love copper chalcedony, chalcedony (pink), chrysopal, chrysoprase, emerald, moonstone, morganite, pink opal, rhodochrosite, rose quartz, ruby, watermelon tourmaline
love of life garnet (rhodolite), opal
love, sorrows of chrysoprase

loyalty/fidelity diamond, kunzite, sapphire, sodalite, tourmaline (indicolite)
lucid dreams (*see* also dreams) emerald, moonstone, zircon
luck agate, ametrine, aventurine, amber, chrysoprase, garnet, malachite, moldavite, moonstone, opal, sunstone, turquoise
lungs amethyst, chalcedony (blue), dendritic chalcedony, fluorite, moss agate, rutilated quartz
lymph/lymph nodes chalcedony (blue and pink), dendritic chalcedony, heliotrope, moss agate

M

madness sapphire, zircon
magic alexandrite, sapphire
magnesium metabolism dolomite, magnesite, serpentine
making up/atonement peridot
manipulation larimar
many-sidedness/variety beryl, tourmaline (verdelite)
materialism moldavite, zircon
maturity agate, rhodonite
meaning/meaninglessness (*see also* meaning of life) copper chalcedony, diamond, rhodonite, schalenblende, topaz
meditation amethyst, citrine, fossilized wood, mookaite, obsidian (black), rainbow obsidian, rock crystal, rose quartz, serpentine, silver obsidian
mediumistic abilities aquamarine, alexandrite, labradorite, moonstone
melancholy chrysopal, thulite
memory agate, aquamarine, calcite, chalcedony (blue), copper chalcedony, kunzite, labradorite, malachite, moldavite, pink opal, pyrite, rock crystal
menopause moonstone
menstruation chrysocolla, lapis lazuli, malachite, moonstone, serpentine, zircon
mental illnesses diamond, sapphire
meridians pop rocks, topaz, tourmaline
metabolism amazonite, amber, calcite, carnelian, copper chalcedony, charoite, fossilized wood, garnet in general, garnet (rhodolite), heliotrope, Imperial topaz, peridot, sardonyx, topaz, turquoise, tourmaline
migraine magnesite, rhodochrosite
milk, production of chalcedony (blue and pink)
minerals, absorption of carnelian
mistakes/failures diamond, epidote, tourmaline (schorl), tourmaline quartz
mobility/motion chiastolite, disthene, fluorite, mookaite, ruby, sugilite

modesty magnesite
money worries moldavite, zircon
mood-lifting ametrine, citrine, rhodochrosite, rutilated quartz, sunstone, variscite
moods (*see also* emotions) chrysopal, dendritic chalcedony, diamond, kunzite, malachite, pop rocks, rhodochrosite, tiger's eye
moods shifts amazonite, chrysocolla, falcon's eye, serpentine, turquoise
mortality zircon
motivation, increase of apatite, amber, chalcedony (blue), chrysoprase
motor nervous system disthene, onyx, sugilite, tourmaline (dravite)
mucous membranes apophyllite, amber, chalcedony (blue), dendritic chalcedony, fluorite, garnet (grossular), moss agate
multiple sclerosis rhodochrosite, rhodonite, watermelon tourmaline
muscle power hematite, tiger iron, turquoise
muscles aragonite, magnesite

N

narrow-mindedness fluorite
nature, spiritual amber, amethyst, jade, moldavite, rock crystal, sunstone
nausea antimonite, dumortierite, rock crystal
neck/throat chrysocolla,lapis lazuli, larimar, sodalite
needs chalcedony (blue), hematite, malachite, morganite, rose quartz
negativity chrysoprase, sunstone, tourmaline (schorl), tourmaline quartz, zoisite
neglect peridot
nerves, motor disthene, onyx, sugilite, tourmaline (indicolite, rubellite, verdelite), watermelon tourmaline
nerves, sensory amethyst, jade, onyx, tourmaline (indicolite, rubellite, verdelite), watermelon tourmaline
nerves/nervous system amethyst, charoite, chiastolite, diamond, dumortierite, fluorite, Imperial topaz, jade, kunzite, lepidolite, malachite, morganite, smoky quartz, sapphire, sugilite, topaz, tourmaline (indicolite, rubellite, verdelite), watermelon tourmaline, variscite
nervous system, autonomous amazonite, ametrine, beryl, charoite, citrine, Imperial topaz, sunstone, tourmaline (rubellite)
nervousness aragonite, beryl (golden beryl), chiastolite, chrysocolla, falcon's eye, magnesite, serpentine, variscite
neuralgia kunzite, lepidolite, sugilite

neurodermatitis chrysoprase, fluorite
neutrality azurite-malachite, rock crystal, copper chalcedony, chrysocolla, nephrite, tourmaline (schorl), tourmaline quartz
nightmares amethyst, chrysoberyl, chrysoprase, garnet (spessartite), tourmaline
non-influenceability dendritic agate, nephrite, serpentine, sugilite, tiger's eye, turquoise
normalization after birth agate
nose/sinuses emerald
nutrients, proper absorption of (*see also* small intestine) carnelian, chalcedony (red), epidote, garnet, sardonyx

O

obesity fossilized wood
observation, talent for charoite, malachite
obsession/possession obsidian
oedema (*see also* water retention) chalcedony (blue), dendritic chalcedony
openmindedness/ receptiveness azurite malachite, amber, chrysopal, fire opal, rose quartz, tourmaline (verdelite)
openness apatite, apophyllite, chalcedony (blue), copper chalcedony, chalcedony (red), emerald, Imperial topaz, pink opal, pyrite, topaz
opinion chalcedony (blue), dendritic chalcedony, lapis lazuli, sodalite
optimism ametrine, chalcedony (blue), opal, sunstone
order aquamarine, diamond, fluorite, pietersite, sodalite
organs, inner ametrine, amazonite, carnelian, sunstone, tourmaline (dravite)
orgasm ruby, serpentine, thulite
orientation, new actinolite
orientation, alignment sapphire, watermelon tourmaline
orientation, spiritual opal (green), zoisite
ovaries (*see also* gonads) opal (green), thulite, zoisite
overacidification biotite lenses, chiastolite, heliotrope, malachite, serpentine, turquoise, variscite, zoisite
overcoming calcite, carnelian, emerald, fire opal, garnet, jasper, sardonyx, sodalite
overview diamond, falcon's eye
overwork epidote
oxygen, supply hematite, tiger iron

P

pain amethyst, apatite, aventurine, charoite, dioptase, falcon's eye, malachite, obsidian, prase, pyrite sunburst, obsidian,

smoky quartz, rhodonite, rock crystal, sapphire, sugilite, tiger's eye, tourmaline (schorl), tourmaline quartz, turquoise, zircon
pain, mental azurite-malachite, rhodonite, turquoise
pancreas citrine, prehnite
panic dumortierite, rhodonite
paralysis rock crystal, chiastolite, rhodochrosite, rhodonite, watermelon tourmaline
paranoia sugilite
parasites amethyst, peridot
pardoning peridot, rhodonite
partnership emerald
passion ruby
past life memories agate
patience actinolite, aventurine, chrysoprase, epidote, heliotrope, magnesite, tourmaline (verdelite), watermelon tourmaline
peace, inner agate, amber, amethyst, apophyllite, chalcedony (pink), dendritic jade, disthene, jasper (yellow), larimar, lavender jade, lepidolite, marble, mookaite, nephrite, prase, rhyolite, serpentine, turquoise
peace, need for pietersite
perception alexandrite, amethyst, ametrine, chalcedony (blue), chiastolite, chrysoprase, dumortierite, malachite, obsidian, rock crystal, sardonyx, sunstone
persistence chalcedony (red), tree agate
perspectives, new (*see* life's perspectives)
pessimism sunstone
pineal gland amazonite, aquamarine, moonstone
planning alexandrite, chrysoberyl, diamond, Imperial topaz
pleasure antimonite, apatite, fire opal, garnet, malachite, opal, pink opal, ruby, thulite
pliability/compliance amber, biotite lenses, kunzite, rose quartz
poetry opal
poisoning (*see also* detoxification) chrysoprase, dumortierite, heliotrope, turitella jasper
positive attitude towards life (*see* life affirming)
posture, upright apatite, fluorite, garnet (melanite), rutilated quartz
potency garnet, rutilated quartz, zoisite with ruby
pragmatism (*see also* thinking, pragmatic) agate, carnelian, dolomite, prase, smoky quartz, tiger iron, tourmaline (dravite)
prediction rock crystal, obsidian

pregnancy agate
prenatal memories agate
presence of mind chrysoprase
pressure, inner apophyllite, moss agate
pride Imperial topaz
problem solving agate, amazonite, carnelian, chalcedony (pink), diamond, garnet, marble, pietersite, sugilite, thulite, tourmaline (verdelite), tiger iron
processing/dealing with/digesting spiritually agate, amethyst, copper chalcedony, fluorite, mookaite, pietersite, prehnite
prostate schalenblende
protection agate, dendritic agate, biotite lenses, heliotrope, jasper (green), lepidolite, nephrite, smoky quartz, serpentine, tiger's eye, turquoise, tourmaline (schorl), tourmaline quartz, watermelon tourmaline
psychiatric illnesses diamond, sapphire
psychosomatic illnesses chalcedony (pink), diamond
purification, physical ametrine, chrysoprase, diamond, lepidolite, peridot
pus calcite, fluorite, heliotrope, mookaite, rhodonite

R

radiation dumortierite, turitella jasper, prase, smoky quartz, rose quartz, schalenblende, tourmaline (schorl)
reactions, speed of Imperial topaz, jade
realism fossilized wood, Imperial topaz, labradorite, onyx, smoky quartz
reality, sense of agate, carnelian, chiastolite
reality, spiritual chrysoprase, falcon's eye, jade, larimar, moldavite, tiger's eye, zircon
realization/insight (*see also* self-realization) azurite, chrysoberyl, diamond, pop rocks
reason amethyst, sardonyx
reasoning/intellect amazonite, azurite-malachite, chiastolite, citrine, dolomite, moss agate, obsidian, prehnite, sardonyx, zircon
recognition/acceptance Imperial topaz
reconciliation prase, rhodonite
recovery aventurine, charoite, emerald, epidote, fossilized wood, moss agate, opal (green), zoisite
red blood corpuscles hematite, tiger iron
reflection azurite, fossilized wood, kunzite, larimar, pink opal
regeneration agate, aventurine, alexandrite, dioptase, epidote, garnet, mookaite, rejuvenation emerald, ruby
relativity zircon

relaxation (*see also* stress, tension) amazonite, aventurine, chrysocolla, dolomite, garnet (grossular), magnesite, smoky quartz

relief tourmaline (indicolite)

rescue stone rhodonite

resignation (*see* courage, lack of)

resistance, power of dendritic agate, chrysocolla, garnet (melanite), turitella jasper, smoky quartz, rhyolite

resistances amber, chalcedony (blue), charoite, garnet, kunzite, thulite

respiratory tract amethyst, apophyllite, chalcedony (blue), dendritic chalcedony, emerald, fluorite, pietersite, rutilated quartz

responsibility for self disthene, larimar, turquoise

responsibility, sense of onyx, tourmaline (indicolite)

restraint, reserve, caution apophyllite, chiastolite, lapis lazuli, moss agate, rutilated quartz

restriction moss agate

retreat agate

revenge rhodonite

reverence/awe chalcedony (pink), chrysopal

revival/stimulation obsidian, ruby

rhetoric chalcedony (blue)

rheumatism biotite lenses, carnelian, chiastolite, emerald, garnet (grossular), labradorite, malachite, turquoise, variscite

rhythms of nature moonstone

risks, readiness to take alexandrite, fire opal, malachite

romance pink opal, rose quartz, thulite

S

sacrificial attitudes amazonite, larimar, turquoise

sadness amazonite, amethyst, chrysopal, epidote, onyx, sardonyx, tourmaline (indicolite), zircon

safety/security agate, beryl, nephrite, tree agate

salt metabolism jade, nephrite

scars rhodonite, tourmaline (schorl)

scattering of attention/diffusion of feelings/distraction opal, pietersite

schizophrenia sugilite

sciatica biotite lenses, kunzite, lepidolite

scurvy apatite, aragonite, calcite

secrecy pyrite

security, feeling of agate, chrysoprase, watermelon tourmaline

seduction/enticement/temptation opal, malachite

seeing/sharpness of vision (*see also* eyes, senses, sensory organs) aquamarine, beryl, emerald, onyx, schalenblende

self-acceptance magnesite, peridot, rhyolite, sodalite

self-awareness amber, dioptase, Imperial topaz, lapis lazuli, onyx

self-confidence calcite, citrine, fluorite, garnet, Imperial topaz, sardonyx, sunstone

self-control chrysoberyl

self-criticism tourmaline (rubellite)

self-destruction rhodonite, ruby

self-determination amazonite, aventurine, fluorite, larimar, peridot, sodalite, topaz, turquoise

self-discipline chrysoberyl

self-expression citrine, dioptase, Imperial topaz, variscite

self-healing power alexandrite, chrysoberyl, larimar, sunstone

self-importance Imperial topaz, morganite

self-knowlege (*see also* knowledge, insight) azurite, rock crystal, epidote, jade, kunzite, peridot, pyrite

self-love magnesite, rhodonite, rose quartz

self-observation chrysocolla

self-pity epidote

self-realization biotite lenses, citrine, dioptase, dolomite, garnet, Imperial topaz, jade, onyx, topaz

self-recrimination chrysoprase, peridot

self-respect garnet (hessonite), rhyolite

self-worth, feeling of actinolite, rhyolite, sunstone

senses alexandrite, obsidian (black), prehnite, rainbow obsidian, rock crystal, silver obsidian, turquoise

sensitivity to weather chalcedony (blue), moss agate

sensitivity/oversensitivity aragonite, falcon's eye, rainbow obsidian, rose quartz, silver obsidian, turquoise

sensory organs (*see also* eyes, balance, ears, nose) agate, aquamarine, beryl, chalcedony (blue), dendritic chalcedony, diamond, kunzite, sardonyx

sensory perception sardonyx, turquoise

sensuality copper chalcedony, emerald, malachite, thulite

serving kunzite

severity chrysoberyl

sexual organs antimonite, chalcedony (blue), copper chalcedony, fire opal, jasper, malachite, rose quartz, thulite, tourmaline (rubellite)

sexuality antimonite, chrysoprase, fire opal, garnet (general), garnet (rhodolite, spessartite), malachite, opal, pink opal, rose quartz, rutilated quartz, ruby, serpentine, thulite, zoisite with ruby

shadow sides obsidian, pop rocks, pyrite

shame pink opal

shock obsidian, rhodonite

short-sightedness (*see also* eyes, seeing, sharpness of vision) aquamarine, beryl (heliodor)

shyness malachite, pink opal

simplicity chrysoprase, fossilized wood, prase, tiger iron

sinus, frontal emerald

skill tourmaline (dravite)

skin agate, amethyst, antimonite, apophyllite, aventurine, amber, calcite, chrysoprase, dumortierite, fluorite, garnet, (grossular), lepidolite, marble, peridot, rhyolite (leopard skin jasper), tourmaline (dravite)

sleep amethyst, aventurine, chalcedony (blue), charoite, chrysoprase, emerald, lepidolite, opal (green), schalenblende

sleepwalking moonstone

slowing down chiastolite

smell, sense of sardonyx, schalenblende

smoking, consequences of chalcedony (blue), dendritic chalcedony, moss agate

smoking, problems with legs due to obsidian, mahogany obsidian, snowflake obsidian

sober, becoming amethyst

sobriety amethyst, chiastolite, onyx, smoky quartz, sapphire, variscite

sociability (*see* community, sense of)

social commitment tourmaline (dravite)

sorrow amazonite, apatite, epidote, nephrite, sugilite

speed fire opal, Imperial topaz

spine garnet (melanite)

spirit of discovery apophyllite, dendritic chalcedony, tree agate

spirituality amethyst

spleen amber, citrine, mookaite, ruby, tourmaline (rubellite)

spontaneity amber, charoite, fire opal, moldavite, opal, rhodochrosite, ruby, schalenblende

stability agate, aragonite, dendritic agate, calcite, chiastolite, dolomite, fluorite, fossilized wood, hematite, mookaite, sardonyx

stamina (*see also* perserverance) aquamarine, chalcedony (red), dendritic agate, epidote, garnet, jasper (red and yellow), tiger iron

state, intensification of rhyolite

steadfastness calcite, carnelian, rhyolite, rock crystal, sugilite

stomach agate, antimonite, amber, citrine, magnesite, rhodonite, serpentine, turquoise, variscite

storytelling, art of chalcedony (pink)

straightforwardness actinolite, aquamarine, beryl, sapphire

strength chalcedony (red), hematite, rhyolite, rock crystal, tiger iron, tree agate

strength/strengthening chalcedony (red), diamond, epidote, sunstone, thulite, tree agate

stress ametrine, antimonite, apophyllite, beryl, chalcedony (blue), charoite, chrysocolla, disthene, epidote, magnesite, morganite, moss agate, peridote, smoky quartz, rhodonite, serpentine, tiger's eye, topaz, tourmaline (schorl), tourmaline quartz, zoisite

strife onyx, rhodonite, topaz

structure fluorite, schalenblende

success ametrine, aquamarine, amber, calcite, epidot, fire opal, Imperial topaz, rhodochrosite

suffering larimar, smoky quartz, rhodonite

sunburn prase

sunny sides sunstone

sunstroke prase

suppression azurite-malachite, citrine, fluorite, marble, nephrite, sodalite, sugilite

suppuration (*see* pus)

survival hematite, schalenblende, tiger iron

swellings amethyst, prase, rock crystal

T

taboos garnet, malchite

take-it-easy stone dumortierite

taste, sense of sardonyx, schalenblende

team spirit emerald

teeth/teething apatite, amber, fluorite

tenderness chalcedony (pink), pink opal, rhodochrosite, rose quartz, watermelon tourmaline

tenseness (*see also* relaxation) amethyst, chrysocolla, obsidian, smoky quartz, serpentine, tourmaline (dravite)

tension agate, kunzite, nephrite, ruby, rutilated quartz, sugilite, tourmaline (schorl), tourmaline quartz

testicles opal (green), thulite, zoisite

thankfulness tourmaline (verdelite)

thinking (*see* reflection)

thinking patterns chrysoprase, fluorite

thinking, abstract schalenblende

thinking, analytical agate, chiastolite, dendritic chalcedony, onyx, prehnite, tourmaline (schorl), tourmaline quartz

thinking, clear/wakeful amethyst, antimonite, smoky quartz, ruby, rutilated quartz, sapphire, tourmaline quartz, variscite
thinking, fast fire opal, fluorite
thinking, logical/rational agate, chrysoprase, citrine, diamond, disthene, kunzite, lepidolite, onyx, tourmaline (schorl), tourmaline quartz, variscite
thinking, simple pragmatic dolomite, hematite, tiger iron
thinking, strategic alexandrite, chalcedony (red), chrysoberyl
thinking, visual tourmaline
thoughts apophyllite, azurite, chrysoberyl, pop rocks, smoky quartz, sapphire, schalenblende
threats (see hostility)
thyroid gland aquamarine, azurite, chrysocolla, lapis lazuli
timing actinolite, fossilized wood
tiredness heliotrope, tiger Iron, turquoise, variscite
tissue, connective (see tissue)
tissues rose quartz, agate, aventurine, ametrine, calcite, carnelian, lepidolite, magnesite, malachite, marble, nephrite, rhodonite, rhyolite (leopard skin jasper), tourmaline (dravite), zoisite
tolerance aragonite, aventurine, copper chalcedony, kunzite, nephrite, tourmaline (indicolite)
tonsils chalcedony (blue), chrysocolla, heliotrope
toxins peridot, schalenblende
tradition, sense of amber, dolomite
tranquillity, quietness agate, morganite
tranquillity, relaxedness apophyllite, aquamarine, copper chalcedony, charoite, larimar, tourmaline (schorl), tourmaline quartz
transformation marble, zoisite
trauma malachite, obsidian, rhodonite
trembling, shaking aragonite, falcon's eye
trust amber, chalcedony (pink), chrysoprase, dumortierite, garnet (rhodolite)
truth/truthfulness chrysoprase, lapis lazuli, prehnite, sapphire, sodalite, sugilite, tiger iron, topaz, tourmaline (indicolite), variscite
tumours azurite-malachite, calcite, fluorite

U

ulcers (see tumours)
uncertainty apophyllite
unconventionality moldavite, opal
understanding chalcedony (blue and pink), citrine, emerald, falcon's eye, fluorite, malachite, rhodonite, rock crystal, sardonyx, variscite, watermelon tourmaline
unrest, inner aragonite, schalenblende, variscite
unselfishness, altruism pink opal
upheavals in life charoite, pietersite
urinary tract nephrite, tourmaline (indicolite)
uterus agate

V

vagina chalcedony (blue), copper chalcedony
vaginal flora chalcedony (blue), copper chalcedony
variety apatite, citrine, heliotrope, mookaite, opal, ruby
verruca (see also skin) amethyst
virtue diamond, sardonyx
virus infections turquoise
vision, far-sightedness aquamarine, beryl, emerald
vision, sense of rutilated quartz
vitality hematite, heliotrope, rock crystal, tiger iron, tree agate
vitamins, absorption carnelian
vocal chords lapis lazuli, sodalite
vomiting antimonite, dumortierite

W

wakefulness amethyst, ametrine, chiastolite, emerald, fire opal, rhodochrosite, ruby, turquoise, variscite
warmth chalcedony (pink), citrine, turquoise
warrior nature jasper, tree agate
warts peridot
water metabolism jade, tourmaline (indicolite)
water retention chalcedony (blue), dendritic chalcedony, jade, nephrite
water, reabsorption of in intestines amethyst
weakness chiastolite, epidote, schalenblende, thulite
wealth, inner dioptase, garnet, topaz
well-being, sense of ametrine, aquamarine, aragonite, azurite-malachite, chrysopal, fossilized wood, hematite, rose quartz
wholeness chrysoprase, obsidian, sodalite, tourmaline
will alexandrite, garnet, hematite, jasper (red), sapphire
wisdom amethyst, lapis lazuli, peridot, sapphire, topaz, tourmaline
worries/carefree apophyllite, amber, chalcedony (pink), charoite, pink opal, rose quartz

work, energy for garnet (almandine), smoky quartz, rhodochrosite
work, pressure of beryl, emerald, morganite
worries about the future moldavite
wound healing amber, calcite, garnet (general), garnet (almandine), mookaite, obsidian, rhodonite, schalenblende

Y

yearning, longing chrysopal
youth, spiritual emerald

About the author

The late Michael Gienger was an enthusiastic mineral collector from childhood and an amateur mineralogist in his teens. Before completing his degree in chemistry at university, he became a student at the School of Natural Healing and also studied different traditional healing methods from Europe, Asia and the Americas. In 1985 he researched the art of healing with crystals and founded a research group on the subject in Stuttgart in 1989, then formed a company called Karfunkel in 1990. This is a large retail firm trading and specializing in healing minerals. He is the founder of 'analytical healing with crystals', a scientifically based therapy that is presented for the first time in this volume. Michael Gienger was also a founder member of Steinheilkunde e.V., a society dedicated to promoting the art of healing with crystals as a recognized natural method of healing.